Thank You!

The University of Regina Rams Football Club would like to thank the following for their financial contribution in making this legacy a reality.

Doug Alexander
Roger Aldag
Ed Bankowski
Paul Barnby
Stan Biden
Wayne Borys
William Brennan
Craig Briere
John Broderick
Donovan Brown
Jason Bula
Roy Crebo
Rafe Chadwick
Gord Currie
Jason Daum
Richard Delnea
Paul S. Dojack
Dr. William Elliott
Mel Fiissel
Frank Flegel
Todd Fuchs
David Gebert
Mike Gebert
Richard Hearn
Harry Hilsden
Terry Hincks
Jim Hopson
Allen Jensen
Dennis Junior
Joe Kanuka
Jim Kenyon
Kevin Kearns
John Konoff
Murray Kyle
Larry Kratt
Larry LeBlanc
Dick Livingstone
Jarrod Livingstone
Valerie Livingstone
Denis Losie
Charles MacDonald
Douglas MacKenzie
Don MacPherson
Gary Mather
Steve Mazurak
Doug McKillop
Brent McConnell
Frank McCrystal
Rick McCullough
Don McDougall
Jill McDougall
Scott Meikle
Robert (Bob) Millar
William Moldovan
Lyle Mosiondz
Charlie Obrigewitsch
Kelvin Ostapowich
Bob Pelton
Dean Picton
Marco Ricci
Brian Roland
Rick Seaman
Tom Shepherd
Randy Smith
Steve Sombach
Darren Steinke
Sheldon Stener
Erwin Strass
Gary Surkan
Norbert Thurmeier
Dan Thibault
Don Tingle
Gary Treble
Doug Tunison
Steve Tunison
Gary Uhren
Dr. Barry Urness
Richard White
Donald Young

The University of Regina Rams Football Club would also like to thank the Saskatchewan Sports Hall of Fame and Museum and the Sask Lotteries Trust for their generous financial support under the terms of the Sport History Project Grant. It would also like to acknowledge the technical assistance offered by the Hall Program Coordinator and members of the Sport History Project Committee at the Saskatchewan Sports Hall of Fame and Museum in preparing this publication.

Sport History Project

Table of Contents

TABLE OF CONTENTS

Bob Hughes

Bob Hughes has had a remarkable career in journalism, most of which has been spent at the Regina *Leader-Post*. Hughes, a third-generation Reginan, started at the *Leader-Post* in 1962 as a copy boy. He moved to the paper's Sports Department in 1964, covering high-school football and the Regina Rams. Hughes worked at the Saskatoon *StarPhoenix* from 1969-70, covering the Saskatoon Hilltops and writing a daily sports column. He was with the Calgary *Albertan* from 1970-72, writing the lead sports column and covering the Calgary Stampeders. He returned to Regina in the summer of 1972 and covered the Saskatchewan Roughriders while writing the lead column in the sports section. Hughes was named Sports Editor of the *Leader-Post* in 1973, a position he held until he was appointed Managing Editor of the paper in 1988.

Hughes became the youngest person ever to be named Publisher of the *Leader-Post* in 1993, at the age of 48. He held that position until 1997 when he was appointed Editor-In-Chief of the *Leader-Post*. In 2000, Hughes was named Executive Editor of the paper. He now writes a daily column on virtually any topic that interests him, the column appearing on page two of the paper.

Hughes is also well known as an after-dinner speaker and a master of ceremonies. He has enjoyed success with daily radio commentary shows and has often appeared on television. He is involved in various charity fundraisers. Hughes was a founding member of both the Gord Currie Youth Development Fund and the Brad Hornung Foundation. He also serves as Vice-Chair of the Leader-Post Carrier Foundation and as Chair of the Leader-Post Christmas Cheer Fund.

Hughes received the Canada 125 Medal from the Governor General of Canada for his community involvement and was also named to the Canadian Football League Hall of Fame, Football Reporters of Canada section.

This is Hughes' first book.

FOREWORD

This is what I have been looking forward to for what seems an eternity. It is Thursday, September 4, 2003. It is 11:30 in the morning and the hottest summer I can remember is lingering on. I have just been for a walk around my condo area and I can tell it is going to be one of those days where you feel smothered in heat. This is the last day that I will write anything for this book and all I am thinking is, I've done it – it's over.

I don't even remember exactly when this started, this book. Most of the people who write for newspapers have within them the desire to write a book. It is mostly because of a passion for writing. Sometimes, it is because there is just something you want to write about. With me, I have always wanted to write a book. That's all. For so many years, a lady in Regina, named Jean Bradley, wrote me little notes when she came across one of my columns in the *Leader-Post* that she had enjoyed. And, always, at the end of her note, Mrs. Bradley would tell me that I had to write a book, that she knew I had a book in me. I will never ever be able to repay her for her faith and her encouragement.

This book started when I went to lunch at Moxie's on Park Street, across the street from the *Leader-Post*. I was with Danny Marce, General Manager of Centax Books at PrintWest; Frank McCrystal, the coach of the Regina Rams; and Paul Barnby, a former president of the Rams, who is one of that organization's most devoted people. They wanted to publish a book on the history of the Regina Rams and they wanted me to write it. It would celebrate their 50th anniversary. I said I would, and now it is finished.

It is very hard to describe what writing a book involves. I thought I had an idea, but I was so wrong. It was far more than anything I could imagine. I think I drove everybody who was around me nuts because I let this book consume me. I started off writing a few hours a day and by the end of it I was writing for much of every day. On top of that, I was also writing my column in the *Leader-Post*. On the last full day of writing, when I had pretty well reached the end of the book, I wrote for 16 hours. When it was finished, my whole body ached and my head throbbed. But I felt as if a huge weight had been lifted off of me. I had often heard the term that writers hunched over their keyboard "sweat blood." Now, I knew what they were talking about.

It is a pretty safe bet that those people who were around me felt the same way. I am not sure I was always all that pleasant to be around. I am sure I drove my friend Danny Marce to the brink of wanting to wring my neck. He kept giving me deadlines and I kept missing them. But he was such a support. He will never know how much his words meant to me. They kept me going, or got me going. He worked as hard as anybody at making sure the book came together the way he envisioned it.

His sidekick at Centax, Margo Embury, was assigned the job of editing my stuff as I forwarded it to her. She is one of the most gifted editors I have ever come across. I still remember the day Danny sent me back a copy of the first chapter after I had sent it into her. "Bob," he said, "this is the one Margo has edited. I've left her changes on there so you can see what you had and what she has done. Don't blow your top." Every page was a maze of notes. But as I read it, I lost all concern that somebody would be editing my stuff who didn't know what she was doing. I had total faith in what she was doing, which is not easy for any writer. She is simply magnificent at what she does.

By my count, I wrote about 127,000 words on the history of the University of Regina Rams. In some ways, it was made easier because I had covered the Rams when they really became what they became – the greatest amateur sports organization ever. That was in 1965, when Gord Currie was brought in from Balfour Technical School to be their coach. So, I was intimately familiar with those years, and I have followed the Rams and written about them ever since.

When somebody writes a book, there are many people involved. I have mentioned the roles Danny and Margo played. I also give sincere thanks to Gary Mather, who has been with the Rams, in one capacity or another, since the 1950s when they were formed. He oversaw the gathering of much of the research I would need. A lot of it also came from Wendy McCrystal, Frank's wife, who had meticulously put together scrapbooks of newspaper clippings and programs, beginning in 1972 when Frank joined the Rams as a player. Norbert Thurmeier, another Rams' executive, also assisted in the researching of this project.

The summer of 2003 is essentially when I wrote the book. It was a summer that I ended up giving away. I only went camping once. For the first time that I can remember, I did not have a game of golf with my oldest son, Geoffrey. There were things I wanted to do with my youngest son, Ryan, that I didn't do, so if I am dedicating this book to anybody, then it is to them. And to thank them for what they have done for me by just being my sons.

If I am dedicating this book to anybody, I also dedicate it to a lady named Loretta Sernowski. I have occasionally referred to her as "the realtor" in my newspaper column because that is what she does for a living. And she does it so well. She came into my life in the summer of 2002. As it turned out, we fell in love with each other, and that love was tested throughout the time I was writing this book. When I'd finished it and told her how relieved I was, she said, "So am I. So am I. In fact, I'm more relieved than you are. You have no idea." I didn't. At the risk of being a little too mushy, she has changed my life, and continues to change my life, in so many ways. She truly provided the backbone for the completion of this book.

I received a lot of support and tolerance and patience throughout the writing of this book. Friends such as Joe Kazeil, Don Wilson, Scotty McLellan, Dick and Val Livingstone, their son Jarrod, Tom Shepherd, Cec Ferguson, Jack Grossman, all were, well, just good friends. There were others. The *Leader-Post* was more than tolerant throughout this.

Nobody should get the idea that I hated doing this book, although I am sure there were times when that appeared to be the case. I didn't hate it. I loved it, even if there was some pain. But then that's the test of a true love, isn't it?

The opportunity to write this book is something I will forever cherish and be grateful for. When you have had as glorious a history as the Rams have had, it is impossible to include everything. I know that. All I can say is, I did the best I could do.

Bob Hughes
September 4th, 2003

INTRODUCTION

It was the Saturday of the 2002 Remembrance Day weekend – November 9th to be exact – the skies were sheeted in grey clouds and there was a wind coming fairly hard from the northwest, which always spells trouble at that time of the year. The weather had turned overnight. Where the temperature had reached a balmy 10°C a few days earlier, overnight, Friday brought a sudden blast of winter. The wind was coming at 28 kilometers per hour and the temperature had dipped to minus 6°C.

As the morning wore on, snow was falling, the white flakes nailing themselves to the artificial turf at Taylor Field, creating a blanket that was 110 yards long and 65 yards wide. A chartered bus carrying the University of Saskatchewan Huskies had left the West Harvest Inn on Albert Street south. They were already in their dressing room at Taylor Field when another chartered bus left a clubhouse at Mount Pleasant Park in the north end of Regina carrying the University of Regina Rams, the players already dressed in their uniforms.

This was not an unusual scene for the Rams. They had made this trip so many times since 1966, when their clubhouse was built on the backs of volunteers, coaches and players. This was not a team used to losing, nor accepting anything other than winning the last game played every season, whether it be junior football or university football. They worked so hard, every year, at building champions, that it had become expected of them. They would want it no other way.

On this Saturday in November, a game would be played that was seductive in its anticipation. There are few rivalries in Canadian sports as intense as that between Regina and Saskatoon teams. For years, the Rams and the Hilltops squared off in junior football. The rivalry sizzled with a white heat. They plain did not much like each other. And neither did the fans. It was not uncommon to see fist fights break out in the stands. Nobody ever won any of them.

The Rams' head coach since 1984, Frank McCrystal, talked about that rivalry as he sat in the Rams' clubhouse before practice one night in 2002. "We used to play the Hilltops a lot. We'd play them four times a year and sometimes we'd play them six times a year. I loved it. It was great. I have nothing but good memories of it. They are all good memories, although I am not sure I realized it then. But I do now. I look back at those times fondly. At the time, when you were a player, you were so young, you just got so caught up in the rivalry part of it you didn't realize how great it really was."

So, when the Rams left junior football at the end of the 1998 season, and went to Canadian college football representing the University of Regina, there was the anticipation of another provocative Regina-Saskatoon rivalry. Thus, the interest in this November playoff game in Regina featuring the Rams and Huskies. The rivalry had not yet taken its final form, if only because these two teams had just been playing each other since 1999, the first year the Rams entered college football. But this game would count for so much – the right to resume the battle for the Vanier Cup for the Canadian college championship. The winner would go on to what amounted to the Vanier Cup semifinal in Montreal the following weekend.

The week of the game was not an unusual one for the Rams. They recognized the importance of the game, that much was obvious. But they also embraced the Ram's tradition which commanded that, when given the opportunity to win a championship, they would seize the moment and make it happen.

Although the Rams were formed in 1954, it was not until 1965 that they became what they are today. In 1965 the Rams were totally reorganized – a new executive, new coaches, and a new attitude. Once they had Gord Currie as their head coach, a man who had achieved legendary status as coach at Balfour Technical School in Regina, where his Redmen won seven straight provincial high-school championships, the Rams had the ticket to success. Currie coached the Rams into the playoffs his first year, thus laying the foundation for the new-look Rams. Theirs was a remarkable story in junior football, unmatched in the whole country. From 1966 to 1998, 33 years of history, the Rams appeared in 17 Canadian junior football championships. They won 15 – 1966, 1970, 1971, 1973, 1975, 1976, 1980, 1981, 1986, 1987, 1993, 1994, 1995, 1997, 1998. If this wasn't a dynasty, nothing was.

If you had wandered into the Ram's clubhouse the week before the game with the Huskies, you could easily paint a picture of nostalgia and tradition. Team pictures and plaques from every era adorned the walls, moments of history in games that had been played; a sense of professionalism pervaded. The only thing I had ever seen that was similarly steeped in tradition was the Montreal Canadiens' dressing room.

So, every night that week, the Rams visited their past as they prepared for their future.

Few professional football teams are as well prepared for games as are the Rams. McCrystal, who had been the head coach since 1984, and who before that spent five years as a defensive co-ordinator, and who before that spent five years as a high-school coach, and who before that spent five years as an all-star linebacker with the Rams, had become as good a head coach as had ever been in the game. He also surrounded himself with a lineup of exceptional assistant coaches, none of them more widely respected than offensive co-ordinator Bernie Schmidt.

Every night that November week, the players met before heading out onto Scotty Livingstone Field for practice. And it was drilled into them what the Huskies would be trying to do to them, and how the Rams could combat it.

There also were moments when McCrystal would gather the team and talk to the players. It was not always about football. Often, it was about history and rising above the crowd to accept whatever challenge was flung your way.

On the Tuesday night, McCrystal talked to his players about Remembrance Day, John McRae and Flanders Field. "On Christmas Day during the First World War, John McRae went out to battle. Before he went he wrote a poem. He said he wanted to be brave and he wanted to be a leader, and he was. He also died. But he accepted the challenges that came his way and looked at them as opportunities. We're facing battle and challenges on Saturday. The only difference is, you guys won't die. You'll wake up on Sunday."

Later, McCrystal talked about why he chose to tell that story to his players. "Using Vimy Ridge in the context of our game against the Huskies wasn't intended to trivialize Vimy Ridge. It was to show that, when there are challenges in life, some people want to succeed, some can't and some don't."

You will often find McCrystal talking one-on-one with his players, scolding them, praising them, helping them, or just talking about football and life. In the dressing room, he will talk to them player by player. "I do more things one-on-one with guys now than I ever did before," he said. "It's because I have the time now. I didn't have the time before because I was teaching."

It's all part of the Rams' philosophy of producing not just good football players and good teams. It is also about producing better people, more productive people, people who will contribute something to society. It also produces a better team feeling, a better sense of being "together" – almost like a family.

In all of the years since 1965, when they were reborn, the Rams have had only four head coaches – Gord Currie, Mel Fiissel, Jerry Zbytnuik and McCrystal. That in itself is remarkable, but such is the ability of the Rams to attract the best. And it ensures that their tradition will continue.

As the snow fell on that Remembrance Day weekend Saturday, the players went through their pre-game warm-ups with an obvious intensity that underlined how importantly each team viewed this game. They left the field for their dressing rooms, disappearing through the tunnel in a stadium that, through the decades, had cradled so many stirring professional and amateur games. Taylor Field is the most fabled football stadium in this country. People have travelled to it from throughout North America, even Europe, just to say they have been to a game in Taylor Field. On this Saturday, the old grey lady of 10th Avenue awaited another game for the ages.

Once the players had left the field, sweepers took to the turf to brush away the snow. Through the puffs of snow that were swept away could be seen the outlines of two figures standing at the south end of the field. They were McCrystal and Schmidt, who usually look as if they just have tumbled out of a clothes dryer. Now, in their warmest winter clothing, they were looking even more rumpled. It was deceiving, because two better coaches you won't find anywhere in the land. As always, before games, they stood and talked. Neither showed any tension. Both seemed relaxed. Not even the snow and the wind bothered or worried them. Their years of coaching had taught them there was not much more they could do, that it would soon be up to the players.

The players were waiting in the dressing room. Some sat in their cubicles, staring at the floor; others walked around; others stood and talked quietly; some were having adjustments made to their equipment. The dressing room door opened, McCrystal walked in and went to the middle of the dressing room. The place went quiet. This would be what they call a pre-game speech, but if anybody expected that Frank would come up with an inspirational, "Win-One-For-The-Gipper" kind of talk, they were wrong. He knew his players were ready. He knew he didn't have to inspire them for a game like this. He knew that they understood what was expected of them. After all, they were Rams.

Frank was methodical in his talk before the game. He reminded them of some of the important things they would have to do to win, mentioned that the winning team would get a trip to Montreal, and then the players and coaches – everybody – bowed their heads and said the Lord's Prayer. The door opened and they headed down the tunnel, out onto the field. The game was at hand. The time was now. This was what Rams' football was all about. And playing in the snow and cold made it all the better. This was how playoff football games should be played.

McCrystal came onto the field, stern-faced, with his toque sitting at its usual lopsided angle, and he took his spot on the sidelines. McCrystal leaves the play calling to his assistant coaches. He has that much confidence in them. Most successful head coaches are like that. Frank spends the game pacing the sidelines, watching the clock, staying up with what is happening on the field, talking to his players and, perhaps, in rare bursts, having words with the officials. On this day, he paced more and more as the game wore on, his face turning a deep red. His words reflected intense frustration. By the second quarter, he looked as if he had swallowed some bad milk. Schmidt was sagging as well. Wearing the headset that connected him to coaches in the press box, Bernie's frustration was shown by how hard he was flicking away the cord that seemed wrapped around him. As he watched the offence stumble and make bad decisions, he could only shake his head and mutter to himself. "What's going on out there?" grumbled a clearly exasperated Schmidt.

What was going on out there was very simple, even if to the Rams and their fans it was shocking. The Huskies took control of the game from the very beginning and, before anybody knew it, they had built a 28-point lead.

The Rams, not ready for what was turning out to be The Nightmare on 10th Street, did not come apart, even when it looked as if they might lose by 100 points. The coaches stayed focused and encouraging; the players stuck up for each other. Before the first half ended, the Rams had mounted somewhat of a comeback, which fizzled when the Huskies struck for a late first-half touchdown.

As the players went into the dressing room at halftime, McCrystal stayed outside in the hallway, pacing now and then, but mostly trying to figure out what was happening and, more importantly, how to stop the bleeding. As he stood there, an assistant coach from the Huskies, Barry Radcliffe, a former Ram himself, came by. As Radcliffe headed into the Huskie dressing room, he mentioned something about Saskatoon getting all the breaks.

McCrystal turned beet red. He muttered something under his breath, his lips tightening in a grim smile. Breaks had nothing to do with it. His team just wasn't playing well. Frank headed into the dressing room, angry. The players looked at him and fell silent. "How bad do you guys want to go to Montreal! We were terrible in the first half, absolutely terrible. They're not that good. I'm telling you they are not that good. Not as good as you are. There are guys on their team that couldn't make our team, and you're letting them get away with this. There's only one way we're going to win this game. They scored all those points in the first half. We have to score just as many in the second half, plus one more, and we have to shut them out."

The door to the dressing room opened and the Rams trooped back out onto the field, into the snow, into the wind, into the cold November day that had started out so promising for them. In the stands two different stories were being told. On the east side, where the Huskie fans were, there was unbridled joy. On the west side, where the Rams fans had gathered, there was still support, but it was muffled by what had happened in the first half. The Huskies themselves were nervous as they came out for the second half. They knew the Rams were good, and they knew the Rams would not roll over and die. They knew about that Rams' tradition. They knew it was real, that it was a driving force.

The Rams gave it a good shot in the second half, trying to claw their way back, but when it seemed as if they just might do it, the Huskies struck again. Finally, the Huskies regained control and they rolled to a 44-28 victory.

Just like that, the season had ended for the Rams. There was nothing they could do but bus it back to their clubhouse and take off their uniforms for the final time in 2002. As they sat in their dressing room, in their clubhouse, there were a number of Rams who felt, who knew, they had let down a tradition. It is always there, that obligation to a tradition. It drives them and inspires them. It is what has made the Rams what they are. It is why players will come to play for them, not only from Saskatchewan, but from all over Canada. They know about the Rams, and when they get here, they find out even more.

McCrystal makes sure of that. At Scotty Livingstone Field, where the Rams practice, there is a hill at the north end of the field. This hill used to be a garbage dump, now it is a hill with grass on it. It sits there overlooking the clubhouse and the practice field, and behind it sits the community of Uplands.

It is a common thing to see McCrystal take the players, all the players, to the top of the hill after practice. When he gets them there, he starts talking. He talks about the Rams' history, their coaches, their players – all those who have gone before them. He looks down on that practice field and reminds them of all the coaches, players, trainers, equipment managers, members of the executive, who have walked on that field since 1966.

He talks of the legendary people who have been involved with the Rams, none more legendary than Gordon Currie, who coached them to their first Canadian championship in 1966, and won five more before leaving the Rams in 1976. Sometimes, McCrystal even brings some of the people he talks about out to Mount Pleasant.

He remembers one special night. "I remember bringing Gord Currie out here in 1993. The players thought he was dead, but there he was, right there among them, on the same field and in the same place that they now are.

Another special person is a nun, Sister Mary Haggerty, who has followed our team for 30 plus years. She calls me on a regular basis to talk about the team, wish us luck, and pray for the safety of our players. Sometimes, the players don't believe these people are real. They think I make them up."

They're not made up. They're as real as life. They do exist in Rams' folklore, a roll call of some of the greatest names in Canadian amateur sport, some of the most successful. There are coaches like Gord Currie and Frank McCrystal, and players like Roger Aldag and Bob Poley, and executive members like Scotty Livingstone and Joe Kanuka and Paul Barnby.

What the Rams have become is what all of those people brought to them over the decades, which is to be the very best you can be.

It wasn't always like that. It surely wasn't. Before Gord Currie and the people of his era took hold of the Rams, it was anything but.

The Rams of the mid-1950s, where the present-day Rams began, that's where the tradition laid down its roots, in soil that had bred failure, had been unable to grow a winner.

The Rams were not always the prettiest thing on the block.

"The poem *Ulysses* determines for our program the means to our end. We seek out new challenges, thrive in times of adversity, and refuse to yield. *A Man of Worth* clearly defines what our hope is for all those who seize the moment to belong. It is the end result of the Ram experience."

Frank McCrystal

A Man Of Worth

To be true, faithful, devout to the ideals of what is a man

To understand and practice the virtue of honesty,
the quality which gives one peace

To have empathy for a less fortunate, suffering soul
and compassion to make a difference in that life

To recognize what needs to be changed and possess
the courage and patience to change it

To be discerning and steadfast in love, the condition all men fear,
yet long for

To be resolute and firm in oneself while owning
the dignity to be humble

To have the will to commit to a cause, the passion
to seize it, holding a vision, pursuing a goal

To believe and trust in a Higher Power guiding the path
of all humanity

To determine what is moral and right and then stand for it

To know what is honour and strive for this cradle of justice

To be perceptive and tolerant of the uniqueness in all people

To be loyal to a friend yet remain bold and brave
in your own convictions

To be cooperative and protective of your planet
in reaching to discover, to know, to learn

To be generous and thoughtful, giving of your life
to better our world, seeking no reward of fame from this gift

To be genuine, to be wise, to be caring is to be a man of worth

Ulysses

It little profits that an idle king,
By this still hearth, among these barren crags,
Matched with an aged wife, I mete and dole
Unequal laws unto a savage race,
That hoard, and sleep, and feed, and know not me.
I can not rest from travel: I will drink
Life to the lees: all times I have enjoy'd
Greatly, have suffer'd greatly, both with those
That loved me, and alone: on shore, and when
Thro' scudding drifts the rainy Hyades
Vext the dim sea; I am become a name;
For always roaming with a hungry heart
Much have I seen and known; cities of men
And manners, climates, councils, governments,
Myself not least, but honour'd of them all;
And drunk delight of battle with my peers,
Far on the ringing plains of Troy.
I am a part of all that I have met;
Yet all experience is an arch wherethro'
Gleams that untravell'd world, whose margin fades
For ever and for ever when I move.
How dull it is to pause, to make an end,
To rust unburnish'd, not to shine in use!
As tho to breathe were life. Life piled on life
Were all too little, and of one to me
Little remains; but every hour is saved
From that eternal silence, something more,
A bringer of new things; and vile it were
For some three suns to store and hoard myself,
And this gray spirit yearning in desire
To follow knowledge like a sinking star,
Beyond the utmost bound of human thought.
This is my son, my own Telemachus,
To whom I leave the sceptre and the isle –
Well-loved of me, discerning to fulfil
This labour, by slow prudence to make mild
A rugged people, and thro' soft degrees
Subdue them to the useful and the good.
Most blameless is he, centred in the sphere
Of common duties, decent not to fail
In offices of tenderness, and pay
Meet adoration to my household gods,
When I am gone. He works his work, I mine.
There lies the port; the vessel puffs her sail:
There gloom the dark broad seas. My mariners,
Souls that have toiled, and wrought, and thought with me –
That ever with frolic welcome took
The thunder and the sunshine, and opposed
Free hearts, free foreheads – you and I are old;
Old age hath yet his honour and his toil;
Death closes all: but something ere the end,
Some work of noble note, May yet be done,
Not unbecoming men that strove with Gods.
The lights begin to twinkle from the rocks:
The long day wanes: the slow moon climbs: the deep
Moans round with many voices. Come, my friends,
'Tis not too late to seek a newer world.
Push off, and sitting well in order smite
The sounding furrows; for my purpose holds
To sail beyond the sunset, and the baths
Of all the western stars, until I die.
It may be that the gulfs will wash us down:
It may be we shall touch the Happy Isles,
And see the great Achilles, whom we knew.
Tho' much is taken, much abides, and tho'
We are not now that strength which in old days
Moved earth and heaven; that which we are, we are;
One equal temper of heroic hearts,
Made weak by time and fate, but strong in will
To strive, to seek, to find, and not to yield.

Alfred, Lord Tennyson

ACKNOWLEDGEMENTS

The University of Regina Rams would like to thank and acknowledge the following for the information, pictures and support in the production of this legacy. We have tried to include all the names of those that have contributed and apologize to those that may have been missed.

Bill Addie
Roger Aldag
Ed Bankowski
Paul Barnby
Dean Barton
Rafe Chadwick
Gord Ciuca
Gord Currie
Hugh Delaney
Bryan Dimen
Ted Dolinski
Bill Dubecky
Bob Fedor
Greg Fieger
Terry Hincks
Jim Hopson
Reg Houston
Dave Howie
Jerry Joynt
Dennis Junior
Joe Kanuka
Bob Kerr
Erwin Klempner
Len Knoll
The Regina *Leader-Post*
Larry LeBlanc
Dick Leech
Bob Leskun
Dick Livingstone
Val Livingstone
Dan Marce
Sue Marshall
Gary Mather
Frank McCrystal
Wendy McCrystal
Rick McCullough
Don McDougall
Jill McDougall
Ron McGuigan
Bob Millar
Gloria Moore
Larry Mueller
Ken Newman
Kristine Pascua
Bob Pelton
Saskatchewan Sports Hall of Fame & Museum
Dave Sawa
Bernie Schmidt
Tom Shepherd
Sheldon Stener
Erwin Strass
Norbert Thurmeier
Rob Vanstone
Garth West
Don Young

THE BIRTH OF THE RAMS

1954

Regina in the mid-1950s was not the city it is now. The downtown was thriving, alive with movie theatres and businesses and small shops, all of which served to attract people to the core of the city every day of the week. But not Sunday, which was the accepted day of rest and worship. Sunday, everything shut down, except for the Balmoral Cafe. People still had to eat on Sunday, so the Balmoral stayed open. The Balmoral, which was owned by Sam and Nick Pappas, could be found in the middle of the west side of the 1800 block Hamilton Street. The 1800 block of Hamilton Street was the soul of downtown Regina. It was where the pulse of the downtown and the city could be found. Hamilton and 11th was where you would find Simpson's department store. For a few weeks in December and January, the large front windows were filled with magical displays of mannequins and sleighs adorned with everything to do with Christmas. They created such an enduring warm atmosphere, it was where families went in the evenings, when it was dark, the displays lighting up their glowing faces, the everyday stresses washed away. You would see them standing there in silence, not wanting to leave.

During the day, on weekdays, you would come across Whistlin' Willie Greer standing at the corner of Hamilton and 11th. He was a cop of long service, whose role in those days was to patrol the downtown, always returning to his post at Hamilton and 11th, and making sure traffic was moving. He smiled and chatted with everybody who came by. He knew most people by their first names. When he wasn't tooting on his whistle at some car illegally stopped, Willie would be passing on any new gossip he had picked up and, of course, talking about the latest in sports.

Further down Hamilton Street were locally owned clothing and shoe stores. The centre of the 1800 block Hamilton was anchored by the *Leader-Post* Building, which is still there, although the newspaper long ago moved out of the downtown. But the twin attractions of the 1800 block of Hamilton were the Balmoral Cafe and the LaSalle Hotel, across the street from the *Leader-Post*. The LaSalle was owned by brothers Jimmy and Harry Kangles, who, like the Pappas brothers, were Greeks. The LaSalle featured a popular restaurant and pub and was the stopover place for professional wrestlers when they made their weekly trips to Regina.

Both of those eating spots were used by the city's coffee crowd on a daily basis. Mostly, you would find Regina's sports personalities in the Balmoral having morning coffee and, later, in the LaSalle having lunch. Coaches, athletes, fans, broadcasters, sportswriters, all could be found trading stories and discussing the day's issues. In those faraway days, everybody knew everybody. It was not unusual to find a Saskatchewan Roughrider head coach having to justify some decision he had made during a recent game.

The topic of most interest in the Balmoral and LaSalle was, of course, the Roughriders. But curling and junior hockey also had moments when they would be front and centre. The Regina Pats always had their fans.

Toar Springstein

This was a time when those who played for the Roughriders stayed in Regina year round, holding down jobs, developing careers, raising families and getting involved in the community. It was that way for Toar

Springstein, a huge man who had toiled for the Roughriders from 1946 to 1952. Springstein, a square-jawed man, was an imposing figure. He lived in what was then the city's north end, which was the area north of Dewdney, bordering Pasqua Street, where the "war-time" houses were. Because he was a Roughrider and because he was so gigantic, I can still remember going over to Springstein's house as a boy. He always had time for the kids who would show up, unannounced, at his back door.

When he played for the Roughriders, Toar Springstein had no idea that ahead of him was a role that would forever change the direction of junior football in Regina. Junior football had a long history in Regina. The Regina Pats Football Club had won a Canadian championship in 1928 and the Regina Dales had won one in 1938. By the mid-1950s, junior football was in a somewhat confused state. There were two teams – the Regina Dales and the Regina Bombers. In 1953, those two teams united and became the Regina Bomber-Dales.

But after the 1953 season, it was decided that yet another change was needed. The Bomber-Dales had hooked up to play in the Manitoba-Saskatchewan Junior Football League along with the Saskatoon Hilltops and the Rods and Wildcats from Winnipeg. Apparently, Bomber-Dales was too much of a mouthful for everybody and, so, on April 23, 1954, a move of great significance was announced at the team's annual meeting.

The headline in the *Leader-Post* of April 24 proclaimed: "New name for juniors." Under that was the subhead, which read, "Springstein to coach Rams."

John Rowand
first Rams' president

And, thus, was born the Regina Rams. The Regina Rams. A name that would, in the years to come, signify accomplishment and excellence. Their first president was a highly successful Regina businessman named Johnny Rowand. Max Amon was the treasurer and Tom Drope the secretary. Also on the executive was Martin Grudnitski, who was credited with naming the team the Rams. These were all well-known Regina businessmen, a tradition that would be maintained throughout the Rams' history.

This was the new look of junior football in Regina. And the job was just beginning.

Wayne Pyne

Springstein, who had been a line coach with the Bomber-Dales, suddenly found himself cast in the role of head coach when Huck Welch left town. Springstein's assistant coach was Wayne Pyne, another former Roughrider. This was a far cry from the coming days when junior football team coaching staffs would exceed seven people and develop coaching into a sophisticated science.

The Rams also announced that April night in 1954 that

they "are looking for a trainer and anyone interested in the job should get in touch with Springstein."

The week after he had been named head coach of the Rams, Springstein showed up one morning for coffee at the Balmoral. The talk immediately turned to the new team name and the new head coach.

"What do you know about being a head coach? You were nothing but a dumb old lineman when you played," chided Tom (Scotty) Melville, the sports editor of The *Leader-Post*.

Toar cut an imposing figure. He was six feet, two inches tall and weighed close to 300 pounds. Springstein looked down at Scotty – he looked down at everybody – and laughed. "I was the only one they could find and probably the only one dumb enough to take the job."

Those were not the easiest of times for junior football in Regina. Although some of the top business people in Regina were running the team, there was not a whole lot of money rolling in. Players had to bring their own shoes, shirts, pants and towels to practice. There really was no such thing as recruiting players. A simple story would appear in the newspaper inviting interested players to show up for practice.

The year before the Rams came into being, the Bomber-Dales had moved into a new clubhouse and practice field that had been used by the Wheat Pool Athletic and Social Club. It was just off Albert Street, bordering Lakeview.

Lakeview was one of the oldest communities in Regina. Running south of Wascana Creek and along Albert Street to about Hill Avenue, it featured some of the finest old homes in the city, most of which are standing to this very day. Mostly to the south, new homes were going up in what would be called New Lakeview as the city grew. The communities of Hillsdale and Whitmore Park were also being developed.

The provincial government owned the land south of Wascana Creek, the stately legislative building overlooking downtown Regina. But Wascana Park was nowhere near as filled with government buildings as it now is. Much of it was empty fields, with fir trees the most dominant feature.

As you headed south on Albert Street, if you looked to the left when you reached 23rd Avenue, where the Tommy Douglas Building now sits in all of its modern elegance, you would have seen fir trees bordering the street. Behind them there was a building that could only be described as a "shack." There are no other words for it. That was the Regina Rams' clubhouse.

Anybody who ever went to the place will never forget it. It was small and made of wood. It had its own smell. The players shared their dressing room with mice, sometimes rats; it always seemed to be cold. There was no heat in the showers. It looked as if it would not withstand the next Saskatchewan wind.

Dick Livingstone, a long-time Rams' supporter and son of former Rams' president Scotty Livingstone, remembers painting the shack as a kid. "We kept falling through the floor, it was so crappy," he said. But the shack was all they had, and that was that. Fortunately, the place never totally collapsed while the Rams were using it, which was through the mid-1960s. No doubt if the thing was still around, it would be condemned as unsafe and turned into firewood. If you stretched your imagination, you could possibly say that the old clubhouse did have character.

Then there was the practice field. It is a wonder there wasn't a serious injury every practice. The field was pockmarked with gopher holes, and on more than a few occasions ankles were twisted and sprained as players caught their cleats in them during workouts. What little grass there was never lasted all that long. It wasn't even real grass. It was prairie grass that had grown wild. There were mounds and dips to catch the unaware as they ran through their drills. This was not life in the fast lane. But, in those days, not a whole lot more was expected. Most of the players were just happy to have some place to play football, a game that marched alongside curling and hockey as the most favoured in Saskatchewan. They didn't know about heated dressing rooms, thickly carpeted green grass practice fields. All they knew about is what they had, and it seemed enough. On those sunny nights of summer, as the shadows grew long with the setting sun, and there was a certain sweetness in the air, the practices were filled with the sounds of plastic on plastic, voices rising, coaches yelling, whistles chirping.

Frank Flegel

Frank Flegel played for the Rams that first year. He was a running back and returned punts. Half a century later the memories are still with him.

He remembers the clubhouse. "It was just a big room, there were no rooms for the coaches or anything like that. We didn't have any lockers, we just hung stuff up on hooks or put them on benches. I don't recall any paint on the walls inside. And I don't remember ever taking any showers there, probably because there wasn't any hot water. We only had two coaches, Toar Springstein and Wayne Pyne. Toar was okay. He swore a lot, legitimately I might add. And I remember just before we played our first game, Wayne Pyne pacing up and down in the shack and saying, 'Don't worry, guys, don't worry, we'll win some games.' Well, that didn't happen." When he left the Rams, Flegel enjoyed a long career in radio and television news broadcasting, becoming one of the best in the business in Regina.

The Rams of 1954 prepared for the season in much the same way the Rams of today get ready. There was a spring camp held for new and old players, and in 1954 Saskatchewan Roughrider head coach Frank Filchock helped out. Then, there was the regular training camp leading into the season in the Manitoba-Saskatchewan Junior Football League.

The year before, the Bomber-Dales had finished last in the league, a league which had produced the 1953 Canadian junior champions, the Saskatoon Hilltops.

Nobody knew just what to expect in the team's first season playing under the "Rams" name.

Training camp attracted about 45 players, a mix of veterans and rookies, and Springstein expressed the optimism that every coach in every sport expresses when a season is about to begin.

But that optimism was short on return. The Rams lost all seven games they played, finished last in the league and, of course, missed the playoffs. The schedule, at times, could be grueling, but everybody seemed to accept it. For instance, can you imagine a football team coming close to the kind of demanding schedules that hockey teams endure – weekend doubleheaders. That was exactly what faced the Rams in 1954. On the Thanksgiving weekend, they played the Hilltops on Saturday afternoon in Regina and then in Saskatoon on Monday. Incidentally, they lost both games.

"That was no big deal, those weekend doubleheaders," shrugged Flegel. "Everybody did it. The Roughriders used to do it when they'd go east, play two games in three or four days. No big deal."

The Rams went into training camp, about three weeks before the season started, with 61 players voicing their intentions to try out, but only 45 showing up. There were a number of holdovers from the 1953 Bomber-Dales and Springstein was counting heavily on them, even though the Bomber-Dales had finished last in the MSJFL. Back for another season were Jack Klein, John Mann, Stan Shoeman, Jack Chandler, Bill Nixon, Al Thompson, Ron Dundas, Regent Smith, Erv Marchtaler, Ed Sheffield, Brian Roland, Pat Chapman, Jack Ashenbrenner, Marv Vandale, Bill Finnegan, Wayne Nichol, Dale Parsons, Gary Larter and Art Uhren. On paper, it looked like a solid nucleus, but Springstein wasn't dishing out any praise, or making any predictions, even as training camp rolled along toward the first game.

Oh, practices and scrimmages were intense enough as Springstein attempted to mould a team that could compete. In one scrimmage, five players were sent to the sidelines for roughing. Springstein was also not sure just who his quarterback would be for the season – Jack Chandler or Al Thompson, with Bev Bell, known more for his hockey prowess, also getting a look. In the end, all three played quarterback during the season.

Finally, the day of the Rams' season opener came – their first game ever under their new name. It was played on Saturday, August 30th in Taylor Field in front of almost 3,000 fans. The Rams, alas, were no match for the Rods, who rolled to a 35-1 victory. The Rams fumbled the ball 11 times and the Rods scored three touchdowns off recoveries. It wasn't pretty, this debut. In fact, it was downright ugly.

John Johns

Not all was lost for the Rams in this opener, though. They got solid performances from ends Brian Roland and Bernie Sebastian. And backs Bill Nixon, Johnny Mann and Johnny Johns provided glimpses of promise that the Rams would be able to run the football with some authority.

Things weren't about to get any easier for the Rams, and Springstein wasn't going to make it any easier for them. Their next opponent would be the defending Canadian champion Saskatoon Hilltops, coached by Bob Arn. Toar ran tough practices all week in the wake of the loss to the Rods, but on the eve of the Saturday game against Saskatoon he outdid himself. Instead of the usual light workout the night before a game, Springstein put the Rams through a tough, long scrimmage. "They'll scrimmage tonight and every night until they get things right," the coach snarled. "When game day rolls by, they'll think it will be a picnic compared to this."

Little did anyone know what this game would mean. Really mean. This Saturday in September of 1954 was the first time that a team wearing the name Regina Rams would play the Saskatoon Hilltops. This would become a provincial rivalry that would eclipse all others, and it would pass through five decades before it ended. Such is the stuff of folklore.

Springstein's hard line in practice throughout the week almost worked. The Rams, still stinging from the tongue-lashing and whip-cracking, were a remarkably different team from the one which had been lambasted by the Rods in the season opener. They went toe to toe with the defending Canadian champions in front of a Taylor Field crowd of more than 2,500 fans. And while they ended up losing, 16-14, at least some hope came out of the game. The difference might well have been two missed converts that would have given the Rams a tie. The first, by Bev Bell, hit the cross bar and the second, again by Bell, was blocked by the Hilltops.

The hope that sprang from that game, though, was short-lived. The Rams next went into Winnipeg to take on the Wildcats. After traveling overnight by train, taking with them only 30 players, the Rams were no match for the Wildcats, taking it on the chin 33-11, to drop to 0-3 on the season and sole possession of last place in the MSJFL. It was there, last place and winless, that they ended the season, their first wearing the banner of the Regina Rams.

The Rams did not have a whole lot of luck that first season, but Bev Bell had established himself as the starting quarterback. The Rams were suffering from injuries to key players and, apart from the injuries, they also were losing players who were attending universities throughout North America. It was the nature of the game that college players, still young enough, could start the season in junior football and then, come September, take off to play for their schools.

There was, of course, nothing especially significant about the Rams' first season, other than it was their first season and should not be forgotten. At the start of their excursion into what would become a long journey, spanning 5 decades, they may well not have won a game, but they did accomplish one significant thing that remains to this day one of the real reasons for their existence. That is, they provided a place for young men to play football at the amateur level beyond high school.

The years that followed exhibited the usual highs and lows of sport, the remainder of the 1950s and into the 1960s set the scene for what would become a glorious future.

Regina Rams' first clubhouse

The Second Season

1955

In the summertime, Saskatchewan is a relaxed place to be. The province moves at a pace slower than usual. In the country, the farmers wait for the rains to come and their crops to grow. In the cities, the heat of the day moves people to the swimming pools or the parks. Families take to the highways to find havens in the campgrounds, or journey to what seem like endless days at the cottage where the lazy hours on the beach give way to the brilliant Saskatchewan sunsets. There also is an annual event that Regina awaits.

In the summer of 1955, Regina welcomed the arrival of the football season with the usual optimism for the Saskatchewan Roughriders blossoming, as it always did and always will, with the first cracking of pads at training camp. Across town, in the tortured clubhouse that was really an old shack, the Regina Rams gathered for their second season under that name. In their debut year in the Manitoba-Saskatchewan Junior Football League, they had not won a game in the seven they played, so nobody knew what would be ahead for them in the seasons to follow. Except, perhaps, their coach, Toar Springstein.

The Rams' first season was not kind, and certainly was not indicative of what would come over the years. They went from defeat to defeat, at times they seemed like lost souls, having to confront the worst of what any team in sports could have to confront – not winning a single game. It was the stuff of a Hall of Shame. So in 1955, just 10 years after the Second World War had ended, and just one year after the B.C. Lions had entered the Canadian Football League, the Rams gathered on the jagged turf of their practice field, just north of the old Campion College at the corner of Albert Street and 23rd Avenue. Little did they know at the time, but in this season they would go on to record a remarkable turnaround. In some ways, they became the Cinderella team in the MSJFL. In a stunning about-face from the year before, the Rams almost hung an undefeated season on the board, losing only once in eight games and finishing first in the Manitoba-Saskatchewan Junior Football League.

There was an incredible leap in confidence within the Rams, essentially because of Toar Springstein, the former Roughrider lineman who was returning for his second season as head coach. Toar was one of those guys who always seemed to be able to find something good about whatever was going on in his life, even if he was head coach of a team that had gone winless in seven games. In 1955, a bold 36-year-old Springstein took to predicting not only Rams' victories before games, but also stating how many points he felt the Rams would win by. If anything raised a red flag in front of the opposition, that was it. The media, the fans and opposing teams ate it up, so unusual was it to hear a head coach make such predictions. Toar could have cared less. He felt he not only had the talent to make the Rams winners, he was also more than happy with his coaching staff and their ability to get the most out of the Rams. Assistant coaches for the 1955 season were Wayne Pyne, in charge of the line, and the quiet Bill Ciz, handling the backfield. Pyne had had a long career as a player with the Roughriders, and his son Rob would, decades later, also

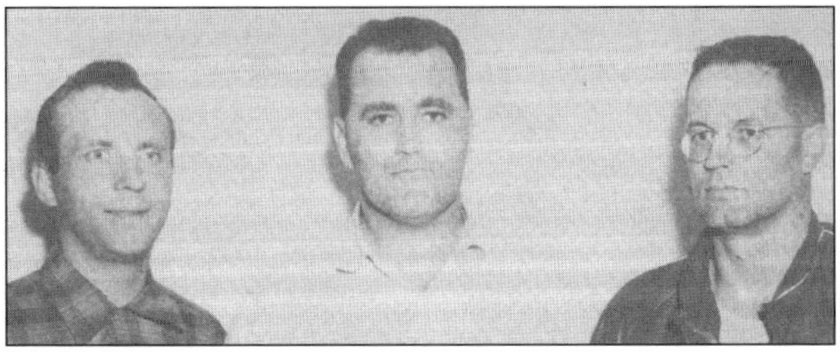

Bill Ciz, Toar Springstein and Wayne Pyne.

play with the Riders. Ciz was a student of the game and eventually went on to become head coach of the Rams. Although only 30 years old, Bill had coached the Dales for four years and the Bombers for three years before hooking up with the Rams. These guys knew their stuff.

There was one other announcement made by the Rams as they prepared to open camp. That was, of course, the completion of the renovations to the clubhouse. The renovations must have pleased the mice who shared the clubhouse with the Rams because they didn't move out. Windows still seemed to be an option in the clubhouse.

The Rams opened training camp midway through July, with a solid nucleus of players returning from the year before. That meant nothing to Springstein, who announced on the eve of camp that "all positions were open." When the Rams opened training camp, there were 67 players on hand, indicating once again that amateur football was alive and well in Saskatchewan.

Springstein figured he could be bold in how he took the team into the season, feeling quite confident that the Rams would quickly develop into the team to beat in 1955. One of the reasons was a twin brother act that came to the Rams right out of Scott Collegiate. Scott Collegiate was one of the oldest high schools in Regina. The red-brick building was well known as having good sports programs and producing solid athletes. In Regina, at that time, north enders considered themselves as the toughest in town. The brother act that came to the Rams in 1955 simply underlined that. They were Jack and Ted Urness.

Jack Urness

Both players came by their football talents honestly. Their father, Al, had been a standout lineman with the Roughriders in the 1930s. Both of these players brought exceptional athletic skills to the Rams, especially Ted, who would go on to a long all-star career with the Roughriders as one of the best offensive centres, if not the best, to ever play the game. Jack did not have the professional potential of his brother, but he certainly had skill and a fiercely competitive personality. He came into camp as the number-one prospect to be the starting quarterback. Other quarterback candidates were Don (Butch) Leskun, who came to the Rams from Balfour Tech, and Fred Wagman, a Campion College graduate. Yes, the same Fred Wagman who would one day head up Cable Regina and become President of the Saskatchewan Roughriders.

Ted Urness

Don (Butch)Leskun

The Rams counted among their holdovers a solid core of veterans from the year before – Pat Chapman, Ed Sheffield, Al Deck, John Johns, Ron Dundas, Bert Vinet, Frank Flegel, Brian Roland and Art Uhren.

Fred Wagman

In the heat of the Saskatchewan summer, training camp became a test of stamina and skill as Springstein put his players through long, rugged sessions that often included a heaping helping of hitting. If the length of the practices was any indication of what it took to produce a winner, then the Rams figured to be more than ready.

The Rams were set to open the 1955 season against the Winnipeg Rods in Taylor Field, and Springstein decided to go with a considerable number of rookies in his 30-player lineup. In fact, the Rams opened the season with 17 rookies, the most notable being Jack Urness at quarterback. Urness was backed up by Butch Leskun, a one-two punch that left Springstein smiling. Wagman simply enhanced the position. Included in the opening-day lineup were some familiar names. Ted Urness won the starting centre spot, backed up by Dale Parsons, who also would go on to a Canadian Football League career, most notably with the Calgary Stampeders. Gerry Kleisinger and Larry Dumelie were in at the fullback position. Dumelie would go on to a career as a defensive back with the Roughriders. Even then, the Rams were a valuable feeder system for the Roughriders. The Rams were deep along the offensive line with nine of 17 linemen back from the previous season.

Larry Dumelie

Ron Dundas

One of them was another future CFLer, end Ron Dundas, who would play for the Saskatchewan Roughriders.

And, so, the first game of 1955 came and there was an excited buzz of anticipation in the air. A crowd of about 1,500 fans showed up in Taylor Field on a Saturday afternoon in late August for the Rams' first game of the season. An entertaining game, it was. A Rams' victory, it wasn't. The Rods won, 6-2, but the Rams served notice they would have to be dealt with before the season was much older.

Jack Urness at quarterback was the big reason for all the good feelings that surrounded this Rams' outfit. In the opening game, Urness established himself as a triple threat performer – running, passing and punting. Throughout the game, Urness moved the Rams within touchdown range, but they couldn't crack a tough Winnipeg defence, which was anchored by future Winnipeg Blue Bomber lineman Cornell Piper.

Dale Parsons

When the game was over, somebody suggested to Springstein that Jack Urness looked like a "real comer." Springstein laughed. "He's already arrived," Toar said.

The Rams were not at all dismayed by an opening-game loss. In fact, they took heart from it, quite happy that they had given one of the top teams in the league a run for it, and had had more than a few chances to put the Rods away. If these Rams lacked anything, it certainly wasn't confidence.

Next up for the Rams were their rivals from the north, the Saskatoon Hilltops. There is no name that can get the hackles on the Rams' backs up quicker than the Saskatoon Hilltops. If a Ram learns anything, it is that he is to hate the Saskatoon Hilltops, or anything with the name Saskatoon in front of it. It just goes with the territory.

Springstein decided to fuel the rivalry. An article in the *Leader-Post* of Friday, September 2, 1955 told the story. It was headlined, "Springstein picks Rams by 10 points." Springstein wouldn't back off when pressed by reporters about whether or not he was serious. "I think we'll beat them by 10 points," he said.

The Labour Day long weekend in Regina was usually the last crack at getting out of town before the first chilly winds of autumn were felt. But this Saturday afternoon game on the Labour Day weekend had a special feeling, and when the Rams and Hilltops kicked off, there were more than 1,500 fans in the stands at Taylor Field.

The game took on a tone of its own, partly because of the Rams'-Hilltops' rivalry, and partly because of Springstein's comments.

Art Uhren

It took until the fourth quarter before the Rams got themselves into a position to nail down a victory. And nail it down they did! The Rams erupted for 14 fourth-quarter points to easily bury the Hilltops, take an 18-6 victory, and surpass Springstein's prediction of a 10-point victory.

The Rams did not throw the ball especially well, but when they did they made their passes count. One went for a touchdown, another set up a touchdown. They were the only two completions Urness, Leskun and Wagman managed as they shared the quarterbacking duties. But the Rams laid out a strong running game that produced 143 yards. Regina's defence, with linemen Dale Parsons, Art Uhren and Gerry Tanouye having standout games, virtually dominated the Hilltops' offence throughout the game.

Gerry Tanouye

The victory was huge for the Rams. It was their first of the season, their first in two years actually, and it was the second straight game in which they had produced a solid performance. The Rams came out of the game with a few minor injuries, but nothing serious, and began preparing for their first road game of the season, against the Rods in Winnipeg.

Springstein, on a roll now, went out on a limb again. When you are six feet, two inches tall and 270 pounds, that limb can be fairly fragile. But it didn't slow Springstein. On a streak after his Hilltops' prediction, Big Toar decided that it would be no problem for the Rams to take out the Rods.

"We're going to win by seven points," he declared on the

eve of the game. "I'm actually being conservative. Some people think we're going to win by more. They're just the league champions, what the heck!"

The Winnipeg game was not without its complications, complications that mirrored the unique challenges junior football faced in those days. Springstein took only 28 players to Winnipeg, and for some it would be their last game. Starry backfielder Glen McDonald would be leaving Regina to enroll at Michigan State University. Fullback Jerry Kleisinger was leaving for Duluth; halfback Butch Miller was on his way to Michigan State. All were former Regina Pats and were headed to American schools to play hockey and get an education.

For the second straight week in a row, it took the Rams some time to get rolling. At halftime they trailed the Rods 5-0, Winnipeg's lone touchdown scored on a blocked kick, recovery and 60-yard run by Rod standout Cornell Piper. Come the second half, Jack Urness seized control of the game. The Rams' quarterback turned in what The *Leader-Post* described as a "spectacular" performance, firing two third-quarter touchdowns to Ronnie Dundas and Jerry Wasnik and kicking four singles. Urness completed only six of 20 passes but they went for 232 yards. As well, when he had to, Urness was a dangerous runner, gaining most of the 123 yards rushing himself.

The Rams, of course, won by more than the seven points Springstein had predicted. They ended up beating the Rods 16-5, their second straight win. They moved into a first-place tie with the Rods three games into the season. The Rams held first place for the rest of the year.

The Rams went into Saskatoon the following weekend and it was no contest. Urness and Leskun shared the quarterback duties for the Rams as Regina hammered Saskatoon 62-7. Lanky end Ronnie Dundas scored three touchdowns for the Rams and Murray Balfour and Gib Forbes each scored two touchdowns. Even in 1955, the Rams attracted players from out of town. One of them was special. Guard Clair Treleaven drove in for practice every day from Milestone. What made this rookie guard special was not just his obvious talent, but the fact that he was only 15 years old. That he was six feet, two inches and 245 pounds didn't hurt, either. And none of the Rams could forget that he was still a growing boy. By the end of the season, he would be a starting guard.

For the rest of the schedule, the Rams were unstoppable, even though they lost quarterback Jack Urness to torn ligaments in his ankle. They went into Winnipeg and Leskun kicked a last-minute convert that gave Regina a 6-5 win over the Rods. Then it was a 12-5 win over the Wildcats, sparked by a two-touchdown performance by Larry Dumelie. The Rams finished off the schedule with back-to-back wins over the Hilltops on the Thanksgiving Day weekend – winning 23-6 in Regina on Saturday and 17-11 in Saskatoon on Monday.

The Rams finished first and received a bye into the league final where they would face one of the two Winnipeg teams, the Rods or the Wildcats. As it turned out, the defending champion Rods beat the Wildcats in the semifinal, which made the Rams happy because they were the team Springstein said the Rams would prefer to play against.

It was no surprise that Springstein again decided to unleash one of his bold predictions for the league final. He figured everything was lined up in the Rams' favour. They had had a two week rest, hadn't lost a game since the first game of the season, and were on an incredible roll. So, Toar told the world the Rams would win by nine points over the Rods.

Obviously, Rods' head coach George Depres had had enough. Responded Depres when word of Springstein's prediction reached Winnipeg: "Regina? We'll murder them, and I mean that."

The Rams went into the game minus only one player from their roster, a solid receiver named Gordon Flaman, who was in Yorkton playing hockey for Bill Hunter's Terriers. Otherwise, they seemed relatively healthy and perhaps a little over-confident. "I'm a little worried about my players getting a little too cocky," said Springstein. "They're the most confident bunch I've ever seen. It's not bad, providing it doesn't get out of hand."

The league final was a two-game, total-points affair, which was a good thing for the Rams because had it been sudden-death their season would have ended on Saturday, October 29. With a crowd of more than 2,500 on hand, the Rods hammered the Rams 24-11 in Taylor Field to take a 13-point lead back to Winnipeg for the deciding game of the MSJFL final.

The Rams' defence had played its worst game of the season. Their tackling was so atrocious that Springstein vowed, "We'll be doing a lot of tackling practice this week." There were few bright lights for the Rams. Halfback Larry Dumelie rushed 74 yards in 13 carries, and

Jack Urness and Ron Dundas hooked up on a number of successful passing plays. But, mostly, it was too little.

After the game, Springstein announced, "I'm not making any more predictions."

Off to Winnipeg the Rams went, and what greeted them was anything but conducive to overcoming a 13-point deficit. The morning of the game, it began pouring rain, and about two hours before kickoff the rain turned to heavy snow. The field was slick, the turf a soggy mess that would steal away any traction the players needed.

With about 100 fans on hand on this miserable November 7 day, the Rams won the battle but lost the war. They beat the Rods 13-12, but it wasn't anywhere near enough to overcome the 13-point deficit. The Rods would go on; the Rams would go home. Right there, Springstein set the benchmark Rams' teams of future generations would live by. Making the playoffs wasn't enough. Playing in the league final wasn't enough. The only thing that mattered was the national championship.

If the 1954 season was significant because it marked the first year under the Rams' name, then the 1955 season was significant because it marked the first year the Rams finished first, made the playoffs and almost won a league championship.

The rest of the 1950s would continue to see the Rams play. There had been some doubt they would be back after the 1955 season, but that worry never materialized. The Rams spent the off-season licking their wounds and getting ready for the next season. They were not yet a dynasty. They had a long way to go.

ON ANOTHER FRONT...

Balfour Technical School was situated on the south side of College Avenue, between Broad and Winnipeg Streets, its back end overlooking a large empty field that stretched all the way to Broadway Avenue. A large red-brick building, in the early 1950s it was one of the most imposing buildings on College Avenue, rising to fortress-like proportions.

Gordon Currie

In summer, the hallways and classrooms of Balfour were empty, the field at the back mostly home to gophers that had the freedom to romp they could rarely find in the heart of a city. But at the tail end of the summer and into the fall, through the winter and spring, Balfour was alive with the sounds of kids getting their education, preparing to grab what life would offer when they passed through those imposing doors for the last time and graduated.

Balfour was not that much different from any high school in the city. It was kept alive by the excitement of young people, whose energy never waned, whose dreams never died, who just by being around painted a smile on the place that would last forever. The kids went into Balfour as nervous freshmen and, if their teachers did their jobs, four years later they left as young men and women, ready to tackle the world, and take on all of its challenges.

In 1950, something happened at Balfour that would forever change its face and, in the years and decades that followed, would change the face of not only Regina, not only Saskatchewan, but also of Canada. That was the year that a young man named Gordon Currie accepted a position as a teacher at Balfour. He would also coach some of their sports teams. Oh, did he coach them. Some day, although nobody knew it at the time, Gordon Currie's genius would also be stamped forever on the Regina Rams.

Gordon Currie coached Balfour Tech Redmen teams from 1950 through 1965, and what was so remarkable about it was that it really didn't matter what sport he was coaching. He brought such incomparable skill, such a wonderful touch to it all that the results he produced will likely never be equaled.

During Gord Currie's years at Balfour, he coached the Redmen to eight provincial high-school football championships, six in succession. At one stage, his Redmen won 40 straight games without a loss.

He coached the Balfour hockey team to three provincial championships. He also coached outside of Balfour, agreeing to handle coaching duties with the Regina Red Sox baseball team. The Red Sox won four Southern Baseball League championships under Currie. Has there ever been a greater amateur coach in this city, indeed in this province, and perhaps in Canada, than Gordon Currie?

Regina's sporting community knew all about Gordon Currie, as the years stretched into decades, stapled together by championships in one sport after another, and his remarkable assembly line of winning championship teams grew and grew and grew some more. Along coffee row, in the Balmoral Cafe and the LaSalle Hotel, they compared Gord Currie with the immortal Al Ritchie, whose time as a coach in Regina was also legendary.

Perhaps, in the 1950s and the 1960s, the thought might have occurred to somebody that Currie might well be suited to coach the Regina Rams. But if the thought did strike somebody on the Rams' executive, nothing was ever done about it. As well, the Rams already had a coach, and in 1956 they were coming off a season in which they had lost only one game. It seemed that they were on their way to nothing but success. There was no need to think of a coaching change.

That would come later. For the present, Gordon Currie remained at Balfour, and the Rams were headed for a stretch of time when they experienced all the ups and downs of any team in any league.

Balfour Tech players salute Currie's 40-game winning streak.

THE WINDS OF CHANGE

1956

The winds of change seemed to constantly swirl around the Regina Rams in their formative years. The expectations for the team to do well were dramatically realized in the teams and players that would follow over the decades. The Rams of the early years had many challenges, the kind that would drive most coaches bonkers. In the early years, they often had to worry about whether or not they would even have enough players to adequately play a game. Stability was not a word that could often be found in their vocabulary. The Rams of 1955 had shown such flashes of promise that, when the 1956 season arrived, they seemed certain there would be plenty of momentum once the schedule started. They were so optimistic that, for the first time in the team's history, they announced they would be selling season tickets. "We've never had a season ticket sale before," said team president Tom Drope, a high-profile local businessman. "But now, after last year's great season, we feel we really have something to sell." It was not exactly a streamlined selling operation in the beginning. There were no mailing lists. Instead, tickets were handed out to players, coaches and members of the executive, and they were to go forth into Regina and sell as many as they could. It was kind of like selling Girl Guide cookies.

But right off the top, before training camp had even started, the Rams were dealt what seemed to be a serious blow to riding that wave of momentum. In 1955, the Rams had surprised a lot of people by finishing first in the Manitoba-Saskatchewan Junior Football League. Even if they had lost in the league final, it was nothing to hang their heads over. They had made their mark.

They were not only a well-coached team, that in the main played to their potential, the Rams were also an entertaining bunch. There was an engaging quality to their team – mostly because of head coach Toar Springstein. He could be a tough, no-nonsense kind of coach, and he knew how to capture attention. Springstein had made it a weekly occasion in 1955, following the Rams' season-opening loss, to come out on the eve of their next game and, not only predict that his Rams would win, but also provide just how many points he expected his team to win by. Of course, Toar was right on the mark for every game, except two – the playoffs. That's when he announced, with his usual good humour, that his predicting days were over.

But more exciting times were to come, involving Toar Springstein and his coaching days with the Rams. During the off-season, Springstein found out his company was transferring him to Winnipeg. What was good for Toar was not necessarily good for the Rams. Nevertheless, the Rams had to find a new head coach. "We suffered a great loss when Toar was moved to Winnipeg," said Drope.

Bill Ciz

The search for a successor did not take long. They went to a long-time high-school and junior-ranks coach named Bill Ciz. Just 31 years old, a draftsman with the provincial government, Ciz brought to the Rams not only experience, but a much softer approach to coaching. There were no flamboyant predictions coming out of Bill Ciz. A tall, gentle man, Ciz was more than happy to be told that assistant coach Wayne Pyne would return to the team in 1956. Pyne, a two-way performer with the Saskatchewan Roughriders, would maintain a meaningful continuity with the Rams as they prepared for the 1956 season.

The players on the roster were no chumps, either. These guys could play. The roster included Danny Banda, a firecracker from the east end of Regina who made up for his lack of size with a competitive spark that could set the soggiest hay on fire. Banda was one of those guys who was too small to play football. But the size of his heart more than made up for any shortcomings in physical stature. Only about five feet, nine inches, and perhaps weighing 160 pounds, the dark-eyed, square-jawed, black-haired Banda ultimately went on to a career with the Roughriders. This was a guy who was ahead of his time in that he was continually working out, keeping his compact body in top-notch shape.

Danny Banda

Of course, there were others on that Rams' team who were significant players and people. There was Garry Ford, a guard who made a name for himself in curling. There was Alf Zimmerman, who years later became a member of Regina's Catholic School Board. Another name people would be familiar with for years was that of Larry Dumelie, who moved on to a career as a defensive back with the Saskatchewan Roughriders, and who in 2003 was inducted into the Riders' Plaza of Honor. The Rams were fortunate to have centre Ted Urness back; Don Leskun was returning as quarterback after winning the Manitoba-Saskatchewan Junior Football League's scoring championship in 1955, as well as being voted the league's rookie of the year.

Alf Zimmerman

There was much for Ciz and Pyne to work with. They also had Jack Urness and Fred Wagman back at quarterback. Urness, though, was coming off knee surgery performed over the winter and was, at best, a question mark for the 1956 season. And a new quarterback named Pete Connellan showed up. He was a Central Collegiate graduate who later made a huge name for himself as the head coach of the University of Calgary Dinosaurs. Gib Wagner was another whose name was associated with the Rams long after he was finished playing. The stocky Wagner, a fire hydrant in cleats, came to the Rams as a guard from Balfour Technical School. Years later, he became an assistant coach to Gord Currie with the Balfour Redmen, and then the Rams. Even back then, there was a familiar pattern emerging. Those who played with the Rams often stayed on when their playing days were over, as coaches or on the executive, as equipment managers or as team managers.

Pete Connellan

Gib Wagner

When Ciz and Pyne opened training camp, they were, as always, faced with the loss of players who had graduated, or simply left junior football for other endeavours. Among the 11 players who had graduated were tackles Art Uhren, Wilf Oberthier and Len Biden, guards Pat Chapman and Erv Marchtaler, ends Brian Roland and Ron Dundas, centre Dale Parsons and halfback Gerry Wasnik. Then, there were others who had left junior football. End Gordie Flaman gave up football for hockey. Murray Balfour, one of the most gifted athletes ever to come out of Regina, didn't turn out for the Rams until the softball season was over, and then he had to make a decision on whether to give up football for hockey. Balfour ended up playing in the National Hockey League with the Chicago Blackhawks.

Some things never change. When the Rams opened training camp in the sweltering heat of July, practice was disrupted and then cancelled on more than a few occasions. "We couldn't run a proper practice because the mosquitoes were very bad," said Ciz. Before that, practice was often stalled or thrown off schedule by the growing cluster of gophers that shared the practice field with the Rams on Albert Street in

Larry Dumelie

south Regina. There were other, ah, challenges. "The field is as hard as concrete," complained Ciz. Also, there were goalposts at only one end, which served up some humour when Ciz held intra-squad games on the practice field. There were – surprise, surprise – no chalk lines.

Garry Ford

The good news for the Rams was that they had fast become a team people wanted to play for, be a part of. When they opened training camp there were 61 players on hand and, for the first time ever, a significant portion of that roster – nine players – came from rural Saskatchewan. "It's gratifying to see the increase from country points," said Ciz. "Interest in the Rams must be spreading." In 1954, the Rams had had only two players from country points – Clare Treleaven from Milestone and Garry Ford from Gray. In 1955, end Ken Nurse, halfback Don Lubiens and receiver Bill Boll came from Fillmore; Gib Wagner came from Craven and Ron Bloom came from Notre Dame at Wilcox.

As training camp wore on and the season opener moved closer, Ciz had no choice but to confront the reality of the times – the conflicts that steadily ate away at his roster. Where 61 players were on hand for the start of the camp, the numbers had diminished to half that figure, and at times fewer, as the Rams headed into August. In those days, junior teams were allowed to register 40 players and dress 28 of them for games. Ciz was worried he would not even have enough players to get to 40.

Of the 35 players out for practice just a few weeks before the season started, eight of them didn't figure to be around to play. Glenn McDonald, Gerry Kleisinger, Mickey Garvey and Fred Cochrane decided to go to college in the United States. Murray Balfour was off to the Montreal Canadiens' training camp; Bill Treleaven chose to attend the University of Saskatchewan; Pete Connellan was headed to the University of Alberta in Edmonton.

Finally, the 1956 season opener arrived. And you would never guess what happened! There must have been something in the air in the stuffy, worn Rams' clubhouse that served to inspire normally quiet people to step up to the plate . . . well, on the eve of the opening game, against the Saskatoon Hilltops in Taylor Field, mild-mannered Bill Ciz must have stepped into a telephone booth somewhere and emerged as Superman. He boldly predicted that the Rams would win the game. "We'll win this game and we'll win some others after that. If the weather's with us, we can run and pass, and we'll win." So there.

The Rams opened the season on the Labour Day weekend with back-to-back games – at home to the Hilltops on Saturday and then in Winnipeg on Monday against the Weston Wildcats. And what a start it was.

By the time the Labour Day weekend had ended, the Regina Rams were undefeated in two games. Playing before a crowd of about 1,200 fans in Taylor Field, the Rams gutted out a 9-8 victory over the Hilltops, then travelled to Winnipeg by bus where, on Monday, they throttled the Weston Wildcats 38-6. The highlight of the weekend was the play of running back Larry Dumelie. While Dumelie's career in the CFL, with the Riders, was as a defensive back, in junior football the quarterbacks gave him the ball willingly and let him run with it. The Rams rushed for 234 yards against the Wildcats. Against the Hilltops, the highlight of the game was a 28-yard touchdown run by Dumelie. According to the *Leader-Post* account of the game, "Dumelie's major score was a beauty. He slashed over left tackle on a quick opener, shook loose two tacklers and reversed his field, going 28 yards to paydirt." Keys to the Rams' running were the play of their offensive line and the ball-handling wizardry of quarterback Don Leskun. Dumelie found out later in the week that he had won the junior football player of the week award, a Jantzen sweater, given by Crossley's Men's Store, located at the corner of Hamilton Street and 12th Avenue.

Despite the 2-0 start, Ciz and assistant coach Wayne Pyne weren't exactly jumping for joy. The usually mild-mannered Ciz was pleased with the victories, all right. But, "The defensive play was poor," said Ciz, "and the pass offence was terrible." So, the coach ordered a full-scale scrimmage two days before their third game of the schedule, in Saskatoon against the Hilltops.

It was a no-contest affair as the Rams jumped their record to three straight wins, slaughtering the Hilltops in a Griffiths Stadium massacre by a score of 35-0 – the second straight lopsided victory for the Rams. "We win two of our next three games," said Ciz, "and nobody can dispute our claim to first place."

Once again, Leskun and Dumelie had big games. Another highlight of the game came from defensive back Danny Banda, whose interception of a Hilltops' pass on the

Regina goalline led directly to another Regina touchdown – the long march left the Hilltops deflated.

Meanwhile, on the streets of Regina, tension was building and interest was developing for another form of entertainment that had a solid following. That, of course, was the weekly pro wrestling card in the Exhibition Auditorium. The highlight of the night was surely the midget tag team match pitting the duo of Tom Thumb and Irish Jackie against Tiny Tim and Lord Littlebrook. Tickets were available at Gillies Agencies.

Paul Nazarchuk

Not all was well with the Rams despite their perfect start to the season. In a bizarre series of events, the Rams learned they had lost both of their offensive centres in the Hilltops' game – starter Ted Urness with torn knee ligaments and backup Paul Nazarchuk with a broken collar bone. Ciz and Pyne immediately began experimenting with other linemen on the roster.

If that wasn't enough, the exodus of players heading off to universities throughout North America began. Defensive back Freddie Cochrane, halfback Glenn MacDonald, end Bill Treleaven, quarterback Pete Connellan, fullbacks Gerry Kleisinger and Denny Cochrane all prepared to bid the Rams adieu. The blow was slightly cushioned by word that players who were attending school in Winnipeg and Saskatoon would play for the Rams when Regina came to town. The Rams also brought in three halfbacks who had been with the team earlier in the season – Gord Mullin, Bill Forbes and Ken Don. Don ultimately went on to play with the Roughriders.

On the eve of their fourth game of the season, in Regina against the Wildcats, a controversy of sorts flared. Winnipeg coach Gerry Mitchell was still stinging from the 35-6 loss the Rams had hung on the Wildcats in Winnipeg, accusing Ciz of taking advantage of the inexperienced linemen the Wildcats were going with, claiming that Ciz instructed his players to "deliberately" go after them.

Ciz tried to stay serious in the wake of this verbal onslaught. "Those Winnipeg guys are ganging up on me. What did I do?" Then, Ciz, tongue-in-cheek, said, "It certainly would help me and the boys to find out which Wildcat tackle is inexperienced and which one isn't." Ciz said he would ask Mitchell to sew an "X" on the sweaters of the inexperienced players before the Saturday game. The *Leader-Post* ran a cartoon of a coach standing beside a large football player. The cartoon showed the coach looking up at the player and saying, "When we play the Rams in Regina on Saturday, you'll wear an X on your sweater. The Regina coach has promised he won't run any plays your way until you gain a little more experience."

Saturday came, and Ciz wished it had never arrived. Not only did he go into the game minus a slew of players who had left the team, and without both of his offensive centres, Dumelie was also absent from the lineup, having injured a knee in practice.

Throw in the Rams' worst performance of the season – nine fumbles and five interceptions – and it was no surprise that the Wildcats won 22-0 before 1,800 fans at Taylor Field. "You worry about having games like this, but you don't want them happening at home. I'm sorry it happened in Taylor Field," said Ciz.

Suddenly, the pressure was back on the Rams. And Ciz said that their next game would represent the Rams' biggest test of the season. It would be against the Winnipeg Rods, the defending league and Canadian champions. The Rods would come to Taylor Field with two straight losses that Ciz said should never have happened. A rivalry had been born between these two teams the previous season when the Rams took a 7-1 record into the playoffs against the Rods and were promptly eliminated. "I can only say it's going to be a long sleepless week around here," said Ciz. "The way things are going around here, I'm afraid I'm going to have a little trouble getting a full team together."

The Rods came to Regina with two players on their roster who were destined for successful careers in the CFL. One was offensive lineman Cornell Piper, who has since been called one of the best Canadians to ever play in the CFL, from his days with the Blue Bombers. The other was a familiar name to Saskatchewan fans. It was Gene Wlasiuk, described by the *Leader-Post* as "a speedy youngster in his third season with the club, the best of a talent-laden backfield."

In a game that was so huge for the Rams, Ciz had his players ready to go. And go they did. Taking control right from the start, the Rams recorded their second shutout of the season, blanking the Rods 16-0. The Rams turned five Winnipeg fumbles and two timely interceptions in a rout highlighted by an exceptional game from quarterback

Don (Butch) Leskun. Leskun's ball-handling magic was amazing, his most glittering moment coming when he made such a great fake to running back Al Zimmerman that the whole Rods' defence was chasing Zimmerman while Leskun had actually given the ball to Siggy Splett, who scored a touchdown with nobody in sight.

As the Rams prepared for their rematch with the Rods in Winnipeg, Ciz made some observations that caused more than a bit of interest in Regina. Ciz said that one of the most difficult things about trying to put together a strong junior team in Regina was the lack of a university in the city. As a result, players were constantly leaving the Rams during the season to attend university elsewhere. Ciz reasoned that if there was a university in Regina, the drain of players would be plugged, and the Rams would indeed become a force to be reckoned with every year.

Meanwhile, at the Exhibition Auditorium, the weekly pro match saw Whipper Billy Watson defeat Regina's Johnny Foti for the world heavyweight (pro) wrestling championship. And Bill Clarke and Doug Killoh, both Saskatchewan products, were lauded for turning in outstanding performances in a 24-7 Rider win over the Winnipeg Blue Bombers.

On to Winnipeg went the Rams. With Leskun again turning in another big performance, the Rams beat the Rods 15-13 to virtually wrap up their second straight first-place finish in the Manitoba-Saskatchewan Junior Football League. First place would be decided on the final weekend of the season. In another Thanksgiving Day doubleheader, the Rams played the Hilltops in Regina on Saturday and in Saskatoon on Monday. It was anything but a homers' weekend. The Rams lost in Taylor Field by a 20-17 score, but needing a victory in Saskatoon on Monday to clinch first place, they ran away from the Hilltops 31-19.

With a bye into the final, Ciz figured the Rams needed something to keep the team sharp, so he arranged an exhibition game with, of all teams, the Notre Dame Hounds of Wilcox, coached by Cy McDonald, who would in the years ahead involve himself deeply in Notre Dame and in provincial politics. The Hounds, with several former Rams in their lineup, came into Regina figuring they had a chance. Guess what? The Hounds scored three fourth-quarter touchdowns to beat the Rams 18-7.

Things were not exactly going well for the Rams. They learned they might have to go into the league final without their standout back Dumelie, who had broken his kneecap, and tackle and kicker Irwin Schmidt, who was bothered by tendon problems in his kicking foot.

The Rams also found themselves at the centre of a political storm in Regina. In a heated debate, sparked by angry exchanges among city councillors, city council voted to allow the Regina Rams to play a Sunday game in Taylor Field. "Never on Sunday" was the theme in those days. Scheduling difficulties in Taylor Field forced the Rams to seek permission to play on Sunday, the only day open to them. Once the Rods had beaten the Hilltops in the semi-final, all the attention was turned to the first game of the two-game, total-points playoff for the league championship that would open in Regina on Sunday, October 28th, 1956.

Despite their earlier misgivings, the Rams were brimming with confidence. They had both their offensive centres back from injuries – Ted Urness and Paul Nazarchuk – and the rest of the roster seemed relatively healthy.

In the first Sunday game ever played in Taylor Field, the Rods took a one-point lead in the total points series with an 8-7 victory. The Rams felt as if they had seen this movie before. One year earlier, they had finished first in the league only to get stopped cold in the league final by the Rods, who went on to win their second straight Canadian championship. Now, the picture seemed about to be repeated.

The following weekend, the Rams went into Winnipeg, confident in their chances because they were, after all, only one point behind the Rods. The weather in Winnipeg turned sour. It rained heavily, turning the grass at Winnipeg Stadium to mush. As a result, the junior game was moved to Alexander Park, which was really a soccer field, and the Rods and Rams played on a field with end zones that were only 10 yards deep. Nobody complained, though, because the soccer pitch at Alexander Park was the best field either team had ever played on.

When the game ended, the Rams had been vanquished again. For the second straight season, the road to the Canadian championship took the Rams to Winnipeg, and they couldn't find a way to get through it. They were starting to look like little kids that had their faces pressed against the candy store window.

With the Winnipeg defence, led by Cornell Piper, playing its best game of the season, the Rods shut down the Rams' potent ground game, controlling Dumelie and putting a lock on quarterback Butch Leskun's passing attack, allowing him only two completions for the whole game. The

Rods won 14-1 to easily take the two-game, total-points playoff, and went on to win their third straight Canadian junior championship. The Rams were again the bride left at the altar.

Gene Wlasiuk, the team captain, was a dominant force for the Rods, playing perhaps his best game of the year. Named the Manitoba-Saskatchewan Junior Football League's most gentlemanly player for the season, Gene scored a touchdown and kicked two converts. He also ran back punts, something he would excel at when he reached Regina and the Roughriders, intercepted two passes, and played the game from both sides of the ball, as a safety on defence and as a running back on offence.

The Rams, mind you, did not go out quietly. As the game wound down, fiery Danny Banda was one of two Rams' players to get tossed out by the referee as tempers flared and frustrations boiled over.

The Rams did come out of the league's individual awards for the season with a trophy. Running back Siggy Splett was a unanimous choice for the rookie of the year award.

For the Rams, their first two years in the toughest junior football league in the country had been a mixture of stunning success and maddening failure. They had every right to feel proud of their two first-place finishes. But it didn't seem to matter when they had twice failed to get out of the playoffs.

Who knew what the coming years would bring. One thing seemed sure, the Regina Rams had established themselves as a force to be reckoned with in junior football.

Ciz Rebuilds

1957

The worn ground of the Regina Rams' practice field at the corner of Albert Street and 23rd Avenue, just north of and across the street from Campion College, where the Tommy Douglas Building now stands, continued to emphasize the ongoing struggle the team was confronted with from year to year. Pockmarked by gopher holes, the field was as hard as a concrete driveway, rarely a week went by that some player didn't catch his cleats and twist an ankle. The clubhouse itself was not the Royal Suite at the Hotel Saskatchewan. You wouldn't use it as a weekend cottage. It was a shack with barely enough room for the players and all of their equipment, a far cry from the clubhouse and practice facilities the Rams of other eras would enjoy on the north side of Regina. The team would never have survived if those early players had expected the facilities presented to players now. But that was all they had and all they knew and, as with every Rams' team in their long history, all those kids wanted to do was play football. How they did it, where they did it, wasn't anywhere near as important as getting the chance to play. So, it was never really an issue in the early days. When they showed up for training camp, they even had to bring their own shoes, shirts, socks and towels.

If anything, you had to own a certain toughness to be a player with the Regina Rams, and you had to accept that to be a Ram meant more than just playing football. You were expected to win. In their first three years in the Manitoba-Saskatchewan Junior Football League, the Rams missed the playoffs only in their first year, 1954. The next two years, they finished first in the league, only to be swept out of the picture in the league final, both times by the Winnipeg Rods. If the Rams had a rivalry in those early days, it was with the Rods, not the Hilltops. The battles with the Hilltops for bragging rights in Saskatchewan would come later, and roll through their dressing rooms like a grass fire on the open prairie.

The Rams of 1957 knew they were in a tough situation right from the beginning. For starters, coach Bill Ciz had to find a quarterback because Butch Leskun had graduated. Not only that, but two stars with the team, centre Ted Urness and running back Larry Dumelie, had accepted scholarships at Arizona University at Tucson. They might be around for a few games, but that would be it. Losing Leskun and Dumelie ripped out of the Rams' offence the dependable one-two punch that was the heart of their running game. But that's junior football. Every year is a rebuilding year in this game, some more so than others. And the Rams did figure to go into 1957 with 15 veterans from the 1956 team.

"We hated to lose Urness and Dumelie," said Ciz, "but at the same time we're actually quite happy to have been able to give them the fundamentals of the game. We're always glad to see a boy move up into college or pro ball. It speaks well for the training he has received from us."

By the time training camp opened, 45 players were on hand. Only 10 of them were returning from the year before, but there were some solid veterans. The previous year's rookie of the year, running back Siggy Splett, was back and so were returning backs Ken Don, Danny Banda, Cliff Uhren, Dan Lubiens and Luke Moser. Ciz was also hoping that quarterback Jack Urness would have

Luke Moser

recovered sufficiently from stomach surgery to take over the number one spot. At six feet, 2 inches and 205 pounds, Urness was described as one of the best quarterbacks to play in the Manitoba-Saskatchewan Junior Football League since Ronnie Adams had played with the Saskatoon Hilltops. Adams, whose nickname was "Rook," went to the Saskatchewan Roughriders when his junior career ended. Ciz received one more blow to his roster as camp opened. One player he had been counting on heavily to return was two-way end Gerry Tanouye, but Tanouye accepted a scholarship at Colorado Springs College, joining Ted Urness and Dumelie in the trek to the United States.

Early in training camp, there was more bad news for the Rams. Jack Urness' stomach problems returned and the Rams had no choice but to figure on playing the season without him at quarterback. That left the Rams with five quarterback candidates – veteran Luke Moser and rookies Ron Blum (from Notre Dame), Bill Sides (Scott Collegiate), Ernie Pappas (from Central) and Gill Collins.

Bill Sides

There were plenty of new faces romping about on the south Regina practice facility. Local high schoolers Lionel Ruhr and Jerry Schmidt (from Campion), Bud Crobar and Bill Wright (from Central), George Jaeger and Mickey Garvey (from Scott), Ed Splett and Chris Batley (from Balfour) and Don Scheffner (from Luther) all caught the eyes of Ciz and assistant coach Wayne Pyne. Out-of-towners who showed well included Bill Boll of Fillmore, Dale Laird of Broadview, Kent Gerecke and Zip Schaeffer from Saskatoon. Laird eventually became equipment manager with the Saskatchewan Roughriders. Another newcomer was Gene Scheibel from Notre Dame, who became a distinguished Regina lawyer and then was appointed a Queen's Court justice.

The Rams found an eye-opener along their offensive line. He was Clarence Long, who, at 300 pounds, was the biggest lineman in Canadian football. Other new players included Ken Culham, Wayne Barber, whose father Gordon had played for the Roughriders, and Ernie Pawliw, who one day became a Major Junior Hockey League referee.

As had become usual, the Rams opened the season with a doubleheader spread over the Labour Day weekend. This year, they opened at home on Saturday against the Hilltops, then played a return match with the Hilltops in Saskatoon on Monday. It was a much-anticipated weekend set of games. The year before, the Rams had beaten Saskatoon in all four games the teams had played against each other. But the Hilltops were now being billed as the team to watch in the Manitoba-Saskatchewan Junior Football League, their roster well-stocked with veteran players. And they wanted a piece of the Rams so badly that word out of Saskatoon was they couldn't wait for the season to begin.

The Rams had received some good news. Jack Urness had recovered from the stomach problems that had flared in training camp and was set to start at quarterback. Urness was a genuine triple-threat kind of quarterback. He could run. He could pass. He could kick. Now, all he had to do, after sitting out the previous season, was find a way to win.

The ever-smiling Ciz was primed for the game, too. With Urness able to play, and with his players having come out of camp virtually injury-free, the Rams' coach had high expectations for the season-opener. "I'm counting on our offence to score four touchdowns," he said.

Well, as the weekend unfolded, Ciz didn't get the four touchdowns he wanted out of his offence. He got something more important. The Rams swept the Hilltops, winning 13-8 in Regina on Saturday and 8-7 in Saskatoon on Monday, riding the often brilliant play of their triple-threat quarterback Jack Urness.

Lionel Ruhr

Urness made good use of rookie back Lionel Ruhr and veterans Alf Zimmerman and Siggy Splett in the weekend games. He also received strong support from the Rams' defence and showed how valuable he could be to the Rams when his quick kick caught the Hilltops off guard and went through the end zone for the winning point.

Next up for the Rams were the Winnipeg Rods, who had opened the season by crushing the Winnipeg Wildcats 27-0 and then losing to the Wildcats 29-7.

The undefeated Rams had been looking forward to this game with the Rods ever since the previous year's playoffs. Taylor Field had never seen a crowd as ready for a junior football game as it was on this September 7 in 1957. The indication that the Rams were catching on in Regina was reflected by the size of the crowd in Taylor Field. About 2,000 fans showed up for the game against the Rods, one of the biggest, if not the biggest, to watch a junior football game in Regina. And they got their money's worth.

The Rams continued their amazing start to the season, this time feeding off an unstoppable running attack that amassed 388 yards to propel the Rams to a 27-14 victory. Showing off the depth of their running game, the two top ground gainers were rookie Roy Crebo, from Notre Dame, with 91 yards in 18 carries, and veteran Alf Zimmerman, with 102 yards in 18 carries. The win came at a price for the Rams. They lost veteran fullback Ken Don with torn ankle ligaments.

Urness again shone at quarterback, shelving his passing game when he realized the Rams could run the ball. Winnipeg coach George Depres was impressed. "They're a better-balanced team than they were last year, especially with that guy Urness at the controls."

The teams would meet again the following Sunday in Winnipeg. And this rivalry was picking up some heat. Following the game in Regina there was a fair amount of chatter about the shoving, punching, kicking and talking that went on between the two teams. The referees chose to allow much of it to go unchallenged. But it certainly set up the rematch back in Winnipeg.

They were ready for the game in Winnipeg. More than 3,000 fans turned up at Winnipeg Stadium to bathe in the glow of a rivalry that had risen to new heights of intensity. And the Rods were ready, too. The key moment in the game, when all fell deathly silent on the Rams' bench, came in the third quarter when the Rams' outstanding quarterback Jack Urness left the game with an injury. The Rams led 15-14, but the Rods put a pair of touchdowns on the board in the fourth quarter to win the game 28-15. The Rams hoped that the injury to Urness was not that serious, that he had given in to fatigue. Still not fully recovered from his stomach problems, Urness had been pounded by the Rods during the game.

As the Rams prepared for their next game, in Winnipeg against the Wildcats, they received a mix of good and bad news. They learned that backs Lionel Ruhr and Ken Don would likely be gone for the season. They also found out, to their delight, that end Gerry Tanouye was returning to their roster from his brief stint at Colorado Springs College. Two-way back Danny Banda had left the Rams for a hockey tryout with the Seattle Americans of the Western Hockey League, but he returned shortly thereafter.

The Rams were beginning to become big draws in Winnipeg. Where over 3,000 fans had turned out for their game with the Rods a week earlier, more than 5,000 fans showed up for this one against the Wildcats. And they got their money's worth.

The Wildcats came from behind to stop the Rams 28-14 in Winnipeg Stadium in a game that was marked by a controversial play. A quick whistle on a punt return, that saw the Wildcats return a Jack Urness kick 122 yards for a touchdown, was allowed to stand, even though the game's referee agreed the whistle had blown. He said there was nothing he would do. The Rams decided not to protest the decision because, if the league upheld their protest and ordered the game replayed, the Rams would not be able to afford the train trip back to Winnipeg. For the second week in a row, Urness did not finish the game, this time leaving with a sprained ankle.

The Rams, who had opened the season so impressively, were now sinking. With two straight losses behind them, they came home to Taylor Field to take on the Wildcats in a return match. On a chilly October afternoon, the game turned into a rout, with Winnipeg blasting the Rams 47-27. Although Urness started the game, his sprained ankle again forced him to the sidelines.

With three straight losses, the Rams headed into the Thanksgiving Day weekend home-and-home series with the Hilltops desperately needing to win to keep alive their playoff hopes. Heading into the weekend, Rams' coach Bill Ciz, not happy with the play of some of his guys in the past three weeks, made a roster change of some significance. He had previously benched the 1956 rookie of the year, Siggy Splett, because he wasn't happy with his play.

Siggy Splett

Splett would play a key role on the Thanksgiving Day weekend. After losing 26-3 to the Hilltops in Regina on Saturday, the Rams rolled into Saskatoon on Monday knowing they had to win the game. They rode the sensational running of Splett to a 30-27 victory before 3,500 fans in Griffiths Stadium, keeping alive their playoff hopes.

The darting, weaving, explosive Splett scored three touchdowns for the Rams. Urness played the whole game at quarterback; his sprained ankle had healed.

But the Rams had left their playoff fate in somebody else's hands, a cardinal sin in any sport. In order to make the playoffs, the Winnipeg Wildcats would have to beat the Saskatoon Hilltops. A Hilltops' win would put the Rams out of the playoffs. It turned out to be a killer situation. The Hilltops rolled into Winnipeg and into the playoffs by beating the Wildcats 25-7, eliminating the Rams from the playoffs.

Dennis Silzer

The season wasn't a total loss for the Rams, though. When the league's individual awards were handed out, the Rams could take some solace in seeing that Urness was named both the league's most valuable player and the all-star quarterback. Bill Ciz was named the all-star coach, and end Dennis Silzer and fullback Roy Crebo were named to the all-star team.

Over the course of the season, the Rams faced many problems, both on and off the field. There was the huge rebuilding job that Ciz and Wayne Pyne had handled so well that they almost took a team loaded with rookies into the playoffs. Then, there was the constant pressure of having to make sure there was enough money to support the franchise. That job fell to president Harry Hilsden, who has been referred to as one of the best Rams' presidents ever. Hilsden's executive was a who's who of Regina businessmen – Tommy Drope, John Gareau, John Malone, Al Wessel, Jack Stewart, Allan Day, Martin Grudnitski, John Roland, Doug Ramsay, Jack Finlayson, Max Amon and Cass Lambrecht. Jack Stewart's name became a fixture in Rams' football folklore. He remained on the team's executive for years and years.

Ted Stawarz
Trainer 1955-1964

The 1957 season marked the fourth year in the history of the Regina Rams, and it was remarkable in so many ways. It will always be remembered for the coaching of Bill Ciz and the quarterbacking of Jack Urness. The question at the end of the season was, how long would it take for the Rams to win a league title, to win a Canadian championship? The answer, my friend, was blowing in the wind, the winds of change that would be coming in the approaching years.

THE RIVALRY BEGINS & HEATS UP

The road between Regina and Saskatoon runs straight northwest, taking the odd bend around some small towns that lie in the flatness of land that is barren of trees but never of scenery. The drive takes only two and a half hours, but the highway had to be twinned because there was so much traffic. At the turn of this century, it was named the Louis Riel Trail to honour the Metis leader's memory. But it could have been called Rivalry Road because this was the link that brought together one of the most tantalizing city rivalries in this country, hotter even than that which crackles between Calgary and Edmonton.

The rivalry between Regina and Saskatoon is that of two brothers, or sisters, who don't much care for each other, but will always find some affection in their hearts for the other, as long as neither is getting the better of the other. That is how it always seemed to be between the Regina Rams and the Saskatoon Hilltops. They played each other so many times over the years – decades even – that it was inevitable a rivalry should grow.

As everything has an end, as did the Rams'-Hilltops' rivalry when the Rams went the university route, so, too, does everything have a beginning. The Rams'-Hilltops' rivalry started very early. It started in the late 1950s in Saskatoon.

Of course, it was a sinister act performed by those who called Saskatoon home that, ah, ignited the flames.

It seems that the Rams had journeyed to Saskatoon to play the Hilltops in one of the many games these two teams played against each other each season – at least four times a year, sometimes as many as six times, and from that materialized the fuel for some explosive moments.

What ignited it was an incident that happened in a game in Saskatoon, likely in 1957 or 1958, nobody seems sure just when. But they do remember the moment. Late in the game, with the Rams on their way to an easy victory, a group of Hilltops' fans, nourished by the grape they had consumed during the game, slipped down to the Rams' bench.

The Rams' equipment manager, Tom McRadu, always brought extra sweaters to games. The Hilltops' fans reached the end of the bench where the sweaters were kept, and set them on fire. An eyewitness, Tom's son Garry, related the following report: "Some of the players saw this occurring and chased them until they caught them and started laying a whooping on them. The only thing that saved the poor Hilltops' boosters was the ball was turned over and these players had to go on the field."

Tom (Midnight) McRadu

The sweaters were not seriously damaged, certainly not as much as were the Hilltops' fans, and the Rams romped to a one-sided victory. They got on the bus after the game and headed down the highway to Regina. The bus trip was noisy, full of the sounds of celebration, not just because of the victory, but also because of the failed attempt of Hilltops' fans to do at least some damage to Regina. When they reached Davidson, the players were hungry so they decided to stop and get something to eat.

The celebration continued in the restaurant, reaching its zenith when Rams' player Paul Yaciw performed a Ukrainian dance right in the middle of the dining room.

It was not the last time Davidson hosted a celebration supper, and it wasn't always the Rams doing the dancing – sometimes it was the Hilltops. It was that kind of rivalry.

Close But No Cigar

1958-1964

Long after the early years of the Regina Rams, when they had been a team starting out with a new name and old frustrations, Bill Ciz could be found Saturday mornings sitting around a table in downtown Regina. It had become a ritual of sorts, this gathering of Reginans in Grothe-Barber Man's Store. Wayne Barber and Laurie Grothe, the store's co-owners, had been in business for years. Wayne's father, Gordon, had had a men's clothing store in the 1800 block of Hamilton Street before he turned it over to his son. Both father and son had played football, Gordon with the Roughriders in the 1930s, Wayne with the Regina Rams in the 1950s.

On these Saturday mornings, in the back of the store on 11th Avenue, there was an old wooden table around which could be found Bill Ciz, Dr. Paul Good, Johnny Sandison, Ron Northcott, Wayne and Laurie, and a variety of people who would wander in and out. This was a place to gossip, trade stories, dissect the latest Roughrider game, talk politics and, sometimes, just to remember. Bill Ciz was a tall quiet man with thin hair, of medium build, and he always brought a warm, friendly smile. He would often talk of the "old days" and the difficulties when he was the head coach of the Regina Rams, which was from 1957 to 1958 and again in 1964. He would talk about how tough it was sometimes to find enough players. He would talk about the practice field and the old shack that served as the dressing room on south Albert Street. He would talk about the financial difficulties the team often faced.

While at the time it may not always have been comfortable to be the head coach of the Regina Rams, it was never a burden to the people who did it. In fact, if anything, it was an important and fulfilling part of their lives. It was something they wouldn't have traded for anything. It was something they would never forget. When you remembered what kind of a coach Bill Ciz was, and then remembered the Saturday morning coffee sessions at Grothe-Barber's, the one constant you remembered about Bill Ciz was that this gentle man truly cared. If there was one thing that Bill Ciz ever got out of coaching the Rams, it was that he was able to play a part in the development of his players, not only as football players, but also as people. That was what he cared most about – that he was able to be a part of making them better people. This was something that would be common to virtually everybody who ever coached the Rams or served on their executive. And so profoundly was this rooted in the team, almost from its beginnings in 1954, that player after player would stay on as an assistant coach, equipment manager or join the executive after his playing days were over. And stay there.

It speaks well of what the Rams were from the very beginning, because there were years when they lost more than they won, when making the playoffs became a challenge, when surviving the playoffs was impossible. You can look it up.

If the years from 1954 through 1957 were the years in which the foundation of the Rams was poured, then the seasons from 1958 through 1964 were when the team's survival instincts – not just on the field, but off it as well – were pushed to the limit. Those with not as much belief in the benefits of junior football might well have turned away and packed it in. But there has always been something special about the Regina Rams. Always. They get into your soul.

There had to be something special for the Rams to have survived. The 1958 season was the start of a tailspin that didn't produce the usual results of tailspins – total collapse. For the next seven years, the Rams developed an itch they couldn't scratch. It was if they were wandering around in circles looking for a way out, unable to find the door. Starting in 1958, and running through the 1964 season, the Rams never had a season in which they won more games than they lost. That was the bad news. The good news was they only missed the playoffs once during that period. What it really meant was this was not Rams' football.

Ciz went into training camp in 1958 having decided that this was going to be a grinding, tough session designed to whip the players into shape and make sure they knew what their assignments were. He hoped to have 18 players back from the 1957 team that had finished last in the Manitoba-Saskatchewan Junior Football League. The Rams had hoped to have Danny Banda, John Klein, Bill Wright, Wayne Barber and Ken Don returning in the backfield. Linemen returning included Jim Dick, Dennis Junior, Dave Howie, Ken Culham, Dennis Silzer, Brian Noonan, Bill Metcalfe, Ernie Pawliw, Doug Lyon, Harvey Campbell, Woody Langfield, Jack Kennedy and big Clare Treleaven. But when the Rams went to camp, both Banda and Don were at the Saskatchewan Roughriders' training camp, and Rider coach George Terlep was impressed with both of them. As it turned out, both Banda and Don made the Riders' roster, and it was the last the Rams saw of them. Banda ended up being named rookie of the year in the west by a single vote.

Dave Howie

Bill Metcalfe

Ernie Pawliw

Woody Langfield

Near the end of July of that year, Ciz found himself facing yet another major problem. The number of players attending practices during camp had rapidly and alarmingly diminished. The Rams had opened camp with about 60 players, but that number had dropped to about 30 for workouts, "I'm going bald as it is," said Ciz. "And this is not going to help."

Ciz at least had more coaching help. Where the Rams had in the past gone with two coaches – a head coach and one assistant – this season he brought in one more assistant coach. Former Roughrider Nick Blum joined veteran assistant coach Wayne Pyne on Ciz' staff.

As was the case in those days, a number of hockey players turned out for the Rams' camp. A couple of Regina Pats showed up. One was Terry Harper, a six-foot, three-inch, 190-pound running back the Rams compared to the Riders' great Bobby Marlow. Observed Blum, "Harper could be a better football player than a hockey player." Harper would eventually go on to a long National Hockey League career, starting out with the Montreal Canadiens. The other Pat working out with the Rams was Gary Butler, who stayed with hockey.

Of the rookies, the one who would make the biggest impact was running back Henry Dorsch from Weyburn. Tough as nails, Dorsch proved to be a versatile player, going on to make the Saskatchewan Roughriders, where he was used as a running back and also played defence. Dorsch ultimately became general manager of the Riders.

The Rams did head into the 1958 season with one major concern. They were worried they might lose their best lineman, the 245-pound Clare Treleaven, who was suffering from back problems.

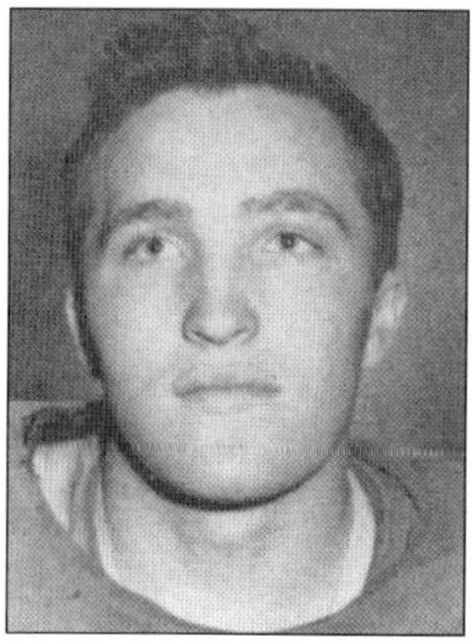

Dymetry Warnyca

The schedule did the Rams no favours. They opened with one of those weekend back-to-back doubleheaders, playing the Saskatoon Hilltops on Saturday in Regina and back in Saskatoon on Monday. Before they could blink, the Rams had fallen to 0-2, losing

19-14 to the Hilltops in Regina and then getting spanked 31-0 in Saskatoon. John Klein got the starting quarterback's job, but the only real bright spot in the whole weekend for the Rams was rookie running back Dymetry Warnyca, who rushed for 110 yards in the first game.

The Rams couldn't afford a third loss, they had to win their next game, at home to the Winnipeg Rods. And the Rams came through. Klein played what *Leader-Post* sports writer Ron Campbell called a "near flawless" game, and the Rams won 6-1. In the process, they lost veteran guard Jack Kennedy with a broken jaw. Warnyca again had a big game, running for 108 yards in 25 carries.

Ciz became infuriated the week following the victory. Some of his players kept missing practices. "Look at that," he fumed one night, "tonight we had only enough players turn out to form one team and leave four extras. How can I convince these guys that you have got to work at this football business? They think that turning out for a couple of practices just prior to a game is all that's needed now." The Rams travelled to Winnipeg to play the Wildcats and Ciz was close to blowing up, or as close as Bill Ciz could come to blowing up. "Here we are, facing our biggest game of the year, and all I can muster up are 25 players and only 15 or 16 of them have any experience."

Henry Dorsch

As it turned out, it was enough. The Rams' defence made a heroic goalline stand, stopping the Wildcats from one yard out on the last play of the game to win 21-15. But the win was not without a price tag. While Dorsch scored his first touchdown of the season, the Rams lost quarterback John Klein with torn foot ligaments; Al Collins tore ligaments in his knee; Warnyca bruised some ribs.

Bill Sides

Desperate for a quarterback, the Rams went to Central Collegiate in Regina for permission to use quarterback Jack Brandt, but the school turned them down. The Rams decided to go with Bill Sides at quarterback against the winless Winnipeg Wildcats in Taylor Field. Three new players had shown up at practice – Marty Collins from Campion and brothers Ed and Bob Jerome. All were halfbacks.

Sides came through. He fired a pair of touchdown passes to Dennis Silzer and Dorsch ran 11 yards for a touchdown as the Rams won 18-6. Terry Harper played fullback and also punted, kicking the ball 14 times – when the snap got to him. Three times in the game the snap from centre sailed over Harper's head.

For the Rams, the win was really their last hurrah. They were hammered 37-7 by the Hilltops in their next game and then lost 20-7 to the Hilltops two days later in a Thanksgiving weekend doubleheader. The Rams closed out their schedule by losing 46-6 to the Rods. Their record was three wins against five losses, but it was good enough for a second-place finish and home field for the semifinal against the Rods. The Rods were favoured to win and go for their fifth straight league championship but, finally, the Rams found a way to beat them. They got a big game out of quarterback Dave Butts; beat the Rods 20-15 to advance to the two-game, total-points final against the still undefeated Hilltops. Butts threw touchdown passes to Dorsch, who also ran for another, and to Dennis Silzer. Regina got big performances out of Dennis Junior, Jack Kennedy, Ken Culham, Morley Fleischhaker, Ernie Pawliw and Bernie Osiowy.

In the week leading to the final, the Rams got some good news when it was announced that Dymetry Warnyca had been named the rookie of the year. After that, it was over as quickly as it had started. The Hilltops won the first game 50-19, took the second game 34-20, and the season was over for the Rams. The Hilltops went on to win the Canadian championship in an undefeated season, something that did not digest all that well in Regina.

The 1959 season was also marked with changes that seemed to move through the Rams like a roller coaster. Ciz had to leave as head coach because of business pressures. The Rams replaced him with Bert Iannone, a former CFL player with Winnipeg, Calgary and the Riders. The short, stocky Iannone had coached for nine years at Campion College in Regina, winning seven intercollegiate titles. Wayne Pyne came

Jack Kennedy

back as an assistant coach and the Rams changed their uniform colours from blue and white to green and white. Training camp had arrived.

Gary Mather

There were some promising new faces. Jack Brandt came in as quarterback from Central. Luther grad Gary Fitz, a highly rated two-way back, showed up. The Rams liked what they saw in Al Collins and Bob McMillan at ends, Morley Fleischhaker and Dale Johnson at tackles, Jack Kennedy and Bill Metcalfe at guards, and Don Peterson at centre. Gary Mather, a smallish running back, arrived from Scott Collegiate and was paired with Dorsch in the backfield. Those two would develop into an almost unstoppable one-two punch. The Rams, though, lost 1958's rookie of year, Warnyca, to a football scholarship at the University of Denver.

But before things got really moving, the Rams were facing such a serious financial crunch that for a while they teetered on the brink of having to shut everything down. Had the Roughriders not bailed them out, there may well have been no Regina Rams in 1959, or beyond. But the Riders agreed to take over "sponsorship" of the Rams, and the Rams' new board of directors would be a mix of Riders and Rams – Gord Milton, Jack Stewart, Al Wessel, Judge E.M. Culliton, Daryl Heald, Bill Ciz and Bill Spicer.

It would not be the last time in their history the Rams' ability to survive was on the line. But, always, a way out would be found, no matter how bleak the moment.

Speaking of bleak, the Rams opened the 1959 season against the Hilltops in Taylor Field, something that seemed to please Ianonne. "What better way to start the season than against the Canadian champions," he said. "We'll get an idea of where we stand." It wasn't the best idea. The Hilltops rolled over the Rams 39-7, putting tremendous pressure on Regina quarterback Jack Brandt. The Rams' only touchdown came on a sensational 95-yard kickoff return by Dorsch. Ianonne threatened roster changes if his charges didn't play better in the rematch in Saskatoon. They did. The Rams came from an 18-1 deficit to force the Hilltops to take their game to another level, which they did. With the crowd of 3,000 in Griffiths Stadium on their feet and roaring, the Hilltops drove the ball 72 yards for a touchdown in the final moments of the game to win 25-23. The Rams got two touchdowns out of speedy rookie Gary Mather, whose first season with the Rams was the beginning of a relationship with the juniors that would span the decades. It is still going on as this book is being written. He is an exceptionally dedicated man.

Next up for the Rams were the Wildcats in Winnipeg and, for the second season in succession, the Rams had lost their first two games to the Hilltops. Under the gun, the Rams responded with a 7-3 win, but they lost star defensive back Gil Graboski with rib injuries. Then the Rams went up against the Winnipeg Rods and it was no contest, the Rams riding the brilliance of quarterback Jack Brandt to a 54-21 victory. The remarkable Mather, a magician of a running back, led the onslaught with three touchdowns, two of them on kickoff returns and one a 40-yard run around the end. Dorsch had two touchdowns and, defensively, the Rams received major performances from defensive linemen Bob Leskun and Ernie Pawliw.

Gil Graboski

Had the Rams finally turned the corner? They'd soon find out because once again they had to face the Hilltops.

Get this. The Hilltops ran the ball right down the Rams' throats, backs George Werezak and Evan Kyba pounding the Rams for a combined 340 yards along the ground in a 46-14 Hilltops' victory. "Our tackling was inept," growled Iannone. "No team should ever pile up that much yardage on the ground against us. No team." Mather again scored a long-distance touchdown, hooking up with Brandt on a 73-yard toss. Brandt also found Dennis Silzer on a 96-yard touchdown pass. By Tuesday night, Iannone had three new defensive linemen at practice – Ray Blender and Rick Purcel, Campion grads, and former Edmonton Huskie Bob Bateman.

The up-and-down trials of the Rams of 1959 continued one week later. Heavy rain turned Taylor Field into a basin of mud and water; the conditions were greasy. The Rams couldn't handle it. The Winnipeg Wildcats could. Fumbling the football 13 times, and losing nine of them, the Rams went down without a whimper by a score of 25-0. The Rams' offence managed just five first downs and a mere 136 yards in total offence.

Despite all of this, the Rams were still not out of the playoff hunt. The next weekend they came from a 12-8 deficit to dump the Rods 24-16, clinch a playoff spot, and move to second place behind the unbeaten Hilltops. A victory over the Hilltops ended Saskatoon's winning streak in a game that was meaningless. By the time they played each other the Hilltops had clinched first place and the Rams had second spot wrapped up.

In what was sounding like an unpopular old refrain, the Rams again failed to go far in the playoffs. On a bitingly cold, late October afternoon in a sloppy Taylor Field, the Rams' offence stalled and they lost 8-0 to the Wildcats in the semifinal. The Wildcats went on to the final and lost to the Hilltops, who then won their second straight Canadian championship.

For the Rams it was another season of unfulfilled promise. "Next year" was becoming an all too familiar slogan.

What a difference a year makes. In 1959, the Rams won three games and made the playoffs. In 1960, the Rams won three games, only this time they didn't make the playoffs. Iannone decided he needed more coaching help and the executive told him he could bring in two more assistants. He hired former standout lineman Harvey Campbell and another former Ram, Tom Fahlman. Wayne Pyne would be back as an assistant coach, having worked under Toar Springstein, Bill Ciz and now Iannone.

Meanwhile, the positive impact Saskatchewan's minor football program was having on the Roughriders was again felt at the Riders' training camp. Former junior players Larry Dumelie, Dave Shaw, Tony Schneider and Ken Don were all invited to the Riders' training camp. Dumelie, Don and Schneider were all from Regina, Shaw from Saskatoon. All but Schneider made the Riders' roster, Tony had opted for a career in hockey.

The Rams opened their 1960 training camp with 60 players on hand. Two of the top new faces were Kevin Kearns, a 200-pound end from Kipling, and Dennis Messier from Notre Dame College at Wilcox. Denny Messier, a hard-nosed fullback, had led the Hounds to the provincial high-school championship in 1959, scoring six touchdowns as the Hounds blasted Saskatoon 71-38.

And for the first time in the team's history, there were as many out-of-towners as there were rookies from Regina trying out for the Rams. Four of them came from Gull Lake. Among the new faces could be found Dale Laird, back again from Broadview, Blaine Norton, Bob Petrie, Orville Fitzgerald, also from Broadview; Ed Bochek of Maryfield, Don McKay of Moosomin, Wayne Strudwick of Fort Qu'Appelle, Tim Woodland from Strasbourg, Jerry LaFontaine of Montmartre, Lyle Sinkewicz of Lampman, Dan Gallagher and Jerry Carline of Moose Jaw.

Regina's well-oiled high-school system continued as a dependable feeder system for the Rams. Jack Slobodan, Vern Simonson, Bill Forrest and Danny Maxim all came from Sheldon-Williams. Stan Biden came from Scott, Dareau Ashenbrenner, Bob Richardson and Bill Belof from Balfour, Stan Agopsowicz from Martin, Dick Weist from Regina College.

Back for another year were Dorsch and Mather. Fighting it out for the quarterback position were Campion grad Bob Mirwald, Gallagher, and holdover Chris Batley. Mirwald later became Dean of the College of Physical Education at the University of Saskatchewan. Dorsch did not last the season, deciding to accept a football scholarship at the University of Denver/Tulsa.

It didn't really matter. The Rams were going nowhere anyway. They couldn't beat the Hilltops, losing 55-0 right off the bat. They rebounded, sort of, with a 20-7 win over the Rods, with Mather scoring one touchdown and Dorsch getting two. Then, it was a 16-15 loss to the Hilltops, a game that was Dorsch's last as a Ram. He had scored five touchdowns in just three games. The Rams were desperate to try and keep him. They even offered to pay for his education if he stayed in Regina. Hank thought about it but felt that because he had told Denver he would accept the scholarship, he had to go through with it.

With Dorsch gone and Mather injured, the Rams were out of gas offensively. Finishing last, missing the playoffs, their season came sputtering to an end. Maybe next year.

The year 1960 also signified the start of a 40-year relationship with a local businessman and supporter, Gerry Welsh. Through his business, Kenridge Men's Store, Gerry donated a suit to the Rams' Most Valuable Player, as selected by the players. This commitment was continued each year up until 1999, when Gerry retired and closed the business.

The 1961 season was not one that offered much hope. The Rams had been hit by graduation and, when they went to camp, they knew not what to expect. Iannone and his assistants, Wayne Pyne, Tom Fahlman and former Rider Martin Ruby, knew they needed to find at least 15 rookies who could start.

Nobody knew it at the time, but the 1961 season would come to be the most significant of all Rams' seasons, because of one addition to the team's roster. And he wasn't even a player. He was R.C. Livingstone or, as he would come to be known far and wide, Scotty Livingstone. Livingstone came onto the Regina Rams' executive in 1961 and was immediately named vice-president. The impact he would ultimately have on the organization would be as profound as it was timely.

R.C. (Scotty) Livingstone

Among the new faces who were playing with the Rams were Leo Ledohowsky, a 220-pound tackle from Broadview, centre Barry Urness, fullbacks Ken Johns and Ron Johnston. Gary Mather was back for his third year and big things were expected from him. Veteran Al Collins, would start the season at centre, anchoring a line that Ianonne called, "the biggest since I've been here."

Al Collins

The Rams won only two games in 1961, but they still made the playoffs. They opened the season with the usual loss to the Hilltops, this time by a score of 19-7, the lone Rams' touchdown coming from fullback Ken Johns. One week later, the Hilltops again beat the Rams, 39-7, on a rainy night in Saskatoon. Again, Johns scored the Rams' only touchdown.

Gary Mather

Ianonne was not impressed with his players, especially noting that too many of them were not in the kind of physical condition they should be. "The ones who aren't in shape are hurting the entire team," he said. "From now on, any player who misses a practice won't play in the next game."

New players also started to show up. Three running backs turned up at practice – fullback Lorne Gale from Balfour, quarterback and running back Ken Tyson, and little Johnny Konoff, another back, both out of Central.

It didn't seem to make much of an impression on the Rams, who at times played as if they would rather be somewhere else. Playing in a howling 50-mile-per-hour wind, the Winnipeg Rods easily out-scored the Rams 26-1 before fewer than 200 fans in Taylor Field. About the only good thing Ianonne could come up with after the game was that he thought the play of defensive players such as Gord Bowerman, Mal Perkins, Al Collins and Vern Simonson was up to par. Otherwise, it was just another lackadaisical performance by the Regina Rams.

A week later, in a driving rainstorm in Winnipeg, the Rams were shut out, 20-0, by the Rods, leaving the Rams in last place at 0-4.

In the middle of September, the Rams decided to take on the University of Saskatchewan Huskies in an exhibition game in Taylor Field. The Huskies had a number of former Rams in their lineup, including quarterback Bob Mirwald, two-way back Gary Fitz and speedster Dale West. Before only a few hundred fans, the Rams won their first game of the season, beating the Huskies 7-6. Mal Perkins was the Rams' workhorse in this game, rushing for over 115 yards in 16 carries. While the game meant little, at least the Rams had finally won something.

Mal Perkins

A week later, perhaps boosted by their win over the Huskies, the Rams went into Winnipeg and took on the equally inept Wildcats. It was no contest. With Gary Mather and Joe Larson each scoring two touchdowns, the Rams

Back (l-r) Don Leader, Ken Johns
Front (l-r) Gary Mather, Terry Shercliffe, Dan Maxim

romped to a 31-9 victory. If the game was memorable for simply more than a win, then it served as a coming-out party of sorts for rookie 16-year-old Rams' tackle Larry Van Moorlehem. In the next few years, Van Moorlehem would develop into one of the most outstanding linemen in Rams' history.

Needing a victory to get into the playoffs, the Rams again teed off on the Wildcats, only this time it was in Taylor Field. With Mather having what was perhaps his best game ever in junior football, the Rams crushed the winless Wildcats 20-3. Mather scored two touchdowns and accounted for 261 total yards, 155 of them along the ground, the rest on receptions. The victory assured the Rams of a playoff spot with two games remaining, both against the Hilltops.

With only 300 fans in Taylor Field, the Rams folded in the face of an explosive, grinding Hilltops' ground game. The Hilltops rushed for 335 yards on the way to a 13-6 victory over the Rams. The regular schedule ended for the Rams in Saskatoon where the Hilltops completed a season sweep over the Rams with a 43-9 victory before 2,300 fans.

The Rams had to travel to Saskatoon for a sudden-death semifinal against the Hilltops. There was little doubt over what the outcome would be. With about 2,000 fans on hand in Holiday Park, which eventually became Gordie Howe Bowl, the Hilltops eliminated the Rams with a 22-13 victory.

For the Rams, it led them into an off-season in which there was a complete overhaul of the assistant coaching ranks and some changes in the team's executive suite. Scotty Livingstone was named president of the Rams and he recruited a Regina chiropractor, Dr. Rafe Chadwick, to the executive. Bert Iannone stayed on as head coach. He brought in four new assistant coaches – Paul Anderson and Russ Haines to work with the line, Nellie Greene and Jack Urness to handle the backs.

Three new quarterbacks were brought into camp in 1962 – Rudy Lipp, a graduate of Campion, Grant Becker, a graduate of Balfour, and Warren Potts, fresh out of Martin Collegiate. Among the players who showed up at training camp for the 1962 season were running backs Bob McAfee, Norm Parisien, Art McAvoy, Danny Maxim and Mal Perkins. The fullbacks were Ken Johns and John Arnot. Kevin Kearns, Dave Wirth and Lyle Sinkewiz were fighting it out for the centre spot. Larry Van Moorlehem, only 17 years old, was back for his second year on the offensive line. Vern Simonson was returning at end as were Alex Smith and Gord Bowerman. But there were some impressive new receivers around as well. Ken McNabb, a two-year all-star at Scott, was there and so was another Scott grad, Andy Schuck, who also was a provincial boxing champion. North enders Bob Walker, whose father, Bob, was the first American to play with the Roughriders, and Ron Cobbledick from Martin turned out at camp.

As usual, the Rams opened the season against their provincial rivals, the Hilltops. This time, the game was in Saskatoon against a Hilltops' team that faced a huge rebuilding job and had a new head coach in Al Ledingham. With rain falling for the first half, the Hilltops overcame a 7-0 deficit with two fourth-quarter touchdowns to nail down an impressive 21-7 victory. With the rematch back in Regina a week later, the Rams were surely wondering if they would ever beat the Hilltops. The game was much closer, but the ending was the same. With the margin of victory coming off a 17-yard field goal by Gord Garvie in the third quarter, the Hilltops hung on to beat the Rams 10-7 before 1,500 fans in Taylor Field. With Rudy Lipp quarterbacking in place of the injured Grant Becker, the Rams' offence had trouble getting a comfortable pace. Ken Johns was the lone bright light for the Rams' offence, scoring the team's only touchdown.

The Rams' next game, at home, was against the Winnipeg Rods, who were coached by former Winnipeg Blue Bomber player, Ray Jauch. Jauch, of course, went on to coach in the Canadian Football League with Winnipeg, Edmonton and Saskatchewan. With the offence still unable to get out of the blocks, it was left to the Rams' defence to

Left to Right: Bill Baker, Bob Lowe, Bob Rupka, Garth West, Ken Huber, Coach Paul Anderson.

rise above the crowd. And rise they did, turning in a performance that had even the Rods singing their praises. But it wasn't enough to get Regina a win. A field goal with less than two minutes to go in the game sent the Rods home with a 10-8 win and kept their undefeated record intact at three straight wins. A week later, in Winnipeg, the Rods had an easier time of it with the Rams. They whipped them 28-13.

All was not well within the walls of the Rams' clubhouse. Throughout their early years, the Rams had always managed to avoid the kind of inner turmoil that can tear a team apart. But not this time. This time it all caught up to them. Throughout the season, Ianonne had taken considerable heat from every direction. When the Rams lost 19-3 at home, all hell broke loose. It was their fifth straight loss. Everybody, including Iannone, had had it.

Immediately following the game, the bewildered Iannone became the first Rams' coach to quit during the season. He was in a hurry to get out. He resigned within hours of the loss. He cut the ties to a three-year association with the Rams in which he was never able to get the team to the next level.

Iannone said he resigned because of "internal criticism and interference," and Bert did not go quietly into the sunset of his coaching career. This is what he told the *Leader-Post*'s Ron Campbell on September 15, 1962:

> It became apparent several weeks ago that because of criticism and interference from the Ram organization I wasn't getting the best possible performance from many of the players. In junior ball, an all-out effort is imperative for a winning combination. A losing season always brings criticism and this I expected. However, such criticism and interference has definitely hurt the morale of the club and particularly the linemen. It is in the best interest of the team that I have regretfully resigned as head coach of the club.

R.C. (Scotty) Livingstone, the Rams' president, quickly accepted the resignation and said that within a day a new head coach would be appointed. Sure enough, within a day, the Rams had named assistant coach Paul Anderson as the new head coach. The tall, soft-spoken Anderson, a former Roughrider and a former Hilltop, whose son Mike was a star lineman with the Riders, was the obvious choice for the job.

Anderson quickly laid down the law to the Rams. "No practice, no play." is how he put it to the players who figured missing practices was not that serious an issue. "Everyone's time is valuable," said the likeable Anderson. "We don't have time to waste on anyone who isn't interested enough to turn out for practice."

Vern Simonson

Anderson's first game as head coach came in Winnipeg against the Wildcats. The night before the game, the head coach was tested when two players missed curfew. So, Anderson benched centre Marty Collins and running back Mal Perkins. The message was delivered and the rest of the Rams seemed to receive it. They went out and hammered the Wildcats, 41-2. Lanky Vern Simonson was the game's star, scoring two touchdowns and catching all four passes quarterback Rudy Lipp threw his way. Simonson also played defensive back, intercepting three Winnipeg passes. The Rams also got touchdowns from Ken McNabb, Joe Larson and Ted Hogan in what were easily their best performances of the season.

The Rams went on to win their last two games and make the playoffs, getting to the semifinal where they lost 21-8 to the Hilltops. But that is not what the season will be remembered for. It will be remembered as the year the Rams went through more in-house turmoil than in their entire history.

The 1963 and 1964 seasons were much the same for the Rams, who were still without any real direction or purpose. In 1963 they were 4-4, made the playoffs, and then got blown out 95-0 in a two-game, total-points series with the Rods. In 1964 they were 3-5, finished second, finally won the Manitoba-Saskatchewan Junior Football League championship, but got hammered 47-8 by the Edmonton Huskies in the Western final.

Perhaps the most significant and lasting thing to come out of those two years was that Scotty Livingstone was definitely putting his stamp on the Rams. He brought to the board of directors people who would be with the Rams for years, even decades, and who, together, would make the necessary moves to turn this team completely around and set the stage for a dynasty the likes of which Canadian junior football had never seen, or experienced. Scotty brought onto the executive Jack Stewart, Ron McGuigan and Joe Kanuka. Their names would be on the Rams' honour roll for years to come.

Paul Anderson stayed one more year with the Rams, giving way in 1964 to a familiar name, Bill Ciz. That 1964 season marked the end to the first chapter in the Rams' history. There was much to be thankful for. The team had established itself and had drawn committed people to its bosom.

FRIENDS OF GORD CURRIE

Joe Kanuka

It is November 15, 2002, and the day is chilly, cold even. I pull into the parking lot at Greko's restaurant on south Albert Street in Regina. They have the best Greek ribs in the world. I am sitting in my car when another car drives up. It is being driven by June Ann Kanuka. She is bringing her husband, Joe, to Greko's and he and I are going to have lunch and talk. I have known Joe Kanuka since 1965. A short man, with eyes that are always alive and searching for something new, he is one of the most innovative, imaginative, stubborn, smart, loyal people I have ever known. I often laugh that he has "Short Man's Syndrome" because he will pick an argument with anybody. He uses his finger as a sword, jabbing to emphasize a point. When he wins, the silliest grin creases his face; his eyes brighten. You always want him on your side.

In the last few years, Joe has had some health problems. He suffered a stroke, which slowed his speech a bit, but not his mind. The other night, in Greko's, a few days before we had lunch, there was a dinner for Joe and June Ann. This was held in their honour because they had decided to leave Regina and move to White Rock, British Columbia, where they would be close to their grandchildren. That night, an area in the back of Greko's was sectioned off for this group. Three long tables were filled with their friends. There was Dr. Rafe Chadwick. There was Tom Shepherd. There was Gordon Currie. Ron McGuigan was there; Norbert Thurmeier was there; Gary Mather was there; Doug Killoh, Jim Toth, Don McDougall and Bob Milton were there. There were three tables full of people. I was sitting at one of the tables when the thought hit me. Every one of these people is here tonight in this great Regina restaurant to wish Joe and June Ann good luck because of one reason. The thread that binds everybody to Joe and June Ann Kanuka, and to each other, is the Regina Rams. That is where they all first came together, became lifelong friends, and made a point of getting together whenever they could, for whatever reason they could find. They liked each other and they loved the Rams. Some of them had played for the Rams. Some of them had coached the Rams. Some of them had served on the executive of the Rams. They were all Rams. They will all go to their graves being Regina Rams.

And had it not been for them, especially the late Scotty Livingstone, who would have loved to have been in Greko's that night reliving the past and planning the future, the Regina Rams might very well not exist. The Rams would never have grown as they have in their 50 years. Heck, they would never have reached 50. Scotty, Rafe, Joe, they started it all. They took a struggling junior football franchise, that was on a swift downhill skid, an organization that was clinging to the edge of a cliff by its fingernails, crying for help, and they pulled it to safety. They gave it a purpose and a roadmap, and then they put all the pieces together. And they gave it life.

That was why I wanted to have lunch with Joe Kanuka. I wanted to find out how it was that the Regina Rams had gone from a team that could never win a national championship to one that never stopped winning them. How is a dynasty born? Where does it start? He was there, in the beginning of the adventure.

The day before Joe Kanuka left Regina to go to a new home somewhere far away, we sat by ourselves at a table in a room at Greko's. Briefly, we ate; mostly, we talked. And this remarkable man sitting across from me, sipping on a glass of red wine, went back into the recesses of his mind – it all came back to him.

Scotty Livingstone was the catalyst, no doubt about that. He had joined the Rams' executive in 1961 and for four years endured the ups and downs, mostly the downs, of the team. At the end of the 1964 season, Scotty couldn't take it any more. He knew, if something drastic wasn't done, the Rams would fold. He had already brought some of his buddies onto the Rams' executive, most notably Rafe Chadwick and Joe Kanuka. So, he had the muscle. And the brains. And, most importantly, the will.

Kanuka was a young lawyer at the time and had just joined a law firm in Regina. He remembers how it all began. "I showed up at work the first day and they tell me, 'Whatever we get, we get from the community so you make sure you give back to the community.' I was working on a case for Scotty at the time and Scotty was talking about the Rams. He said he had told the Roughriders they weren't doing anything for the Rams. The Riders told Scotty that if he thought he could do better, why didn't he take them over. Scotty told them, 'You gawd-damn right I will.' And he did. Then, he got really involved. And, of course, he got me involved. I went back to the law firm and told them I was involved with the Rams. They told me the Rams were nothing but a bunch of juvenile delinquents. I said, 'You told me to get involved in the community. The Rams don't get anything from the community. This is what I want to do.' The firm pretty well had to let me do it."

Livingstone had thought hard about what it would take to make the Rams more than just a football team. He wanted to turn them into an organization that was well respected, was a winner, was a huge part of the community, was something people would be proud to be associated with and support. He wanted to inject vibrancy and purpose into something he was worried would turn into roadkill if something huge wasn't done. And soon.

As far as Scotty was concerned, there was only one saviour out there who could accomplish all of this. Only one.

Gordon Currie had been a long-time amateur coach in Regina. By the mid-1960s he had already achieved legendary status. He had coached the Regina Red Sox baseball team to championships. A teacher at Balfour Technical School, he had coached the Redmen to hockey championships. But the role that he was best known for was that of head coach of the Balfour Tech Redmen of the Regina Intercollegiate Football League. The Redmen were the most dominating high-school football team in the whole province. They had once built a 40-game unbeaten streak. They had won seven provincial championships under Currie. Nobody could ever come close to them. Game after game, season after season, the remarkable Gord Currie produced teams that just couldn't be stopped. He was an educator who loved sports and saw that through sports the young people under his wing could learn values that would stay with them throughout their lives.

Scotty knew he had to have Gord Currie as the coach of the Regina Rams.

Joe Kanuka remembers. "We decided we had to get a high-profile guy. Scotty said, 'Let's get Gord Currie.' So we took Currie to lunch at the Assiniboia Club." Scotty Livingstone, Rafe Chadwick and Joe Kanuka were with Currie that day.

They told Currie of their plans and offered him the head coaching job.

"Well, I can't tell you I'm not interested. I am interested."

"We want to pay you to do the job," Livingstone said.

"Well," smiled Currie, "that would be something."

Knowing that Currie was ready to leave high-school football and take on a new challenge, Livingstone made his next move.

"Scotty went straight to the Roughriders and told them that we were going to get Gord Currie as our coach. He told them we could get him for about $3,000. They told Scotty that if the Rams ever gave anybody anything, they would never hear from the Roughriders again."

Joe Kanuka smiled as he recalled that moment:

"Scotty was a leader. And he got things done. Scotty came out of that meeting with the Riders and he was mad over the whole thing. 'Fuck 'em!' he said. We went straight to Gord and told him we would raise the money ourselves. We told Gord what had happened.

" 'Well,' said Currie, 'that makes my decision easy. I'm with you guys.'

"I turned to Livingstone, who was wearing the grin of a cat who had just caught the biggest mouse in the world. 'Scotty, how are we going to raise the money?'

" 'Easy,' said Livingstone, 'We have to put together a program.' We went to businesses in Regina and told them the story and they all said they would support us. Every one of them. A little while later, the Riders came to us and said they wanted to support us. They gave us $10,000. They wanted us to stop going to the community for advertising – we had so much support. We told them to forget it, and keep their money."

Once the announcement was made that Gord Currie would be the next head coach of the Regina Rams, everything took off. The year was 1965. Joe Kanuka will never forget that year.

"We had such great support. We'd go see business people for help. Anybody who said they wanted to think about it, or didn't want to do it . . . we'd tell them, 'Look we're going to build a brand new clubhouse and we're going to put up a plaque and that plaque will be hung in the clubhouse forever and on that plaque will be the names of everybody who supported us, who donated to us. You don't want your name on it?' " Kanuka giggled. "We always got the money."

For Gordon Currie, the challenges were obvious. So much faith had been placed in him that it might have caused a mortal man to buckle. But Currie welcomed the new challenge. This was a man who had come out of Notre Dame College in Wilcox, where he was taught by the immortal Père Murray, the Priest of the Prairies. If Père taught his students anything, it was to have and maintain faith in themselves, that no mountain was too big to climb, no ocean too wide to swim. If you believed it could be done, then go do it.

Gord Currie was never worried. Not for a second. That was why he was Gord Currie. That was why Scotty Livingstone had wanted him so much. He was the only one.

THE CURRIE ERA BEGINS

1965

The prairie wind swept hard across the land and into the city in the summer of 1965, licking the moisture from the ground and leaving it dry and cracked. The sun was high in the sky. You could feel its baking heat go into your skin. You thought for sure your skin would bubble from the heat. The breeze was hot and thick. Wascana Park was filled with people lying in the shade of trees that had all been planted by the city's early visionaries. Kids played touch football on the lawn in front of the Legislative Building. Parents pushed their toddlers along the shores of Wascana Lake. Traffic moved at a leisurely pace through the main park roadway. Along Albert Street, where the clubhouse and practice field of the Regina Rams could be found, a sense of excitement and anticipation filled the air. The Rams were about to begin training camp in their 12th year. But never, not even at that first camp in 1954, had there been so much to look forward to. The new head coach of the Rams, Gordon Currie, was in charge. There was such a buzz you could hear it hissing through the pine trees along Albert Street.

In their first 11 years, the Rams had gone through five head coaches, one of them twice, looking for somebody who could mould them into champions. Now, they had little doubt the Chosen One had arrived on the scene, found in a manger as it were. The buildup to Gord Currie taking over the Rams was extravagant, with overwhelming promise. But why not, after all, the man would deliver. Right? He always had. Currie had put together a stunning success record coaching amateur sports teams to championships, mostly at Balfour Technical School in Regina where he was best known as head coach of the remarkable Redmen football team. They had once won 40 games without a loss. When Rams' president Scotty Livingstone got Currie to agree to coach, there was one condition. Currie wanted to

Jerry Joynt, Gerry Probe, Ken Wheeler, Scotty Livingstone, John Holash

stay on as coach of the Redmen for one more season, He had a group of players he respected, almost loved, and 1965 would be their high-school graduating year. He felt he owed it to them to stay on for their final season. So, in the most amazing of years, 1965, Currie and his two assistant coaches, Al Relkey and Gib Wagner, coached both the Rams and the Redmen.

1965 would take a partnership of people to yet another level in a relationship that would bind them as friends throughout their lives. As well, Currie brought in other friends to work the dressing and trainer rooms for the Rams. The ever-grinning Alex Kerr came on board as equipment manager and Lloyd Dobie moved in as trainer. The executive of the Rams also took on a new look with Dr. Rafe Chadwick as president, the impish Joe Kanuka as vice-president and Scotty Livingstone as past-president. Ken Culham, Kevin Kearns, Vic Moore, Jack Stewart and Ken Wheeler rounded out a Rams' executive that would shepherd the team throughout its most magnificent turnabout, the beginning of a dynasty that would seem never to end. Above anything else, all of these people shared common ground in that they were committed to the Rams, were successful in their careers, would do whatever it took to provide Currie and his staff with whatever support they needed to do the job. Beyond even that, there had to be fun involved. Of that happening, there was never any doubt.

The driving force was the one-of-a-kind Scotty Livingstone, the high-pitched, occasionally salty-mouthed former Royal Canadian Navy man who never understood the meaning of the phrase, "It can't be done." Scotty's rants and raves were well known throughout Regina, but his charming sense of humour always smoothed out any wrinkles the gruff side might have created. He was a doer, that's all. And Livingstone's legacy and name lives through the Rams to this very day. The practice field in Mount Pleasant Park was named in his honour. His son, Dick, and Dick's "former spouse, best friend, mother of his children and current partner," Valerie, are involved with the Rams, Val as a member of the board of directors. Their son Jarrod, confined to a wheelchair, attends virtually every Rams' practice and game, and occasionally accompanies the Rams on road trips.

Football in Regina was at the zenith of its popularity at the time. The Regina Intercollegiate High School Football League was attractive to fans and students alike, and the brand of ball played was high. The Roughriders were hitting their stride in what would be a dynasty of their own. Eagle Keys had taken over as Rider head coach, replacing Bob Shaw, and it came none too soon. Had Shaw stayed on, neither of the Roughriders' greats, Ron Lancaster or George Reed, would have. But they clicked with Keys, and the rest, as they say, is history. The Riders would win the Grey Cup in 1966, their first ever. Keys and Currie would become close friends, so similar were they in their personalities. Often, a night of talking about football, kids, life, anything, would end with Eagle's wife, Joyce, making the two highest profile coaches in the province a warm breakfast and then sending them to sleep.

The seasons 1965 and 1966 are bound together in Rams' folklore. In those two years everything came together for the Regina Rams' organization and gave it its real identity, its roots and, perhaps most importantly, its tradition.

Gordon Currie brought one overriding quality to the Rams. He was a winner. He hated losing. He refused to lose. As mild-mannered and temperate as he might appear on the outside, inside burned a competitive fire that could blow the top off a volcano. He did not have to prove anything to the Regina Rams' players. Indeed, they had to prove a lot to him. Or they wouldn't be Rams for long. As the season wore on, they discovered this. The days of players taking time off practice, missing practice, not giving everything they had were long over. The 1965 season was when Currie nailed that in place. The problems that had plagued Springstein, Iannone and Ciz in earlier years would be no more.

"Being new to the club, my assistants and I feel we are starting from scratch and therefore can truthfully say all positions are open," said Currie on the eve of the Rams' training camp, midway through July of 1965. When camp opened at the Albert south practice facility, there were close to 60 players on hand.

Currie was far from taking over a loser. He was simply taking over a team that couldn't go the distance in the playoffs. Even though the Rams had won the Manitoba-Saskatchewan Junior Football League championship the year before (winning just three of five games over the course of the schedule), they hadn't gone any further, losing to the Edmonton Huskies in the Western final.

When Currie showed up for his first training camp, he was blessed with considerable talent. Back for another year were such players as Barry Aldag, the first Aldag out of Gull Lake to play for the Rams; Moose Jaw running backs Garry Andrews and Barry Radcliffe; Gord Ciuca, a Balfour prod-

Gord Ciuca

Barry Aldag

Cam Clark

Larry Van Moorlehem

uct; big Cam Clark; a bulked-up Ron Cobbledick; end Ken McNabb; running back Dave Orban; fifth-year lineman Larry Van Moorlehem; the sensational running back Ken Walters, a rookie this year; Kamsack product Don Bahnuik. Both Aldag and Bahnuik went on to long careers with the Saskatchewan Roughrders. Cam Clark, sadly, died shortly after retiring from a long career as an educator.

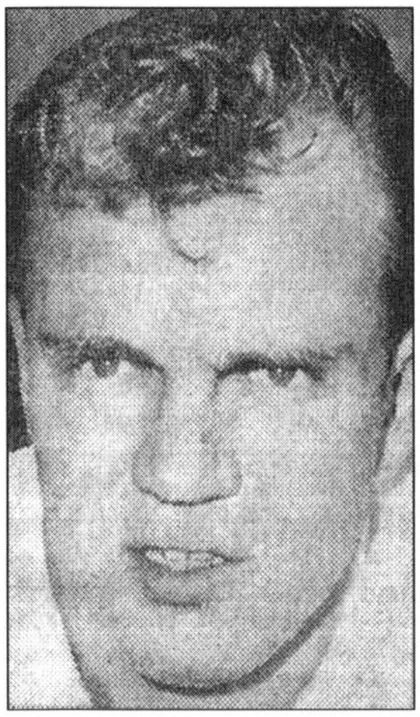

Dick Leech

Those were but a few of the players who made an impact on the Rams in 1965. The 1964 season, by the way, was the last season the Rams went through any schedule without having won more games than they had lost, until the century turned and the Rams entered Canadian university football.

When the Rams went into camp, Currie found that the situation was more one of utilizing the players coming to his system than the coaches having to go out, find new talent and completely rebuild. There was talent, and one of the main areas of concern was solved almost from the day camp opened. The quarterbacking position. There was no problem. Grant Becker would be the starter, everybody knew that, and in Dick Leech and Gerry Dobra, also Balfour graduates, there was sufficient backup strength. If they got into a pinch, Garry Andrews could fill in.

The Rams seemed so solid in their running backs there was almost too much to handle. Leading the way was the 1964 rookie of the year, Dave Orban, a Balfour grad, who had added 20 pounds to his 190-pound frame and was a cinch to play fullback. But early in camp, Orban broke his leg and missed most of the season. Fortunately, the Rams had another Balfour grad in camp, Ken Walters, a tough-nosed rookie, running fullback, who would set the league on its tail in 1965. With Walters at fullback and Andrews and Barry Radcliffe as halfbacks, the Rams were looking at one of their best backfields ever.

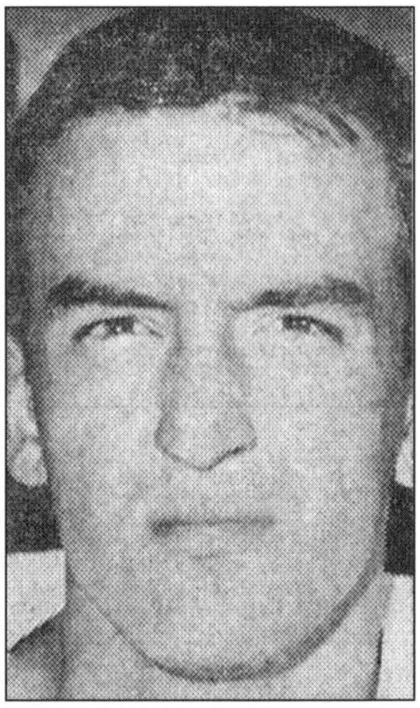

Dave Orban

The offensive-line assistant coach, Gib Wagner, figured he also had himself the talent and size to provide the running attack with the necessary freedom to operate. Guys like Van Moorlehem, Paul Cocks, Cam Clark, Ken Huber and Barry Aldag were big enough and mobile enough to give any rival defence problems.

The defence also figured to be experienced and strong. Returning were Pat McAvoy, Al Lott, Bill Luzecky and Bob (Peahead) Walker. They joined a clutch of rookies that Currie, Relkey and Wagner felt comfortable with. "We've got real man-eaters," said Wagner. "We have about three guys who can play both ways."

By the time the Rams closed training camp and Currie had made his final cuts, even more players had surfaced that the Rams felt confident about. There was Ray Legault, younger brother of Saskatchewan Roughrider Len, Rod Smith, Vic Zipchian, Bernie Brandt, Murray Redhead, Paul Cocks, Larry McGrath, Daun Daum and Al Chase.

The Rams opened the season with the Hilltops, who had in their lineup running back Steve Molnar. Molnar eventually went to the United States on a scholarship and then onto a lengthy career with the Roughriders, where he gained the label as "the best backup in Canadian football," and played on the same team as George Reed.

Al Relkey

On the eve of the opening game, Currie and his coaches looked back on camp. They rated Garry Andrews as the "biggest find." Said Relkey, "The first time I saw him, he was playing baseball with the Moose Jaw Regals. This kid has size, energy, and hits the line hard. Our timing in the backfield is almost there. By the time we get a game, we should be hitting the line like shots."

Currie's coaching philosophy had nothing to do with trick plays or filling the air with footballs. It was about fundamentals, learning the fundamentals of the game, understanding the importance of timing. How could you play football if you couldn't run, tackle, catch or block? Currie teams rarely won because of anything tricky they pulled off. "If you have good fundamentals and good execution, you'll be okay," he would say.

Ken Walters knew all about it. He had been a star fullback at Balfour under Currie. He graduated, took a year off football to see if he could be a hockey player and, now, with Currie coaching the Rams, Kenny couldn't wait to get back. A gifted athlete, Walters cracked the Rams' starting lineup as a fullback between Andrews and Radcliffe, two Moose Jaw products. "Ken Walters," said Currie, "was one of the best high-school fullbacks of his era."

Hilltops' coach Al Ledingham had an equally high opinion of his team heading into the 1965 season. He not only had Steve Molnar coming out of his backfield, he also had linebacker Don Seaman playing in a leadership role. Ironically, Seaman and Walters both met the same fate. Both died relatively young, many years after their junior careers had ended.

There was plenty of excitement in Regina the night of the home opener. The Rams brought in Lieutenant-Governor R.L. (Dinny) Hanbidge for the opening ceremony. They unveiled two new groups of cheerleaders and a 36-piece band. There was even halftime entertainment.

Garry Andrews

With a crowd of 3,000 on hand in Taylor Field, a crowd some said was the biggest in Rams' history, Gord Currie played his hand for the first time. And it was vintage Gord Currie football. You'll find it filed under Here We Come, Stop Us If You Can. And the Hilltops couldn't.

Unleashing a running game that snapped with Andrews, popped with Walters and crackled with Radcliffe, the Rams rumbled 84 yards in 14 plays for a touchdown the first time they got their hands on the ball. That was pretty well all she wrote.

Unveiling a running game that totaled 352 yards, the Rams won their season opener with the Hilltops 26-10. Radcliffe, Walters and Andrews all scored touchdowns. Walters rushed for 160 yards in 22 carries; Radcliffe had 105 yards in 15 carries; Andrews got 70 yards in 18 carries. The Rams' defence, led by rookie end Gord Cuica, were like hungry lions that had just come out of the bush. They hunted down Hilltops' quarterbacks Ralph Schoenfeld and Murray Richardson all day long.

"They just beat the hell out of us," is how Ledingham summed it up. "They don't fool you, they just overpower you." Said Hilltops' assistant coach Bernie Custis, "The turning point was the first time they got the ball. They simply pushed us aside and marched right down the field for a touchdown. It gave them all the momentum they needed and we never recovered."

Next up for the Rams were the highly rated Winnipeg Weston Wildcats, in Winnipeg. But now the Rams were on a roll, and they flattened the hometown Wildcats 37-20, again leaning on their running game to do the damage.

For the second straight game, it was Kenny Walters who shone the brightest. Walters and Radcliffe each scored two touchdowns, but it was Kenny's running ability that had them talking throughout the league. In his first game as a junior he had rushed for 160 yards – now he had his feet wet and knew what it was all about. So, against the Wildcats he took the ball from quarterback Grant Becker 35 times and ran for 211 yards. "Winnipeg's defence was tough but we found a couple of weaknesses and Walters did the rest," said Currie.

The Rams headed for home to prepare for a game against the Hilltops in Saskatoon. Still smarting from the season-opening spanking, Ledingham vowed his team would be tougher this time out. Oh, really?

The Hilltops were obviously not aware that a Gord Currie-coached team, regardless of the sport, had not lost a game in Saskatoon since 1952. And it wasn't going to happen this trip, either. The Rams, their running game continuing to hum along, rushed for 323 yards on the way to a shutout, 29-0, slaughter.

Barry Radcliffe

This time it was Radcliffe who led the ground assault. Radcliffe, who also handled the placekicking chores for the Rams in 1965, rushed for 116 yards. Walters got 95 yards and Andrews 76 yards.

"Those were such great days," Radcliffe recalled years later, when he had settled into a role as a capable assistant coach with the University of Saskatchewan Huskies. "Gord Currie was a great, great coach to play for. And we had pretty good talent. That backfield of ours was tough to stop, we could hit defences in so many ways. The coaches made us think that we just couldn't lose if we all did our jobs. I will never forget those years. They're still a very big part of me."

As they headed toward the halfway mark of the schedule, undefeated in three games, the Rams faced a big challenge in the Winnipeg Wildcats, who were on their way to Taylor Field. The Wildcats, who had lost earlier to the Rams, didn't feel the Rams were as good as their 3-0 record might indicate. They also were confident they could shut down Regina's running game. Oh?

With Gary Andrews scoring two touchdowns, and the Rams displaying an effective balanced offence, Regina romped to a 21-9 win in Taylor Field before 3,000 fans and took a solid grip on first place in the Manitoba-Saskatchewan Junior Football League.

With Barry Radcliffe rushing for 103 yards, and quarterback Grant Becker completing 12 of 18 passes for 193 yards (to go with 183 yards rushing), the Rams were just too much for Winnipeg to handle. Becker threw for two touchdowns – one to Andrews and the other to end Ken McNabb.

Grant Becker

The Rams' unbeaten streak was about to come to an end as they journeyed to Saskatoon for their third meeting of the season with the Hilltops. At first the Rams looked as if they were on their way, building a 15-1 halftime lead. If you looked at the game statistics, you might have concluded the Rams were easy winners. The Rams had 21 first downs, 325 yards rushing, 101 yards passing. Walters ran for 201 yards. But the final score told the real story. The Hilltops won 20-16 – Regina's winning streak was over.

The Rams were far from finished. In fact, the next weekend they went to Winnipeg, hammered the Rods 53-7, clinched first place, and took parts of the Manitoba-Saskatchewan Junior Football League record book apart.

Ken Walters set a single game rushing record with 258 yards, driving his season total, with two games left, to 970 yards, which was a league season rushing record. The Rams ended the season with a loss to the Hilltops and a win over the Rods before heading into the playoffs.

Walters ended the season with a record-breaking 1,287 yards rushing. He was named the league's rookie of the year, the second year in a row a Ram had won the award. Not only that, but 11 Rams were named to the all-star team – Walters, Ken Huber, Barry Aldag, Ken McNabb, Grant Becker, Radcliffe, Van Moorlehem, Cam Clark, Neil Robinson and Garth West.

Ken McNabb

For those keeping track of such stuff, Currie's Balfour Tech Redmen were undefeated in four games, nobody in the Regina Intercollegiate Football League was close to them. Their offence was the key to their success. Quarterback Richard Seitz, fullback

Ken Newman and halfbacks Mel Fiissel and Stan Mustatia couldn't be stopped. The Redmen had a ground game that could strike from all directions. Sound familiar? You might want to remember the names of Seitz, Newman, Fiissel and Mustatia.

The Rams and Wildcats headed for a league showdown in a two-game, total-points playoff that opened in Winnipeg after the Cats had eliminated the Hilltops in the semifinal. Currie had some concern about what his offence's timing would be like, considering they had had two weeks off.

"We appear ready in practice, but it will be a lot different when you run against something other than the wind," he said.

The game gave Currie something to worry about. Ahead 17-16, with less than a minute to go in the final quarter, the Rams gave up a 52-yard touchdown pass that carried the Wildcats to an upset 23-17 win and a six-point lead in the series heading back to Regina.

For the first time in the season, Currie let his players have it. "We played dumb football," he said. "There are too many guys on this club that still don't appear to think that it takes 60 minutes of solid team play to win in this league. We made mistakes that you don't see in peewee football." Currie also let some of his individual players have it, too. He was especially incensed when Garry Andrews carried a pass from Becker 64 yards to the Wildcat one-yard line. The Rams thought Andrews was in the end zone. They argued. One of them, end Ken McNabb, argued a little too much and the Rams took a penalty for unsportsmanship-like conduct, moving them back, and they failed to score. "Sure I thought Garry was in for a touchdown, but the official ruled him dead on the one. So what? We had that big first down and three chances of going over for the major. What happens? We get a talking penalty. Imagine that. It's our first of the season and what a time to come."

When the Rams got back to Regina, they saw another side of Currie. They scrimmaged Tuesday, Wednesday and Thursday nights. "I want them back in the right frame of mind. In the playoffs, you don't get second chances," he said.

It was a wakeup call. It worked. The Rams fired on all cylinders, cutting loose an unbelievable passing and rushing attack that rolled over the Wildcats like an avalanche roaring through a picket fence. The total offence tallied 622 yards – 396 on the ground and 226 in the air – as the Rams won the game 60-21 and the series 77-44. Walters and Radcliffe each scored three touchdowns; Radcliffe also added five converts. Walters rushed for 171 yards and Andrews, playing what Currie described as his best game of the year, ran for 125 yards. The Rams also got Dave Orban back for the game, Recovered from his broken leg, Orban got a few shots at fullback, scoring a touchdown on a three-yard run. But his biggest moment was an electrifying 58-yard kickoff return he was one step away from turning into a touchdown.

"The boys wanted to win it and they played the kind of football they're capable of," said Currie. "Our offence couldn't have played much better than they did. But our season is not done yet."

No, it wasn't. The Rams had two more steps to take – giant ones at that. They would have to go to Edmonton and defeat the defending Western Canadian champion Edmonton Huskies. Win that one, and they would be but one win away from taking the *Leader-Post* Trophy, emblematic of the Canadian championship.

Meanwhile, back at the ranch, Currie was taking his Balfour Tech Redmen into the Regina high-school playoffs. His masterful juggling act of the Redmen and the Rams had produced an undefeated high-school team and a junior team that had produced one of the most amazing rushing attacks ever seen.

The Rams had a tough time getting to Edmonton. They were scheduled to fly. But, at the last minute, they had to take a bus to Saskatoon and then get on a passenger car hooked onto a slow freight train for an overnight trip.

When they arrived for the game, the weather had turned sour. There was a gale-force November wind knifing through Clarke Stadium, and then heavy snow began to fall, whipping up a good old-fashioned western Canadian blizzard.

Although they were leading 10-7 late in the third quarter, the Rams couldn't hang on. The Huskies came back, chewing up one Rams' mistake after another, and went on to win the Western championship 28-10. They went on to win their fourth straight Canadian championship. The Rams went home to lick their wounds.

"Penalities killed us," said Currie. "We couldn't catch any breaks. We had a good season, but we'll have a better one next year."

For Currie, the football season wasn't over. Gord's schedule with the Rams had never seen a game conflict with the

Balfour Tech Redmen. But now he was cutting it close. The Rams lost to the Huskies on a Thursday in Edmonton. The Redmen were playing Saskatoon in the provincial high-school championship on Friday night in Taylor Field, having swept undefeated through the city playoffs, and then beating Moose Jaw's Riverview Royals in the southern final.

Currie came back to Regina with his team. He boarded the train in Edmonton for the all-night trip across the black prairie, the rumbling train throwing up white clouds of snow powder as it surged south to Regina. It was a long trip, and when you lose it can also be a lonely trip, but Gord Currie was not going to let the trip slip into silence. And, so, on that train, as its lights beamed through the wintery black night sky, it was a time to feel good about the season. And everybody did.

As far as Currie was concerned, the season may well have fallen short of the ultimate goal. But strides had been taken and attitudes changed, and given what was on the way from Balfour Tech, he was sure in his own mind that 1966 would be a good season.

In Regina, it was a chilly November night. It was not the oppressive cold you can get at that time of the year; it was simply a gentle reminder that winter was lying in wait. The lights had been turned on in Taylor Field. They could be seen from everywhere in the city at that time of year. They formed an umbrella of brightness over Taylor Field that was visible from Highway 11, which was carrying the Saskatoon high-school fans on their way to Regina. They came for the fun of high-school football, and to see if their team would be the one to put away this football King Kong that Gord Currie had created at Balfour Technical School.

As time went on, people came into Taylor Field. They brought blankets and sleeping bags and thermoses filled with, of course, hot chocolate. High-school football had captured keen interest, and what better way to celebrate it than to go to a provincial championship in a province that had every right to boast of its football heritage.

It was after supper, I remember that, when the players from both teams came through the long dark tunnel and onto the field that had been graced by the likes of Ron Lancaster and George Reed, Danny Banda and Gene Wlasiuk, Doug Killoh and Henry Dorsch. They took to the end zones and began their warm-ups. The game was now near at hand.

In downtown Regina, a train pulled into one of the grandest stations in the country and slowly screeched to a halt. It was carrying, among other passengers, the Regina Rams. They were a bleary bunch as they struggled off the train to be taken home. One of them, Gord Currie, was taken to a car and driven west on South Railway Avenue. He looked as if he had slept for hours, and had just returned from a month at a health spa.

On the field, the players were running their drills. Ken Newman, Mel Fiissel, Stan Mustatia were taking handoffs and pitchouts from quarterback Rich Seitz. Little Doug Griffith was standing off near the hashmarks. He was a flanker, and in the Balfour offence he would rarely see the ball. He was just there.

I was standing just outside the tunnel that night. I was the high-school reporter for the *Leader-Post*, and we were all wondering if Gord Currie would get back in time for the game. Near the end of the warm-ups, Currie came walking through the tunnel. He came out into the lights of the greatest football stadium in the world. He looked out onto the field and he could see his Balfour Tech Redmen going through their paces. The thought occurred to him that this would be the last game he would ever coach in high-school football. It was the end to an era. "Are they ready?" Currie said. "Good, then get them into the dressing room. We've got a game to be played here tonight."

In the moments before his final high-school game of the year, his final high-school game ever, Currie spoke softly to his players. When they came from the dressing room, their eyes shone like the stars in a northern sky on a clear winter night and there was a blush on their cheeks. They moved onto the field, cleats clacking on the pavement. The game was over before it began. The Redmen won, 63-9.

The Gord Currie era in high-school football was over. Now all he had to worry about were the Regina Rams, and taking them to the highest level of all.

CURRIE'S HIGH-SCHOOL ERA ENDS

When Gordon Currie's career as a high-school coach had ended, I wrote the following column, which appeared in the *Leader-Post* of November 17th, 1965:

> Balfour Tech Redmen won another provincial championship Friday night, but at the same time they lost a guy who was largely responsible for moulding them into the champions they were. They lost a man who has enjoyed more success than any other amateur coach in the country – Gordon Currie. Currie, a soft spoken disciplinarian whose methods in coaching earned him only wide-spread respect and many championships, said after Balfour's 63-9 win over Saskatoon in the provincial final that this was his last year as head coach of the Redmen. Currie this year signed a two-year contract to coach the Regina Rams and led the Manitoba-Sakatchewan Junior Football League champs into the Western Canadian final.
>
> Currie obviously felt the strain of two full-time coaching jobs and decided that next year he would devote his coaching talents entirely to the Rams. Although Balfour suspected that Currie would call it quits after this year, the news still came as a shock. The likeable coach has ended his career at a very crucial time, at least as far as the school's football team is concerned.
>
> Graduation, a direct cause of ulcers to high school coaches, has claimed the best Balfour backfield ever, several key linemen and defensive halfbacks. Balfour has faced gigantic rebuilding tasks before but without Currie there to guide the rebuilding it seems the job will be even bigger. Few will argue with Currie's success in moulding top teams and even fewer will argue about Currie's success in developing football players. A native of Seamans, Currie has been teaching at Balfour for 18 years and has coached various high school teams from Tech for 14 of them.
>
> Since Currie took over as coach of the football Redmen, he has chalked up eight provincial titles, eight southern titles, and nine city titles. Before that he coached the junior footballers, and won the city title the two years he held the post.
>
> He headed Balfour's hockey team, winning six city titles and three provincial titles. He coached the Regina Red Sox of the Southern Baseball League for five years and winning the championship three times and the pennant four times. For two years, he coached a city Little League team to two city championships.
>
> The effect Currie has had on hundreds of youngsters in this city could never be expressed in words. He has been more than a coach, he has been a friend of his players. The Wascana Kiwanis Club honored Currie by naming him Regina's Dad-Of-The-Year in 1963. But the biggest reward Currie has gotten has been watching the happiness his kids have gotten out of winning.
>
> Reflecting back on his title-winning championship teams at Balfour, Currie rates this year's edition as one of the best. "This team definitely had the best backfield that I have ever coached," he said. He rates Mel Fiissel, a first-stringer for the last four years, as his best halfback ever. "Mel is one halfback you can count on at all times. He gives 110 per cent effort out there, always putting himself before the team." Currie's departure from high school football will be felt, but don't be surprised if he isn't back out at the 1966 Balfour training camp, lending a hand in developing another championship team.
>
> Just prior to Currie's announcement Friday night that he

Gord Currie

was resigning as head coach, the Balfour dressing room had taken on the appearance this year that it has at about this time for the past six years. Full scale bedlam prevailed as players, many with tears in their eyes, raced around, threw coaches in the showers and happily began their celebration of the team's conquest over Saskatoon earlier in the evening. For many, it would probably be their last victory celebration together. Some would abandon football completely, others would begin the quest for the few available football scholarships while others would be contemplating tryouts with the junior Rams.

Balfour this year will lose about 20 players off their squad, mostly first-stringers. Heading the list are fullback Ken Newman, halfbacks Stan Mustatia and Mel Fiissel, linemen Dick Lupastian, Bill Deal and Ken Pielak, and defensive backs Al Johnston, Rod Brown, Gary Chapelle and Doug Griffith.

The Redmen had made headlines over the years but it wouldn't have happened had it not been for great team efforts and a fellow named Gord Currie.

The Foundation Is Laid

Gord Currie was wearing his baseball cap with the bold R crested on the front. His face had the fresh ruddy look that was always there. I could see him standing on the bow of some Canadian navy destroyer, slicing through the waves of the North Atlantic, peering into the morning mist. He had served in the navy during the war, nothing unusual about that. The navy was filled with Saskatchewan kids who found at sea the same open vistas they had found at home.

In the year 1966, I was not covering the Regina Rams as a full-time beat. Ron Campbell was handling that. I was still covering high-school sports for the *Leader-Post*, and through that I had become friends with Currie. I had also come to know and become close friends with some of the Balfour Tech players who, in 1966, had graduated and were following their head coach into his second season with the Rams. So, when Campbell was away, or needed help with coverage of the Rams, I jumped right in.

The year 1966 was one of the most remarkable in the history of the Rams. For starters, Currie's status had stirred up new excitement in junior football in Regina. His incredible gift of creating championship teams was well known. His reputation as a coach and as an educator in the Regina Public School system provided the Rams with the kind of credibility that would open many doors for the organization among businesses in town. And the Rams would need that.

When Scotty Livingstone had come on board the executive of the Rams a few years earlier, anybody who knew him realized that nothing would ever again be the same for the Rams. Livingstone brought into the executive some of his pals. Guys like lawyer Joe Kanuka, chiropractor Rafe Chadwick, banker Peter McCaffrey and Reg Forsyth all followed the Pied Piper of Junior Football onto the Rams' executive. What they all had in common, and what all the others who would come on board had in common, was that they got things done. They knew that it would take considerable effort to get the Rams to where they felt they should be. But they were going to do it.

Getting Currie was the first step, a huge leap forward. "You know," I would say to him, "you're a legend. A living legend at that."

Currie would always laugh. "What's a legend?"

"You're a legend."

"I don't know what a legend is. Is a legend some guy who just hangs around for a long time and gets a little lucky?"

"Yeah," I would say, "that's what a legend is."

Gord Currie was comfortable in most situations. There was only one thing that could happen where his face might go bright red and you could see him squirming. He always had trouble handling any situation where there was too much praise being heaped on him, where he found himself being treated as some sort of coaching genius. He would do everything in his power to deflect the praise.

"What am I?" he would ask, and then he would answer his own question. "I'm an ordinary guy. I get up in the morning, I shave and shower, I go to work. I teach kids. I have to cut the lawn every Saturday. I go grocery shopping. Sometimes, I have a little too much to drink. My wife gets mad at me the same as anybody's wife gets mad at them. I'm not wealthy. I have to work for a living. I coach kids because it's fun. I enjoy the coaching because of the friendships you make that will last a lifetime. I've always said that if you can go through life and count on your hand the number of really good friends you have made, I mean really good and true friends, then you are a very lucky person. If you have just one, you are lucky. This coaching stuff, people put too much importance on it. I'm not any smarter than any other coach. I'm probably dumber than a lot of them. I've been lucky in that I've been able to coach really good athletes and really good people. But it was never me that went out and played the game. They had to play the game. I just try to stay out of the way."

Whatever.

Almost as soon as they got involved with the Rams, Livingstone and The Rat Pack hit the streets. Currie's name was the catalyst as they hit one business after another, looking for money and support of any kind so they could build a new clubhouse for the team. Not just any clubhouse. But the best clubhouse they had no money to buy.

The Rams wanted the clubhouse built for nothing. Their logo should have been an outstretched hand. They wanted everything donated. Material, labour, everything. And so, Scotty and his crew hit the streets running, their outstretched hands reaching across the oak desks of some of the most powerful and wealthy people in town. They brought the tireless Erwin Strass onto the executive. Owner of a construction company, owner of several apartment blocks, Strass was a guy who truly loved Regina and loved football. "Erwin," Scotty would tell him in the high-pitched voice he used when he got excited or wanted to have fun with somebody, "you've got more money in your pocket than I'll ever have in my lifetime."

Strass' role was to oversee the construction of the clubhouse, which would be located in north Regina, near the refinery, at the base of a large hill that had once served as the city's garbage dump. Strass' instructions were to get it built for nothing. Remember, these were mostly a bunch of guys who were wedded to the bottom line and profit margins in their professional lives, and they were going after donations from people and companies who were of the same cut.

Erwin Strass

The key selling point, the deal closer, virtually every time they came up against a reluctant businessman was, simply, the threat of embarrassment. "Okay, don't give us anything," Scotty would blurt, his face turning red and wearing the best "kicked dog" look he could muster. "But this clubhouse will get built. There's no doubt about that. And when it does get built, we are going to put a huge plaque right at the main entrance. And on that plaque will go the name of everybody who donated to the building of the clubhouse. That plaque will be there forever. You don't want your name on it?"

With Strass directing traffic, the clubhouse went up, piece by piece. "Everything we got was free," Kanuka remembers. "Everything. Including the steel from Ipsco. Jack Turvey gave that to us."

The clubhouse was put up, nail by nail, in one of the most incredible scenes in this city's history. Members of the executive, their children and wives, coaches, players, trainers, water boys, equipment managers, friends, would come to Mount Pleasant Park every day and work on the clubhouse. It was all volunteers. They were people who had jobs and families to take care of. But they still found time to help out at the Rams' clubhouse. It was built on blood, sweat and charity. The Rams had dared to dream.

The dream rose, day by day, up from the ground, until it became reality, a solid, enduring monument to the kind of dedication and devotion it took for the Regina Rams to become what they did become. When people care enough, anything is possible.

The clubhouse became the envy of not only every other junior football organization in the country, but also more than a few professional teams. Even the Saskatchewan Roughriders looked a little jealous. The Riders were still located under the stands at the exhibition grounds racetrack, and practiced on the track's infield. The Rams had their own clubhouse with a practice field right out the door, fully lit, of course, with donated light standards. This fine facility would, very appropriately, be named after Scotty Livngstone following his passing in March of 1991.

In 1966 the community embraced the Regina Rams. That year found the Regina Rams not only backed by businesses and the people of this city, it was also a year of stunning success.

That year also saw the Rams embark on an ambitious fund-raising venture intended to raise their profile and status. They decided to have a sports dinner during the late winter, and they booked the Regency Ballroom in the Hotel Saskatchewan. They needed a draw to sell tickets. So, they landed the great Chicago Bears running back Gayle Sayers. The dinner sold out.

But a funny thing happened to Sayers on his way to the podium. Joe Kanuka beat him to it. Kanuka's role was to bring greetings to the crowd on behalf of the Rams and thank the people for their support. Instead, Kanuka went a step, or two, or perhaps even three, beyond that. He chose instead to, ah, loosen up the crowd with his sense of humour. And the more laughs Joe got, the more jokes he told. The Rams' executive were looking for a hook. Sayers was beginning to look for the door. Joe kept going. Finally, he grew weary and gave way to Sayers, who had a tough act to follow, but managed to do what the Rams had brought him in to do. The dinner became an annual event and continues as an important fundraiser for the Rams to this very day.

Adding it all up, the year was something to remember. A big fundraising dinner. A brand new clubhouse. What possibly could top all of that?

Well, just wait.

Illustration by William Argan

The Championship Season

1966

Every year in junior football, one thing is for certain. Nothing is forever, and everything will change. Graduation, players moving on to other teams, scholarship offers from colleges in the United States, they all combine to rob junior football teams of their players. It is simply a part of the game. So even though the Rams of 1965 showed plenty of promise, there was no promise that all would remain the same come 1966. The executive knew, the coaches knew, everybody knew the Rams would be losing some key players, if only to graduation.

Don Bahnuik

Barry Aldag

It is quite possible that the 1965 graduating crop of Regina high-school football players was the best ever. Certainly, it was among the most talented. High-school football in the mid-1960s had steadily heated up, thanks in part to the added interest in football in Charlie Leibel's Regina minor football leagues, the dedication to kids' football from the likes of Murray Sawa and, of course, the continued growth of football teams in rural centres. Six-man and nine-man football teams could be found throughout Saskatchewan. So far, two of the most notable Rams' players to come from small town Saskatchewan, and go on to careers in the Canadian Football League, were the Riders' Don Bahnuik, from Kamsack, and Barry Aldag, from Gull Lake. This procession of talent from the country into Regina would continue.

Gordon Currie knew, going into the 1966 season, that while he would have a lot of serious talent returning from 1965, he also would have to plug some gaping holes. And the biggest hole of all was at quarterback. Grant Becker had graduated, and there was no obvious successor.

Richard Seitz

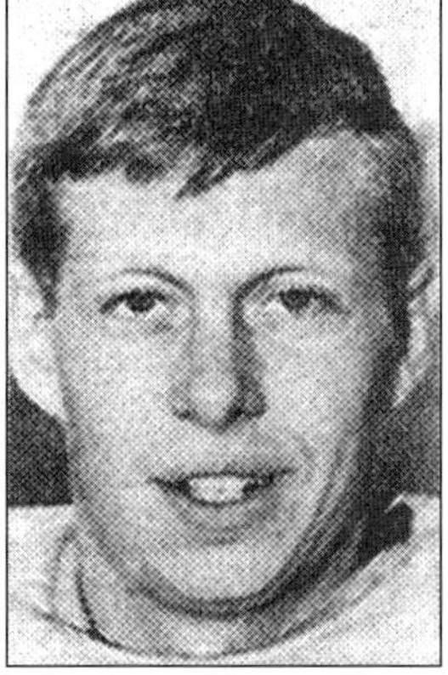

Doug Morice

The Rams would have to find one among the rookies. And Currie knew all about his top two rookie quarterbacks. One he had coached at Balfour Tech. The other he had coached against. Richard Seitz, a sturdy left-handed ball-handling magician, was Currie's starting quarterback at Balfour. Doug Morice, the better passer of the two, came to the Rams from the Scott Blues. The adjustment from high-school football to junior football was major, especially at the quarterback position, but patience was something Currie had loads of, especially with the kind of talent he saw in Seitz and Morice.

And Currie also knew that there would be a real mix of veterans coming back to go the extra yard when the going got tough.

For starters, Walters, Andrews and Radcliffe were all returning,

Ken Huber

leaving the league's best running game in 1965 intact. Dave Orban was coming off a broken leg. Barry Aldag, Paul Cocks, Ken Huber and Larry Van Moorlehem were all back on the line.

It was the crop of rookies that had Currie and his assistant coaches, Al Relkey and Gib Wagner, excited. They were familiar with virtually every one of them from their coaching days at Balfour, either having coached them or coached against them.

Larry Van Moorlehem

Al Johnston

From Balfour came defensive backs Rod Brown and Al Johnston. There was big Bill Deal from Balfour to play centre, guard Dick Hearn, flanker Doug Griffith, and lineman Bill Salloum. Other rookies, who would wear the mantles of starters with the Rams in the future, were guard Stan Crawford from Sheldon-Williams, flanker Bob Hornsberger from Scott, lineman Bob Millar from Sheldon.

Stan Crawford

Not only that, but Balfour's vaunted running game was on its way to the Rams' clubhouse: Fullback Ken Newman, who had the build of a fire hydrant; halfback Mel Fiissel, who packed both power and speed in a tank-like body; Stan Mustatia, a tall gliding runner who could also break open a game. Together, at Balfour, with Seitz at quarterback, they were simply unstoppable. Now, they were still together at the camp of the Regina Rams.

The Rams of 1966 had it pretty good compared to the Rams' teams that had gone before them. That was the year they left the rickety clubhouse on south Albert Street, where you figured the wind could blow it over at any time. And that was the year they left the gopher-hole-mounded practice field that, in 1965, had often forced Currie to move practices to King's Park in Lakeview. The rats could have the old clubhouse. The gophers could romp undisturbed. The Rams were moving up in the world, all the way to the north end of Regina where the new clubhouse and the new practice field waited for them.

Also waiting for them was the season of all seasons. The 1966 season was when the Regina Rams finally crossed the threshold that had been denied them for too long. They took an appealing batch of veterans, threw in some of the most talented rookies any junior football team had ever seen, and Currie stirred it all together. What came out the other end was the Rams' first Canadian junior football championship. The *Leader-Post* Trophy came home to Regina and took up residence in the new clubhouse.

It was a November for the ages. The Rams beat the Montreal Notre-Dame-de-Grace Maple Leafs in the national championship game in Saskatoon, 29-14. The game was played on November 11, the margin of victory was 15 points. Fifteen days later, and 15 years after they were last in a Grey Cup game, the Saskatchewan Roughriders won their first Grey Cup. They beat the Ottawa Rough Riders 29-14, the margin of victory again 15 points. Fortunately, the so-called magic of the figure 15 didn't last. It didn't take the Rams another 15 years to win another Canadian junior championship. Mind you, the same couldn't be said of the Roughriders.

With some significant changes being made to the roster, the Rams did not explode out of the gate in 1966 like Secretariat at the Kentucky Derby. It was more like the son of Secretariat taking his first steps. Although they won their season opener 12-9, against the Hilltops, the Rams flopped

Richard Seitz and Gord Currie studying film.

about for a few games after that, getting shut out 23-0 by the Hilltops in Saskatoon and losing 15-12 to the Winnipeg Weston Wildcats in Winnipeg.

It's not that the Rams didn't have their good moments through those first few games, showing flashes of what was to come. In the loss to the Wildcats, two rookies out of Balfour got their moments in the sun. Running back Mel Fiissel capped a 50-yard Rams' drive by scoring from two yards out, and linebacker Bill Locke intercepted a pass and returned it 44 yards for a touchdown. It was obvious that Currie was going to give his new players as much experience as he could. Rich Seitz, out of Balfour, Doug Morice, from Scott, both got turns at quarterback, each bringing a different flavour to the position.

In the 23-0 loss to the Hilltops, which dropped the Rams' record to 1-2, neither Seitz nor Morice was able to get much of anything going, giving up four interceptions. The Rams also turned over the ball seven times. Not pretty. Not what you would expect out of a Gord Currie-coached team.

But there was no panic among Currie or assistant coaches Al Relkey and Gib Wagner. There was anything but panic. In fact, there was confidence.

"I'm not worried about it," said Currie. "The mistakes we are making are things that will be corrected. And it is going to take time for some of our rookies to find their way in junior football."

"It doesn't matter a lot what you do now," was how Relkey put it. "It's what happens at the end of the season. Win that last game that is played, everybody is happy."

The Rams found themselves in almost a must-win situation when the undefeated Wildcats came to Regina for a Taylor Field date. Lose this one, and depending on what happened elsewhere in the Manitoba-Saskatchewan Junior Football League, the playoffs might suddenly be pushed out of reach for Regina.

Currie knew this. There have been few coaches in any sport who were as gifted as Currie was in giving a message to his players. His pre-game talks were legendary. His words were so powerful they were capable of lifting his players from terrible performances to a level where they became unstoppable. So, before they took on the unbeaten Wildcats, Currie reminded the players of what they were capable, what was expected of them, and that only they could determine what kind of a game they could play.

Players from his teams still recall some of the words he used to inspire them as they prepared for big games, or when they were locked in the grips of a slump."I remember one game where we were behind at halftime and hadn't done anything right," recalled one former Ram. "He came into the dressing room at halftime and he pulled this piece of paper from his pocket. He said it was from a guy who once played for the Rams. Gord read from the telegram. The player talked about how great it had been to be a Ram, about how it had prepared him for his life. He said he had learned values such as discipline, determination, dedication, not letting your teammates down, stuff like that. He talked about how playing for the Rams meant never letting down your teammates, always giving everything you had in every game. He went on and on about how playing for the Rams meant so much and that you took away from the experience what you had put into it. By the time, he had finished we were so pumped up we would have run through the walls to get back on the field for the second half. Of course, we came back and won the game easily. It was only later that somebody asked him if he really got that telegram at halftime. Gord admitted he hadn't, but he said that's what the guy would have said if he had sent one."

Occasionally, Currie would come into the dressing room before games, or at halftime, and talk to his players about friendship. He would take his customary position in the middle of the room, his hands often clasped together in front of him, and sometimes he would look up, as if he was getting a message from somewhere out there. "You know," he would say, "Life is full of experiences and relationships. If at the end of the day, you have learned from those experiences and become a better person for it, then it has been worth it. If, through your life, you can look back and say that you have one really special friend, then you are saying something. If you have more than one true friend, then you are very lucky. I think, to tell the truth, that I am the luckiest person in the whole world. I look around this dressing room and all I see are nothing but friends. I look around this room and all I see are my friends. I am the luckiest person in the world." No more needed to be said. The players would rocket out of the dressing room like race cars leaving the starting line at the Indianapolis 500.

When the Rams faced their first real test of the season in 1966, against the undefeated Wildcats, there was no question Currie and his staff would have the team ready. And ready they were.

For the first time all season, the Rams' offence was solid

and methodical, if not that exciting, and the defence was tenacious and prickly as the Rams stopped the Wildcats 18-3 to climb right back into the thick of the playoff hunt.

Fullback Ken Walters displayed the slashing, driving form which a year earlier had carried him to record-breaking rushing yardage, gunning for 102 yards. Richard Seitz had a game at quarterback that indicated he was finally comfortable with the position. And defensive end Gord Ciuca showed why he was one of the most feared defensive ends in the league.

"That was a big win," said Currie. "I'm afraid that if we had lost, the playoffs may have been out of reach. The boys played well, the best they have played all year."

Ciuca was simply sensational at defensive end. The respected Balfour grad twice bulled through the Winnipeg offensive line and knifed down Wildcat quarterback Bob Rye with jolting tackles, one of which produced a Rams' touchdown. Gord was a big, easy-going kind of guy. In later years, in Regina, he operated the family-owned Belgian Cleaners and cultivated a moustache that would make a walrus envious.

Gord Ciuca

Meanwhile, back to the game. Walters scored both Regina touchdowns, on one he ran down the field, recovered his own punt, and ran it in for a touchdown. Ken Walters was one of the most gifted running backs this province has ever produced. That he wore George Reed's number 34 when he was with the Rams was no coincidence. Ken Walters was the George Reed of junior football.

The 1966 season was obviously going to be somewhat of a struggle for the Rams as Currie and his staff continued to put the pieces together, remaining patient with the rookies they knew would be worth the wait. The very next game was back up in Saskatoon against the Hilltops. This rivalry was off and sizzling. These teams didn't like each other, and it would be that way forever.

The yo-yo season continued. Hot off their win over the Wildcats, the Rams on that Saturday night were no match for the Hilltops who took it to the Rams 22-14.

In the steamy Rams' dressing room after the game, there was a steady flow of players slowly going to where trainer Lloyd (Doc) Dobie had set up his table. "There's always more injuries when you lose," said Dobie.

Outside, in the cool night air, Currie, Wagner and Relkey stood around talking about the game. Holiday Park, which became Gordie Howe Bowl, sits overlooking a golf course and is next door to Cairns Stadium. The field is dug into a bowl in the ground, with the stands curving down both sidelines. The turf, as the season moves on, wears until there is little but hard dirt running down the middle, with strips of turf along the sidelines. The lighting has a sunset darkness to it, at best. But it was a charming place to watch a game, and a tough place for visiting teams to win in. Inevitably, the visiting team would spend a considerable amount of time bemoaning the hometown officiating they were sure was a part of the fabric of the stadium.

"It's always tough to win up here," Currie said. "But I thought we played well. The mistakes we made were quickly capitalized on by Saskatoon. Saskatoon is a good team and turning our mistakes into points was a strong indication of it." Currie walked back into the dressing room, stood up on a bench, and told his players, "Well, we got beat . . . but we're not out of it. Get changed and let's go eat."

The Rams came off the loss by producing their most prolific offensive game of the year, rushing for 501 yards and outlasting the Winnipeg St. James Rods 42-39 before about 2,000 fans in Taylor Field. But the game carried a price tag. Fullback Ken Walters went out with an ankle injury, but not before he had rushed for 162 yards in 20 carries.

Ken Walters broken ankle.

Rookie Ken Newman came in and the Rams' offence didn't miss a beat with the bull-necked Newman rumbling through the Rods' defence for 142 yards in 19 carries. It turned out that Walters had broken his ankle, and Newman was suddenly called on to carry the load at fullback. Newman was up to the task. It is likely that there was never a more determined running back in Rams' history than Kenny Newman, who did not have exceptional speed or a bunch of deft moves. What he had was the kind of size and strength and thick legs that never stopped churning. "It was like trying to tackle a tank," is how all-star Hilltops' linebacker Jim Seaman put it.

With Walters gone, Newman's first starting role against the Hilltops saw the Rams win 20-5. The 200-pound Newman rambled for 125 yards in 26 carries. The Rams' offence was its crisp best, the blocking of guards Barry Aldag and Larry Van Moorlehem clearing openings for Newman and halfbacks Barry Radcliffe, Garry Andrews and Mel Fiissel. The win put the Rams into a tie for first place with the Wildcats with one game left in the schedule.

The Rams closed out the season in Winnipeg against the Rods. It was a blowout. This close to a league championship, the Rams were not going to be denied. The Rams ran up 30 first downs and 489 yards rushing on their way to a 64-31 victory and first place in the Manitoba-Saskatchewan Junior Football League.

Cam Clark

Newman bulled his way 165 yards in 27 carries and scored a pair of touchdowns. Andrews scored three touchdowns. Big Cam Clark blocked a Rods' punt. The Rams were on a roll, three straight wins under their belt, the end to the Canadian championship dream clearly within reach.

And it was in Saskatoon, in the first game of the two-game total-points league final, that the Rams truly hit their stride, saw that the knotting of rookies to veterans had produced a team that truly must be reckoned with. With 3,000 fans packed into Gordie Howe Bowl, the Rams came from behind on a Sunday afternoon to take a seven-point lead with a 21-14 victory.

The Rams had trailed 13-0 just 23 minutes into the game, after a couple of costly fumbles, and for a while it looked as if they were destined to fail. "We made enough glaring mistakes and fumbles to make any team quit," said Currie, "but the boys fought it off. The will to win was the difference out there."

Ken Newman

The Rams' running game again backboned the victory. They rushed for 330 yards with Newman getting 117 of them and Radcliffe 105. Currie also had high praise for Fiissel, who only carried the ball twice, but gained 70 yards – 53 of those yards coming on an explosive 53-yard run on a second and nine play from the Rams' two yardline.

But perhaps the most telling story of how far the Rams had come came at the quarterback position. Seitz started the game, as usual, but he injured a hip on the first series of the game and was out for the rest of it. Doug Morice, another rookie, who was a starting defensive back, came in and did a superb job, controlling the Rams' offence with the poise of a veteran. As noteworthy was the fact that Morice continued to play in the defensive backfield. This was the type of football players the Rams had in 1966, the year of the big breakthrough.

Back in Regina a week later, the Hilltops were no match for the Rams. The Rams' defence came up with a near perfect performance. With 12 rookies starting, with Seitz back at quarterback, they shut out the Hilltops 17-0 in Taylor Field. It pushed the Rams onto the western junior final against the Edmonton Wildcats.

The Rams, as usual, had laid out their ground game against the Hilltops, rushing for 302 yards. But it was the defence that shone the most. Linebackers Bill Locke and Dick Hearn were outstanding. The defensive backfield of Rod Brown, Daun Daum, Bernie Brandt and Doug Morice choked the Hilltops' passing attack, with Brown intercepting two passes.

Bernie Brandt

Van Moorlehem, who played two ways, had what was described as the best game of his junior career. "Van has to be our leader," said Currie. "He's the Atchison of this club." Ron Atchison was a defensive tackle with the Roughriders who came to the Canadian Football League after a storied career with the Saskatoon Hilltops. So revered was Atch in Saskatoon that the Hilltops' practice facilities were named after him.

Currie knew he would need more of the same when the Rams played the Wildcats in the Western final. That the game was in Taylor Field was a bonus. That the Rams had won four straight games was momentum. Come game time on that Sunday afternoon, the day before Halloween, the weather was more a trick than a treat. Or at least at first. The infamous Saskatchewan winds were blowing and both the Wildcats and Rams had serious concerns about which team would best adjust to them.

Anybody who has ever been to a football game in Regina knows that if that wind is howling, it can muster the strength to either carry the football all the way to Wilcox or send it right back to where it came from. It took until the fourth quarter before the direction of the game turned in Regina's favour. And not until the Rams' Vince Germann had kicked a pair of singles, and not until the Rams had scored a safety touch did they snatch the biggest victory so far in their history. They beat the Wildcats 17-14 to advance to the Canadian junior championship for the *Leader-Post* Trophy. It would mark the first time since 1938 that a Regina team had made it that far. In 1938 the Regina Dales had won the Canadian championship.

The championship game would be played in Saskatoon's Gordie Howe Bowl, giving the Rams a short distance to travel plus the bonus of playing in a park they knew.

To get past the Wildcats, the Rams got a big game out of rookie running back Mel Fiissel, who picked up a pair of touchdowns, and had a standout game, rushing for 73 yards and picking up another 22 yards on pass receptions.

The wind was gusting at 55 miles per hour, with the score tied at 14-14, late in the fourth quarter. The Rams' Cam Clark broke through the Wildcats' line and smashed Edmonton quarterback Joe Petrone into the end zone turf for a safety touch that put the Rams ahead 16-14. The Rams got the ball on the ensuing kickoff and, with the wind at his back, with 45 seconds left, Germann booted a 47-yard single that clinched the win.

For Scotty Livingstone, Joe Kanuka, Rafe Chadwick and other Rams' executives, who by now were howling their ecstacy in the stands of Taylor Field, the victory and the season was a vindication of all they had put into turning around the Regina Rams. But the best was yet to come.

That the Rams were going to Saskatoon to play for the Canadian junior championship on Friday, November 11th caught Regina by its shoulders and shook it to life. An enormous caravan of cars, carrying people to Saskatoon, was on Highway 11 the morning of the game. A three-hour pep rally on the paved link between the two cities was something the province had never seen before.

Rod Smith, Cam Clark, Ken Huber, Gord Ciuca, Larry Van Moorlehem

FIRST NATIONAL CHAMPIONSHIP

It was a grey November morning that dawned on Remembrance Day of 1966 in Saskatoon. There was a chill in the air, but not the biting cold you might expect that time of year in Saskatchewan. In the Executive Hotel, on the edge of downtown, Gordon Currie was up early. So were his assistant coaches and even some of his players. More than a few of them had had trouble sleeping. Currie was excited. These were the days in his coaching career that he loved, when the challenges were huge and the clichés were trotted out. No tomorrow. Do or die. One chance.

Dave Orban

There are teams and athletes who never get to play for championships. Some of the greatest athletes in the world never got to compete for the ultimate championship in their sport. Gord Currie made a career of winning championships. It was that simple. So, on this November 11th in 1966, this simply represented another championship opportunity.

The Regina Rams, born in 1954, had never had a season in which they had gone the distance. But that changed in 1966. On Friday, November 11, 1966 in Gordie Howe Bowl in Saskatoon, they came to their defining moment. They went up against the Montreal Notre-Dame-de-Grace Maple Leafs for the Canadian junior football championship in a game that was as unpredictable as it was remarkable.

With a crowd of 4,500 fans packed into Gordie Howe Bowl, many of them having made the journey from Regina, the air crackled with the kind of electricity that only games like this can generate. If the Rams had had their resilience as a team tested all season, it had never been tested as it would be on this holiday afternoon.

Before the fans had a chance to settle into their seats, even before Rams' president Scotty Livingstone had the chance to complete his customary fun bets with the opposing team's executive, the first touchdown was flashed up on the scoreboard. A stunning, but beautifully executed 103-yard touchdown return off the game's opening kickoff by Montreal's Frank Belveredge momentarily knocked the wind out of the crowd and shook the Rams.

Where a play like that could put a team on its heels, this one seemed only to jolt the Rams awake, fortify them. It was as if a wakeup call had been delivered. They were not going to be handed this thing on a platter. They would have to go get it. And go get it they did. They stared that moment of adversity in the face and never looked back. By the end of the first quarter, the Rams were ahead 15-7; they led 21-7 at the half; there was no scoring in the third. The Rams put it away in the fourth quarter, winning 29-14 to take the *Leader-Post* Trophy back to Regina.

Only twice before had Regina teams won the *Leader-Post* Trophy. The Regina Pats Football Club, coached by Al Ritchie, won it in 1928 and the Regina Dales, coached by Paul Dojack, won it in 1938.

The Rams won this game in 1966 for two main reasons. One was their rushing game, the other was a tenacious defence that simply smothered Montreal's offence. The Rams' ground game, guided by the smooth Richard Seitz, a rookie quarterback now playing with the poise of a veteran, was easily the best in the country. Maybe, one of the best ground games ever. It didn't seem to matter if Ken Newman or Dave Orban was playing fullback; it didn't seem to matter if Mel Fiissel, Barry Radcliffe, Stan Mustatia or Garry Andrews were at halfback. They were as unstoppable as an avalanche.

Stan Mustatia

The Rams that November day in 1966 painted a portrait of running football that was one for the ages. They rushed for 374 yards on the hard-worn ground of Gordie Howe Bowl, the blocking of Van Moorlehem and Barry Aldag opening huge holes in the Maple Leafs' defence. The piston-legged Newman churned for 106 yards; Orban had 99 yards; Fiissel slashed for 93 yards; Andrews, who played middle linebacker for most of the game, found time to rush for 54 yards. The Rams hardly threw the ball at all, gaining but 60 yards in the air.

Rod Smith

The Rams' defence never gave Montreal's offence a chance. They held Maple Leafs' all-star running back Tommy Dyce to 84 yards rushing, and held Montreal's total ground game to 134 yards. Montreal couldn't throw the ball against the Rams, ending up with minus six yards passing yardage. The Rams' defence was led by linebackers Bill Locke, Andrews and Dick Hearn. Tremendous pass rush pressure came from ends Gord Ciuca and Rod Smith.

When it was all over, a beaming Currie stood in the hallway of the Rams' dressing room, his smile growing wider as the noise from his celebrating players grew louder and louder, washing over the now empty Gordie Howe Bowl like a warm tropical wave on that chilly November day. Rams' executive Reg Forsyth, Scotty's eternal sidekick, handed Currie the *Leader-Post* Trophy and Currie took a sip of the champagne that it held. He talked about his assistant coaches and his players. He had nothing but praise for his players and their devotion to not only the season, but especially to this game.

"I knew at breakfast this morning that the boys were ready. You can sense these things. The only thing I was worried about was that we might be too tense and we were. But that touchdown on the opening play just brought us back to reality and from then on we played extremely well."

Few people who were at that game truly had any idea of the meaning of the victory. It was right there that the foundation was dug and the tradition planted for what the Regina Rams would become. They became a winning organization that day, one that expected to win and would never come to accept that it couldn't. Currie would coach the Rams through the 1976 season and not once would the Rams miss the playoffs.

In 1966, the good times started to roll.

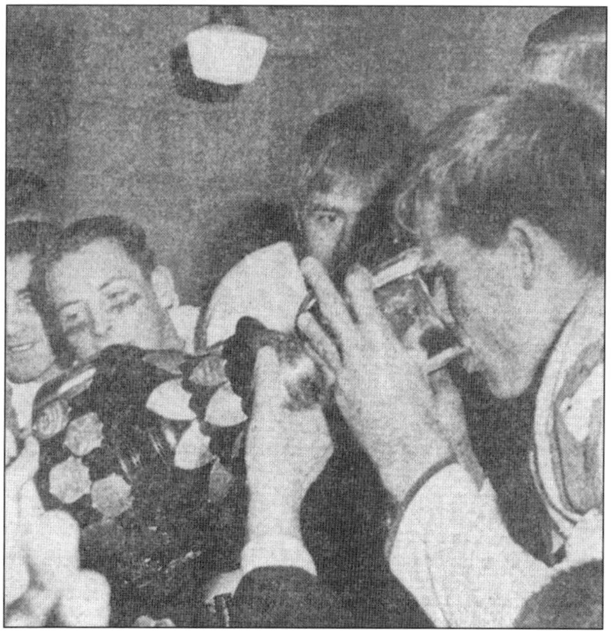

Moving Toward Excellence

1967-1969

The happiest of endings would be if you could say that having won their first Canadian junior football championship, the Regina Rams never stopped winning them. Well, in some ways there was something to that. Over the years and decades that followed 1966, the Regina Rams won more than their share of Canadian junior championships. They became the showcase organization for junior football in the country, a group plugged into the legend of Gord Currie and tapping into the finest minor football system in Canada, that being the one that runs from one end of Saskatchewan to the other. Of course, the Saskatoon Hilltops also had access to that same system, and in a three-year stretch from 1967 through 1969, the Hilltops had the Rams' number once the playoffs rolled around. The road to the Canadian championship passed through Saskatoon in 1967, 1968 and 1969, and not once in those years were the Rams able to break through the Hilltops' blockade.

Jim Charter

Brian Closs

Wayne Borys

When the Rams won the *Leader-Post* Trophy in 1966, it marked the end to the junior football careers of a number of players. The most notable who graduated from the junior ranks were linemen Barry Aldag, Larry Van Moorlehem and Paul Cocks. Also wrapping up his junior career was Garry Andrews, who had excelled as a running back and a middle linebacker. Those four graduations left bigger holes than one would naturally expect with the loss of experienced and talented players. The Rams also lost the leadership of those four players.

But if 1967 was the year those four left, it also was a year in which talented new faces appeared on the Rams' radar.

Big Wayne Borys, a tall, agile lineman, came from the Sheldon-Williams Spartans. Jim Charter, Bill Deal and Frank Ens arrived from Balfour – Charter a guard and tackle, Deal a centre and Ens a defensive end. Lanky George McLeod, a defensive end from northern Saskatchewan, opened more than a few eyes when he showed up. Brian Closs was another in a growing line of players to make the trip from Moose Jaw to play for the Regina Rams. Closs was a six-foot, three-inch, 230-pound defensive lineman whose easygoing nature off the field belied the toughness he took to the turf on game day.

If anybody out of Regina's high-school league came into camp with rave reviews, it was Campion's Don Schmidt. One of the most versatile players around, Schmidt played running back, took a turn on defence, and punted. He was as good a team player as the Rams would have. He was a standout performer who often brought courage to the game. Perhaps his most outstanding moment came in a

1966 playoff game against Balfour, a game that stretched brilliantly into overtime. Near the end of an overtime quarter, Schmidt was resting on the bench, having played most of the game on both offence and defence. He could barely walk, let alone run, but he kept finding ways to get back on his feet and back into the game. With the outcome of the game on the line, some of Schmidt's teammates helped him back onto the field to punt the football. His kick went far enough that it counted for the winning single and brought to an end Balfour's reign as high-school champions. Watching the game that autumn night in Taylor Field was Notre Dame's Père Murray. Murray grabbed me in the press box and asked me to take him over to Campion College. "I've got to meet that kid," Père said. When we got to Campion, Père burst through the dressing room doors, yelling in that raspy voice of his, "Where's Schmidt! Where's that Schmidt kid!" Père found Don sitting on a bench near the far wall. Père rushed over, hugged him, and told him that the game he had played that night against Balfour was "one of the greatest individual efforts of courage I have ever seen." When Don Schmidt showed up at the Rams' camp, Currie and his staff knew what they were getting. No surprises there.

Don Schmidt

The most surprising rookie came from Shaunavon, a southwestern Saskatchewan town not far from the Gull Lake home of the Aldags. Ron Nicolson was about six feet tall and packed a rock-hard 200 or so pounds with him. He could run with the wind. But he was about as green as the lawns in Shaunavon.

Gord Currie remembers him. "He had the size and he was as fast as just about anybody on our team. But he was raw. Yikes, he had so much raw talent that you knew it didn't matter how long it took to get him to use it in a proper football sense, it would be well worth it."

Luckily, Currie had just the coach to do the job. Gib Wagner had left the Rams' coaching staff after the 1966 season due to business pressures. Currie went out and brought in Doug Killoh to handle the linemen. He couldn't have found a better coach.

The soft-hearted, gruff-talking Killoh came from Regina's east end. He had played junior football in the days of the

Ron Nicolson

Doug Killoh

Dales and Bombers, then went on to a Plaza of Honor career with the Roughriders, playing alongside the likes of Ron Atchison and Bill Clarke. Killoh also was an exceptional hockey player. It took Killoh a year or so, but in the end he turned Nicolson into one of the top defensive ends in the league. His speed and his quickness were always his biggest strengths, but once Ron learned the finer points of the game, he was spectacular. He was virtually impossible to block one on one.

The Rams went into the 1967 season filled with the typical optimism generated by winning a championship. They felt they had what it takes to win a second straight championship. And, if they could get to the national final, it would be played in Regina in November. What more could you ask for than a winning season capped by a title-winning final game right in your own backyard.

For the Rams, in 1967, the road would be a rough one, at times. In the year Canada celebrated its centennial, the

Rick Seitz, Ken Newman and Mel Fiissel

Rams opened the season on the road, traveling to Saskatoon to take on the Hilltops. The rivalry had heated up, and its temperature had risen even higher when the Rams had won the Canadian championship the previous year in Saskatoon's football park. They had used the Hilltops' dressing room to boot.

So, when the Rams hit Saskatoon for that first game, the Hilltops were ready for them. Compounding everything was that the Rams chose their season-opener to play perhaps their sloppiest football game since Currie had taken over as head coach.

They played as if they would have rather been somewhere else. They couldn't get any kind of sustained offence going. Their defence couldn't handle Saskatoon's short crisp passing game. And the Rams managed to take penalties at the worst times. They ended up losing, 27-13. Twice during the game, Rams' players forgot to go on the field during changes; twice the Rams found themselves with only 10 players out there.

"That's what we needed," said Currie, ever searching for the proverbial silver lining in the black clouds. "It gave everybody a chance to know how the guy beside him plays."

For the Rams, the highlights were brief. Mel Fiissel scored a pair of touchdowns and Ken Newman was the top rusher with 98 yards. Moose Jaw's Rod Smith showed himself a capable receiver, catching four Richard Seitz passes for 64 yards.

Rod Smith

The Rams had a tough week at practice as they prepared for a rematch with the Hilltops back in Regina. So much for coming back at the Hilltops. The Rams flopped again, for the second straight week. This time, the game was marked by the Rams' inability to put the ball into the end zone, and Saskatoon escaped from the Queen City with a 9-4 victory before 3,500 fans in Taylor Field.

The Rams knew what was coming. All of a sudden, they were getting awfully close to putting themselves in danger of missing the Manitoba-Saskatchewan Junior Football League playoffs. The Rams were headed for the Labour Day weekend where they would be playing two games in three days.

When they had won the Canadian junior football championship, the Rams had received an invitation to play the junior AKO Fratmen in Windsor, Ontario in an exhibition game on the Saturday of the long weekend. There was a bit of history made in Regina on the Friday, the day the Rams flew to Windsor. The first DC9 jet to fly out of Regina carried the Regina Rams to Windsor. The Rams were treated royally in Windsor, taking in the sights of nearby Detroit on the Friday before their Saturday afternoon game with AKO.

The timing of the Windsor trip couldn't have been better as far as Currie was concerned. It gave the team the opportunity to spend the whole weekend together. They could use the Windsor game as a tuneup for their Monday game in Winnipeg against the Wildcats, get some of the wrinkles out of what had been thus far an inconsistent team. The Rams did show some flashes of their former fire in Windsor, even though they lost the game 16-12.

By the time they hit Winnipeg, you could sense something different about the Rams. They were more relaxed and more focused on the task at hand. They had learned the hard way that winning a Canadian championship doesn't mean a thing the following season.

The Rams came out with all guns blazing against the Wildcats on Monday. They took the lead near the end of the first quarter and never looked back, scooting to a 27-12 victory.

Russ Marchuk

It took a big effort from the Rams' offensive line to get the ground game going again. And Ken Newman cashed in on his best game so far in the season, rushing for 131 yards and scoring two touchdowns. Richard Seitz had a remarkable game at quarterback. His play calling and ball handling kept the Wildcats off guard throughout the whole game. Even the kicking game was in sync. Punter Russ Marchuk averaged over 41 yards per punt, including a booming 67-yarder.

The Rams were back on track.

And they kept it going. A week later, in Taylor Field, the ground attack exploded as they steamrolled to a 51-0 victory over the Winnipeg St. James Rods. Veteran halfbacks Mel Fiissel and Barry Radcliffe each scored a pair of touchdowns, and Seitz scored a touchdown on one of his patented quarterback options. The Rams were off and running.

Riding a two-game undefeated streak, the Rams took their act to Saskatoon the following weekend, anxious to gain some revenge for the season-opening loss they had suffered at the hands of the Hilltops. With a crowd of 5,800 fans shoehorned into Gordie Howe Bowl, the Rams exploded for 19 points in the final minutes of the first half and won the game running away, 29-15.

Newman had his best game of the season, scoring 10 points himself, rushing for 153 yards, and laying plenty of hurt on any Hilltop who got in his way.

"The only way you can expect to beat the Rams is to keep their offence off the field," said Hilltops' head coach Al Ledingham. "If you don't, you could be in for a long day."

The city of Regina was clearly embracing the Rams. The previous year had been a great one for football. The Rams had won their first *Leader-Post* Trophy. The Roughriders had won their first Grey Cup. Football fever was at a volcanic peak, with both teams looking capable of repeating in 1967.

Living off the momentum of a three-game winning streak, the Rams came home to Taylor Field to face the Wildcats. A Rams' victory would clinch a playoff berth. In front of a record home crowd of over 10,000 fans, the Rams were taking on a desperate team in the Wildcats, who had to win to avoid being eliminated from the playoffs.

Fighting like the cornered cats they were, Winnipeg came back from a 16-point Regina lead to run away with a 35-20 victory. They beat up the Rams in virtually every phase of the game, manhandling both the offensive and defensive Rams' lines. The Rams turned over the ball seven times, six on fumbles. "You can't expect to win when you turn over the ball that many times," an obviously unhappy Currie said. "We had the opportunity to nail down a playoff spot. Now, we've made it tough on ourselves."

The Rams could not afford another loss. And Ken Newman, their hard-nosed fullback, wasn't about to let it happen again. Currie had spent much of the week trying to find a reliable placekicker. Then, Newman showed up at practice one night with a square-toed right cleat in his hand. He said he'd do it, and he did.

At home to the Hilltops, it was the Kenny Newman show. Newman kicked a pair of field goals and converted the

Ken Newman

touchdown he had scored as the Rams beat the Hilltops 13-6. Newman also rushed for 69 yards, somewhat off his usual standards. But Radcliffe picked up the slack, gaining 127 yards along the ground.

As it turned out, the Rams' playoff hopes hinged on what they did in Winnipeg, the last game of the schedule, against the Rods. The Rods, once the kingpins of Canadian junior football, were now the doormats of the Manitoba-Saskatchewan Junior Football League, and they were easy pickings for the Rams.

With Newman scoring 20 points, rushing for 128 yards and catching two passes for another 39 yards, the Rams won 38-7. Mel Fiissel scored a pair of touchdowns. Rich Seitz had his best passing game of the season, throwing for 223 yards and firing touchdown strikes to Fiissel and Stan Mustatia.

Stan Mustatia

It wasn't going to get any easier for the Rams. They would face the Hilltops in a two-game, total-points series for the league championship. The first game was scheduled for Regina's Taylor Field. The Rams felt good about the playoff. They had won their last two games against Saskatoon.

But the Hilltops turned the tables on the Rams. They beat the Rams at their own game. They rushed for 306 yards while holding the Rams' ground game to just 76 yards, Newman getting 64 of them.

Ledingham, who had lost his share of games to the Rams, was having trouble containing the obvious delight he felt over having walked into Regina's backyard and leaving with an 18-point lead. "We haven't got it wrapped up yet," he said, "but the 18-point leading going into the second game in our park is a mighty nice thing to have."

Currie knew his Rams were up against it, big time. "We seem to have to do things the hard way this season and this time we are really behind the eight ball. That 18 points isn't impossible to overcome, but . . ."

But it was impossible. The Hilltops scored on their first possession and went on to win the game 25-9 and the series 50-16. The season, although disappointing in its ending, was not without its rewards for the Rams. The unstoppable Newman was named the league's most valuable player, his season's total of 1,079 yards by far tops in the league. And Rod Smith was named the most gentlemanly player.

The Rams, who finished 1967 with five wins and three losses, posted an identical record in 1968, in a season which saw them go without such stars as Ciuca, Locke, Radcliffe and Fiissel, who had graduated. But they also had their annual infusion of new talent which assured the Rams they would field a competitive team. They had been firmly established as a team to play for. Their Canadian championship in 1966 and their winning records since Currie had joined them in 1965 magnified their appeal to young football players.

Ron Scrimbitt

Bob Johnstone

Bill Pastuch

Monte Ziola

When they opened training camp in the summer of '68, the new crop was highlighted by quarterback Mike Hill from Campbell, back Bob Johnstone from Sheldon-Williams, linebacker-running back Ray Manz from Campion, and back Billy Pastuch, lineman Dieter Pelzer, receivers Ron Scrimbitt and Henry Schubach, all from Balfour. The versatile Monte Ziola showed up from Campion and lineman Don Tingle came from Campbell.

The Hilltops had also tapped into Regina's high-school scene, emerging with the top graduating player of the lot. Dave Pickett, a quarterback out of Campion, went to Saskatoon to enroll at the University of Saskatchewan. In his first year there he won the starting quarterback job for the Hilltops. Pickett went on to guide the Hilltops to some of their best years ever before moving on to the University of Saskatchewan Huskies. There he was named the Hec Creighton Trophy winner as the outstanding Canadian college player.

As usual, the Rams opened the season with back-to-back games against the Hilltops. Saskatoon marched into

Regina and beat the Rams 28-18. But a week later, back in Saskatoon, the Rams took a piece out of the Hilltops, winning 24-8. The difference from one game to the next for the Rams was twofold. They pressured Pickett relentlessly and also got their running game going. Newman, coming off his MVP season, was his usual unstoppable self. In fact, the resourceful fullback-placekicker scored all 24 Regina points.

The Rams won their second straight game the following weekend in a bizarre finish that produced a 19-13 Regina victory. With the score tied at 13-13 late in the fourth quarter, the Rams were at the Winnipeg Rods' 24 when Bob Johnstone, who had played a standout game as defensive back, was sent in by Currie to punt for the winning single. Johnstone's punt was fielded by Darcy Normand in the end zone. Normand went to kick it back out, but it didn't go far enough. And a Rams' backup linebacker, Tom Ireton, an unlikely hero, was there to fall on the ball for the winning touchdown.

Don Schmidt

Back in Regina, a week later, it was no contest. The Rams shut out the Rods 33-0, the spark coming when Currie chose to alternate rookie Mike Hill and veteran Richard Seitz at quarterback. With Don Schmidt, Bob Hornsberger and Newman all producing big plays, the Rams put together their most balanced offensive attack of the season, and set up the third meeting of the season between the Rams and Hilltops.

The Hilltops made no secret of what their plans were for the Rams. They had to stop Newman. The plan was sound. The execution was a little flawed. Newman rushed for 118 yards, Don Schmidt had another 63, and the Rams were on their way to their fourth straight win, this one coming in Saskatoon. The irony of the night was that it wasn't Newman's pile-driving legs that decided it. It was the square-toed boot he wore on his right foot. With 10 seconds left in the game, Newman kicked a 17-yard field goal for the winning points.

Hilltops' coach Al Ledingham was not amused. He could be heard screaming at his players at halftime. "You know every single play in their playbook," Ledingham shouted. "There's no excuse for not stopping them."

The Rams clinched a playoff spot a week later in one of the goofiest games in their history. Just hours before game time Saturday, heavy rain began to fall. About an hour or so before kickoff, the City of Regina told the Rams they would not be able to play on Taylor Field's grass. The city did not want the turf ruined for the Roughrider games. So, the game against the Winnipeg Wildcats was moved to Mount Pleasant, where the Rams kept their heads above water to win by a 2-0 score.

Rams' president Ken Wheeler was not the least bit amused at the last-minute notice, and he teed off on the City of Regina. "This is ridiculous. We've got to come up with a better solution than finding out just before game time where we're going to play."

Scotty Livingstone, hearing of Wheeler's tirade, thought it might not be a good idea for the Rams to start criticizing City Hall. Into the fray jumped Scotty. "We've got to make one thing clear. We're not taking a swing at the city for telling us to get out of there on Saturday. We agreed before the season started that if they felt we'd damage the field on a rainy day, we'd go."

Whatever. One thing was for sure. It was the Rams' last hurrah for 1968. They were blasted 40-13 by the Hilltops and quarterback Dave Pickett a week later. Then, a week before the playoffs began, the Rams were upset 19-10 in Winnipeg by the Wildcats.

The season officially came to an end for the Rams when they once again lost to the Hilltops in the two-game, total-points league final, this time by a combined score of 48-32. The Hilltops found their game in the playoffs, with Pickett and receiver Al Rankin tearing apart the Rams' defence, and fullback Archie Thomson establishing a ground game.

For the Rams, it was back to the drawing board. "We found out that the Hilltops are the best team in the league," said Currie. "There was no doubt about that. We know where we have to get to if we want to beat them."

For Seitz and Newman, it was their last season in junior football, their glorious careers with the Rams were coming to a close. Both would look back on those days as among the greatest in their lives.

As some junior careers ended in 1969, others were just starting. In this year the Rams continued to make improvements, hoping they would be enough to catch the Hilltops.

Currie's ability to entice graduating high-school players to the Rams continued. Among the more notable of the new faces at Mount Pleasant was that of lineman Jim Hopson, who would some day enjoy a career with the Saskatchewan Roughriders. Linebacker Tony Husli was another new face in 1969. And the second of the Nicolson brothers from Shaunavon showed up. Oh, did he show up! His name was Alex and, although he might have been Ron's baby brother, he was anything but a baby when he hit camp. Alex packed 280 pounds on his six-foot frame. And if his size wasn't enough to catch some eyes, then his speed certainly was. Like his brother Ron, Alex was, plain and simple, fast. Both Alex and Ron would make the Manitoba-Saskatchewan Junior Football League all-star team in 1969.

Wayne Pyne had been an assistant coach for the Rams during their early years. Now, his son Rob showed up at the Rams' camp. Once his junior career was over, Rob followed in his dad's footsteps and also went on to play for the Roughriders.

Gary Wilson

Kim Ziola

Gary Wilson, a graduate from Thom Collegiate, made the team and, although short, he became one of its top defensive backs. The second of the Ziola brothers, Kim, lined up with Monte in 1969.

No matter what else the Rams had, it was a given they would always have a ground game. With Mike Hill at quarterback, the Rams opened the season at home to the defending champion Hilltops. With Rick Ackerman rushing for 125 yards, the Rams carved out a 27-6 victory. Ackerman, Bill Pastuch and Ray Manz scored the Rams' touchdowns as the Hilltops, with quarterback Dave Pickett, made far too many mistakes to contend with Regina on this day.

The Rams' running game took off a week later in Winnipeg in a 38-0 whipping of the Wildcats. The speedy Bobby Kerr exploded for 180 yards rushing, mostly on bursts around the ends, while Ackerman bulled his way up the middle for 132 yards.

A week later, the Rams hung their second straight shutout up on the board, this time devouring the Winnipeg Rods 61-0 in Taylor Field. Ackerman scored three touchdowns, Flanker Ron Scrimbitt scored two touchdowns and backs Don Schmidt, Bill Pastuch, Rob Pyne and Garry Wilson each scored one in what was at this point the most lopsided win in Rams' history.

Suddenly, the Rams looked as if they were unbeatable. In three straight victories, they had given up only six points. And now they were on their way to Saskatoon, licking their chops at another shot at the hated Hilltops. The Rams feasted again, this time winning 19-4. A week later, in front of 5,000 Taylor Field fans, the Rams won their fifth straight game, this time trampling the Rods 26-1. Currie was again alternating his quarterbacks, this time spelling off starter Mike Hill with Barry Polowick. Rookie Dave Seeley, injured in training camp, played his first game at running back and churned for 71 yards in 12 carries.

Dave Seeley

The rivalry between Saskatoon and Regina was about to move to a new level when the two teams locked horns in Saskatoon. The Rams could hardly wait to board the bus to Saskatoon for this one, feeling quite smug about their undefeated season. In Saskatoon, the Hilltops could hardly wait, either, for another shot at the Rams. Gordie Howe Bowl was filled for the Saturday night game, about 5,000 fans crammed into the place.

They got their money's worth. Somewhere between Regina and Saskatoon the Rams forgot what it took to win. Hilltops' quarterback Dave Pickett, as good a short passing artist as there was, picked apart the Rams' defence as no team had picked it apart all season. And halfback Gord Remmen had a career game, rushing for 194 yards, as the Hilltops stopped Regina's undefeated season with a 32-0 wakeup call.

The game turned into one of the roughest ever played between the two teams. There was everything from kicking to gouging. Despite the outright fights that broke out, the only surprise was that there were no player ejections.

A week later, the Hilltops came to Regina, and for the second week in a row they again beat the Rams, this time by a 13-9 count.

It set up what was becoming an annual meeting of the two teams, battling for the league championship. The Hilltops, who had gone on to win the Canadian championship in 1968, were looking to repeat in 1969. The Rams opened the two-game, total-points final with a 7-3 home victory, but a four-point lead wasn't much of a gap for the Hilltops to have to close. Hilltops' coach Dean Dickson, a former student of Currie's at Balfour Tech who had taken over from Ledingham, was only concerned about making sure his Hilltops were ready for Regina.

They were. The Hilltops simply had too many guns for the Rams to handle. Pickett was the best quarterback in the league, and he showed it down the stretch. The defence, led by linebacker Jim Seaman, was suffocating. Stan Polak gave the Toppers the best kicking game in the country. The Hilltops won the second game of the series 20-14 to take the total-points affair 23-21. They sent the Rams back to the drawing board yet one more time.

Al Relkey coaches players Rod Brown, Al Johnston, Bill Locke and Bill Pastuch.

THE DYNASTY TAKES OFF

1970

The coach nearly always arrived at the clubhouse in the north end of town in a bit of a hurry, a few minutes late for practice. He would park his car in the lot, stroll through the doors, always with a smile on his face, and he would stop and talk with trainers, equipment managers, players, assistant coaches.

"Okay," Gord Currie would say, as the eager-to-practice players began heading out onto the field, their cleats clicking as they went down the hallway, "what are we doing tonight." One after another, the coaches would talk about what they wanted to do at practice. "Okay," said Currie, "then let's go do it." And out they would go.

Sometimes, members of the media were waiting for Currie to do an interview. Most times, he was a terrible interview, especially if they were looking for excitement. He had a way with words that made you think you were back in school getting a lecture. Often, if he was in a hurry, he would tell me, "You write it. Just make up my quotes. You know what I want to say. And you're better at it than I am anyway."

There were always voices of optimism at any Regina Rams' practice, no matter what. Currie would roam about from one set of players to another set of players, clapping his hands and speaking words that rang with encouragement and confidence. Sometimes, he would talk to a group of players, or to individual players. He always knew something about them, or their families, because he genuinely cared about them.

He always found good in people, even when others might have stopped looking for it. There was one running back who got into a fistfight with a cop. Currie wasn't about to abandon him for that. "The guy's a tough guy, he's not a bad person. In fact, he's darn smart. He's just tough and if he gets himself in a spot where he thinks he has to prove it, then he will," Currie said.

Another talented football player had come from a difficult home life and, as time went on, after his playing days, he found himself in one jam after another. He ended up in jail. One time, his mother phoned Currie. She said she had received a letter from her son, who was in prison in Manitoba. The son wanted her to send him a Rams' sweater. Currie got one and it was sent to the prison where this kid Gord Currie had coached was behind bars. "The Rams were probably one of the few things in his life that he enjoyed, one of the few things that was good for him. He was never any trouble for us. To ask for a sweater shows he does care about things. He's not a bad guy. Some day, he'll straighten himself out," Currie said.

For Gord Currie to give up on anybody, to write anybody off as hopeless, was something I never saw nor heard. And I have known him since 1964. He is the most decent, honest person I have ever met. His players picked up on this and they would do anything he asked them to do because, above everything else, they trusted him. When Currie ran for politics and was elected as a MLA for Regina in the Progressive Conservative government of Grant Devine, he lasted only one term before he had had enough. He simply could not stand the "politics" of politics. It was that simple. He wasn't capable of playing the games politicians play. So he did the only thing he could do. He left.

"There was always something special about him," Mel Fiissel once said. "It was like he was royalty, as if there was an aura around him." Fiissel was a star running back for Currie at Balfour Tech and then with the Rams. When his playing days ended, he played for a while with the Regina Buffaloes, a senior team, as did Ken Newman and a few other former Rams. There was some humour attached to his days with the Buffaloes. "I played through high-school football and then with the Rams," he said. "I never got hurt. One year with the Buffaloes and I got my nose broken." But Mel stayed close to the Rams. He helped out with the equipment duties, that sort of thing, just to be around. In 1970, he joined the Rams as an assistant coach, joining Al Relkey and Doug Killoh on Currie's staff. Fiissel and Currie formed a friendship that ran deep, and is strong to this very day. Fathers and sons don't always have what these two shared.

Mel Fiissel

Al Relkey

The 1970 season marked one in which the championship juices really began to flow through the Rams. Since Currie had taken over as head coach in 1965, they had danced in the winners' circles, but with one exception they had never made it to the big dance, the Canadian championship.

All that would change in 1970. There is never any specific reason for these things happening in sport. They just happen. There has to be talent. But talent is not always the answer. Why, in 1970, would the Saskatchewan Roughriders win 14 of 16 games and then lose in the playoffs to the third-place Calgary Stampeders? There has to be good coaching. But good coaching doesn't always guarantee anything. No, there is no set formula. It just all comes together. It just all clicks. And that is what happened with the Rams in 1970.

It was the start to a remarkable string of victories. From 1970 through 1976, the Rams would put together three undefeated seasons, two seasons in which they lost only one game, appear in six Canadian championship games and win five of them. If that isn't something to write home about, then nothing is. No team in Canadian junior football could match them. They were so far ahead of the pack it was almost boring. The 1970s marked the third decade in which Gord Currie had coached sports, and eventually the time came when enough was enough. Currie stayed with the Rams through 1976, retiring after he had won yet another Canadian championship.

The 1970 season provided the Rams with a harvest of riches in graduating high schoolers who flocked to Mount Pleasant in the swelter of July for the Rams' training camp. It was a group from which would ultimately come some of the greatest Rams ever, some of whom would stay on long after their playing days were over.

There was John Broderick, who developed into a running back capable of breaking games open. There was Bryan Dimen, a teardrop of a football player from Balfour Tech who made up for his lack of size with a rare football intelligence and a fierce competitive spirit. So talented, so versatile was Dimen that it didn't matter where he was playing – in the defensive backfield or at quarterback – he was the best there was on the field.

Jerry Orban was a tough-as-nails offensive lineman who possessed an exceptional work ethic and a love for football. He enjoyed an all-star career with the Rams and then became a line coach. From there he stayed close to the team by appearing as the colour commentator on Rams' radio broadcasts.

Dave Sawa brought with him the toughness all the Sawas possess, as well as raw athletic ability. His father, Murray, had long been a tireless worker for minor football in Regina, making sure there were teams and a league for kids to play in. It was only natural that his kids would also get involved in football, and a number of other sports as well.

Even though the Rams had been beaten by the Hilltops in the league final in 1969, they moved into the 1970 season brimming with confidence. They figured they were strong at quarterback with Mike Hill and Barry Polowick. They knew they had a dynamic running game in Bobby Kerr and Rick Ackerman. Fact is, the Rams figured they were solid everywhere. It would just be a matter of when they put it all together.

It didn't take long. The Rams opened the season against the Hilltops with 2,000 fans in Taylor Field. You could hear the explosion all the way back to Saskatoon. The Rams scored 55 points in the second half, on the way to a 64-0 lacing of the Hilltops, who had lost most of their top players from the 1969 Canadian championship team.

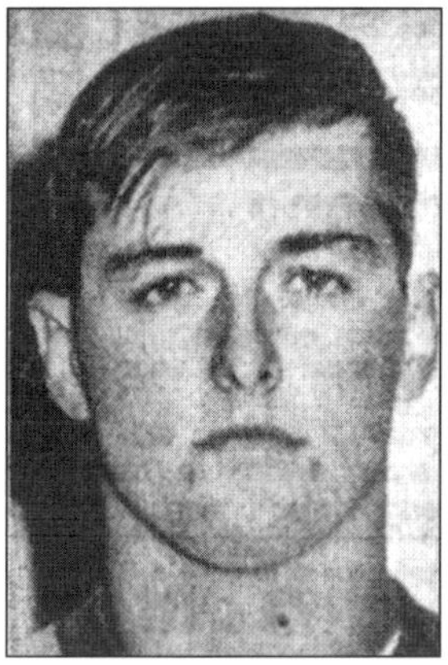

Rick Ackerman

Ray Manz

Alex Nicolson

Tony Husli

The Rams did it through the air. Polowick came off the bench in the second half and he just couldn't miss. He threw touchdown passes to Henry Schubach (twice), Peter Schaefer, Terry Renwick and Ray Manz. Schubach was developing into one of the most capable Rams' receivers ever. His height, ability to get open and his sure hands were too much for most defences to handle. The Rams rang up 324 yards passing and threw in 169 along the ground as they totally dominated the Hilltops. Saskatoon came into the game boasting that they had a strong running game. Could have fooled the Rams. The Regina defence so controlled the Hilltops' offence that Saskatoon ended up minus 34 yards rushing.

Could anybody stop the Rams? Well, yes, as a matter of fact. A week later, at home, the Rams couldn't handle the Winnipeg Hawkeyes who edged them 23-22. It was a surprise, mostly to the Rams. But they got their act together in the rematch in Winnipeg, unveiling their ground game in force.

Running backs Ken Fiissel, Mel's younger brother, Rick Ackerman and the explosive Bobby Kerr tore through the Hawkeyes' defence with the ease of a lawn mower slicing through grass. The Rams won 35-24. The nimble-footed Fiissel, who was more known as a soccer player with Regina Concordia, showed off his stuff, weaving for 93 yards on 12 carries. Ackerman ripped for 148 yards on 19 carries and Kerr had 43 yards on 10 carries. Regina's offensive line, backboned by guard Jerry Orban and tackle Don Tingle, had it all. And with the kind of running backs the Rams had, there was a clear incentive to block. Regina's defence was nothing to pass over, either, dominated by end Brian Closs and the huge Alex Nicolson at tackle. Linebackers Gary Wilson and Tony Husli, backs Rob Pyne and Ray Manz excelled on a team that had more than its share of talented juniors. Monte Ziola hit with the force of somebody twice his size.

Bob Kerr

Bob Kerr

By the time the schedule had ended and the playoffs were set to begin, the Rams had rung up a six wins and two losses record. And while they finished second to the Winnipeg Hawkeyes, the Rams had no shortage of confidence heading into the two-game, total-points Manitoba-Saskatchewan Junior Football League championship series. They had had a solid season with few missteps, and had survived a series of injuries that had challenged their backup players.

The Manitoba-Saskatchewan Junior Football League had earned the deserved reputation of being by far the best in the country. Its champions, whether they be the Rods, the Hilltops or the Rams, dominated the national finals. The league was the envy of the rest of the country for the top-notch talent and good teams it produced. So, it was that the toughest playoff matchups every year were in the league finals. If you got through that one, chances were you were on your way to the national final.

In 1970, the two-game final was a treat for both fans and players alike. The Rams knew the Hawkeyes would be tough, and they knew all about the Cinderella story the Hawkeyes were starring in. The Hawkeyes had joined the league in 1970, replacing the Wildcats' franchise. A first-place finish in their first year served notice that they would be a team to contend with come the playoffs. The Hawkeyes, who came from Winnipeg's juvenile league, counted their share of top-level talent in their lineup. The biggest name belonged to that of receiver Gord Patterson, who went on to the University of Manitoba Bisons and then to a long and productive CFL career with the Blue Bombers.

The series opened in Winnipeg, and the weather took a turn for the worse. An October winter blast blew through the city. Combined with the endless wind that Winnipeg is known for, the day dawned chilly and stayed that way.

The Hawkeyes handled the wind and cold better than the Rams. They won the opening game by a 30-21 score to take a nine-point lead back to Regina for the deciding game in the series. If the truth be told, the Rams were fortunate to be down by only nine points. Only a late fourth-quarter touchdown on a dazzling play by Wilson and Kerr had brought the Rams to within nine points. Right after Winnipeg had scored a touchdown, Wilson took the kick-off, ran it back 50 yards and then flipped it to the bullet-fast Kerr, who carried it the rest of the way for the major.

The Rams had been down in the game right from the start, with Patterson scoring off a touchdown pass from quarterback Bud Harden. Don Schmidt, plagued by leg injuries for much of the season, scored a pair of touchdowns for the Rams, who headed back to Regina knowing they had a tall mountain to climb.

Don Schmidt wins MVP.

Currie was not happy with what he had seen from his team in Winnipeg. Dropped passes, botched assignments and a lack-luster performance from some of his veterans stirred him to as much anger as was possible for Gord Currie to express. He decided to bench all-star defensive end Brian Closs for the start of the second game in Regina's Taylor Field. Closs, in his last season in junior football, reacted the way Currie had hoped he would. When Currie put the big guy into the game, Closs turned in one of his best, if not his best, performances of the season. But, then again, so did the rest of the Rams.

On a sun-splashed Saturday afternoon, the Rams came roaring back, winning the game 26-16 and the two-game series 47-46.

There were a lot of reasons for the Rams' turnaround. Schubach, Pyne, running back Dave Seeley, Manz, and punter Rocky Treleaven all turned in sensational performances. The versatile Pyne moved from defence to offence, setting the tone for the game when he made an amazing touchdown catch of a Polowick pass, with a Hawkeye draped all over him.

For the Rams, this would be the toughest competition they would face on the journey to a Canadian championship. They took their act on the road; travelled to Vancouver where they beat the Meralomas 49-21 in the western semi-final; travelled to Edmonton and uprooted the Huskies 29-11 in the western final. That sent them into the Canadian final. The game was scheduled for November 11th in Taylor Field, against the Burlington Braves. The Braves were largely an unknown quantity. But the Rams did know this, they would be a well-coached, tough bunch. Their head coach was Bernie Custis. Included in their lineup were two players destined for long Canadian Football League careers. John Bonk was a linebacker with the Braves, and he would enjoy an all-star career as a centre with the Winnipeg Blue Bombers. And placekicker Ian Sunter would make a name for himself doing the same thing for the Hamilton TigerCats, his most memorable moment coming when he kicked a late field goal to beat the Saskatchewan Roughriders 13-10 in the 1972 Grey Cup game in Hamilton.

The Rams were more than a little nervous about just what they would be facing from Burlington. The Braves hadn't lost a game all season long. They came into Regina with a 15-0 record and a scoring machine that had produced 78 touchdowns, about five TDs a game. The Rams watched a tape of the Braves' eastern championship win over Montreals' Notre-Dame-de-Grace, and came away more than a little impressed.

But all that information, the undefeated record, the glowing scouting reports, served only to feed Currie with more fuel to make sure his players were not only physically ready for the game, but also mentally. He talked about how good Burlington was, and said it simply meant another big challenge for the Regina Rams. Were the Rams about to let a team from Burlington walk into their stadium and snatch a national championship from them?

Well, there were 11,000 fans in Taylor Field that afternoon, and after the opening few moments of the game they were indeed wondering if Burlington wasn't going to be too much for the Rams to handle. Early in the first quarter, the Rams' Monte Ziola had trouble handling a Burlington punt. He fumbled it, the Braves recovered, and before the game was six minutes old they were ahead 7-0.

After that, the first half was a battle between two strong teams. The Rams settled down, and so did the Braves, and it became a test of wills. The Rams scored two second-quarter touchdowns to take a 13-7 lead into the halftime break, but neither team could claim it was in control. It was still a see-saw battle.

Once Currie got his charges behind the closed doors of the dressing room, he delivered one of his inspirational speeches. The players took in every word. When they hit the field for the second half, their feet weren't touching the ground. The Rams were off and . . . as always . . . running.

Oh, were they running, Right off the bat, with the roaring crowd of 11,000 sounding more like 30,000, the Rams took the game by the throat and shook it. When they talk about how the Rams' reputation grew in national championships, performances such as the one that was unveiled on November 11, 1970 in Taylor Field are what they are talking about.

On their first series of the second half, Rams' quarterback Barry Polowick unleashed the running game on the Braves. Eight plays and 80 yards later, Richard Ackerman culminated the drive by sliding into the end zone from three yards out. After that, the Rams never stopped. With

Henry Schubach

Dieter Pelzer, Jim Charter, Rae Pratt and Henry Schubach clearing the way, Ackerman, Don Schmidt and Bob Kerr ran freely.

The Rams went on to smother Burlington 39-8 in one of the most one-sided games ever played for the *Leader-Post* Trophy. Their ground game totaled 396 yards and they posted 34 first downs. Ackerman was named the game's most valuable player. Small wonder. The slick fullback rushed for 181 yards on 31 carries and scored two touchdowns. Schmidt, like Ackerman, was playing his last game as a junior. He carried the ball 21 times, gained 134 yards and also scored two touchdowns. Kerr, the speed back, gained 72 yards in nine carries in what was also his final game as a junior.

Rams' quarterbacks Barry Polowick and Mike Hill threw only 13 passes between them, completing six, with the versatile Schubach catching three of them, one for a touchdown.

For the Rams, it was a memorable way to start the 1970s. As it turned out, it was just the beginning.

Barry Polowick (12), Rick Ackerman (31), Bob Kerr (27), Jim Charter (65) and Don Schmidt (16).

FIRST UNDEFEATED SEASON

1971

This is how it was in the spring of 1971. You could get a double room at the Georgia Hotel in downtown Regina for less than $10 a night; the Army and Navy was selling dresses for $1.39; Mid-Town Used Cars was offering a 1970 Pontiac Grand Prix for $3,650. And there was a changing of the guard on the national level of junior football.

The Regina Connection was taking over.

The impact that the executive of the Regina Rams had had on the organization in Regina was now being stretched, stretched to where it would, in April of 1971, find itself being asked to participate on a national level. When Scotty Livingstone and his gang moved into the executive suite of the Rams, it marked a new beginning. The timing was perfect. The Rams needed the new blood. And, so, they got it. They also got the best junior football coach, ever, in the history of the game, a brand new clubhouse that had more than a few professional teams drooling and, of course, they ended up with a successful image that others wanted to tap into.

At a meeting of Canadian junior football operators in Regina in 1971, the Rams' Joe Kanuka was elected the national chairman of junior football. Dr. Rafe Chadwick, who had also come to the Rams with Livingstone, was named president of the Manitoba-Saskatchewan Junior Football League. Chadwick, a soft-spoken man, was a tireless worker on behalf of the Rams. His contributions were often forgotten because of his quiet nature.

As well as those moving into positions of influence, Ron McGuigan was named secretary-treasurer of the national body. McGuigan was cast in the same mould as Chadwick. He was quiet and so low-key that he was taken for granted. But few who have been involved with the Rams have done as much over the course of their history as this man who was affectionately called Magoo. Another tireless worker for the Rams, and also for minor football in Saskatchewan, Jack Stewart, was returned as secretary-treasurer of the Manitoba-Saskatchewan Junior Football League for the 20th year.

The Rams clearly had become the dominant organization in Canadian junior football. And if there were any doubters out there, then the seasons from 1971 through 1976 erased the concerns.

The 1970s marked perhaps the greatest string of Rams' successes in their history. Beginning with the 1970 Canadian championship, the Rams stepped it up a notch and – BAM! – they defined the word "dynasty." Year after year, victory after victory, they took over junior football in a way never seen before.

From 1971 through 1976, the Rams won 43 league games, lost only five games, tied two, and won four national championships. And they did it with an ever-changing set

Rafe Chadwick and Scotty Livingstone

of players, that being the law of the junior football jungle, where every fall one batch graduates and every summer new blood is pumped into the green and white.

The 1971 season was a ground-breaker for the Rams. They never lost a game, posting an 8-0 record in league play, demolishing the Winnipeg Hawkeyes 72-31 in the Manitoba-Saskatchewan Junior Football League two-game, total-points final, smothering the Edmonton Huskies 48-7 in the western semifinal, whipping the Vancouver Meralomas 34-12 in the western final, and teaching the Burlington Braves another lesson, 42-13, in the Canadian championship.

All that despite a major rebuilding job, caused by the graduation of many of their greatest players from that 1970 team. One of those who had graduated was running back Don Schmidt. Gord Currie didn't want to lose somebody of Schmidt's caliber, so he added him to his assistant coaching staff of Al Relkey, Doug Killoh and Mel Fiissel.

The Rams were undefeated in 1971 for obvious reasons. They had the talent. Once again, the high-school system in Saskatchewan spit out one outstanding player after another, and most of them trooped on over to Mount Pleasant where the air reeked of winning.

Larry LeBlanc

Take a look at some of the rookies who not only showed up that season, but also started. There was lineman Ron Cherkas, a Kamsack native who would eventually play in the Canadian Football League with both Saskatchewan and Winnipeg. There was Terry Hincks, a tough offensive lineman, and center Larry LeBlanc. LeBlanc enjoyed an outstanding career with the Rams, ultimately serving on their executive, becoming president. He was perhaps the key figure in the Rams leaving junior football and joining the University of Regina.

Steve Mazurak

Steve Mazurak was another in that year's crop of rookies. At six feet, three inches, Mazurak was a natural as a receiver, and that's what the Rams had in mind for him. He became one of the most consistent receivers in league history, and then became a starting wide receiver with the Roughriders. Brian Saip was another rookie that year. Saip brought his considerable frame, over 250 pounds of it, to the Rams' line, and he fit right into the Rams' scheme of things as well.

Mix that crop of rookies with such veterans as defensive back/quarterback Bryan Dimen, running back Ken Fiissel, running back Gord Glass, lineman Jim Hopson, linebacker Tony Husli, linebacker Larry Kratt, lineman Jerry Orban, lineman Dieter Pelzer, two-way star Rob Pyne, defensive back Gary Wilson, and you have the ingredients for an undefeated season. Cherkas would be named the league's rookie of the year in 1971 and Pyne the most valuable player.

And, of course, the usual handful of rural Saskatchewan players were on hand, Cherkas being the most notable. Defensive tackle Marv Messner of Spring Valley and fullback Bob McKenzie of Watrous were both seeing their first action in 12-man football. And Tom McCord had followed his brother Archie along the yellow brick football road, coming over from Moose Jaw. Tom also would stay with the Rams long after his playing days were over, eventually becoming a team president.

Ron Cherkas

The Rams opened the 1971 season with a performance that sent a shudder through the rest of the league. In a lip-smacking feast, they intercepted . . . count em! . . . 11 Saskatoon passes and laid a 56-7 licking on their rivals from the Hub City. The game saw Currie use three players at quarterback Hill, Dimen and the versatile Pyne – and they guided the Regina offence smoothly. Mazurak and running back Gord Glass each

Marv Messner

scored a pair of touchdowns, with running back Rich Storey and receiver Pete Schaefer getting one each. Eight different players shared the interceptions. Larry Kratt, Tony Husli and Rocky Treleaven each intercepted two passes, with Pyne, John Broderick, Manz, Dave Sawa and Doug Zimmerman each getting one.

The Rams shut out the Winnipeg Hawkeyes 38-0 in their next outing, then went to Saskatoon to take on the Hilltops in front of 2,300 fans. Once again, it was no contest, the Rams winning 30-10. Nothing gave the Rams more pleasure than to bury the Hilltops in front of their hometown fans. The game turned when Currie inserted the veteran Mike Hill at quarterback. Dimen had started the game at quarterback, with Hill starting at cornerback on defence. Dimen was struggling, so Currie moved Hill to offence, and his passing was just too much for the Hilltops to handle.

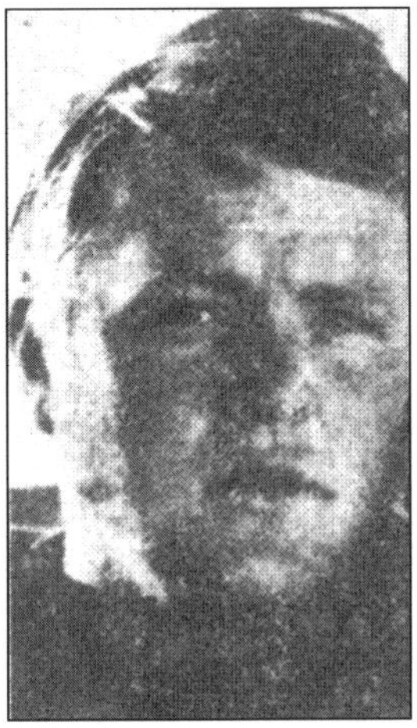
Jim Hopson

The Rams went from victory to victory after that, with Hill, Dimen and Pyne all getting time at quarterback. The Rams closed out the regular schedule with a 66-0 hammering of the Winnipeg Rods to set them up for their equally unstoppable playoff run. That game, though, did give them some cause for concern. Both Hill (concussion) and Dimen (shoulder) had to leave the game.

It would be the Rams and the Hawkeyes in the two-game, total-points league final. The Rams took the opener in Winnipeg 39-24. Coming back to Regina for the second game, cold weather and snow was waiting for the teams. The folks at Taylor Field were anxious about what a game would do to their natural turf, so the Rams were booted out by the City of Regina and they played the game at Mount Pleasant. In frigid weather and damp snow, the Rams bulled their way to a 33-7 win and a 72-31 series' triumph. While this was a total team victory, one player rose above the rest and had his best game of the year. Halfback Kim Ziola scored three touchdowns for the Rams, including an electrifying 92-yarder on a pass from Hill. The diminutive Ziola rushed for 150 yards behind the offensive line of centre Dieter Pelzer, guards Jerry Orban and Jim Hopson, and tackles Roy Shiplack and Blake Walker.

For the second straight year, it was the Rams and Huskies in the western semifinal. The Huskies' whole game plan was geared to stop Regina's running game. And Edmonton succeeded, better than anybody else had managed. "The trouble was," said Currie, "they left themselves completely vulnerable to the passing game."

Mike Hill

Did they ever. Mike Hill had the best passing game of his junior career to date. He completed 19 of 22 passes for 404 yards and five touchdowns as the Rams won 48-7 before 3,500 fans in Taylor Field. Ziola caught five passes for 155 yards and three touchdowns, and Mazurak pulled in 11 catches for 111 yards.

When the game was over, the *Leader-Post*'s Jim Wagman asked Currie if the Rams' game plan had called for a passing attack. Currie laughed. "What game plan? We aren't that systematic that we use any plan. We just go into a game and find out what works and then we stick with it until it stops working."

The Rams found out about November weather in Vancouver when they travelled there for the Western final against the hometown Meralomas. It poured rain, and the Rams had some trouble handling the ceaseless buckets of water that streamed from the swollen grey skies. They actually had trouble handling the ball. In all, the Rams fumbled 11 times and Vancouver recovered four of them. Not until the third quarter did the Rams begin to take control. It was the defence that established a grip on the game by continually repelling the Meralomas' offence. Offensively, running back John Broderick ran for 145 yards as the Rams went on to win 34-12.

Currie actually felt that the point spread was not indicative of the closeness of the game. "That was as good a ball club as you are going to see. They are big. People think we are big, but they probably average 230 pounds along the line."

The Rams would have to go on the road to win their second straight national championship. So, on Saturday, November 13, they found themselves in Ivor Wynne Stadium in Hamilton to once again face the Burlington

Gord Glass

Braves. It really didn't matter where the Rams were. Hamilton. Timbuktu. Carlyle. Or Avonlea.They were just too good.

With running back Gord Glass gaining 176 yards along the ground, and Mike Hill and Steve Mazurak hooking up for one completion after the other, the Rams rolled to a 42-13 victory in a game that saw Glass named as the most valuable player.

Saskatchewan Premier Allan Blakeney was on hand to watch the game, and he later went into the dressing room to tell the players, "You are the greatest team." The Rams were simply too strong in too many areas for the Braves. Mazurak turned Burlington's defence inside out, scoring three touchdowns in a phenomenal performance that had pro scouts drooling. Kim Ziola again exploded for a big play, this one a touchdown romp after Mazurak flipped the ball to him on a flea flicker play with Hill. The Rams had used the play throughout the season. "It worked every time except once," said Ray Manz. That one time, it gained 45 yards. The other four times Ziola scored touchdowns. "Not working" in the Rams' vocabulary meant it didn't result in a touchdown.

Gary Wilson had a stunningly strong game at defensive halfback, knocking down passes and making tackles from start to finish.

The game marked the 19th straight that the Rams had won, dating back to the 1970 season.

In his column in the *Leader-Post*, writer Jim Wagman talked about some of the things he had seen and heard in covering the Rams in 1971. Here are some excerpts from that column:

> The success of the Rams, who won their first Canadian title in 1966 when they defeated Montreal Notre-Dame-de-Grace 29-14, can be attributed to many things, but the main one would have to be head coach Gord Currie and his assistant coaches, Alf Relkey, Doug Killoh, Don Schmidt and Mel Fiissel.
>
> The coaches seem to have a natural way when it comes to handling the boys and one incident that happened after the Rams won the Manitoba-Saskatchewan Junior Football League final reflects this.
>
> Rams were undressing in their clubhouse at Mount Pleasant following their victory over the Winnipeg Hawkeyes on a snow-covered, wind-swept field. Versatile lineman Terry Hincks and Brian Saip both approached Currie and shook his hand. "Gee coach, it's great to be with a winner and thanks for giving us the chance."
>
> Saip later sat down and expressed his views. "I was involved in a car accident at the start of the year and my knees were banged up pretty bad. As I was lying in the hospital, I felt I was definitely finished for the year. But coach Currie came up to the hospital and told me that as soon as I was recovered my job would still be waiting for me. That gave me a lift and, look, I'm playing now."

Brian Saip

> Not only do the Rams act as gentlemen on the field, but also off the gridiron. They have no problem checking into the same hotel year after year when they are on the road. At the Viscount Gort Hotel in Winnipeg, they received quite a compliment. "I am amazed this club is so well organized when they check in here, they are well disciplined and we never have any trouble with them," said a lady behind the desk. "They are young and they act better than some professional teams that stay here."

Wagman wrote about a few more things, but his column illustrated that in order to have a reputation as a team of strong character and discipline, the Rams had to act the part. And they did.

For 11 players, 1971 represented their last year in junior football. Graduating were Mike Hill, Terry Renwick, Doug Zimmerman, Ray Manz, Dieter Pelzer, Jerry Orban, Tony Husli, Rob Pyne, Gary Wilson, Ken Fiissel and Rick McCullough.

The torch would now be passed to the 1972 edition of the Regina Rams.

Mike Hill, Jim Hopson, Rob Pyne and Coach Currie.

THREE IN A ROW?

1972

With two straight national championships under their belts, and an undefeated string of 19 straight games, dating back to October of 1970, the Regina Rams went into the 1972 season knowing there would be plenty of big holes to fill. They also knew they would have a good crop of rookies from which to find tomorrow's stars, and they hoped some of them would develop today.

But not even the Rams' coaching staff really envisioned the kind of new talent that landed in their camp in 1972. Of a group that included Jack Lichtenwald, Ted Dolinski, Lenny Knoll and Randy Labatte, there were three names that are rather significant to this very day. You may have heard of them.

Roger Aldag

One was Roger Aldag.

One was Bernie Schmidt.

One was Frank McCrystal.

Aldag had followed in his brother Barry's footsteps, coming into Regina and to the Rams from Gull Lake, a small southwestern town situated on a rise in the land beside the Trans-Canada Highway. That region – Gull Lake, Shaunavon – had one of the best minor football programs in the province. It may well have been only nine-man football, but the area had produced four all-star performers with the Rams. Roger and Barry Aldag, and Shaunavon brothers Ron and Alex Nicolson. All four received tryouts with the Saskatchewan Roughriders, and two of them, the Aldags, made the Riders' roster.

Roger Aldag had the build of a tank, and was just as solid. He was about six feet tall, and he seemed to be just as wide. He looked as if his neck had gotten lost somewhere between his head and his massive shoulders. His legs were like California redwood trees. He was quick. And he was as competitive as a cornered badger. When the Rams got him, they knew they had a good one. They just didn't realize how good he would turn out to be. He went on to have a Hall of Fame career with the Saskatchewan Roughriders as an all-star guard, play on one Grey Cup championship team, have his sweater number, 44, retired by the Riders, and be named a Schenley award winner as the outstanding offensive lineman in the Canadian Football League. He arguably was the best Ram ever. Quiet and soft spoken, Aldag could be a ferocious blocker on the field. He backed down from nobody. While still playing with the Rams, he also attended Roughrider training camps, where his one-on-one battles with such seasoned pros as Ralph Galloway and Jack Abendschan were legendary. "He might still be a junior and he might be a little green, but when you go one-on-one with Roger you had better have your chin strap done up and be prepared for a long battle," remarked then Rider quarterback Ron Lancaster. Aldag had only one gear in his transmission. It was forward. There was no reverse, and certainly no neutral or park.

All of a sudden, the Rams were being blessed with outstanding flankers. There was Steve Mazurak, who had come to the Rams in 1971 and was unstoppable. In 1972, along came Bernie Schmidt. Sleepy-eyed and deceptively slow-moving, Schmidt had wonderful hands and, even more importantly, a built-in feel for and understanding of the game of football. He was one of the best ever at understanding offences and at reading defences. He would eventually develop into one of the best offensive minds in the game. He was also a solid defensive back. Years after his playing career was over, Bernie joined the Rams as an assistant coach. He developed into such a talented coach that few, if any, could figure out why some Canadian Football League team never came calling to offer him a job. Bernie didn't do everything in a slow-moving fashion, mind you. When he and his wife decided to start a family, they started off with twins. If that wasn't enough, they decided to have another child. They ended up with another set of twins.

Bernie Schmidt

If you had taken a look at Frank McCrystal at the 1972 training camp, the inclination might have been to ask him, "You want to play what?" He would have replied, "Linebacker."

Not tall. Not big. But quick, as tough as nails and relentless, McCrystal would indeed go on to become a linebacker with the Rams. Pound for pound, he was likely the best linebacker to ever play for the team. He started his rookie season. And his affiliation with the Rams didn't end with the end of his playings days. He eventually became an assistant coach and then a head coach. Ultimately, Frank McCrystal's name would be mentioned in the same breath as Gord Currie's when the topic of conversation turned to great amateur football coaches in Canadian history.

Frank McCrystal

Yes, 1972 was to be quite a year.

But in the end, it was not the kindest year for the two big football teams in the province, the Rams and the Roughriders.

If 1966 was marked by the happy coincidence that the Riders and Rams had both won their national championships by identical scores, then 1972 carried with it a painful irony. Both the Rams and Riders made it to their respective national finals. Both faced teams from Hamilton. And both lost those Canadian championship games. The Riders lost, 13-10, to the Hamilton Tiger-Cats in the Grey Cup game in Hamilton. The Rams lost, 33-8, to the Hamilton Hurricanes in the Canadian championship game in Saskatoon.

Everything seemed to be coming up roses for the Rams in 1972. There were 92 players who turned out to training camp, the largest number ever. And Currie was blessed with four good quarterback candidates. Bryan Dimen was back, Barry Polowick had returned after a year at the University of Saskatchewan, and rookies Augie Bernstein and Len Knoll had turned up at camp.

Terry Hincks

The Rams opened the season with a 27-3 victory over the Hilltops, with rookie fullback Don Wilde rushing for 114 yards and Dimen playing most of the game at quarterback after Polowick had broken his wrist early in the game. The Rams added one more win, 46-10 over the Winnipeg Hawkeyes, with Dimen, Bernstein and Knoll all getting the chance to play quarterback. Mazurak hauled in four catches for 120 yards.

The Rams' winning streak was stopped at 23 straight when they ventured into Saskatoon and lost 18-14 to the Hilltops, but it certainly wasn't the end of the world. The Rams wouldn't lose another game through the remainder of the regular schedule, finishing the season with a 7-1 record and another first-place finish.

And it set the stage for another Rams'-Hilltops' playoff clash, the usual two-game, total-points affair. The Hilltops, having at least beaten the Rams once, had some confidence going into the playoffs, hoping that home field in the opening game would give them an edge.

With Jim Hopson doing the blocking, and Rick Storey the running, the Rams came at the Hilltops with guns a blazin'. The Rams won the first game 31-22. The explosive Storey returned a kickoff 97 yards for a touchdown and broke a 70-yard run for another on a night in which he ran for 163 yards in just eight carries. He was clearly the difference in a game in which the Hilltops made far too many blunders to win; a game in which neither Rams' quarterback, Knoll or Polowick, could really get anything going. Nevertheless, taking a nine-point lead with the final game back in Regina wasn't a bad reward for the night's efforts.

Dessert came back in Regina a week later. The Rams, whose hatred for the Hilltops was now at an all-time high, never gave Saskatoon a chance. They smothered the Hilltops' offence and blew apart the Hilltops' defence on their way to a 43-8 massacre that gave them the total-points series by a 74-30 count. Now, the road to the Canadian championship went through Regina, and it was the Hilltops who couldn't get through.

The Rams again went with Knoll and Polowick spelling each other off at quarterback, and it produced a magnificent offensive show. Six different runners put together 405 yards rushing, with Storey leading them all at 109 yards in 10 carries. John Broderick and Stu Scalf scored two touchdowns each, with Lorne Hubick and Steve Mazurak getting one apiece. The Rams' offensive line of centre Larry LeBlanc, guards Hopson and Hincks, and tackles Blake Walker, Roy Shiplack and Brian Saip backboned the offensive display with textbook blocking.

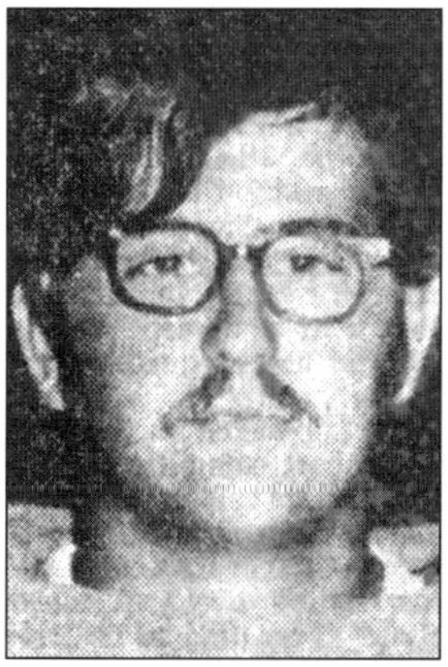

Blake Walker

Defensively, the Rams' line and linebackers shut down the Hilltops. Hopson and Hincks played both ways, joining Aldag, Tom McCord and Saip on the Rams' five-man front. Inside linebacker Frank McCrystal had an outstanding game. He was so on the nerves of Hilltops' quarterback Kirk Houston that, after Rich Delnea had intercepted a Houston pass, Houston turned and tried to kick McCrystal, who had cracked him as he threw the ball. McCrystal didn't react. He just smiled, turned and walked away as the referee threw a flag at Houston.

Assistant coach Mel Fiissel said it all when the game and the series had ended. "Gee, it's nice to beat those Hilltops. I just love it."

Once again, the Rams would find themselves playing the Vancouver Meralomas on the road to the Canadian championship. This time, the game was slated for Taylor Field. The Rams were fully expected to win, again.

Three nights before the game, Currie sat in the Rams' clubhouse and quietly talked about what was expected of the team he had first come to coach in 1965.

"People take for granted that we should win every game. It's one of the prices we pay for winning. People who belong to our executive, fans, even our players to some extent feel that winning becomes your right. Nothing could be further than the truth. The difference between winning and losing is dependent on a number of factors, the least of which is ability. The most important of all is the underlying thinking and character of the team. It sounds like an intangible but it's a very real thing. Athletes are not that far apart on ability. But they must have that quality that binds them together and keeps them from panicking under stress. They must have confidence in themselves as individuals and in their teammates. It's arrived at over a period of time. A football team in many ways is like a country, like Canada is a melting pot of divergent cultures, people and beliefs. A team can become a melting pot of divergent personalities, some of whom have to mellow in small ways in the best interests of the whole thing. This is the secret of the whole thing."

Just three days before the game against the Meralomas, the league's all-star team was named. The Rams put 14 players on the 24-player lineup – Dimen, Broderick, Hincks, Hopson, Shiplack, Walker, Schaefer, Aldag, McCord, Kratt, Sawa, Delnea, Knoll and Mazurak.

Tom McCord

John Broderick

Larry Kratt

Dave Sawa

It was David and Goliath all over again. The Meralomas had the superior size, but the Rams ended up with the Western championship. On a cold day in Taylor Field, the Rams rode the quarterbacking of Polowick and Knoll, and the sensational running of John Broderick – three touchdowns, 170 yards along the ground – to a 57-14 victory. The Rams rushed for 383 yards. Stu Scalf scored two touchdowns and Storey got one. Not to be left out, the Rams' defence struck paydirt too, with Rich Delnea and Bernie Schmidt each returning interceptions the distance.

When the game ended and the Rams had been bused back to their Mount Pleasant clubhouse, they did something they hadn't done in two years. The players got together and gave the game ball to Gord Currie."He's such a great coach, what can you say?" offered co-captain Jim Hopson, who wore a patch of blood across his forehead. "He's just so great. We were so prepared for this game, so totally prepared. We knew everything about them . . . everything."

The Canadian final was played on Saturday, November 11 in Saskatoon's Griffiths Stadium. The Rams against the Hamilton Hurricanes. The Hurricanes beat up on the Rams by a score of 33-8.

As Gord Currie had said, winning is not a right exclusive to the Regina Rams.

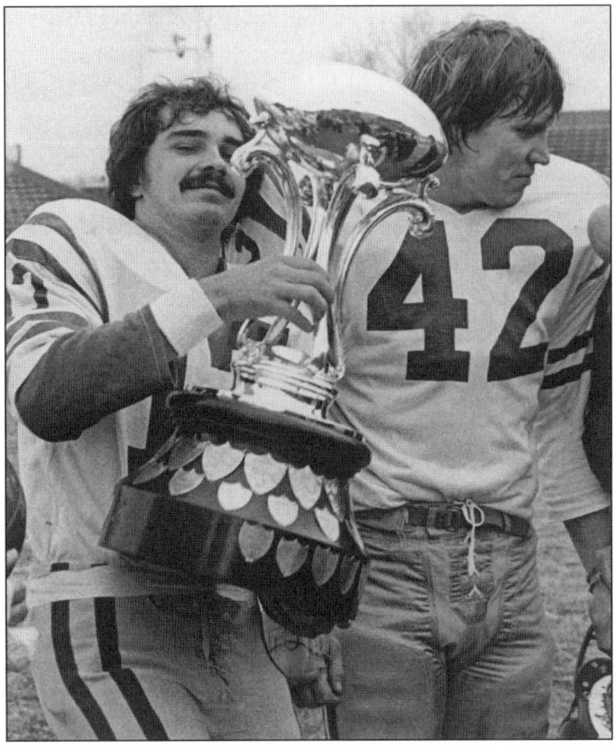

Len Knoll and Roger Aldag

THE ECSTASY AND THE AGONY

1973-1974

Through the winter and spring of 1973, the Regina Rams, players and coaches, did a slow boil. As summer approached it almost turned into a blind rage. Of any loss they had suffered in their 18-year history, the one in November stung the most. There had been little doubt that they possessed the talent to win the Canadian junior championship, but somewhere on the bus ride home from the 1972 championship game in Saskatoon, they had lost something. They lost whatever intangible it is that takes teams over the top. Instead, the Rams were simply mediocre in the Canadian final in Saskatoon, and the Hurricanes denied Regina a third straight national championship.

The empty feeling didn't leave the Rams. They chewed on it throughout the off-season. When the call to training camp came, they couldn't wait to get there.

But, first, Gord Currie had to plug a huge hole. Doug Killoh, his capable line coach, had spent the winter wrestling with whether or not he wanted to return for another year. In the spring, he told Currie he had decided he wanted to retire from football. Currie didn't want to accept the resignation, so he told Killoh to wait until training camp started. Currie was hoping that the summer weather and training camp would be enough to entice Killoh into staying. But Killoh stuck by his decision. So Currie went out and brought in former Rams' guard Jerry Orban to join the staff as a line coach. Orban had been an outstanding offensive lineman for the Rams, and the fact that he was a teacher in Regina made him all the more appealing to Currie. The Rams' other assistant coaches, Mel Fiissel, Don Schmidt and Al Relkey, were all returning.

The 1973 season turned into another special year for the Rams. They didn't lose a game, tied one, and finished in first place with a 7-0-1 record. They won the Manitoba-Saskatchewan Junior Football League's two-game, total-points playoff with ease, beating the Hilltops 88-42. But once out of their league, the Rams were pushed to the limit in every playoff game. Once again, they faced the Vancouver Meralomas, only this time it was no walk in the park. The Meralomas had improved year after year after year, and in the western semifinal they came close to upsetting the Rams, losing 30-28. The Rams went on to beat the Edmonton Huskies 19-17 in the Western final, and it took a stunning performance from their defence for the Rams to win the Canadian championship. With all their regular quarterbacks injured, the Rams' defence and special teams worked a miracle in a 9-0 shutout of the Ottawa Sooners in the national final in Ottawa's Lansdowne Park.

Len Knoll

While the Rams had lost a number of key players to graduation, they still had a solid bunch of veterans returning in 1973. Quarterback Len Knoll was back, as was quarterback and defensive back Bryan Dimen. Veteran Augie Bernstein and rookie Dave Osiowy were the other quarterbacks at camp. Where the Rams were strong was on the line, where players such as Larry LeBlanc, Terry Hincks, Roger Aldag and Tom McCord were back for another year.

The Rams opened the season in Saskatoon against the Hilltops, stealing a 9-8 victory. The Hilltops had beaten the Rams in every statistical department except the one that counted.

Back in Regina for the rematch, the Hilltops again ended up returning home feeling they had left one on the table. The final score was 15-15. The game was decided on a somewhat controversial coaching decision. The Hilltops somehow managed to snatch a tie from the jaws of victory. With the score tied at 15 apiece, and the Hilltops at the Rams 22, with time for two more plays, Saskatoon coach Jon Rechner decided to punt the ball and win the game with the single. But for some reason, he chose not to use his regular punter, Jeff Orchard. Instead, he told quarterback Kirk Houston to kick it. Houston's punt went almost straight up in the air, traveling just 20 yards. Rams' Dave Sawa caught it at the two and killed the clock. This time, kissing your sister wasn't so bad.

The Hilltops had outplayed the Rams through three quarters, then the Rams came alive. Trailing 15-0 going into the fourth quarter, the Rams' Len Knoll got the offence moving – first, firing a 34-yard touchdown toss to flanker Bernie Schmidt, then finding the dependable Ted Dolinski on a 10-yard TD pass. Greg Johnson converted both majors to

Bernie Schmidt

bring the Rams within a point. Then, with less than five minutes to go in the game, Johnson boomed a 62-yard punt that went for the tying single, leaving Rechner to come forth with his ill-fated decision.

"Orchard was worn out and he takes too long getting the ball away," he said. "Besides, Kirk kicks a higher ball and we didn't want to give them a chance to get it out."

The Rams went into the game with three running backs injured. Currie was just plain happy to get a tie out of it.

Before the game, he had said, "We're injured. Our linemen are too small, our backs are too small and we've only got one quarterback."

Hilltops' assistant coach Jim Seaman reacted by saying, "I've heard all about their injuries and everything else. And you know what it is? It's the old Currie psych job, that's what it is."

A week later, the Rams found themselves in a slaughter in Winnipeg against the pitiful Rods. No, make that the pitied Rods. The Rams killed them 80-13. Anybody who wanted to could score for the Rams. Halfbacks Rick Storey and Ted Dolinski each scored three touchdowns; fullback Dwayne Thurmeier and flanker Bernie Schmidt got two apiece; quarterback Len Knoll and defensive back Don Young each had one.

While Currie realized the opposition wasn't much, he still singled out defensive linemen Roger Aldag, Tom McCord and rookie Bryan Illerbrun for the game they had played. "Roger played his best game," said Currie. "We've expected big things out of him and maybe now he's turned the corner." Illerbrun was a 16-year-old, 250-pounder who had come to the Rams from Estevan.

Currie used the game to give defensive back Jack Lichtenwald some time at quarterback, a move that would pay off down the road.

What came next was likely the turning point in the Rams' season. They went into Saskatoon and whipped the Hilltops 31-16, mostly on the precise short passing game of Knoll, who took apart the Hilltops' defence with the precision of a surgeon. Knoll established the Rams' running attack right off the bat, using Storey and Thurmeier to put the Hilltops on their heels. Then, he flattened them with his passes to Dolinski and Schmidt.

Rechner looked like he had been run over by a train. "You can't take anything away from the Rams," the Hilltops' coach said. "They've got a great team."

The win virtually wrapped up first place for the Rams – they would clinch it the following week with a win over the Winnipeg Wildcats – and then it would be time to get ready for the playoffs. Rechner's observation that the Rams were a "great team" was reinforced when the Hilltops came to Regina. With Len Knoll playing the best game of his career so far, according to Currie, the Rams hammered the Hilltops 57-7 in a game that meant nothing to either team.

The game also had one other noteworthy occurrence. A rookie from Hudson Bay, Bob Poley, played a fair amount, and Currie was more than a little impressed with what he saw.

The two-game, total-points playoff once again pitted the Rams against the Hilltops. Even though the Rams had won two of the four games against Saskatoon, tying the third, the Hilltops were given more than an outside chance at beating Regina.

The Rams sauntered into Saskatoon looking to lay another licking on the Hilltops. What they got was the scare of their lives. The Hilltops came up with a solid effort, and had they been able to control the Rams' running game, they might very well have come up with a victory. But Thurmeier rushed for 136 yards and the Rams eked out a 34-28 victory to take a six-point lead back to Regina for game two. The victory saw the Rams lose quarterbacks Knoll (broken ankle), Dimen (gashed forehead) and Lichtenwald (sprained ankle), and running back Rick Storey (dislocated shoulder). Rechner said that was what Saskatoon was trying to do. Hurt the Rams. "The object of this thing is to put the opposition out of the game . . . with clean hits."

The Rams had no trouble getting themselves ready for the Hilltops in game two. They felt that it was a cheap shot that had broken Knoll's ankle, and they weren't about to forget it. "I've been telling the other linemen all week 'Remember what they did to Lenny.' We've got a few scores to even up," Terry Hincks said.

They did. With neither Knoll nor Lichtenwald able to play, the Rams let Dimen play his first full game at quarterback. The pint-sized Dimen shone. And Ted Dolinski turned into a scoring machine. Dolinski scored five touchdowns and converted them himself for a 35-point night in a 54-14 Rams' victory before nearly 5,000 fans in Taylor Field. In all, the Rams gunned for 609 yards in total offence.

Currie was reluctant to talk about any individuals. But he did marvel at Rick Storey's contribution. Storey had dislocated his shoulder in Saskatoon, but in the week between games he somehow healed enough that he was able to play. "Everybody deserves the credit for this win," said Currie, "but Rick really played an outstanding game, considering his injury. I think all the talk about Saskatoon beating us physically in the first game, and their momentum after coming on in the second half in Saskatoon helped some of our players heal a little faster than usual."

Ted Dolinski and Randy Labatte

The journey to the national final now moved into its heart-stopping chapter. First up for the Rams were the Meralomas. Currie sent assistant coach Don Schmidt to Vancouver to scout the Meralomas and Schmidt came back totally impressed. They had size, speed, receivers galore, a good quarterback and were a well-disciplined team. Schmidt knew that anything but the Rams' best would not get the job done.

When the Meralomas hit Regina, they downplayed everything that Schmidt had to say about them, opting instead to shower heaping helpings of praise on the Rams. What transpired at Taylor Field that Saturday afternoon in the western semifinal wasn't for the faint of heart. The whole game was an adrenaline rush.

The Meralomas came out of the gate fast, stunning not only the crowd of 2,000 fans, but also Currie. Before the game was five minutes old, the Rams had fallen behind 14-0. But the Rams didn't panic. Dimen got his short passing game and quick-striking running game working and by halftime the Rams had not only clawed their way back, they had taken an 18-14 lead into the dressing room. Dolinski, Darryl Puscus and Stu Scalf all had their moments, slicing through for big gains.

The Rams kept the Meralomas on their heels in the third quarter, Dimen's machine striking time after time. By the

Bryan Dimen

end of the third quarter the Rams were at full throttle and their lead had ballooned to 30-14. While the Meralomas may have been down, they certainly weren't out. They came off the canvas in the fourth quarter with the power of a heavyweight champion. Vancouver quarterback Dan Smith and his favourite receiver, a speed merchant named Rick Price, hooked up time and time again throughout the game. Price caught eleven passes for 252 yards. It was the one he didn't catch that decided the game.

Trailing 30-28 late in the game, the Meralomas had the ball at the Rams' 49, not close enough to try a field goal. They needed one more play to try and get it close enough for the capable Eddie Thomas to kick the game-winning field goal. Yes, the same Ed Thomas who went on to a long National Football League career with the Detroit Lions.

Smith again went looking for his favourite receiver, Rick Price. The ball was well on target when, out of nowhere, Rams' defensive back Darrel Herauf, who had had fits all day trying to cover Price, stepped in front, went high in the air, and came down with the interception of his life. The Rams ran out the clock, and it was off to Edmonton to play the Huskies in the western final.

Meraloma coach Ed Murray couldn't believe that his team had lost. "I really thought we would come in here and whip their butts," he said. "You can't take anything away from them. They're a great team, but I've felt this was the best team we've ever had."

Currie was more relieved than anything. "This may just be the best junior football team I've ever had the pleasure of rubbing shoulders with," he said. "I have to admit I prayed a bit before the game. But I prayed a lot more during it."

The last time the Rams and Huskies had met in the western final was 1971 when the Rams won 48-7. The Huskies vowed they would be raining revenge on the Rams this time around. Edmonton quarterback Dave Kornder let the world know about the Huskies. "Spirit, good attitude and depth at all positions," he said. "We've got quite a few people who've played Regina before and we all figure it's high time we won it all."

The game started off with a bang. The 2,500 fans in Clarke Stadium must have thought they were going to be in for an offensive show. The Rams opened with Dimen engineering a 19-play, 81-yard touchdown drive that ended when Stu Scalf scored from two yards out. The Huskies took the kickoff and went 75 yards in 18 plays to tie the score. After that, the defences held their own, with neither team really getting themselves into an offensive roll. The Huskies led 14-7 after the first quarter; there was no scoring in the second, and at the end of three quarters Edmonton held a 17-13 lead. While the Rams only scored one touchdown in the game, there was always Ted Dolinski to turn to.

Teddy turned the game the Rams' way with his field goal kicking, scoring the only points of the fourth quarter. Dolinski's first field goal of the quarter came just three minutes into it, nailing one from 17 yards out to cut Edmonton's lead to 17-16. The game-winner was from 39 yards out. The Rams' bench went crazy when his kick sailed through the uprights with only about four minutes to go. The Rams were off to the national final in Ottawa against the Sooners. They had survived the charge of the Meralomas; they had timed the moment of decision just right against the Huskies.

Nothing, obviously, was going to come easy for the Rams. Three days before they were to meet the Sooners in Lansdowne Park, Lichtenwald came limping into the clubhouse. The Rams' backup quarterback had stubbed his toe in a home accident, and now he was listed as doubtful for the Canadian final. With Knoll a definite non-starter because of his broken ankle, and now Lichtenwald, Dimen knew he was all the Rams had.

In their entire history, the Rams had never faced such overwhelming odds as they did in this game. It took every ounce of courage and character for them to survive what they survived in this November 10th Saturday afternoon game that was being shown on national television. The pride and the stamina of the Regina Rams was in full display across the country.

The Rams went into the game with only one healthy quarterback, Bryan Dimen. Backup Jack Lichtenwald had broken his toe, but he was dressed and was ready to try to play in the defensive backfield. Nine minutes into the scoreless game, the unbelievable became reality. Dimen, back to pass, was hit hard and driven into the turf. He didn't get up. He had broken his collarbone. He was done for the day. Lichtenwald would have to play quarterback. A fireman by profession (he became Regina's fire chief), Lichtenwald knew what was expected of him when Currie sent him into the game. Don't make any mistakes.

As Dimen was being helped off the field, he implored his teammates, "You guys better go out there and win." He stayed on the bench the rest of the game, shouting encouragement, talking to Lichtenwald.

Dave Sawa intercepts a pass.

Rams' assistant coach Mel Fiissel said he had never been through anything like it. "It was unbelievable. When Bryan came off, the guys on defence said, 'That's it, we can't let them score.' And when we got that safety touch, one of the defensive linemen said, 'Okay, that's all we need. That's all we need.' And that is all we needed." The safety touch came at the 3:44 mark of the second quarter. It was the margin of victory.

At halftime, Currie talked to his players about friendship, that friendship means you have to go out of your way when a friend is in trouble, or needs your support. He talked about Lenny Knoll's injury, about Bryan Dimen's injury, about the courage of Jack Lichtenwald. "I want you players to remember Bryan Dimen and Len Knoll. I want you to remember that they helped us get here. I want you guys to go out in the second half and win this game for them."

The Rams' defence turned in a heroic effort. Linebackers Don Young, Larry Kratt and Frank McCrystal harassed Ottawa quarterback Mark McCloskey from start to finish. Defensive back Greg Johnson made a huge interception. He also single-handedly shut down a reverse play that had touchdown written all over it until Johnson showed up. But the one guy on defence who rose above all the rest was back Dave Sawa. He played a game for the ages. He intercepted two passes, turned back every sweep Ottawa tried. He was just being a Sawa, that's all, throwing his 155 pounds around with reckless abandon. He was named the game's most valuable player.

The Rams' offence managed only 132 yards in total and Lichtenwald threw only five passes, two of them being intercepted. The Rams' touchdown came when Bernie Schmidt glided 94 yards on a punt return. The Rams won, 9-0. The two points were enough. The touchdown was just gravy.

Currie was amazed at what he had watched. "Every kid had to put everything he had into this game. And Jack Lichtenwald. He just got back from an ankle injury and then he broke his toe this week. Jack doesn't pretend to be a quarterback, but he did an amazing job."

Upstairs in the press box, watching the game, was longtime Ottawa Rough Rider star and Canadian Football League Hall of Famer Bobby Simpson. Simpson had never seen the Rams play and he had never met Gord Currie, but as he sat there, Simpson began talking about the game that was still going on below him.

"You know something, Gord Currie has to be the most outstanding football coach I have ever seen in my life. Ottawa will never win anything because they don't have a Gord Currie."

The Rams came back to Regina bleary-eyed and tired, but they were carrying with them the *Leader-Post* Trophy, and that was what the whole season had been all about. They were back on top, where they felt they belonged, and they could hardly wait for the 1974 season to start.

Although graduation of 1973 took its usual toll, this year's group of graduates had a different twist. Bryan Dimen was a major loss, his wonderful career with the Rams, in which he did everything he was asked, and more, was now at an end. Three other stalwart graduates, however, were gone but not out of junior football. Horrors! Does this mean that they had defected to another junior team?

In a nutshell, the Rams' host league, The Manitoba Saskatchewan Junior Football League, was the only league in Canada to not raise their age limit to 22 that year, they stayed at 21. With their Rams' eligibility lapsed, and no university team in Regina (yet), Saip, Hincks and Sawa were faced with the option of quitting football or playing with another junior team in another league.

Terry Hincks

The Vancouver Junior Meralomas, after years of frustrating losses to the Rams, recruited these three starters. Would it pay off for Vancouver?

The Rams had a strong, strong team heading into 1974. Knoll was back, and healthy. He still had Bernie Schmidt and Ted Dolinski to throw to. Rick Storey to hand the ball off to. Jack Lichtenwald to turn to in time of desperation. The line was steeped in strength and experience. Aldag, Poley, Illerbrun and McCord all were returning. McCrystal returned as a linebacker. And Doug Killoh came back as an assistant coach, after taking the 1973 season off. There was one other change in the coaching staff. Don Schmidt had left as an assistant coach, but his loss was tempered somewhat by the return of Killoh.

The Rams went into the 1974 season as clear favourites to again win a national championship. And why not? They literally had everything it took to go the distance. For the second straight year, they roared through the Manitoba-Saskatchewan Junior Football League without suffering so much as a loss. They nailed down another first-place finish with an 8-0 record – nobody seriously challenged them all season.

New players such as Preston Young, Tim Almas, Jim Kenyon and Erwin Klempner fit right in. And Currie continued his practice of making sure every player learned both offensive and defensive roles. "He's always done that," said Lichtenwald. "He wants people ready in case of injuries. At our practices, we'll have defensive backs running offensive plays, and running backs playing defence. It's one of the reasons we are successful, that we can handle injuries and not lose too much because of it. It's a great way to do it."

By the time the playoffs rolled along, the Rams were indeed rolling. Like a scene from an old movie, it would be the Rams and the Hilltops in the two-game, total-points league final. It was also like watching the movie Titanic, where everybody knew the ending but still watched it. The Rams, mind you, never tired of tormenting the Hilltops. So, torment them they did. The Rams took Saskatoon out of the playoff picture 77-21 over the two games. Life was normal.

From there, they took on the Edmonton Huskies in the western semifinal and beat them 19-10 and, sure enough, the Meralomas were once again waiting for them in the western final.

The game was played in Vancouver's Empire Stadium, and it wasn't pretty. Those dark, thick Vancouver clouds rolled in and opened up – there was heavy rain throughout the first quarter.

The Rams were at their best and at their worst in that first quarter. They controlled it. They had seven first downs. They gained 123 yards. They ran 22 plays to the Meralomas' nine. But the Rams also fumbled away the football time after time. They lost five of seven fumbles.

They couldn't cover on punt returns, giving up a touchdown on one of them. It was just a horror show, and there was nothing they could do to turn it off. Or turn it around.

"If it was just one or two players having problems, you could fix that," said Currie. "But it was everybody. Every player on this team at one point or another made a mistake. And you can't win on the strength of one quarter. And that's all we played . . . one quarter."

The Meralomas ended up winning 17-11, handing the Rams their first loss since the 1972 Canadian championship game against the Hamilton Hurricanes.

As equipment manager Norm Fong put away the soggy gear for the final time that season, team manager Norbert Thurmeier was munching on a pizza. "You know," he said, his eyes wet, "on the bus ride home after every one of our wins this year, I couldn't help but wonder what the losers were thinking."

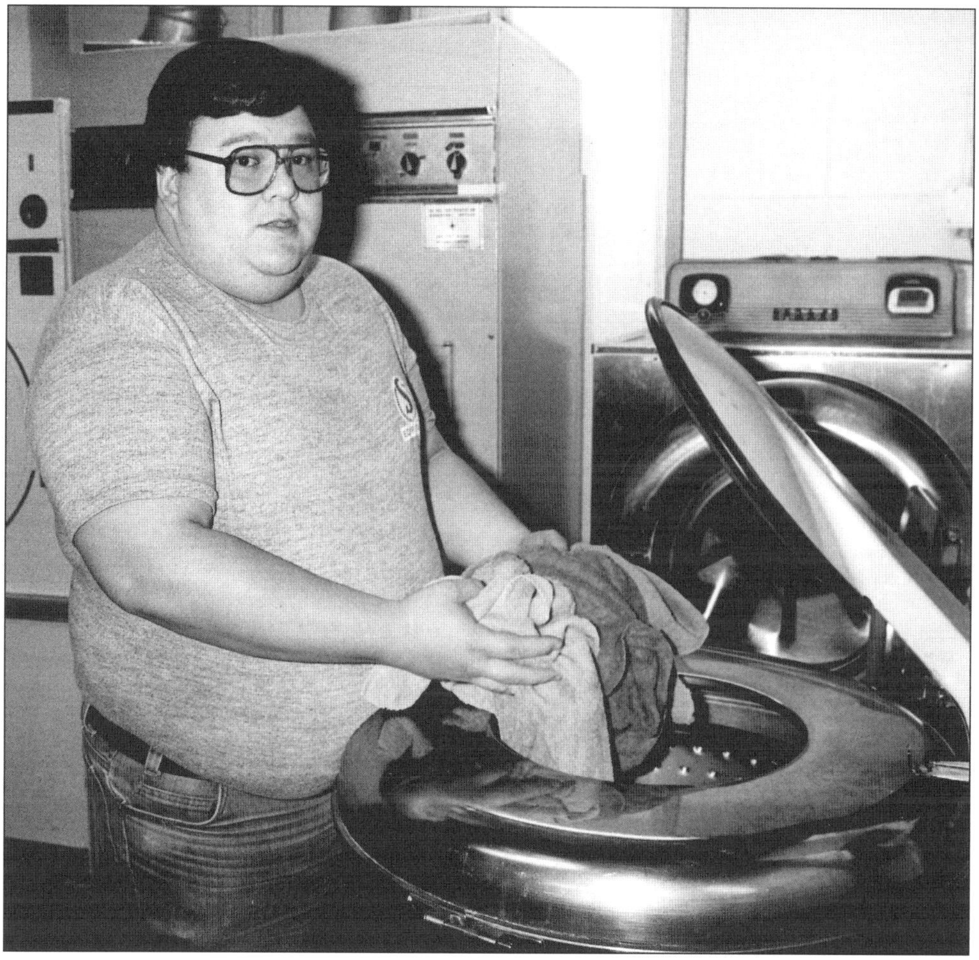

Norm Fong

ERA ENDS ON TWO WINNING NOTES

1975-1976

In the mid-1970s, Currie knew that his time as Rams' coach was drawing to a close. It was not that he was bored with it, but he had been coaching for a quarter of a century, and he was feeling more and more that it was time for him to step aside and enjoy the rest of his life with his family. Anybody who has never coached can't grasp the hours and hours it takes. For five months of the year, there are no days off. For the rest of the year, it is getting ready for that five-month season. As well, Currie continued to work in the education system. He was principal at Campbell Collegiate. His years of coaching had stolen time from his wife, Shirley, and his children. He also felt that somebody else should get the chance to feel the excitement and sense of fun he had felt.

He had begun to think seriously about retirement in 1975. The year before, the Rams had been beaten in the Western final by the Vancouver Meralomas. But they would come bouncing back in 1975.

With a roster that included veterans Lenny Knoll at quarterback, back Ted Dolinski, linebacker Frank McCrystal, linemen Roger Aldag, Bob Poley and Tom McCord, the Rams had a solid foundation. They were also surrounded by the promise of players such as Bruce Lipinski, Mark Constable, Les Ludwig, brothers Craig and Jim Kenyon, Scott Meikle, Gene Larocque, Kerry Berryman, Gerry Fellner and Kelvin Derkson.

For the first time since 1970, the Rams did not finish first in the Manitoba-Saskatchewan Junior Football League in 1975. For a change, the Hilltops nailed down top spot and, once again, the Hilltops entered the playoffs more than a little confident that this would be the year they would put the Rams in their place.

But, if there was any team the Rams had no trouble getting themselves up for, it was the Hilltops. The depth of this rivalry was out of sonar range. The intensity with which these two teams went after each other would have blown the glass out of any heat gauge. "We don't like them and they don't like us," was the general theme song for these two. There were times when it would get so wound up that guys like Alex Kerr, who was a Rams' equipment manager before joining the executive, Norm Fong, who succeeded him, and Jim Francis, the Rams' colourful long-time trainer, would find themselves in furious debates with the Saskatoon fans during the games.

The Rams went into the playoffs with a 6-3 record. The opening game of the two-game, total-points final would be held in Regina, with the Hilltops getting home field for the second and deciding game. It didn't matter. The names hadn't changed. And the results didn't change. The Rams brushed aside their northern rivals 86-33, more than doubling the score on them, once again cutting the Hilltops out of the playoffs, as they had done so many times before.

With Knoll finding his form, and veterans like Aldag and Poley on top of their game, with receivers like Fellner and Dolinski cashing in on their talents, the Rams caught fire in the playoffs.

They again tangled with the Edmonton Huskies and brushed them aside 35-25. Then it was off to Hamilton for another Canadian championship game against the Hurricanes.

Ted Dolinski

Len Knoll

Knoll came through with one of the best games of his Rams' career, firing the ball with pinpoint accuracy. The Rams rolled to another Canadian championship victory, thumping the Hurricanes 38-19. It was Regina's fifth Canadian championship in 10 years. Knoll was named the game's most valuable player.

There were changes galore coming for 1976. The Manitoba-Saskatchewan Junior Football League died after the 1975 season. The Rams and Hilltops joined the Alberta Junior Football League and a new name was born. The league became the Prairie Junior Football Conference. There were eight teams – the Rams, Hilltops, Edmonton Huskies and Wildcats, Calgary Colts and Mohawks, Red Deer Packers and Medicine Hat Rattlers.

But the real story of 1976 was that it was definitely going to be Gord Currie's last year as head coach. That storied career was about to come to an end. And how do you put the wrap on something like that? The only way the Rams knew, that's how.

The Rams may well have been in a new league, with more teams and better competition. But they were still the Rams and Gord Currie was still their coach. And, so, in 1976, the Regina Rams started a new adventure in junior football, welcoming the competition, and looking forward to continuing as the dominant presence in the sport.

Gary Mather

The Rams and Hilltops had come close to being orphans in the football world. With both of the Winnipeg teams out, the two Saskatchewan teams had two options. One was to find another team to join their league, the other was to apply to join an existing league.

George Hambley was Rams' president in 1975. He did most of the preliminary work on the Rams' application. When his successor, Gary Mather, showed up at the annual meeting of the Alberta Junior Football League in Medicine Hat, everything was finalized. The Rams and Hilltops were delighted. "That's wonderful," said Hambley, a devoted volunteer for the Rams, whose rich sense of humour and positive outlook endeared him to everybody who knew him. He felt this new league would develop into the best in Canada, as the Manitoba-Saskatchewan Junior Football League had been for so many years.

Some things don't change. The Rams would open the season against – who else? – the Saskatoon Hilltops. The Rams would find out soon enough just what was ahead of them. They had lost, through graduation, Ted Dolinski, Roger Aldag, Don Young, Bernie Schmidt and Tom McCord. But new starters such as Balfour's flashy Maurice Butler, Sheldon-Williams grad Greg Nesbitt, and running back Steve Donnison gave the Rams the usual dose of optimism going into camp. And there was one bright light from out of town, Bill Lozinski, who came to the Rams from Hudson Bay, the home of Bob Poley. Lozinski was a receiver who had played only nine-man football. His awkward running style caused him to drop some passes he should have caught, but the Rams never gave up on him. Throughout training camp, former Rams Darrell Puscus, Bernie Schmidt and Bryan Dimen worked with him, and he soon caught Currie's eye. "He'll play some this year, that's for sure," Currie said.

When the Rams got to Saskatoon to open the season against the Hilltops, all they had heard was that the Hilltops had virtually every player back from the year before, and they were faster, smarter, bigger, stronger and, of course, better.

And for the first two quarters it looked as if they were right about everything. The Hilltops had taken a 17-8 lead. Currie had a chat with his players at halftime, suggesting they start concentrating and stop making mistakes. They listened. And they did both. The Rams exploded for 26 points in the third quarter and went on to win 41-24. Knoll got his passing game going in the second half, firing strikes to Butler and Tim Almas. Knoll clicked on 17 of 29 throws for 214 yards and four touchdowns.

The Rams' home opener against the Calgary Mohawks had a similar storyline. The Rams waited until the third quarter to put the game away, this time scoring five touchdowns in the last six minutes of the quarter on their way to a 51-4 thrashing of the Mohawks. Knoll was again on top of his game, throwing for 403 yards and three touchdowns. Butler caught nine passes for 151 yards and a touchdown and Fellner had five catches for 186 yards and two touchdowns. Things were going so well that a little linebacker named Frank McCrystal even rushed the ball – four times for 29 yards.

Next stop for the Rams was a ten-hour bus ride to the Alberta burg of Red Deer. There the Rams unveiled their newest running back, Corey Elson, who had come to the Rams from Estevan and was as green as they get. But with starter Les Ludwig injured, the Rams decided it was time to start Elson and see what he could do. What he could do was amazing. Elson carried the ball 18 times, gained 222 yards, scored three touchdowns and the Rams won 61-7.

Kelvin Derkson also had a solid game running, picking up 94 yards in 11 carries, and Greg Fieger got the ball three times and rushed for 56 yards. In total, the Rams' rushing game gained 385 yards. Knoll threw for another 273 yards for a 600-yard plus outing. With that, the Rams rode the bus back to Regina, ten hours worth, carrying with them an undefeated record. It wouldn't last long.

One week later, the bubble burst. The Rams went into Edmonton, lost Knoll with an ankle injury, and lost the game 10-7 to the Edmonton Wildcats. With Rookie quarterback Bob Moore (and, briefly, Bruce Lipinski) trying to get something going, the game was turned over to both defences, and they both shone. "I don't think you'll ever see a harder hitting game than this one," said Fiissel. "You have to give both defences a lot of credit."

There was a logjam in the standings at the halfway mark of the schedule. The Rams, Wildcats and Hilltops were tied for first place with 3-1 records. The Colts, Mohawks and Rattlers were right behind them at 2-2. Things were getting interesting.

The Rams returned to Taylor Field to take on the Huskies.

Greg Fieger

On a cloudy, grey sort of day, with Knoll on the bench, in uniform, but not starting because of his wounded ankle, the Rams came up with their best overall effort of the season.

Rookie Tom Parker started at quarterback. Currie was prepared to put Knoll into the game if he had to, but Parker's performance was beyond all of Currie's expectations. Parker, mostly a defensive back, called a flawless game, throwing for 251 yards and operating a running game that produced 273 yards as the Rams rolled to a 44-13 win.

Ludwig was the top ground gainer for the Rams, rushing for 151 yards on 18 carries, and Fieger was the top receiver, with four catches for 155 yards, one of them a 92-yard touchdown.

The Rams would not lose another game the rest of the schedule. They went into Calgary and beat the Mohawks 30-20; came home and outscored the Hilltops 49-35 in a game that produced a total of over 1,000 yards in offence; beat the Medicine Hat Rattlers 62-15 in Taylor Field, in their last game of the schedule, to clinch second place. The loss to the Wildcats gave Edmonton first place.

Just a day before the playoffs were to begin, Currie made it official. This would definitely be his last season as a coach with the Rams. "Actually, I had made up my mind at the end of last season," he said. "I was going to quit then. But I got caught up in the fever of the new league. I told Doug (assistant coach Doug Killoh) that it was up to him. If he stayed on for another year, so would I." Killoh stayed on. So did Currie. But this would be it. And it was.

The Rams opened the playoffs at home to the Mohawks in a sudden-death semifinal game. The Mohawks were no match for the Rams. With Knoll back at quarterback, the Rams rolled to a 47-0 victory. The same weekend, the Wildcats ousted the Hilltops 28-21 to set up an Edmonton-Regina showdown for the league championship. Knoll tuned up for the final by throwing for 274 yards, with Fieger catching five passes for 117 yards.

In what many thought would be a barnburner, the Rams played the role of opportunists, pouncing on every Wildcat mistake and turning those mistakes into a 62-28 victory to win the first ever Prairie Junior Football Conference championship and the Dr. Paul Schwann Trophy that went with it. Schwann was a long-time Regina doctor who had worked with the Rams for years and with a number of Regina high schools. Labatt's Brewery donated the trophy in his memory, and it was awarded every year to the league champion.

Of the Rams' 62 points in the PJFC final, 49 of them were the direct result of punt and kickoff returns, interceptions, a fumble, a blocked punt and a flubbed kick. The Wildcats held the Rams' offence to 305 yards in total. But special team plays like Gerry Fellner's 67- and 83-yard kickoff returns, Maurice Butler's 82-yard punt return and Bill Lozinski's 62-yard punt return did the Wildcats no favours.

Next up for the Rams were their old pals, the Vancouver Meralomas. The Meralomas had dumped the Rams from the playoffs two years earlier, and now were back in the Western final. The game was scheduled for Regina's Taylor Field. Conceivably, it could be Gord Currie's last game as a Rams' coach. One win away from the Canadian championship, that's what it was all about.

The Rams knew very little about the Meralomas, and it was beginning to worry Currie. The unknown can escalate fears of defeat and tie knots in the players' performance levels. Two nights before the game, Currie gathered the team together in the Vagabond Hotel in south Regina. He wanted to talk to them. He talked for an hour. He talked about the people who had played for him down through the years. He talked about their greatness, and the qualities that made them great. He talked about how important it was to be a team player, to accept every challenge, to be afraid of none, to always rise above the crowd, because that is what makes champions.

Jerry Orban

"We really needed something like that," said assistant coach Jerry Orban. "We need something to pull everybody together. And that was it."

The Rams went out two days later and they buried the Meralomas 48-0 before 4,800 fans in Taylor Field. The game was over before it began. The Rams were headed for the national championship, which would be played on Saturday, November 13, 1976 in Taylor Field, beginning at 7:30 p.m.

Playing a football game at night, in mid-November, in Saskatchewan, presupposes no promise of good weather. But this season and the playoffs had been so perfectly scripted, how could the weather not cooperate? The night was crisp and clear. You could see the lights of Taylor Field reflecting into the sky from all over the city. They seemed to announce that something special was happening in this place, on this night. And there was something special, beyond the Regina Rams playing the Hamilton Hurricanes for the Canadian junior football championship.

This would be the final time Gord Currie would come through the cold, damp tunnel on the west side of the field, out into the bright lights and onto the playing field as the head coach of the Regina Rams. A coaching career that had spanned 26 years was about to end.

The Rams dressed at their Mount Pleasant clubhouse and took the bus to Taylor Field. Hundreds of fans were walking through the gates and into Taylor Field, underneath the concrete stands and up into their seats. By the time they all got there on that Saturday night in November, they numbered 10,000, and they were making more noise than anybody had ever heard at a Rams' game. It got louder and louder as the game wore on. The sounds of that night rolled across the city, rumbling their excitement.

Currie came to the field as usual. He was wearing his Rams' baseball cap. He had on a white shirt with a striped tie, a sweater, with a Rams' windbreaker over that. He was wearing dress pants and dress shoes. All eyes were on him to see if there were any telltale signs that he was feeling the uniqueness of this moment. There weren't. He was there for the same reason he had always been there. To coach. And this game was no more special to him than any other.

He could tell, just by looking at his players, just by walking among them, that they were ready. And he suspected the

Jerry Orban, Gord Currie, Gerry Fellner

Hurricanes were ready too. Championship games bring out the best in individual players and in teams. He figured that would happen on this night.

The *Leader-Post* headline the day after the game was spread across the whole top of the page. In bold black letters it read:

"The perfect end to Currie's fabulous era"

There was a large picture of Currie standing in the Rams' dressing room after the game. The championship trophy was at his feet. He was holding the game ball the players had given him. On page one of the *Leader-Post* there was another story, headlined:

"Perfect gift for Currie"

There was a picture of Bob Poley, wearing a smile you could see all the way back to Hudson Bay, and he was embracing the trophy.

But you had to be there that night. You had to be in Taylor Field to see that game, sense its electricity and feel its emotion. That was how championship games were supposed to be played.

The final score, 45-23 for the Rams, hints at a blowout. It was anything but. Getting there was the fun. It was as gut-wrenching, nerve-wracking a game as any Currie had ever coached. And Taylor Field, the old grey lady of 10th Avenue, which had held in its cradle many great moments from years gone by, had another one for the ages.

The Rams opened the game as if they were going to run away with it. Less than three minutes into the game, Gerry Fellner grabbed a 20-yard throw from Knoll and, with the moves of a snake and two huge blocks from Maurice Butler and Greg Fieger, turned it into an 87-yard touchdown. The rout was on. No it wasn't.

The Hurricances had one of the toughest defences in Canada. They gave up only an average of six points per game. For the rest of the first half, the Rams scored only five points. They were in a battle. And Hamilton's offence was coming to life. Quarterback Joe Fabiani, who had quarterbacked the Hurricanes to a 33-8 win over the Rams in the 1972 national final, went to the air. By halftime the Hurricanes were ahead 14-12. Early in the third quarter, their lead had increased to 20-12. By the time the teams got to the fourth quarter, the Hurricanes held a 20-15 lead.

There is only one way to describe the Rams in the fourth quarter. Brilliant. In that amazing quarter alone, Knoll completed 11 of 13 passes, including touchdown tosses of ten and three yards to Butler and eight yards to Fellner. Tim Almas returned an interception 19 yards for a touchdown. Rich Reitmeier kicked a 40-yard field goal. And the Rams' defence smothered Hamilton's offence.

Knoll ended up with 25 completions in 40 throws for 428 yards and four touchdowns. Fellner was named the game's outstanding offensive player for his unbelievable running ability after he caught the ball. He caught eight passes for 245 yards. Butler had seven catches, Fieger had six.

"I can't describe the feeling verbally," said Currie. "You know, we talked before the game about the power of a stick-to-it attitude, but you can do all the talking you want and it doesn't do any good unless the players go out there on the field and play with their hearts. It was that kind of attitude, that kind of feeling multiplied times 40 that gave us the win."

When it was over, the players picked Currie up and carried him off the field on their shoulders. The crowd of 10,000 rose in the November night and gave him a standing ovation. Even some of the Hurricanes stayed on the field and applauded.

It made you wonder if maybe Currie would change his mind. Maybe, he would come back, for just one more year.

Bob Poley

Gord Currie & Roger Aldag.

THANKS FOR THE MEMORIES

Gordon Currie retired as the Regina Rams' head coach following the 1976 Canadian championship game. The Rams won. I think they won it for Gord Currie. They knew it was his last game as coach, there was no way they would dare send him out with a loss. They knew what he was. They knew what he had done. When the game was over, the Rams' executive fretted for months over how they could properly honour this man who had done so much for them. He had taken over as head coach in 1965. He had not only saved the franchise. He had made it the best in Canada. He set tremendously high standards for anybody who came after him. He made the Rams what they are today. Finally, the Rams' organization decided how to honour this man of men, this man for all seasons and all reasons. Joe Kanuka, who had been there in the beginning of the resurrection, said the Rams should hold a dinner for Gord Currie. So, they did. The dinner was held on October 29, 1977, in the Canada Centre in the Regina Exhibition Grounds. There were 1,300 people in attendance. It was, at that time, the biggest dinner ever held in the province of Saskatchewan. Letters of congratulation came from all levels of society.

Prime Minister Pierre Elliot Trudeau sent a letter. In part, this is what he said: "It is indeed fitting that his many friends should gather to pay homage to Gordon Currie. He has given unstintingly of himself in coaching the Regina Rams, the Regina Red Sox and high school athletics. I know that many young people who have been inspired by Gordon Currie deeply appreciate his dedication. He has made a great impact on sports in Regina."

Saskatchewan Premier Allan Blakeney wrote: "I am certain that many young people who were fortunate enough to work with Coach Currie at one time in his career consider that experience as a significantly important one."

One of many.

Regina Mayor Henry Baker wrote: "Dedication to youth can best describe Gordon Currie. He is a man who has generously devoted his professional and recreational time and his knowledge to the young people of Regina . . . a man whose direct influence on the lives of his students and athletes will far surpass his outstanding record of coaching championship teams in football, baseball and hockey."

The speeches were permeated with nostalgia, steeped in praise and kept in perspective by the man being honoured. Gordon Currie, as humble and honest and decent as always, was not about to let that night go to anybody's head. So, he thanked the people at the dinner, he thanked his wife, Shirley, he thanked everybody in his family, he thanked Scotty Livingstone for talking him into coaching the Rams, and he gave all the credit to his assistant coaches, the executive and, mostly, to the players. All of them. Every one of them. They were always the reason he was there. For all those 26 years.

Gord Currie

There was a program produced that night. It was given to the 1,300 people who attended. It has become somewhat of a collectors' item. I had been asked to write a column for the program. I did. It was one of the most draining columns I had ever written. Sometimes, when you are a columnist, you will write something that is just for yourself. This was one that pulled tears from my eyes, knotted my stomach, challenged my endurance. It took me hours, then days, before I was reasonably happy about it. All I wanted to do was write a column for that program that would meet the expectations of Gordon Currie. All he ever asked of anybody was that they give their best. That is what I did, coach. On that occasion, at that time, I did my best.

This is the column I wrote:

> It was one of those moments which seem to eclipse eternity, which stays with you, in your heart and in your mind, where it counts, lingering as a warm reminder to the greatness of the man, Gord Currie.
>
> On a November night in 1976, there was a chill in the air and the wind whistled down the centre of Taylor Field. Its gates wide open, thousands of people were flocking through, dressed in snowmobile outfits, wrapped in blankets, heads barely visible through toques and hoods and stuff you wear in the west when the warnings of winter are sounded.
>
> They were still driving in the parking lots, walking into the stadium, opening their thermoses and snuggling into their seats, when the moment drew near.
>
> For the Regina Rams and the Hamilton Hurricanes, this November night in 1976 in this place they called Taylor Field, well, this game was what it was all about. It was for the Canadian championship, the ultimate for both of them, the Holy Grail of junior football.
>
> For Gord Currie, it was the end of a fabulous era.
>
> After more than a quarter of a century of coaching in baseball, hockey, football and, life, he was retiring.
>
> This was his last game, win or lose.
>
> Underneath the stadium, where the walls are grim and cold looking and where water was dripping from above, the two teams had gone to their dressing rooms and they were waiting.
>
> This is when it is the worst. This is when the nerves crawl up the players' stomachs and knot in their throats and there is so much tension it is incredible.
>
> In a little room down the hallway, the coaches and the team captains and the referees were together, going over some of the rules, deciding who would kick off and that kind of stuff.
>
> Currie was there, wearing that green parka with R-A-M-S across the back of it and this running back from Hamilton, named Mike Biljetina, was looking at Currie.
>
> They had never met and likely would never meet again, but what this kid from a city far removed from Regina said would last forever in the minds of anybody who heard him say it.
>
> "Mr. Currie," Mike Biljetina said, "I am really sorry I never got the chance to play for you."
>
> It said it all.

You can go blurry-eyed, cross-eyed and short circuit your vocabulary attempting to put into words what Gord Currie has meant to the people and teams he has coached and guided.

All the words of praise fit.

But this kid from Hamilton painted the real picture. He was one of the unlucky ones. He didn't get to play for Gord Currie.

Where did it all begin, this stuff that legends are made of? Where was the foundation laid, the seed planted, which gave Gord Currie his incredible grip on the formula for success? That is what his life has been in sports. Success.

Ask him and he will tell you that Père Athol Murray and Al Ritchie had something considerable to do with Gord Currie's philosophy on life.

Both came into contact with him when he attended Notre Dame College in Wilcox. But there was something before which must have played a role in the ultimate product.

Perhaps, it was that Currie was born in Semans and lived in places like Pinky and Quinton. They were small places and people in small places always seem to be closer to the earth and to reality and they always seem to develop a greater need to be closer to other people.

Currie was like that. He needed people. He needed friends. He cherishes them, whether they be young, middle-aged or old.

But it was especially with the young that he excelled. His influences on them were many, the part he played in the development of their lives outstanding, the dedication he threw into helping them ride out the rough times, handle the good times, and more importantly, develop considerable character.

All through his coaching career, he inspired his teams and his players to excel, to reach beyond what they felt was their limit, to attain the ultimate in whatever it was they were searching for.

He has taken lives which were pointed towards disaster and turned them into something meaningful. One way or another, he has had an effect on every kid who ever played for him.

It began in 1950, this terrestrial kind of coaching career Gord Currie built.

Most of it was at Balfour Technical School, where he was also a teacher.

He coached the Balfour hockey team to three provincial championships. He coached the Regina Red Sox to four Southern Baseball League championships.

He coached the Balfour Tech Redmen to eight provincial high school football championships, six of them coming in succession. At one stage, his Redmen won 40 straight games before losing.

At the time he won his seventh high school title, the Regina Rams were at a crossroads in their history.

They practiced on a rocky field beside Albert Street in the shadows of the legislative grounds and their dressing room was small, and falling apart, and their equipment was bad, and their image not much better.

Something had to be done. So, it was with improving that image and everything else in mind that Scotty Livingstone and Rafe Chadwick and Peter McCaffrey went to Gord Currie, the high school coach, and talked him into coaching the Rams.

In 1965, he coached both the Rams and the Redmen. The Redmen won their eighth provincial title. The Rams got to the Western championship game.

The era had begun.

From 1965 until 1976, the Rams won six Canadian championships, a new clubhouse was built, a new image constructed, and a success story born that rivalled any, anywhere, in Canadian amateur sports history.

Under Currie the Rams won 109 of 136 games and in 1976 Currie was named the outstanding amateur coach in Canada.

He could have won it every year and nobody could have argued.

When you become as successful as Gord Currie has in sports, people wonder what it is that makes it that way, what the recipe he used was, what almost divine powers did he possess that made his teams almost unbeatable.

He was just Gord Currie, that's all.

He was a motivator.

His talks to his players were sometimes electrifying, often gripping, always inspirational. His ability to use words that came from the soul lifted his Balfour and Red Sox and Ram teams to such heights they became virtually unbeatable.

He would draw on history and use it to illustrate how success and goals were achieved. He would give them lessons. And they learned through him, not just about football, but about life.

He has reduced some of his players and some of his assistant coaches to tears, so emotional were his pleas for them to be successful in achieving their destinies.

That belief in themselves carried the 1976 Rams to their victory over the Hamilton Hurricanes on that chilled November night in Taylor Field.

Trailing 14-12 at halftime and 20-15 after three quarters, the Rams exploded for 30 points in the fourth quarter and won, going away, 45-23.

When it was over and they had retreated to their clubhouse at Mt. Pleasant and the players had given Gord Currie the game ball, people became misty-eyed.

The man who has carved out an incredible record during his 26 years of coaching hockey, baseball and football stood in the middle of the dressing room, surrounded by his players and his coaches, holding the ball, a massive trophy in front of him, and he spoke to them, really, for the last time.

He thanked them and he praised them and he told them they were the greatest team he had ever coached.

While he spoke, the awesome presence this man commands was evident. "Gord sort of has an air about him," Mel Fiissel, his assistant and successor would say. "It's like an air of royalty, like he's important. You look at him and it just seems like he is good."

There are cities and towns and places all over Canada that never get to experience a Gord Currie.

Regina was very lucky. They had him as a coach for 26 years.

He was a winner and a teacher and there is a tendency to keep trying to find ways to adequately thank him. There is none, really.

"Too much emphasis has been placed on what I've contributed," he said, "and not enough on what I've gained. Coaching has contributed to my educational growth. I'll tell you, a person can gain a great deal more basic knowledge about people by coaching them than he can by taking all the courses offered. It's maybe sort of barbwired knowledge, but it's more in touch with reality."

Ask him about his championships, and he almost shrugs them off.

"I think the most important thing about coaching is being able to give players something of lasting value," Currie said. "A coach's accomplishments should be related to how much his players have grown as people, how much strength of character they've developed."

His contribution, then, was priceless.

Bob Hughes and Gord Currie

BIG SHOES TO FILL

1977

What does a small boy from Earl Grey, Saskatchewan want to grow up to be? A hockey player? A Brier curling champion? A teacher? A doctor? A farmer? Earl Grey is a small village not far from Regina. It is about 65 kilometres north of Regina and about 40 kilometres east of Rowan's Ravine Provincial Park. It is located in gentle rolling prairie just above the great Qu'Appelle Valley. Its population is usually around 300 people.

Mel Fiissel

It is fair to say that nobody from Earl Grey ever, as a boy, wished he would grow up to be the head coach of the Regina Rams. Mel Fiissel was born in Earl Grey and when he was young the family moved into Regina, settling into the city's north end. He attended Imperial Public School on Broad Street, then Balfour Technical School. He was always a good athlete and a solid student.

When he went to Balfour, he became a first-string guard with the Redmen basketball team. He was a sprinter with Balfour's high-school track team. But where he excelled, where his love for the sport took him, was the Balfour football team, perhaps the most successful high-school football team ever.

Only about five feet, eight inches, and packing about 180 pounds, Fiissel became a starter right off the bat and, for four years, the Redmen were unbeatable. It was there that Fiissel first came across Gord Currie. Currie came to regard Fiissel as perhaps the best athlete he had ever coached. "You never had to worry about Mel," Currie said. "He always gave everything he had. And he is a great person." Currie was the only coach Fiissel ever played for in football. When Currie went to the Rams, Fiissel followed him, then stayed on with the Rams, first as an assistant equipment manager, then as an assistant coach. The two became close friends.

When Currie left the Rams after the 1976 season, the obvious choice to succeed him was Mel Fiissel. Mel was very similar to Currie in that he believed good, fundamental football, with the emphasis on execution, was the best way to produce a winner. Fiissel was also a great believer in the Regina Rams and their role in Regina's sporting scene.

But, who would want to follow Currie's act? Who, in his right mind, would want to replace a man who was a coaching legend?

Mel Fiissel, that's who.

Mel had always held Currie in the highest esteem. "Gord had a lot to do with turning my life in the right direction," Fiissel said. But he didn't for a minute think he was Gord Currie. The opportunity was there to be the head coach of the Regina Rams, and Mel jumped at it. The most important thing about Fiissel was, he was his own man. He had his own style. And he would stick with it. He wasn't going to change.

By 1977, the Rams were well established; they had enormous appeal to graduating high schoolers. Kids were showing up from all over Saskatchewan. This was the place to be and the team to be with.

When Mel Fiissel opened his first training camp as head

Jerry Orban, Bryan Dimen, Jerry Zbytnuik, Mel Fiissel.

coach, in the stifling heat of a Saskatchewan summer, there were at least 100 kids, 108 registered, streaming out of the clubhouse and onto the practice field. Mel still had a deep well of experienced players back from the 1976 team – Bob Poley,. Bryan Illerbrun, Greg Nesbitt, Greg Fieger, Maurice Butler, Tim Almas, Terry Read, Vern Ell, the Kenyon brothers, Jim and Craig, Kerry Berryman, Brent McConnell, Bill Lozinski, Kevin Harle, Clarence Sacawayacappo. So, not having a contender wasn't something the Rams had to worry about.

Fiissel had as strong a coaching staff as there was in the league. Killoh had retired from the Rams when Currie did. But Jerry Orban stayed on as line coach and he was joined on the assistant coaching staff by former Rams' quarterback/defensive back Bryan Dimen and long-time high-school coach Jerry Zbytnuik.

How far they would go would depend on the huge hole that had been left at one position. Quarterback. You can have the best-looking restaurant and most tempting menu in the world, but if you don't have a chef, you have nothing. Or, as Hilltops' coach Paul Schoenhals once put it, "Just because you have the animals doesn't mean you have a circus."

When the Rams lost Knoll to graduation after the 1976 season, they were left with a gaping hole. About half-a-dozen replacements for the number one spot showed up in training camp, but it didn't take long to slice that number down to two veterans – Thom Parker and Bob Moore. Parker had played more, as Knoll's backup, but he was still an unknown quantity. As well, the Rams also saw the first in a string of brothers who would play for them over the coming years – Kelly Hamilton, turned out to get a look at quarterback. He would end up as a starting running back.

The Rams got through training camp and the exhibition season feeling comfortable with virtually all avenues of their roster. But the quarterback question remained unsolved in that they still were not sure just what they would have once the shooting was for real.

As had become a tradition, the Rams opened the season against the Saskatoon Hilltops, this game scheduled for Taylor Field. This was a game both head coaches were looking forward to, the rivalry between these two teams was still hot.

Hilltops' head coach Paul Schoenhals, a fiery, competitive guy, figured his team had the potential to get to the Canadian championship. He put a lot of emphasis on the season opener. "This is what junior football in Canada is all about," Schoenhals said, "playing the Regina Rams. That's the team you measure yourself against."

If this was the game that was going to be the measuring stick, the Rams came out of it on the short end, by a long shot. In a game that turned into a comedy of errors, the Rams might just as well have stayed in their dressing room. The Hilltops played the role of opportunists, and hammered Regina 44-9. All but one Hilltops' touchdown, their last, was set up by Rams' mistakes. The Rams lost four of six fumbles, served up three interceptions, had two punts blocked, and were caught flat-footed on a fake punt.

Bill Parker

On this day, if anybody had told the Rams they were all wet, they would have been right. Literally. Well, at least one of them. It seems that on hot days, and this was a warm August day, Rams' centre Kevin Harle had developed the habit of taking buckets of ice water and pouring them over his head during the halftime break.

"He was so wet we couldn't use him at centre in the third quarter," said Fiissel. "That's what happened on our first series of the second half when we fumbled. The quarterback couldn't hang on to the ball, it was so wet."

By the time the Rams had played their second game of the season, people had every right to wonder if part of the Rams' game plan was to turn the football over. In Calgary, against the Mohawks, the Rams floundered their way through the first half. It looked as if it might be a repeat performance of what had happened in the first game against Saskatoon. Parker did not have a good first half. He threw three interceptions. The difference between this game and the first game was that the Mohawks didn't take advantage of the gifts. They scored only three points in the first half and went into their dressing room at the halftime break trailing by four points.

The game actually turned late in the second quarter when the Mohawks attempted a somewhat misguided play. Facing a third down at their 16 and leading 3-0, the Mohawks sent in their punt team. But Calgary coach Jim Silye, a former Stampeder, decided to call a fake punt. The play was stuffed when defensive stars Dave Hall and Bruce Lipinski were waiting for punter Bruce McAlsan as he tried to run around the end. The Rams took over on the 18, and it took Greg Fieger two passes from Parker to get the ball into the end zone. That was it. The Rams came alive, and kept it going in the second half to win 20-3. Poley and Illerbrun had big games along the Rams' defensive line. But perhaps the most encouraging thing for Fiissel and his staff was the overall play of Parker at quarterback. He completed 17 of 33 passes for 244 yards.

Greg Fieger

The Rams were tested the following week at home to the Calgary Colts. They got a solid game from their offence. With Parker in a groove now, the Rams chalked up 22 first downs, 194 yards rushing and 295 yards passing. But the hero of the game was placekicker Rich Reitmeier. He kicked five field goals, including the game winner from 18 yards out, and the Rams won 22-20.

If there was a hard-luck team in the Prairie Junior Football Conference, it was the Red Deer Packers. They just couldn't win for losing, and it was rarely pretty. They came into Regina wondering just how bad a licking the Rams would lay on them this time. They found out soon enough. It was bad. The Rams rolled to a 67-6 victory. The Rams had fun that night. Three running backs rushed for over 100 yards each – Corey Elson got 144, Len Antonini had 114 and Kelly Hamilton 109. In all, the Rams rushed for 500 yards, averaging 10 yards a carry.

By now, the Rams were on a real roll, but they would soon face their biggest test since playing the Hilltops in the season opener – in Edmonton against the Huskies, who with Forrest Kennard at quarterback and his brother Trevor, an outstanding placekicker, felt they were returning to their glory days. The Rams flicked aside the Huskies as easily as flicking aside a lady bug.

With everything working, the Rams gained the most yards they had ever gained in their history – 723 in all – as they beat Edmonton 41-13. The score actually flattered the Huskies. The Rams rushed for 488 yards and threw for another 235. This, after the Huskies had taken a 10-6 lead. But in the second quarter, Parker got the Rams' offence into gear. In that quarter, the Rams piled up 313 yards in offence, with Parker clicking on eight of 12 passes for 186 yards. Three of his completions went for touchdowns – twice to Maurice Butler from 42 and 10 yards out and once to Bill Lozinski from 25 yards away. The Rams had built a 33-10 lead by halftime, and there was no stopping them.

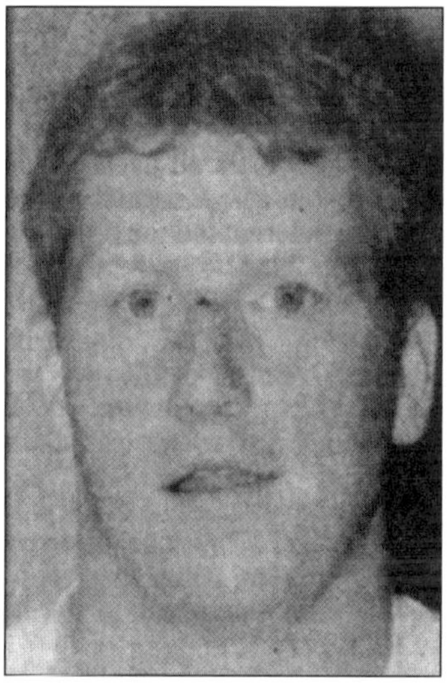

Len Antonini

Elson and Hamilton both rushed for over 100 yards. The offence, mind you, continued to turn over the ball too much for Fiissel's liking – three interceptions and four fumbles. Defensively, the Rams smothered the Kennard brothers, with Bruce Lipinski intercepting two passes and Jim Kenyon getting one.

The bus ride back to Regina, usually long and boring, was filled with the sounds of a team that was sure it had put it all together and was taking dead aim on yet another Canadian championship. And around the league, there was talk that the Rams were still the team to beat, that they might very well be unstoppable.

"The big difference for us now is confidence," assistant coach Jerry Orban said.

"We had a lot of new guys," said Fiissel, "and it takes a while for everything to come together. There's no reason now why we can't challenge for the Canadian championship."

The Rams continued their run to the roses the next weekend, traveling to Medicine Hat where they laid a licking on the Rattlers, 54-0.

The victory left the Rams tied for first place with the Wildcats and Hilltops, all with 5-1 records. Before 10,000 fans in Taylor Field, on an October Saturday night, the Rams and Wildcats clashed. And it turned into the one of the most physical games of the season, with the Rams winning a head-knocker 19-14. Once again, Rich Reitmeier came through for the Rams, kicking four field goals, two in the pressure-packed fourth quarter, providing the margin of victory. But the Rams also got a huge play out of Bob Poley, who was playing tight end. He scored a touchdown on a sensational run after taking a pass from Parker. Fieger was Parker's favourite receiver, catching six passes for 95 yards.

Rich Reitmeier

The win set up a first-place showdown with the Hilltops, in Saskatoon, in the final game of the regular season schedule.

As the game approached, Fiissel looked back on the season and felt that a major difference was how the rookies had come through. He was especially happy with the play of Kelly Hamilton, who had nailed down a starting spot in the offensive backfield, and others such as

Kelly Hamilton

Tim Probe

Dave Badowich, Len Antonini and Tim Probe. Other rookies who had played their way onto the Rams' roster, and had spelled off the starters on defence, were Dan Taylor, Larry Mueller and Rob MacLachlan.

There were plenty of hard feelings developing as the final game approached. Hilltops' offensive lineman Don Sachs threw down the gauntlet to the Rams, warning them they had better not think they were coming into Saskatoon to lay a licking on the Hilltops. "They've probably improved, but we've improved more," said Sachs. "They're good, but we're better. They just ended their dynasty, we're just starting ours."

There were 4,000 people in Gordie Howe Bowl that October night when the Hilltops answered the bell. The problem of turnovers that had plagued the Rams all season long reared its ugly head again. Interceptions, fumbles, and something the Rams hadn't seen all season long – one dropped pass after another – keyed Saskatoon's 30-3 victory that clinched them first place in the PJFC. The Rams ended up second and drew the Wildcats in the semifinal in Taylor Field.

The end to the season came swiftly enough. The Rams continued to have turnover problems. Even though they played as well as they had all season long, it was the fumbles and interceptions that put them under. The Wildcats won 35-24, and the Rams went home.

It wasn't a season they would remember with fondness. Meanwhile, after one year as head coach, Fiissel said he was thinking of stepping down. He had a young family and a job, and combining that with coaching was trying at the best of times. The winter would be long and hard as he fought with himself over what to do.

PASSING THE TORCH

It was in the dead of winter in 1978, during the darkness and the knifing cold, when the wind and snow are numbing, that Mel Fiissel came to grips with his future. On Monday, January 30th, the Regina Rams held a press conference. They announced that Mel Fiissel was resigning as head coach after just one year at the job. I first came to know Mel in 1965 when he was playing high-school football at Balfour Technical School. We became close friends almost right away. When he announced his decision to leave the Rams, I knew how gut-wrenching it had been for him to come to that moment. We had talked about it for months, but in the end his desire to spend more time with his family, his four girls and his wife, Sandra, won out. He was that kind of a person. On Monday, January 30, 1978, I wrote the following column that appeared the next day in the *Leader-Post*:

Mel Fiissel

> On this cold night in 1967, with a chilly wind swirling the dirt into tiny, sometimes blinding pockets of dust, Mel Fiissel stood in the middle of Gordie Howe Bowl and cried.
>
> This was his final game as a player with the Regina Rams and his career had ended in defeat in this playoff game to the Saskatoon Hilltops and when you had given as much of yourself as Fiissel had that night and were found still wanting, then defeat carried with it a special kind of anguish.
>
> The year before, in 1966, he had been a rookie halfback with the Regina Rams and they had won the Canadian championship to officially mark the beginning of the Gord Currie era and for four years before that, from 1962 to 1965, he had been a halfback with the Balfour Tech Redmen and they had won four straight provincial championships.
>
> When people talk about the Gord Currie era in Regina sports, the talk is of winners and championships. Well, as much as anybody else, Mel Fiissel was a vital part of all that. He was a winner and he was a champion, a leader and a follower, a teacher and a learner.
>
> Since he graduated as a player with the Rams, he has been their equipment manager, a scout on occasion, an assistant coach, and last year he became the successor to Gord Currie when Currie retired as the head coach.
>
> There were easier acts to follow than the one Currie left

behind and the pressure on his successor was obvious. But when Fiissel took the job, he did not look on it as taking over. It was more a matter of just continuing what had been done.

The pressure was for others to worry about.

The fun of coaching, the good-time associations with the players and his assistant coaches, were enough for Mel.

The job he did in just his one year as the head coach of the Rams was a remarkable one. Gone from the 1976 Canadian championship team were a dozen starters, most of whom had been of star quality.

Yet, despite what was obviously a rebuilding year, the Rams rose and finished second in the tough Prairie Junior Football Conference.

Their reputation, their name, what they had become and

Mel Fiissel

were all about for the last dozen years or so had not changed.

When they were defeated by the Edmonton Wildcats in the semi-finals, ending their season before they thought it should end, Fiissel stood in the middle of the dressing room and did what he had done in 1967. He wept. His pride was not false.

He had a feeling it might be his last moment as a coach and he was right. Last Thursday, he decided to quit as head coach of the Rams and for the first time since 1962, he will be out of football.

"I'm going out as a coach the same way I went out as a player, "he laughed. "As a loser."

His decision to leave wasn't reached hastily. It was the result of three years of thinking about it. "I've been saying I was going to quit for three years now," he said. "I have fought with myself for the last three months about it. And now that I have made up my mind, I miss it already. But, you know, ever since I have been married, I haven't had a summer or fall off. I have just reached a stage where I want to spend more time with my family . . . It's been a long, long-time since I got into football, hasn't it?"

What bothers you most about somebody like Mel Fiissel leaving something like the Regina Rams is that teams and organizations in amateur sport crave people like him.

There are not enough of his kind to go around. They give so much of themselves, with their only reward not a monetary or tangible one, but a deeper, inner one.

"If somebody asked me what the Rams and what football and what the years I have spent in it meant to me," Fiissel said, "I would say that it's the people I have met. It's not the clubhouse, or the football, or the championships, or the games. It's the people. It's people like Gord Currie and Doug Killoh, people I would never have gotten to know without football. It's the friendships."

It is generally conceded that the new era of the Rams began in 1966 when they won their first Canadian championship. Mel Fiissel was the last link from 1966.

Yeah, junior football in our city is the lesser for his loss.

The Driving Forces

In all of the years that I have written about or just watched the Regina Rams, one thing stood out. It is likely the bottom-line reason for the success of this organization. That is, the caliber of people the team has attracted to its executive levels.

Some members of the executive have been former players, who once bitten by the Rams' bug never got over it, and would do anything to ensure that the words success and Rams would always be mentioned in the same breath. Others came to the Rams in a variety of ways. They were brought on board by friends who were already on the executive, or they just wanted to get involved.

A number of these people stand out in my mind as being towers of strength and soldiers of fortune in the Rams' history. I will never be able to mention all of them in this book. But some of them I remember for their extraordinary contributions. And some of them I remember for the dedication they brought to the Rams, a dedication that at times was religious in its zeal.

There was R.C. (Scotty) Livingstone, perhaps the one man who ignited the fire that still burns within the Rams to this very day. Scotty was the guy who spearheaded the drive to get Gord Currie to coach the Rams in 1965, the year in which this organization found its flight path and really took off. He was the guy who wanted a new clubhouse built, at no cost.

Scotty's years with the Rams were always underlined by success and fun. Nobody had more fun at being with the Rams than he did. There was no game Scotty ever thought the Rams would lose, and long into the nights, in smoky hotel rooms, Scotty could be found making wagers on his beloved Rams, and telling stories. He would take on everybody in those friendly arguments over how good the Rams were, from mayors of other cities to executive members of other teams. Nobody did more for the Regina Rams than he did, and when he died a huge piece of Rams' history went with him.

Scotty Livingstone

It was Scotty who recruited Erwin Strass to the Rams' executive. That was in 1966, when Livingstone and Joe Kanuka, another tireless Rams' executive member, decided there had to be a clubhouse built. Strass was a down-to-earth construction company owner who loved football, and Scotty wanted him to be in charge of building the clubhouse.

"He expects this thing to be built for nothing," I can recall Strass telling me in 1966.

"Yes, he does," I said.

And, it was. But it would never have happened had it not been for the work ethic, the ingenuity and the drive of Strass. It became a 24-hour-a-day project for him. He was out there from start to finish, supervising, advising, helping out himself. The clubhouse sprang from the ground on the wings of the generosity of the business community and others in Regina who shared the Rams' dream in the beginning.

When I think of Rams' executive members whom I admire, the name Gary Mather comes up. Mather has been a lifelong Ram. He played for them and has been a member of the executive ever since, including serving time as president. Nobody is more devoted to the Rams. Quiet and resourceful, Mather continues to carry the Rams' flag.

There was Bob Millar, a former player who joined the executive. Millar was the president of the Rams when the expansion to the clubhouse was built in the late 1980s, and remains with them to this very day. A Regina lawyer, he can be found selling 50-50 tickets at the Saskatchewan Roughrider home games, which is an important part of the Rams' fundraising efforts. Norbert Thurmeier is another who has held every executive position and remains active today.

Norbert Thurmeier

You could never mention the history of the Rams without mentioning Tom Shepherd. Tommy Chuckles has likely given more hours of himself to football in this province than virtually anybody I have ever known. Whether it was with the Rams or the Roughriders, Shepherd had a huge talent as a fundraiser. His contributions to the Roughriders' lottery and Plaza of Honor dinner are legendary.

Tom Shepherd

Shepherd's work on behalf of the Rams yielded extraordinary results. When the Rams started up their annual mixed sports' dinner, he was brought on board by Livingstone. Together, those two sold more tickets to more dinners than anyone else. Shepherd's other role with the Rams included babysitting Scotty and Reg Forsyth through various fundraising efforts, most notably the dinners, until the events were sold out. This included keeping the pair away from refreshments, a task that usually drove Shepherd to distraction but is still the stuff of stories told today.

Gary Uhren has served the Rams for years and years, most notably as the team's manager, but also on the executive. Gary was one of those guys who truly enjoyed virtually every day with the Rams, giving freely of his spare time, and giving of his time when likely he should have been doing something else. I have always looked upon him as one of the background heroes of the Rams' organization. Without people like Gary, the Rams would not be what they are today.

Gary Uhren

Larry LeBlanc played for the Rams and became a member of their board of directors, and he's still there. LeBlanc was the Rams' president when the team decided to leave junior football and join the University of Regina. It took a lot of work and a lot of convincing of many within the Rams' organization, but in the end the vision LeBlanc had turned out to be the right thing for the Rams, for the University of Regina, and also for football in Canada.

Paul Barnby seems always to have been a Ram. Barnby has been president of the team and on the executive in a number of roles. He is another who thoroughly enjoys the time he spends on Regina Rams' business. He is to the Rams as Tom Shepherd has been to the Roughriders . . . tireless and relentless.

Don McDougall, Bob Milton, Rafe Chadwick, Ron McGuigan, Tom McCord, Bob Pelton, Dave Howie, Gary Treble, Jack Kennedy, Ed Bankowski, Doug McKillop and Rick McCullough, are others who also stand out when you talk about dedication to the Regina Rams.

Don McDougall

The list of those who served the Rams and Canadian junior football is endless. But I would be remiss if the name Jerry Joynt wasn't included. The cigar-chomping Joynt was president of the Rams in 1972 and 1973, but perhaps is best known nationally as

Ed Bankowski

Tom McCord

Rafe Chadwick

Doug McKillop

the first president of the Canadian National Junior Football League, from 1974 to 1978. During his administration, the league grew to 33 teams and five leagues. Joynt also was president of the Canadian Amateur Football Association in 1982 and 1983. As with virtually every other Rams' executive member, Joynt served on one Rams' committee after another. It was the Rams' way.

What they have done for the Rams may not be all that exciting to the guy on the street, but what they have done, what many of them are still doing, determined what the Rams became and still are – one of the most successful amateur sports organizations in the country. It is not something that happened by accident.

Rick McCullough, Bob Millar, Bob Pelton, Paul Barnby.

THE Z-MAN TAKES OVER

1978-1979

If there is the perfect word to explain the success the Regina Rams have enjoyed since 1965, the word would be "continuity." From the executive suite to the coaching level, the Rams have always been able to bring people into the fold who genuinely care about them and look upon involvement with them as more of a passion than a duty.

It is remarkable that, since 1965, the Rams have only had four head coaches – Gord Currie, Mel Fiissel, Jerry Zbytnuik and Frank McCrystal. Each of them brought their own special touch to the Rams, and each made lasting contributions to the team and the organization. Not one of them failed. They were what the Rams were all about.

Jerry Zbytnuik

When Fiissel retired after the 1977 season, the Rams put together a small committee to find a successor. President Bob Milton, the tireless Don McDougall and former assistant coach Jerry Orban knew immediately who they wanted. It was Jerry Zbytnuik, who had joined the Rams only the year before as an assistant coach to Fiissel. Zbytnuik called the moment when Fiissel hired him as one of the happiest of his life, and one of the great thrills of his life.

Zbytnuik didn't accept the head-coaching job until early in March, even though the Rams had offered it to him almost immediately after Fiissel resigned at the end of January. "My initial gut feeling when the job opened up was that I would love to do it," he recalled. "It seemed like the next step for me as far as football was concerned, but the big factor for me was my family and the support I got from my wife. That was what really made up my mind."

Cam Clark

Zbytnuik had a long history in amateur football in Saskatchewan. He had played with the University of Saskatchewan Huskies, and he had coached the Miller Marauders in the Regina Intercollegiate Football League for a number of years before joining the Rams. He was well known and well respected in minor

Gerry Harris

football. This move by the Rams would pay off down the road.

Zbytnuik put his own fingerprints on the Rams. Dimen stayed on as an assistant coach, but two new faces joined the coaching staff – Gerry Harris, a long-time coach at Luther College in Regina, and big Cam Clark, who had played for the Rams in the 1960s and who was an assistant coach to Zbytnuik at Miller.

The new Rams' coach also wanted to change the focus of the Rams. In recent years, and mostly because of quarterbacks like Len Knoll and Thom Parker, the Rams had developed a passing game that became the bread and butter of their attack. Zbytnuik wanted to build a stronger running game and not have to rely on the pass as much. "We've got Greg Fieger, Corey Elson and Kelly Hamilton all coming back," he said. He wanted to get back to the days when the Rams' ground game pounded the opposition into the turf. But early in training camp, Elson went down with torn knee ligaments.

The Rams would be without two of their more experienced linemen in Bob Poley and Brian Illerbrun, who were both latched onto by the Saskatchewan Roughriders. Illerbrun still had another year of junior eligibility to go, but the Riders wanted to make an arrangement where he would practice with the Riders and play with the Rams. But, the Rams felt such a deal just wouldn't work. Greg Nesbitt was the lone player returning to the defensive line.

Greg Nesbitt

The Rams figured they would have to find a new quarterback. Thom Parker, who had come on the year before, announced that he was forsaking the Rams to play for the University of Calgary Dinosaurs. But two weeks into training camp, the Rams got some good news. Parker had changed his mind and was returning to the juniors.

The Rams opened against the Hilltops. They lost to the team everybody figured would take the league title, and then they put together back-to-back wins that were not pretty and left Zbytnuik worried about his offence. Nevertheless, it kept the Rams in the running for a playoff spot.

Fieger, Butler, Lozinski and Parker all seemed to be finding their comfort zones in the new system that had been established with the coaching change. As long as the effort was there, there was not going to be panic in the coaching ranks.

The Rams' running game took hold against the Medicine Hat Rattlers. The Rams' rushed for 410 yards in a 42-6 win before 4,000 fans on a cool mid-September night in Taylor Field. Running backs Len Antonini (25 carries, 212 yards) and Les Mironuck (18 carries, 124 yards) had the biggest games of their careers.

But there was more to the Rams' success than an improving offence. The Rams' defence was nothing short of spectacular. Through four games it had been virtually unbeatable. No team, including the Hilltops, was able to gain more than 250 yards in offence against the Rams and no team was able to complete more than half of the passes it put up.

The Rams were gaining momentum as the season moved on. And they were starting to explode offensively. They smashed the Edmonton Huskies 63-20, scoring eight touchdowns, with Fieger getting three of them. Fieger caught seven passes for 114 yards and averaged 41.5 yards per punt.

Next up for the Rams were the Wildcats. It would be the tough game the Rams felt they needed before taking on the Hilltops. The Wildcats had gone on to win the Canadian championship in 1977, thus consolidating the accepted feeling that the Prairie Junior Football Conference was the best league in Canada. The Wildcats had lost 12 starters off that team, eight of whom were all-stars, but Edmonton coach Jim Lazurak was as good a coach as there was in the PJFC, and he had moulded the 1978 team into one that had to be rated as a serious contender.

Well, if it was a tough game the Rams wanted, it was a tough game they got. In a cold and windy Clarke Stadium in Edmonton, the Rams prevailed 14-13, to set up a first-place showdown with the Hilltops a week later in Regina. After Rich Reitmeier had missed three earlier field goal attempts, the Rams desperately needed a fourth-quarter field goal to win the game. He made the one that counted, which was really what he was best at. He was a pressure kicker, and when the Rams needed him, he answered the call.

It was back to Regina to get ready for yet another showdown with the Hilltops. The Hilltops had beaten the Rams 21-14 earlier in the season, and the Rams had been itching to get back at them. But if this was an itch the Rams wanted to scratch, they must have figured they had seven years to do it.

The Rams got bombed 29-1 by the Hilltops on a night that was totally dominated by Saskatoon. No contest, this one. The Rams finished second and would meet the Wildcats in the semifinal in Regina.

Probably, the most improved team from the start of the season to the finish in the PJFC was the Edmonton Wildcats. They had improved and improved with such imperceptible steadiness that the other teams hadn't really noticed.

When the Wildcats reached Regina, they were ready to turn it on. And turn it on they did. Gobbling up three Rams' fumbles and putting together a balanced attack that left the Rams reaching for air. The Wildcats ended the Rams' season with a 40-12 win in Taylor Field. For 11 members of the Rams, it was an especially tough pill to swallow. This was their last game in junior football. They were graduating. Gone, and leaving behind some amazing accomplishments, were defensive tackle Chuck McDonald, defensive backs Vern Ell, Bruce Lipinski, Tim Almas and Greg Jones, quarterback Thom Parker, wide receiver Bill Lozinski, linebacker/kicker Rich Reitmeier, linebacker Dave Hall, and offensive linemen Kevin Harle and John Hartung.

If there was any highlight for the Rams, it was the presentation of the Gordon Currie Youth Development Fund bursary. The fund had been created the night of the testimonial dinner held to pay tribute to Currie. More than $17,000 had been raised that night to start the fund. It is still handing out annual bursaries to young Saskatchewan people as this book is being written. The first ever winner of the bursary was Rams' defensive back Bruce Lipinski.

For the Rams, the off-season of 1978 was one in which there was a fair amount of reflecting. This was the second straight year the Wildcats had walked into Taylor Field and ended the Rams' season in the semifinal.

The Rams came into 1979 on a note of optimism. Despite losing 11 players to graduation, they still had a solid core of rookies showing up for training camp. None would turn out to be more important than the second Hamilton brother to wear a Rams' uniform. This was Marshall Hamilton, and the best was ahead of him. In Marshall Hamilton the Rams would unveil another solid quarterback in a list of good quarterbacks that included Grant Becker, Richard Seitz, Lenny Knoll and Thom Parker. Hamilton was 21 years old when he came to the Rams. He had spent four years at Yale University where he had played hockey while earning a degree. Making the switch from hockey to football was no big deal. "I come from a football family," he said. "(brothers) Kelly and Marty are with the Rams, Pat plays at university in San Diego and Chris is at O'Neill High School." Before the season was over, Pat, a defensive back, would have left San Diego and joined the Rams. There was talk the Rams should change their name to the Brothers Four.

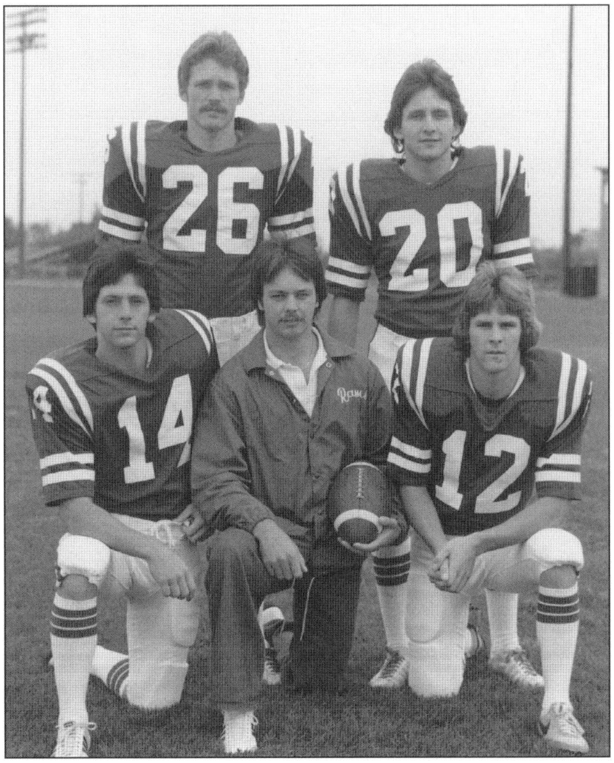

The Hamilton Brothers
Kelly (26), Pat (20) Chris (14), Marshall and Marty (12)

It was not that Zbytnuik was unhappy with what had happened in his first year as head coach. Quite the contrary. "It was a good year," he said. "but it was short lived." The Rams had their usual share of veterans returning.

Marshall's older brother, Kelly Hamilton, was back along with wide receiver Tim Probe, guards Paul Richardson and Wayne Mulligan, tackles Glen Farrow and Blair Thompson, centre Greg Wilchuck and quarterback Tim Garvin. Kerry Berryman, who could play both sides of the line, was also back.

Defensively, the important returnees were linebackers Cal Sikorski, who was named the league's rookie of the year in 1978, and the chatty Larry Mueller. Lineman Greg Nesbitt and halfbacks Bill Parker and Tim Wiens were also back. Others, like lineman Blair Buscis, linebacker Randy Smith and backs Les Krentz, Daryl Baiton and, yes, another Hamilton brother, Marty, provided some depth and experience.

Tim Wiens

Marshall Hamilton and rookie Tim Spelliscy joined Garvin and Parker in the quarterback derby, while ex-Campbell Tartan, Doug Currie, Gord's son, was looking for a running back spot. A new highly-rated high-school player, a linebacker, also showed – Tim McGeough from O'Neill. He'd win a starting position.

Zybtnuik also brought in a rookie assistant coach. You may have heard of him. His name was Frank McCrystal. He had been a linebacker with the Rams, and he turned his lack of size into an asset, buzzing all over the place, becoming one of the quickest and surest linebackers on the roster. He was also a Ram through and through.

By the time the season was ready to start, two things had become clear. The rookie, Marshall Hamilton, had virtually won the starting quarterback's job. And the Rams would

Cal Sikorski

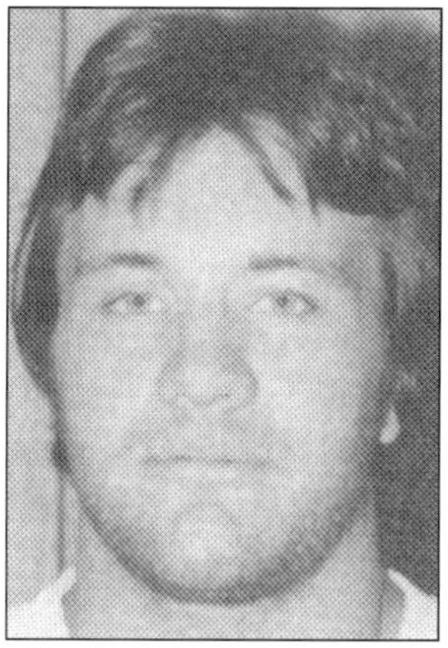

Larry Mueller

open the season against . . . wait for it . . . the Saskatoon Hilltops. Surprise! Surprise!

No, the surprise would come in the game. What a surprise.

It caught the Rams off guard. It caught the fans off guard. And Taylor Field was filled with the sounds of silence, just moments after it had been rocking with the music of a Rams' win.

Here's what happened, in one of the most bizarre finishes in the Rams' history. Late in the fourth quarter, really late, the Rams had possession of the football at the Hilltops' 18. It was third and four. The Rams' were leading 25-18. There were 26 seconds left in the game. What do you do? Run one more play, kill off as much time as you can, and give the ball to the Hilltops on downs deep in their own end? Try a field goal into a strong wind? Punt it through the end zone?

For the first time in his career as Rams' head coach, Jerry Zbytnuik was called on to make a decision that would decide the outcome of a game. He chose to punt the ball. Fieger took the snap from centre. To get it through the end zone for a single, he would have to punt it 44 yards. He came up six yards short. The wind, remember. The ball went to Brian Peberdy 20 yards deep in the Hilltops' end zone. The Rams might have remembered Peberdy from the second quarter when he returned a Fieger punt 103 yards for a touchdown.

Peberdy took the punt and started to run. He ran. He ran some more. And he ran some more after that. The crowd was going crazy. The Rams were chasing him. He kept running. Hilltops' coach Paul Schoenhals was running down the sideline with him – Peberdy jetted on by. He was still running. He ran for 130 yards and he didn't stop until he had reached the Rams' end zone. The convert tied the score at 25-25. As far as anybody in Taylor Field was concerned, the Rams had snatched a tie from the jaws of victory. It marked the fifth straight league game in which the Rams had not beaten the Hilltops, a streak stretching back two years.

That touchdown put a damper on the words of praise that were due the Rams, especially quarterback Marshall Hamilton. In his first start in junior ball, the kid had displayed signs of what was to come once he got comfortable in the role. He guided an offence that produced 22 first downs, 251 yards rushing and 120 yards passing. He completed eight of 16 passes and threw one touchdown. He also rushed for 69 yards. He looked as if he would be the whole package.

The Rams needed something to get their confidence back up. They got it from the schedule makers. The Medicine Hat Rattlers came to town and, as usual, the Rams gorged themselves on this football feast. It was 60-3 Regina. The Rams had 29 first downs and 610 yards in total offence. Everybody played well. Everybody played. The Rams' coaching staff could have gone up and down the bench, asking if there was anybody who hadn't had a big gain, sent them in, and not worried about a thing. This was a walk in the park. The next time these two played each other, back in Medicine Hat, the Rams won 68-10.

The Rams were turning into an explosive team. Ask Johnny Bright, the one-time Hall of Fame fullback for the Edmonton Eskimos, who in 1979 was coaching the Edmonton Huskies.

The Huskies came into Regina, and Bright was sure they could give the Rams a game. They ended up losing, 47-7.

"I have never, ever experienced anything like that before. I just couldn't believe it." Those were the words Bright used when the game ended. He wasn't talking about the game. He was talking about the first quarter. You can talk about teams coming out of the gate fast, getting the jump. But the Rams had a start that was so fast radar might not have been able to pick it up. The Rams opened the game by scoring 37 points in the first quarter alone. Fortunately, they cooled off after that, otherwise they might have out-scored most NBA teams.

The Rams nailed down first place when they closed the schedule with a win over the Hilltops in Saskatoon.

Wouldn't you know it? The Rams and Hilltops met in the sudden-death final for the Prairie Junior Football Conference championship. The game was played on a cold, snowy, windy night in Taylor Field in late October, so cold that only about 800 fans turned out to watch.

The Rams took it to the Hilltops right off the bat, shutting out Saskatoon 32-0 in a lopsided contest that saw Marshall Hamilton give one of the best play-calling displays of the season. "The biggest difference between our two teams is Marshall Hamilton," said Schoenhals. "Whenever they needed something, Marshall went and got it. He's smart, he's quick and he keeps coming up with big plays."

The win put the Rams into the Western semifinal, where they easily disposed of the Winnipeg Fort Garry Lions, 54-7. Two playoff games, and they'd given up only seven points.

That sent the Rams into the Western final. Waiting for them were the Vancouver Meralomas. The Rams were again on their game, cruising to a 45-21 victory and running up 504 yards in total offence. Fieger, Currie and Antonini all had solid games rushing the ball. Marshall Hamilton clicked on 12 of 19 passes for 215 yards. Seven different receivers caught passes from Hamilton and eight players took turns running the ball, including Larry Mueller, normally a linebacker.

The win sent the Rams into the Canadian championship against the Ottawa Sooners.

Before the national final was played, the Rams found themselves being showered with individual awards. Zbytnuik was named the coach of the year. Marshall Hamilton was named the most valuable player. Fieger was named the outstanding offensive back. Brent McConnell was named the outstanding offensive lineman. Kerry Berryman, who had made the switch from offence to defence, was named the outstanding defensive lineman. And Marshall Hamilton was named the rookie of the year.

With all that going for them, how could the Rams possibly be denied the Canadian championship?

Nothing's for sure. Whatever the formula was that the Rams had been mixing on their way to the national final in Hamilton, they didn't bring it along with them. In a game earmarked by some incredible mistakes, the Rams were never even a shadow of their former selves, They lost, 13-9, to the Ottawa Sooners. Fumbles hurt them. But what really did the Rams in was their punting game. It just wasn't there. Once, the snap from centre sailed over Fieger's

Marshall Hamilton

Greg Fieger

Brent McConnell

Kerry Berryman

head. Another time, the ball went low between his feet. A third time, Fieger simply dropped the snap.

To make matters worse, Marshall Hamilton was injured on the second play of the game. He suffered a painful hip pointer. "He couldn't come off his foot," said Zbytnuik. "He was throwing strictly with his arm. He couldn't run. And he could only throw short passes."

So close. Yet so far. It had been a stirring season. But in the end, the Rams were left with their faces pressed against the candy store window. That was the Regina Rams' story as the 1970s drew to a close.

Another Peak . . . Another Valley

1980-1981

Seen from the top of the hill in the north of Regina, on the edge of the Ring Road, are the helmeted figures of the youth of 1980, the year of the Rams, the start of a new decade in the life of this most storied of franchises. It is summer and the wind is sweeping over the crest of the hill I am standing on, and then down the slope and onto the practice field. There are well over 60, maybe even 70 of them, all dressed in their practice gear. The coaches are among them. Off to the south end of the field, there are a few members of the executive, a couple of former players, long-time trainer Jim Francis, and Les Rody the equipment guy. Jerry Zybtnuik, the head coach, is patrolling the practice, the intensity and excitement he brings to the team racing with the speed and noise and the blur of a jet engine at full throttle.

The Rams could hardly wait for the 1980 season to start. In their loss to the Ottawa Sooners in the Canadian championship the previous November, they had stopped short of the goal they felt in their hearts should have been easily achievable. They did not want to make the same mistake again. Borrowing the motto of Notre Dame College in Wilcox, Struggle and Emerge, they came to training camp and they came ready.

Only a trickle of players had graduated from the 1979 team, which meant the rebuilding would not be as extensive as it usually was. Quarterback Marshall Hamilton was the biggest loss. He had only played one season for the Rams, but his play was exciting and effective, smart and, at times, sensational. Also gone were Berryman, a two-way lineman, and back/punter Greg Fieger.

The Rams had lots of talent coming back. Two veteran all-star linemen – Clarence Sacawayacappo on offence and Gregg Nesbitt on defence – were returning. Running back Doug Currie, a natural, and Kelly Hamilton would give the Rams a strong running game.

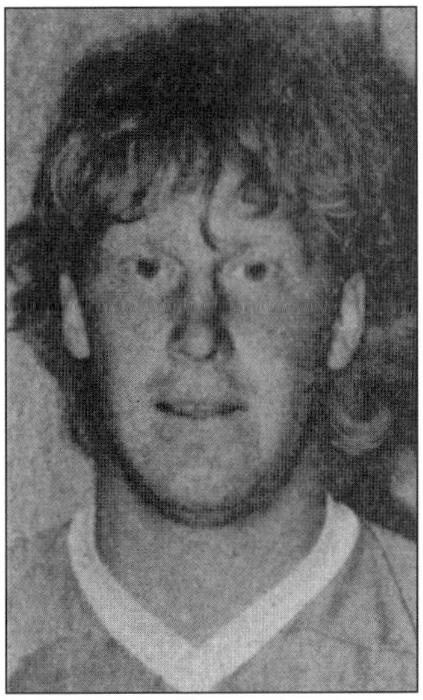

Doug Currie

The biggest question mark was at quarterback. Eventually, the Rams went with two rookies – Chris Hamilton and Keith Hiller. It was a move that would pay off.

It took the Rams a while to get going, but slow starts and picking up steam as the season progressed was nothing new to them. You can look it up. With Gerry Harris and Cam Clark coaching the offence, and Frank McCrystal coaching the defence again, there was stability where it was needed most. McCrystal was fast developing into an outstanding defensive coach. He was aggressive and he was innovative. And what set him apart even more was that he had a feel for what the players could do. He knew what it took to win. He had played for Gord Currie from 1972 through 1976. The Rams had won 35 games, lost only five, and tied once during that period. They had also won three Canadian championships.

But now it was 1980 and Frank was coaching. The Rams had a linebacker named Tim McGeough who, in a nutshell, was hell on wheels when he hit the field – not that big, but quick and tough. McCrystal figured the best way to get the most out of McGeough was to just play him. His main responsibility was to find the ball, and then take care of whoever had the misfortune of carrying it. Tim also used his quickness to block kicks, something he did with regularity. There were side effects, mind you, to his aggressive all-out play. One was, you could count on McGeough to take either a roughing or a talking penalty once a game. It was something easily overlooked given the contributions he made to the Rams.

Tim McGeough and Frank McCrystal

Zbytnuik remembered McGeough for years after he had left the Rams. He called him the "most intense player" he had ever coached.

The Rams opened the season with a 35-33 loss to the Hilltops in Saskatoon. Three games into the season, the Rams had a mediocre record of 1-1-1, but they would suffer only one loss the rest of the way, finishing the schedule with a 7-2-1 record and finishing in first place in the Prairie Junior Football Conference. The Rams' train was about to leave the station, and a Canadian championship was waiting for them at the other end.

First, the Rams had to get out of the PJFC, and that meant getting by the Edmonton Huskies. The final, sudden-death, was scheduled for Taylor Field in late October. It was a typical Saskatchewan autumn day. A grey canopy hung over the field, but it yielded no snow; there was a wind, and it was chilly.

The Rams wasted no time in gunning for the championship. This is what they were all about. They scored their first touchdown less than two minutes into the game, built an 11-0 first-quarter lead, led 11-3 at the half, 25-10 after three quarters, on their way to a decisive 33-10 victory.

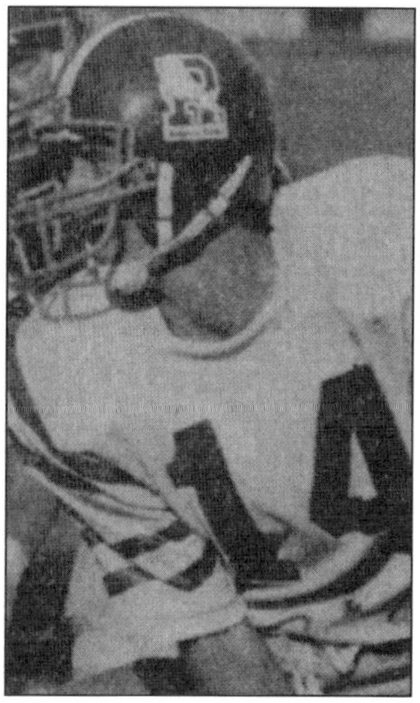

Chris Hamilton

Chris Hamilton played the whole game at quarterback, the second year in a row the Rams had put their faith in one of Hamilton brothers at quarterback. He threw the ball 19 times, completing 10 throws for 88 yards. But it was the Rams' ground game that spearheaded the offensive attack. The Rams rushed for 365 yards, piled up 27 first downs, and had two players rush for over 100 yards – Doug Currie with 126 and Chuck Toth with 102. Chris Hamilton also gave the Huskies fits with his own running, taking off 12 times for 70 yards.

But the key to the victory was the Rams' defence. They set the table for the offence to do its thing. "The first thing we had to do was take away Edmonton's running game," Zbytnuik said. "If they established the run, they would be free to pass. They tried to run and we stopped them." McCrystal's defence did the job, smothering the Huskies, and holding them to 157 yards in net offence. They intercepted four passes and recovered four fumbles. The defence also had five quarterback sacks.

The Western final was again slated for Vancouver. Once again it was the Meralomas the Rams were facing to see who got to play in the Canadian championship in Regina's Taylor Field. The Rams knew one thing for sure. The weather would be lousy when they got to Vancouver. And it was.

The rain fell, the artificial turf at Empire Stadium turned slick, and the Rams knew that the only thing that was going to keep them from going under was to stick with their game plan, which was, essentially, to run the football. The Rams had nothing but trouble with the greasy field and the rain that fell heavily throughout the first half. The Rams fumbled the ball 10 times. They only lost one fumble, but it hurt their momentum. After three quarters of play the Rams were ahead by only nine points, 14-5.

It was in the fourth quarter that the Rams came alive. They had worn the Meralomas down with their relentless rushing game, and it showed in the final quarter. First, Len Antonini scored on an 18-yard pass from Chris Hamilton, then Sikorski kicked a couple of singles. A final touchdown by quarterback Keith Hiller on a six-yard run sealed a 28-5 Regina victory.

Doug Currie, who was lighting it up in the playoffs, had a tremendous game, given the kind of night it was. He carried the ball 17 times for an amazing 167 yards. "Doug is our workhorse," said Zbytnuik. "All we have to do is give him the football. He gets the job done. Tremendous athlete. And the more work he gets, the better he is."

One more step, that's all the Rams had to take to achieve their season's goal. But it would be the biggest, most difficult step of all. And when you get into a sudden-death game for the national championship, there are no guarantees.

That the game would be played in Taylor Field assured the national final of a big crowd, a crowd that would be predominantly Rams' fans. The Rams would be playing the Hamilton Hurricanes, familiar foes in the national championship.

The Rams had kicked into full gear at just the right time of the year. The enthusiasm that Zbytnuik had brought rubbed off on his players. There is no better way to describe him than to let one of his players do it.

Larry Mueller played linebacker for Zbytnuik with the Rams. "He was a great coach," said Mueller. "He was aggressive. He was just what we needed. He and Frank (McCrystal) had the same attitude towards football. They wanted to be aggressive. I think that's why he left Frank alone with the defence, he knew what Frank would do. We used to call Jerry Tick-Tick-Boom! He'd go absolutely crazy during games. We had to put him upstairs (in the press box) once because he got so wound up. Then, you'd hear all this shouting and yelling in the stands and you'd look up, and here he'd be, coming down to the bench."

Zbytnuik's push, and his incredible will to get the best he could out of everybody, gave the Rams the kind of heart that carried them through rough times in 1980. He made them believe that no matter what happened, as long as they stayed the course, the end results would be favourable.

By the time they reached the national final, the pieces had all come together. Chris Hamilton had steadily improved at quarterback. The offensive line, anchored by Clarence Sacawayacappo and Wayne Mulligan, blew holes in the Hurricanes' defence and allowed the Rams' running game to take off. Doug Currie, Rodger Hutchinson, Chuck Toth, Rod Sisco, Dave Arsenault and Kelly Hamilton all hammered the opposition from their running back positions.

The defence came together around nose guard Greg Nesbitt and the ends who flanked him, Julien Hulet and Lyle Mosiondz. Linebackers Cal Sikorski, Larry Mueller, Tim McGeough and Randy Smith formed the best linebacking crew in Canadian junior football. Bill Parker was the heart of the defensive backfield, intercepting eight passes over the season. In that same backfield, guys like Tim Wiens, Les Krentz, Mel Ell and Frank Macera came through big when they were called on. The kicking game was in solid hands with Dave Badowich and Sikorski. There were no weak links in this chain.

Dave Badowich

You had only to be at that last game of 1980, on Saturday, November 8th, to see it for yourself. A crowd of 10,000 fans saw it. The Rams did it all that afternoon against a tough but out-matched Hurricane team.

With quarterback Chris Hamilton again at his best, the Rams piled up an efficient net offence of 286 yards, 265 of it along the ground. Currie had 95 yards and Toth 89 yards. Toth made the play of the game when he found his way into the end zone on a nice run from seven yards out in the third quarter. The touchdown, which capped a 60-yard march, put the Rams ahead 23-12, and that was too much of a lead for Hamilton to overcome. Included in that 60-yard drive was a daring fake punt on third and 12 at the

Hamilton 34 which saw Badowich take off and gain 14 yards for the first down, with change to spare. The Rams went on to win 26-15.

It wasn't easy for the Rams. They fell behind twice in the first half before getting a 16-12 lead on the board, heading into the dressing room at halftime.

The Rams' defence swarmed the Hurricanes. They recorded seven quarterback sacks and held the offence to 176 yards. Nesbitt was named the defensive player of the game and Sacawayacappo was named the offensive player of the game.

The Sweet Taste of Victory

It was the seventh time the Rams had won the Canadian junior championship since 1966. For Jerry Zbytnuik, it was especially something to remember. It was his first championship as a head coach. He did it in his third year. "I have achieved a personal goal," he said. But, mostly, he talked about the effort it took from his players to do what they did. He had never been a part of anything like it.

When he took the job, Jerry had thought he would give it two or three years. He actually had decided that if the Rams won the Canadian championship in 1979, he would retire. But, now, there was no question he would be back in 1981. No question at all. He had been bitten by the Rams' bug. And his wife, Donna, supported him. "Football is an important part of his life, and so it's important to me too," she said.

And the Rams were about to put forward a team that just couldn't be stopped. It doesn't matter what level you play any team sport, there will always be competition and hidden pitfalls you can't forecast waiting to leap out and bite you. The Rams were no exception. Teams they thought should have won Canadian championships didn't, not because they weren't good enough, but because they weren't good enough at the time when they had to be. It's what drives coaches grey. Former Saskatchewan Roughrider great Ron Lancaster said the hardest thing for any athlete to learn is how to win.

The 1981 team was an exception. From the very beginning, this team was ear-marked for immortality. It had everything Zbytnuik could ask for in a team. It had exceptional experience, with some of the greatest juniors ever returning from the 1980 Canadian championship team. Players such as quarterback Chris Hamilton, Len Antonini, Dave Badowich, Wayne Mulligan, Julian Hulet, Hal Wilkie, Tim Wiens, Doug Currie, Kelly Hamilton, Calvin Sikorski, Larry Mueller, Tim McGeough, Bill Parker, Rod Sisco. It was a deep, deep well of proven talent the Rams could draw on as they went about the pressure-packed business of defending their Canadian championship.

The Rams wasted little time in establishing that, until somebody walked up and took it from them, they were the champions and it was going to stay that way. This team was confident, but it wasn't over-confident

"We had a lot of guys who were really good players," Mueller remembered. "We played well as a team. We had everything, experience, all the stuff you had to have. And we didn't think we could be beaten."

They couldn't. The Rams went through the 10-game schedule undefeated. Nobody could touch them. Hamilton ran the offence as smoothly as any Rams' quarterback had. And the defence was everything you figured it would be, given the talent and experience there was.

By the time the Rams hit the playoffs, it was as if they were playing in a league of their own. And, in some ways, they were.

They opened the playoffs by hammering the Saskatoon Hilltops 29-0 in the semifinal. The Hilltops had worried the Rams, come that playoff game. These two teams never had any problem getting ready for each other. But on this day, it was no contest. The Rams next took on the Edmonton Huskies in the Prairie Junior Football Conference final. The Huskies were a more experienced team than they had

Len Antonini

been the year before when the Rams had beaten them. But, then, so were the Rams. The Rams sent the Huskies home with their tails between their legs, hammering out a 33-10 victory.

The Rams were getting almost as accustomed to having to play the Vancouver Meralomas at some point in the playoffs as they were to having to play the Hilltops. And, sure enough, come the Western semifinal, there were the Meralomas, ready to take another shot at the Rams. There was no comparison. The Rams hit the field running, and by the time they had finished they'd mopped up the turf with the Meralomas in a 59-22 victory.

The only thing standing between the Rams and a berth in the Canadian final was the Winnipeg Hawkeyes, and the Rams had their first shaky game of the playoffs, shaky for them. They still won, 30-20, and it was on to the Canadian championship. Once again, the Hamilton Hurricanes came out of the east. The dream season for the Rams had a happy ending. They scattered the Hurricanes 46-24 to win their second straight Canadian championship in an undefeated season.

Zbytnuik couldn't have asked for a more wonderful year. "Everything went well for us as a team. They played well as a team and we were able to play a lot of players," he said. "The team had enough character and ability to overcome every obstacle. I was so proud of them."

Larry Mueller, Chris Hamilton and Bill Parker.

A DOLLAR SHORT

1982

They won't let you forget who you are. From the very moment a player puts on that Regina Rams' uniform, he is a somebody. A somebody who is expected to win. That is what has driven the Regina Rams since 1965, when Gord Currie took over an average football organization and transformed it, almost magically, into a dynasty. Players knew that when they came to the Rams. That was likely what drew them there. You had to be good and you had to be competitive; you had to be willing to sacrifice your individual desires for the betterment of the team. That was the gospel, according to the Rams. The Ten Commandments were – WIN x 10.

When the 1982 Regina Rams went into training camp, they had lost some key players, but they had a number of guys who were ready to step in. Gone were linebackers Cal Sikorski and Larry Mueller, defensive tackle Bernie Knoll, end Julien Hulet, defensive backs Bill Parker and Tim Spelliscy. Halfback Kelly Hamilton and fullback Doug Currie were the biggest names to graduate from offence. Also gone was kicker Dave Badowich.

The most notable returnee on offence was quarterback Chris Hamilton. On defence it was fiery linebacker Tim McGeough.

In all, the Rams lost more than a dozen players to graduation. "It's not like we have to bring 18 guys in off the street," said Zbytnuik. "We have players who have paid their dues. The reason we kept them around is so they would be ready when their time came. Well, their time has come."

One of the most impressive of the rookies was running back Terry Cochrane. Cochrane had played high-school football in Regina with the Campbell Collegiate Tartans and had then gone to the University of British Columbia Thunderbirds. A good-sized kid, he was a game-breaker with plenty of speed and the kind of moves a belly dancer would kill for. Cochrane became a starter in his first year. The Rams opened the season with Cochrane in Kelly Hamilton's vacant slotback position.

Ron Lancaster Jr.

What the Rams had to find right away was a backup quarterback for Hamilton. Rob Bresciani and Ron Lancaster Jr. came to camp, having played the position in high school. Lancaster, the oldest son of the Roughriders' Little General, won the job as backup. The Rams also added a new assistant coach. Bernie Schmidt, who had played for them, returned as an assistant. It marked the beginning of a long coaching relationship with the Rams, one that is still going on.

The Rams opened the season at home, not against the Hilltops as was a tradition of sorts, but against the Edmonton Huskies. Not all that sure what kind of team they would have when they played a game, the coaches developed some mild concerns early in the first quarter. The Rams were sluggish. They were probably lucky they only trailed 1-0 after the first quarter. With four minutes to go in the first half, the Rams were behind 11-7. But in that four-minute span, the Rams caught fire and put together two rumbling touchdown marches that gave them a 20-11 lead at the half. They simply clicked into higher and higher gears after that, opening the season with a 44-18 victory before just 400 fans.

The Rams' offence was hitting on all gears, once it got going. They had 34 first downs and 598 yards in total offence. The Rams' ground game rang up 412 yards. Cochrane led the way, slashing for 220 yards on just 15 carries. Veterans Rod Sisco and Terry Eisler had 67 yards and 55 respectively. Chris Hamilton continued to keep defences off balance with his running, taking off 13 times for 45 yards. Hamilton was also on target with his passing, completing nine throws for 183 yards. It was the kind of opening performance that indicated the Rams had found a team that promised great things ahead.

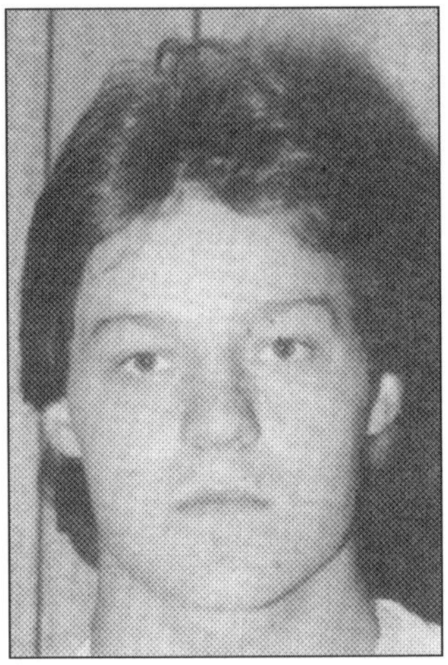

Terry Eisler

The Rams just kept winning. But not everything was going their way. They lost Hamilton at quarterback with bruised ribs. That meant Ron Lancaster Jr. suddenly found himself in a starting role, ready or not. As they headed to their fifth game of the schedule with the Calgary Cougars in Taylor Field, the Rams were on an incredible run. They hadn't lost a game – league or playoff – since September of 1980, a string that was at 25 straight when they took on the Colts. It went to 26, just like that. The Rams won, 35-0.

And the man of the hour was Terry Cochrane. They knew he was good when he came to them. But few knew he was this good. He set a Prairie Junior Football Conference single-game rushing record by peeling off 298 yards in 21 carries. He averaged more than 14 yards per carry. He scored three touchdowns. There were 5,000 fans in Taylor Field that day who witnessed it.

Terry Cochrane

Lancaster, who had been the quarterback at Campbell Collegiate when Cochrane was there, also had a remarkable debut as a starter. "The run was working so well, we just stuck with it," he said. "We thought that if we could get the running game going, we could start throwing the ball. But we never had to throw it."

Zbytnuik had said when he became head coach of the Rams that he wanted to return the Rams to the days when the running game was the dominant part of their offence. He was staying true to his word. The Rams had a running game. And, at times, it was all they needed. Or so it appeared.

The Rams headed into Saskatoon, flaunting their winning streak in front of the Hilltops, who were sitting with a 3-2 record. With a crowd of 3,500 in Gordie Howe Bowl, on a Saturday night in September, the Hilltops did something no other junior team in Canada had been able to do since 1980. They beat the Regina Rams. They beat them, 31-21. They beat them with a swarming defence and a controlling offence.

The Hilltops' offence, with quarterback Tony Gagnon playing flawlessly, and the explosive Dan Servetnyk doing just that, exploding for big gains, tore through the Rams like ripping up a flimsy piece of paper.

Cochrane was the lone Ram who did any damage. He scored two touchdowns. He rushed for 155 tough yards on 23 carries. Lancaster, unable to find any holes in the Hilltops' defence on this night, completed only seven of 20 passes for 72 yards – most of the yardage coming on completions of 44 and 16 yards to Marlowe Pelletier late in the game.

"Their defence contained our outside run and they wouldn't let us run on the inside, either. That doesn't leave much, does it?" Zbytnuik said.

Jerry wasn't sure how the loss would affect the Rams. The Rams had a good week of practice as they prepared for the next game, in Edmonton against the Huskies. Asked what he expected of his team in the wake of their first loss since 1980, Zbytnuik replied, "I expect them to be mean."

Oh, they were all of that. They came out snarling, then started biting, and before the first quarter was over the Rams were ahead 20-0 as Lancaster got his running game going. The Rams buried the Huskies 52-8. The running game produced 379 yards with Cochrane rushing for 128 yards.

Next up for the Rams was a game that had all the makings of being The Grudge Match of the year. It would be in Taylor Field against the Hilltops. Once this game was played, people wondered if the Hilltops had the Rams' number. The Toppers came into Regina and went home with a 15-7 victory, giving the Rams their second loss of the season.

The Rams ended the season with an 8-2 record, but the two losses to Saskatoon cost them first place. They went into the playoffs in second place. But, they would have Chris Hamilton back at quarterback.

The Rams, obviously looking ahead to a showdown in the final with the Hilltops, survived the semifinal with a lackluster 18-13 win over the Edmonton Huskies in the semifinal.

Then, came the showdown of the season, in Gordie Howe Bowl in Saskatoon.

With 3,500 fans in Gordie Howe Bowl on a chilly October afternoon, the Hilltops came firing out of their dressing room and threw down the gauntlet. The dangerous Servetnyk, one of the greatest to ever play the junior game in Canada, took the opening kickoff and returned it 110 yards for a touchdown. The Hilltops came alive. The Rams were stunned. Gradually, the Rams began to get their offence moving. Several times, they were within striking distance of the Saskatoon end zone. But they couldn't finish it off. At the halftime break the Rams found themselves staring down the loaded barrel of a 16-1 Saskatoon Hilltops' lead.

There was plenty of soul searching going on in that Regina dressing room at halftime. They knew they were getting closer and closer to a humiliating end to a season that had shown such promise.

The third quarter saw a different Rams' team. Starting at their own three, the Rams marched the length of the field. With each first down they gained confidence, and they capped the drive when Terry Eisler plowed into the end zone from one yard out.

Momentum was beginning to shift. On the next Hilltops' series, Rams' backup defensive back Gord Marceca came into the game when starter Mark Becker was injured. The Hilltops' Gagnon went after Marceca right away, to test him. Whoops! Big mistake. Marceca stepped in front of the receiver, intercepted the pass, and returned it 25 yards to the Hilltops 17. From there, Chris Hamilton hit Pelletier for the touchdown. The Rams had scored two touchdowns in just 36 seconds of the third quarter.

Marlowe Pelletier

The game was turned right there. But the Hilltops were not dead yet. With just minutes left in the game, and the Rams now leading 21-17, the Hilltops made a last bid to put together a drive into the Rams' end zone. But the Rams' defence dug in and made one big play after another. Then there were no more big plays to be made because the clock had run out and the Rams had once again won the Prairie Junior Football Conference championship.

Gord Marceca did not play a lot, but he came up with the interception that turned the game around and found himself in a philosophical moment in the dressing room. "Now, I know what being a Ram is all about," he said. "Now, us rookies know what it means to wear this uniform. It means you never quit."

Saskatoon head coach Blaine Knoll gave full credit to the Rams for the win. "You have to give them full marks. You can always look back and pick out things that might have changed the outcome, but you certainly can't deny that the Rams played well. They're a good football team. They came back, and that's what you expect of them. They never doubt that they can rally. They never think they can lose. You know that you are playing against that mental state. It's a great aspect for a team to have. It's going to be tough to beat them forever as long as they have that."

That Rams' aura is something that is intangible. It is not something a coach can teach. It comes only with time. It comes only with success. It comes only with an organization that breeds consistency and always deals from strength.

It is always there. But it doesn't mean that the Rams will always win, regardless.

The 1982 season would not end on a happy note for the Rams. They left Saskatoon with their biggest win of the year, and a week later left Vancouver with their biggest loss of the season.

They went up against the Renfrew Trojans from Vancouver, surprise champions of the Big Four Conference in British Columbia.

In Empire Stadium, in the rain, the Rams may well have had the aura that Knoll had mentioned, but they didn't do the rest, which was to play well enough to win. Renfrew won, 17-14. The Rams' defence played a strong game in the western final. But the offence just didn't have it. And more confusing was that the Rams got away from their running game. Cochrane only carried the ball eight times, a stunning surprise given that he had set two Prairie Junior Football Conference rushing records in 1982. The difference was, the Rams just could not finish off what they had started. Eight times they moved inside Renfrew's 45 yard line, and eight times the Rams turned over the ball. Hamilton himself threw four interceptions.

It wasn't a pretty ending. And for the first time in four years, the Rams would not be in the national final.

YET ANOTHER VALLEY

1983

Jerry Zbytnuik is standing on the practice field at Mount Pleasant. It is the summer of 1983. The Regina Rams have just opened training camp. There is a soft, warm wind lightly brushing his face. *Leader-Post* photographer Pat Pettit is taking his picture, a picture of a man of medium height wearing a baseball cap, his face showing the smile that quickly turns into a large grin, making everybody feel he is their friend.

At first glance, he looks as if he is a school teacher, which he was, or a plumber, which he wasn't. He looks as if he would never get mad at anybody, that he is one of those people who can take what life sends his way and deal with it so capably. He is a decent guy, a very decent guy. He has a wonderful family and a wife, Donna, who supports him so much she should get a medal. But inside Jerry Zbytnuik there is a competitive fire that rages, and the minute he hits a football field it explodes. He is one of the most competitive coaches you will ever find. And he is driven to succeed. It is why he is the head coach of the Regina Rams. It is why he has had success as the head coach of the Regina Rams, kept the tradition going, built upon it.

In 1982, the Regina Rams did not get to the Canadian junior championship. They failed, losing to the Renfrew Trojans. In 1983, they did not want this to happen again. So, as Jerry Zbytnuik stood on the practice field that night, watching training camp, he was quietly confident his team would not fail this time. He had so many players returning from 1982, who still had a bad taste in their mouths from the previous season, that he felt motivating this team would be no problem. It would be a matter of picking the right players to take a run at what the Rams are always expected to take a run at, the national championship.

It's not that the Rams hadn't lost some key people from the 1982 team. Tim McGeough's junior career ran out of years, and his was a big hole to fill, not just for the talent and hustle he brought to the position but also for the leadership he provided. Safety Tim Wiens was a big loss off the defence. Backup quarterback Ron Lancaster decided not to return, even though he was eligible.

The Rams, though, had a wealth of talent coming back. The offensive backfield of Chris Hamilton, Terry Cochrane, Rod Sisco and Terry Eisler was back. And the offensive line figured to be bigger, stronger and even more experienced with two new faces. Todd Lewis had spent four seasons with the University of Saskatchewan Huskies and had a tryout with the Roughriders before deciding to join the Rams. Randy Duncan had spent the previous season with the Simon Fraser University Clansmen. These guys came to camp with such rave reviews that the Rams didn't know if they would play them on offence or defence.

The Rams opened the season still nursing their wounds from the 1982 loss to the Renfrew Trojans. They hammered the Edmonton Huskies 52-7, with Terry Cochrane having a huge game and Hamilton playing as if he was on some sort of a mission. "We played the first quarter of this game as if it was the fifth quarter of the game against Renfrew," said Cochrane. The Rams had 535 yards in total offence, 323 of it on the ground. Cochrane rushed for 93 yards in just six carries,

Terry Cochrane

caught three passes for another 53 yards, and returned two kickoffs for 124 yards, one of them a 101-yard touchdown run. Marlowe Pelletier also returned a kickoff 91 yards for a touchdown.

Most impressive was how sharp the Rams were offensively, how crisply their defence played, and how perfect their special teams were. For a team one game into the season, they seemed light-years ahead of themselves. "You work at things, you work at things, you work at things, and pretty soon it becomes habit. If you execute right and if you have the right people it's bound to pay off," said Chris Hamilton.

A week later, the Rams continued to roll, traveling to Calgary and beating the Colts 26-21. The Rams needed nine unanswered points in the fourth quarter to grab the win. Cochrane again had a big game, spinning for 176 yards rushing. Gord Marceca had his best game as a defensive back, intercepting two Rob McNab passes.

But, if anybody was thinking that the Rams were going to cakewalk it back to the national final, then the Saskatoon Hilltops had something to say about that. The Hilltops came into Regina with a 1-1 record to face the Rams, who were unbeaten in their first two games.

Here's the statistical story of this wipeout. The Rams' offence totaled 523 yards to Saskatoon's 435. The Rams had 28 first downs to the Hilltops' 21. The Rams rushed for 320 yards, Saskatoon had 196. The Rams had 77 plays, the Hilltops 53.

Final Score: Regina 25 Saskatoon 50.

Say what?

Say there are times when statistics are for losers.

The Rams had no polish, and they made one huge mistake after another. Couple that with the hot hand Saskatoon quarterback Tony Gagnon was dealing from. The Rams couldn't do anything right because they were doing virtually everything wrong. In a scant two minutes of the second quarter, the Hilltops scored 15 points to take a 28-11 lead, and that was all she wrote. "What can you say?" said a visibly taken aback Zbytnuik. "Those two minutes before the half killed us."

The loss took away from an outstanding rushing performance by Cochrane, who hit for 218 yards on 24 carries and scored a pair of touchdowns. Cochrane also fumbled a kickoff in his own end zone, which Saskatoon recovered for a touchdown.

The Rams did make up for the loss in some ways. They hammered the Calgary Cougars 56-13 the following weekend, and Cochrane had another one of those eye-popping individual performances that turned the record book upside down. He rushed for 340 yards on 19 carries, breaking by 42 yards the single-game record he had set a year earlier. The Rams also broke the league's single game rushing record of 500 yards, which they had set in 1977, by running for 575 yards. They also broke their own team single game total offence record of 735 yards with a total of 770 yards against Calgary.

You would think that after a win like that, where records fell like pins in a bowling alley, the rest of the PJFC would be trembling in its boots. Not so. While the Rams feasted on the weaker links in the league in 1983, the buffet wasn't so plentiful when they came up against the Hilltops or the Wildcats.

The Wildcats were slowly establishing themselves as the cream of the crop in the PJFC, and when they came into Regina to play the Rams midway through September, they came knowing this was a game they had to win if they were to be taken for real. The Rams took a 17-15 lead at halftime, but that was it. The Wildcats took over in the second half. They huffed and they puffed and they blew the Rams over. The final score was 42-17 for the Wildcats, and now there were serious questions being raised about the Rams.

Edmonton coach Dalton Smarsh, for one, figured he had heard enough about the Rams and their tradition and their supposed aura. At halftime, he let his players have it. "I told them it's time to start playing football. All this stuff about the Rams, it's mental. I told them if you just play football, they're a football team too."

Even Zbytnuik knew what the gauntlet meant when Smarsh threw it down. The easy wins against the Calgary Colts and Cougars and Huskies were mentioned. "Those wins don't mean anything if you can't play with the big boys," he said.

The Wildcats totally shut down the Rams' vaunted running game. They held Cochrane to a mere 26 yards. They pressured Hamilton with a fierce blitz all afternoon. "They just gave us a lesson in football," said Zbytnuik. "I was disappointed in our offence. It's as if they expect Terry to do it all. Well, if he's having an off day, we've got other good backs and they have to step up and do the job. They didn't."

This was serious stuff that was happening to the Regina Rams. They were starting to lose the automatic respect, even fear, of the other teams in the league. It wasn't so automatic any longer, and it was being openly talked about. The Regina Rams weren't what they had once been.

Perhaps the message did get through. The Rams started winning again, beating the Huskies, but until they defeated the Hilltops or Wildcats, there would still be doubts about them. That test would come on September 25th in Saskatoon.

The Rams had lost the first meeting between the two teams 50-25 in Regina, so there was no problem in getting them motivated for this game. The Rams, smarting from that and stinging from the loss to the Wildcats a few weeks earlier, were desperate to re-establish themselves as the kingpins of junior football.

In a game that could only be described as electrifying, the Rams needed a 75-yard touchdown strike from Chris Hamilton to the speedy Marlowe Pelletier in the fourth quarter to take a 28-24 victory over the Hilltops. The play was set up when Hamilton made a superb fake to running back Terry Eisler that froze the Hilltops' defence and allowed Pelletier to turn it on and and break into the clear.

There was no particular key to the game, other than that the Rams were able to cut down on their mistakes and make the big plays when they needed them. The Hilltops did a good job of containing Cochrane, especially linebacker Larry Wruck, who shadowed Cochrane all afternoon. But Hamilton picked up the slack by running the ball himself. Nine times he took off, gaining 59 yards in all, but, more importantly, giving the Hilltops defence one more thing to worry about.

The Rams closed out the season with a 6-2 record that ensured them of a second-place finish in the PFJC.

For the Rams, the playoffs would represent the biggest tests they had faced in more than a few years. First up would be the sudden-death semifinal against the Hilltops. If the Rams could get by that one, the Wildcats would be waiting for them in the final.

Larry Wruck was one of the greatest linebackers to play in Canadian junior football. He was the heart of the Hilltops' defence. The Hilltops had this knack of being able to produce linebackers. Players such as Wayne Shaw, Don Seaman, Jim Seaman, all had outstanding junior careers, and both Shaw and Don Seaman enjoyed careers in the CFL with the Roughriders. Wruck had an illustrious career with the Edmonton Eskimos.

Wruck had been given much of the credit for the Hilltops' ability to control Terry Cochrane. But the week of the semifinal, the Rams had no qualms in saying that Larry Wruck did not scare them, that they would continue to run their offence and take him on, and the Hilltops' defence.

Barry Wilkie

The Rams won the semifinal, 30-22, in Taylor Field on a cool, crisp sunladen afternoon in which the tone was established on the opening kickoff. The Rams' Barry Wilkie roared down the field and laid a block on Wruck that was so punishing anybody who watched it could feel the jolt.

Zbytnuik saw it happen. "If there was a single point where someone said 'Based on one play, are you going to win or lose?', it would have been after that play that I would have said we're going to win. Barry has done that all year. He's been our man on special teams who goes down and just raises havoc. He went down and went after their best player – Larry Wruck – and he laid a hit on him. That was a pure unselfish team play."

Wruck was shaken, but he hadn't become the linebacker he was by not being able to come back from it. The Hilltops did a reasonable job in containing Cochrane when he rushed with the ball, holding him to 64 yards in 16 carries. But Cochrane hurt them in other ways. He returned seven punts for 151 yards, including one for 87 yards.

Hal Wilkie

The Rams' defence was outstanding, and provided the moment that decided the game. Hilltops' quarterback Tony Gagnon, often a thorn in the Rams' side, threw a dangerous pass early in the fourth quarter. Rams' defensive back Hal Wilkie, Barry's brother, intercepted it and ran it back 50 yards for the deciding touchdown.

That victory was nice. But they had yet to beat the Wildcats, and now they would get their chance, for all the marbles.

Zbytnuik felt his team was much improved from earlier in the year, that team maturity had arrived. "Our reputation may not matter as much any more to the Wildcats because they've already beaten us once. So, it's been neutralized. As far as we go, we've got so many young people that, really, they're here to build the name. We mention that the Ram tradition is a great thing but you can't ride on its coattails. What you have to do is become a part of it by working hard. I think we got caught up in that earlier in the year where, just because we were the Regina Rams, we may have thought we could step onto the field and everybody was going to lay down. They don't. What happened, because we're the Regina Rams, everybody plays that much harder. They want to beat you that much more."

In as hard hitting a game as anybody could remember between these two teams, the Rams just couldn't cash in on the chances they had, and their defence had trouble holding the Wildcats' offence when it needed to. The Wildcats ended the Rams' season with a 35-28 victory in Clarke Stadium. Edmonton's offence ran up 594 yards, while the Rams were held to 335 yards. Hamilton didn't have a sharp game throwing the ball, completing only nine of 23 passes, and he never really was able to get the ground game going. Cochrane was held to 85 yards and the Ram's running game was held to 208 yards, which by their standards wasn't good enough.

For the second season in a row, the Rams had fallen short of their goal. Some of the heartache of the loss might have been tempered by the announcement that Cochrane had been named the most valuable player in the league, the outstanding offensive player of the year and was a unanimous choice to the all-star team. And that defensive back Hal Wilkie was named the outstanding defensive player and an all-star, that guard Brent Taylor was the outstanding offensive lineman and an all-star. That offensive tackle Reiny Dundas was an all-star.

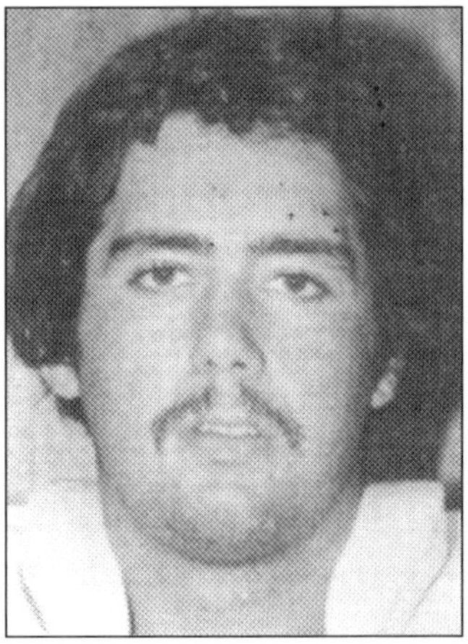

Reiny Dundas

But a loss is a loss is a loss. And when you are the Regina Rams, failing to even get out of your league makes the pain even more intense.

The winds of change would soon be blowing through the Rams' clubhouse.

THE McCRYSTAL ERA BEGINS

1984

The Rams had ended their 1983 season in October. For the next two months, Jerry Zbytnuik went on a soul-searching mission that at times tore at his insides, and at times was as clear as a mountain lake. When he took the Rams' job as head coach in 1978, he intended that it would last only a few years. But the deeper he got into it, and the more he enjoyed it, and the more he got out of it, the longer it had lasted.

But in this off-season, he was thinking that maybe the time had come to step aside and get back to a normal life. Once Christmas had passed, his decision was made. He was resigning as head coach. "I had been thinking for quite awhile whether I wanted to do it for another season. Once you start searching, when that type of commitment is required, you realize it might be hard to do a proper job. And my time with the Rams has been a good experience. I felt I was leaving on a personal high and didn't want to spoil that by possibly staying longer. I wanted to be sure of what I was doing before I made the final decision, that's why it took as long as it did. I wanted to be sure it was the right decision and that I could live with it."

Zbytnuik had never done anything in his life that he had enjoyed as much as coaching the Rams. And his record, what he had contributed, showed that he was the right choice when he was hired in 1978. He had been an assistant coach the year before under Mel Fiissel, who had replaced Gord Currie. During his time as coach, the Rams had won four conference titles, three western titles and two Canadian championships, the most recent in 1981 when the Rams were undefeated in 15 games. His regular-season won-lost record was 43-9-2. His playoff won-lost record was 16-4.

Ram's president Bill Nelson said that Zbytnuik's successor would come from within the organization. It meant that one of the four assistant coaches would be the next Ram's head coach – Frank McCrystal, Bernie Schmidt, Cam Clark or Gerry Harris. Harris took himself out of the running when he announced that he, too, was leaving the team.

Frank McCrystal

The obvious choice was McCrystal. The 30-year-old was a Ram through and through. He had been with the Rams for 10 years, first as a player, then as an assistant coach. He had spent five years as an outside linebacker and he had been an assistant to Zbytnuik for five years.

Nobody knew it at the time, but for McCrystal, a teacher at McGuigan, this would turn into a lifelong job that would generate one success after another. In fact, the Rams would become so successful that, eventually, they would outgrow junior football and move on to university football.

It did not take McCrystal long to put together his coaching staff. Clark decided not to return. So, McCrystal kept Bernie Schmidt and added Rick Seaman, Jerry Orban and Doug Zimmerman. Orban had played with the Rams from 1968-71 and had been an assistant coach to Currie and Mel Fiissel from 1973-77. Zimmerman had also played with the Rams. Seaman came from the Campbell Tartans of the Regina Intercollegiate Football League. He would later bring on board former Ram's linebacker Tim McGeough.

Bernie Schmidt

Rick Seaman

Jerry Orban

Doug Zimmerman

McCrystal quickly put his stamp on the Rams. "I don't really see a lot of changes," he said. "But there are going to have to be some changes because of the whole football thing over the last few years. We're going to go down the field with the ball. You're going to see the ball in the air. We're not going to go from sideline to sideline for three yards a crack. The ball is going to be in the air."

The Rams, then, would have to do it without Terry Cochrane and Chris Hamilton. Cochrane had decided to return to the University of British Columbia to finish his education. Hamilton was also devoting more time to his education and to piano playing, at which he was gifted.

The biggest hole would be Cochrane, a running back the likes of which the PJFC had never seen before. But McCrystal was confident the Rams could replace him. They had veteran Terry Eisler back and, in training camp, players like Jason Belisle, Cliff Rusconi, Dan Johnston and Jim McDowell were impressive. As far as a quarterback went, there was one rookie whose name would long be remembered by Rams' fans, Central Collegiate grad Dean Picton. But the Rams figured they would start the season with Tim Hammond, who had been with the Rams the year before as a defensive halfback. McCrystal was high on both kids.

"Hammond is an athlete who has had a lot of success in his athletic endeavours. He hasn't played quarterback for two seasons, but he's progressing by leaps and bounds. And Picton is going to be outstanding, he really is." said McCrystal.

McCrystal could hardly wait for his first year as head coach to get underway. "We're solid, we really are. If there's one thing this team has, it's a system that provides people to fill in. When someone graduates, we've got someone with two years experience ready to step forward."

McCrystal felt his offensive and defensive lines were the strengths of the team. The offensive line had Kevin Ostapowich, Steve Sombach, Tim Relke, Russ Turgeon and Brian Eltom, who was the only rookie on either offensive or defensive lines. The defensive line had the unstoppable Dave Gebert, Kevin Peyson, Ron Senger and Al Hendren, all bringing size to the line.

Al Hendren

The Rams opened the season against the Edmonton Wildcats defending Canadian champions. Through two and one-half quarters, the Rams struggled, their offence stuck and sputtering. They were behind 13-5 at halftime and, in his first start at quarterback, Tim Hammond was playing as if he would rather have been somewhere else. The thought had also crossed McCrystal's mind that maybe there should be a change at quarterback. Dean Picton was warming up on the sidelines. "I turned to Bernie (Schmidt) and I told him that if things didn't start to happen, we were going to have to make a change."

Tim Hammond

Then, night turned to day, and Hammond suddenly got back on track. As Picton was warming up, Hammond got the Ram's offence moving. He took the Rams on a 98-yard march that ended with Eisler scoring on a seven-yard run. The Rams then went for a two-point convert, which was successful when Marlowe Pelletier took the ball from Hammond and then threw it back to him in the end zone. Tricky stuff, that.

The Rams were on their way now. "It was amazing," said McCrystal. "We really were about to make the change at quarterback."

Terry Eisler

Before the game was over, Hammond had thrown touchdown passes of 20 yards to Mark Kent and 78 yards to Eisler. Both were converted by rookie kicker Mike Lazecki. The Rams also got their ground game going with Belisle rushing for 92 yards and Eisler 66 yards. The Rams won 28-13.

It was a good way for the Rams to start the season.

And they kept right on going. They went into Saskatoon for their second game, a one-sided whuppin' they laid on the Hilltops. With Belisle and Eisler churning out the big yardage. Belisle rushed for 99 yards and Eisler for 133 yards, the Rams won 49-39. Mind you, it wasn't all Rams all day. The Rams had built a 28-0 lead by the halfway point of the second quarter, but then Saskatoon erupted for 26 straight points in the last half of the quarter, before the Rams settled down and ran away in the second half.

Pelletier, who had turned into as dependable a Rams' receiver as any, took in five passes from Hammond for 147 yards and Eisler caught six for 115 yards. Hammond had a strong game, completing 14 of 22 passes for 298 yards.

The Rams ran their unbeaten streak in 1984 to three wins, but McCrystal was livid after the game that saw them beat the Edmonton Huskies 21-16. He stormed into the dressing room after the game and tore a strip off his undefeated team. "They're not playing up to their potential. They're believing what people are writing about them. They're taking their headlines onto the field with them." McCrystal had become so steamed in the first half that he pulled Hammond off the field and put Picton into the game. Hammond returned in the second half, played better, and the Rams won.

The Rams just kept going after that. They hadn't had an undefeated season since 1981. They were about to have another one. By the time the season ended, the Rams had locked up first place with an 8-0 record, and everything seemed back to normal in the Mount Pleasant clubhouse.

Mark Kent

As the season wore on, one Ram who began to emerge as a superstar was Mark Kent. McCrystal couldn't say enough about him. "Mark just may be our most valuable player. Mark's able to play defensive back, slotback and quarterback. He's our punter and he's our holder on place kicks. He's one of the team captains and, as a matter of fact, he probably understands the game as well as any of the coaches. I just can't say enough about him. He's a competitor, he's an all-round citizen, and he certainly is a Regina Ram. He'll do anything, and has done everything that we, as coaches, have asked. He's just the type of young man you'd be proud to have as a son."

Another player who brought a lot to the Rams was kicker Mike Lazecki. A big, easygoing type who always wore a smile, Mike turned into an outstanding kicker whose big-league leg and attitude took him to the Canadian Football League. He was tragically killed in a car accident in 2002 near Brandon, Manitoba.

If there was anything about the 1984 season that made it special, it was that the Rams were once again sending waves of fear throughout the Prairie Junior Football Conference. And nowhere was it being felt more than in

Mike Lazecki

Saskatoon, where the Hilltops were getting the impression they had seen this movie once before. Hilltops' head coach Blaine Knoll was getting the feeling that all his players were thinking about were games with the Regina Rams. "In the past, we've spent too much time thinking about the games with Regina," he said. "We have a tendency of looking two or three weeks ahead to those games. I want them thinking about the other teams too."

The Rams, of course, couldn't have been more delighted to hear they were once again getting on the Hilltops' nerves.

In their final meeting of the schedule, in a game that would give the Rams first place if they won, with two games still to go, McCrystal got a pleasant surprise. He found out that Dean Picton was developing into a strong quarterback faster than he had thought would happen.

Dean Picton

With Hammond struggling somewhat, McCrystal sent Picton into the game for the second half, with the Rams trailing 3-1. Picton put together a big-game kind of game, using Belisle (117 yards) as the force on the ground, and scoring a touchdown himself on a nifty run off a rollout. The Rams went on to win 17-10 and clinch first place. McCrystal couldn't have been happier about Picton's play. "Over the past couple of weeks he's just been outstanding in practice. He understands the offence and he throws a good ball. But he's just out of high school and that's a big step for him and we're not going to put him in there and put that much pressure on him. We're going to allow him time to develop."

For Picton, the game was an eye-opener. "I finally realized what the rivalry was about," he said. "When I got in there, it was pretty intense, quite a bit more than the usual game."

As the playoffs approached, the Rams received a bit of bad news. Their team doctor, Frank Samuels, had decided to leave Regina and go to Hawaii to continue his career in medicine. Dr. Samuels had been the Rams' doctor for 18 years and the Roughriders' doctor for 13 years. He said, "I've enjoyed working with the Rams because I've come to meet and know so many people. The fellowship is something I cherish."

If anybody needed a doctor, it was likely the Hilltops, who came into Regina on a cool soggy day in late October to take on the Rams in the Prairie Junior Football Conference championship game. The Rams emerged with a 19-15 victory in a game that was decided in the trenches, and because of the pounding taken by quarterback Tony Gagnon. Gagnon came into the game injured, and he was easy prey for the Rams.

"We knew he was hurting," is how Rams' linebacker Don Gorski put it, "and we had to hit him. We never knew if he had the ball or not. We just kept hitting him."

Jason Belisle had hit full stride in the playoffs. He had gained 210 yards in the Rams' 31-24 semifinal win over the Edmonton Huskies, and piled up 124 yards against the Hilltops before leaving the game in the second half with an injured hand. Terry Eisler, perhaps the most underrated and unselfish Rams' player ever, picked up the slack, turning in a game that saw him rush for 150 yards and score a touchdown.

Hammond played the whole game at quarterback and turned in a solid performance, guiding a ground game that ate up 335 yards and completing six passes for another 106 yards. Gagnon completed only five passes.

Four days later, Blaine Knoll quit as head coach of the Saskatoon Hilltops.

At the time, the Rams were preparing to travel to Vancouver to take on the Richmond Raiders for the Western Canadian championship. They couldn't wait to get there. In Regina, it had been snowing and the temperatures were dropping. The Rams practiced through the bad weather, but it wasn't easy.

McCrystal knew little about the Raiders, except that they had size and toughness. He had tried to get some game films from Richmond but had come up empty-handed. Meanwhile, the Raiders had scouted the Rams in their game against the Hilltops.

They must have learned something valuable. An undefeated season went down the drain as the Raiders launched a huge running back named Mike Van Geel against the Rams. Richmond romped to a 45-28 victory. Van Geel gained 159 yards as the Raiders pounded their way to the Canadian championship.

There were a lot of things that had happened in the game that determined the Rams' fate. One was the ground game. Another was a 77-yard touchdown run by Van Geel on the first play of the second half. Another was two costly interference calls against the Rams. "Take away those three things, it's a different game. Those cost us 21 points," said McCrystal. Another was the punting of Richmond's Paul Osbaldiston, who averaged 57.7 yards a punt and denied the Rams field position all afternoon.

McCrystal handled the loss well. "I can't be disappointed. I tried to find something positive about it, and that's not tough to do after a 10-1 season. But I can't be satisfied with defeat. This is a courageous team. They are not quitters. I believed, right until the minute flag went up, that we would win."

In the Rams' dressing room, there were tears flowing from tired faces. "The worst thing about losing was seeing Frank's face. We let him down," said Laurence Larkin, a Rams' player who would be back in 1985.

SECOND STRAIGHT 8-0 SEASON . . . BUT

1985

Not even Gord Currie could match Frank McCrystal's record in his first two years as head coach of the Regina Rams, if all that was counted was the regular season schedule's results. In fact, there are likely very few coaches in the history of sport who could say their teams were as successful as Frank McCrystal's. Just don't bring up the playoff records in those first two years. They are to cringe over.

When Currie took over as head coach of the Rams in 1965, they won six of eight games and finished first in the Prairie Junior Football Conference, won the league championship, then lost in the Western final. His second year, 1966, the Rams won five of eight games, again finished first, and went on to win the Canadian junior football championship.

McCrystal became head coach of the Rams in 1984. Through the eight-game regular season schedule, the Rams were undefeated and finished in first place. They won the Prairie Junior Football Conference championship, then were defeated in the western final. His second year as head coach, 1985, the Rams again breezed through the eight-game PJFC schedule without suffering a loss. Come the playoffs, the Rams were beaten in the league championship game. Two seasons, a 16-0 record, and not a whole lot to show for it. This was painful.

Of anybody, McCrystal felt those playoff eliminations the most. There is no other reason for the season than to get to the national final and win it. "We never talk about anything but that, from the start of every season," he said. It was like spending months trying to get a date, and then falling asleep on the big night.

When the Rams went to training camp in 1985, they went with a fair amount of confidence that this could be the year they would win their first Canadian title since 1981. They had more than the usual number of players returning, plus the coaching staff of McCrystal, Bernie Schmidt, Jerry Orban, Doug Zimmerman, Tim McGeough and Rick Seaman was intact and with a year's experience together under their belts.

It was significant that both quarterbacks from 1984, Tim Hammond and Dean Picton, were back, which gave stability at the most important position on the field. Mind you, it didn't last all that long. Hammond came down with mononucleosis – he would definitely miss the season opener and could be out until the end of August. But even that didn't slow the Rams' enthusiasm for the season because Picton was still there, and his rapid progress as a rookie the year before had surprised everybody.

Jason Belisle

Ed McQuarters Jr.

The Rams' outstanding running back from 1984, Jason Belisle, returned to training camp bigger and, presumably, better. Belisle, who was named the PJFC's rookie of the year, had added 50 pounds to the 145 he had played at. The Rams had also added fullback Joe Mahnic, a graduate of the University of Saskatchewan, Rob Bresciani, also from the U of S, and Ed McQuarters Jr., a guard whose father was an outstanding defensive tackle for the Roughriders. The younger McQuarters came to the Rams from Minot State College. McCrystal wasn't sure where he would play Bresciani, who had been a quarterback in high school and an all-Canadian receiver with the Huskies. The Rams also had offensive tackle Kelly Handy, a six-foot, three-inch, 279-pounder who, when the football season was over, joined the Regina Pats as an enforcer, of course.

Jim Francis

There was one significant change. Long-time trainer Jim Francis, the Wizard of Gauze, had retired, ending a 14-year stint with the Rams. The white-haired Francis, always quick with some quip, had been a trainer with the Rams under four coaches – Currie, Fiissel, Zbytnuik and McCrystal, and he was well respected within the sports world. The desire to spend more time with his wife, Sharon, and his children brought him to what was a tough decision.

The Rams knew that the Hilltops would be fielding a team that, while run by new head coach Kevin Scott, had a big plus in the fact that this would be quarterback Tony Gagnon's sixth year in junior football.

The Rams went into their first game with both Hammond and Belisle not playing. Hammond they knew about. Belisle had to sit out because of a neck injury picked up in training camp. But the Rams did not miss a beat. They had their usual truckload of running backs waiting to play.

This time, it was Rich Sutcliffe who got the nod. That it came in the Rams' first game of the season added even more pressure because it was important that the Rams got off to a good start. They did. They beat the Calgary Colts 60-29.

Picton directed what was perhaps the most balanced Rams' offensive attack seen in years. The Rams passed for 320 yards and rushed for 303 yards. Picton hit on 15 of 27 passes for 310 yards and four touchdowns. Picton also ran seven times for 44 yards and scored two touchdowns. Sutcliffe had 139 yards rushing on just 18 carries and also scored a touchdown. Bresciani served notice that he was the receiver everybody thought he was. He caught eight passes for 121 yards and two of them went for touchdowns. He also got a brief look at quarterback, completing two of three for 10 yards, just in case something happened to Picton before Hammond returned. Bresciani was another in a line of outstanding slotbacks, following the model established by Kelly Hamilton and Terry Cochrane.

There was something about Picton that gave the team much confidence. He was an excellent high-school quarterback, a beautifully deceptive ball handler, good on his feet, and while he may not have had as much strength in his arm as Hammond, he had enough. It wasn't as if he was throwing wounded ducks. Picton wanted to take full advantage of the opening created by Hammond's illness. He wanted to make it tough on the coaches to put Hammond back in as the starter when he came back. "It's a break for me," said Dean. "I get my foot in the door. If I play well, the coaches will have to make a decision. But it's pretty well up to them."

McCrystal relished Picton's competitive streak, and he knew that Dean's play could make it a tough decision when Hammond returned. "We have nothing but confidence in Dean. He's throwing the ball well, he's always been a great ball-handler and he's a smart quarterback. He can read defences," McCrystal said.

Hammond dressed for the Rams' second game, but there was still some doubt about whether or not he was strong enough to play much. Picton's second start of the year came in Edmonton against the Wildcats. The final score –

43-15 Rams – wasn't a true reflection of what had happened in the game. What had happened was, the Rams unveiled their explosive side. Their offence was not the chop-chop-chop . . . Timber! – sort of wear-you-down-with-body-blows-and-you'll-eventually-buckle style.

The Rams had three huge plays in the game. It was enough. There was an innocent-looking swing pass to Bresciani that turned into a 100-yard touchdown run. "I broke a tackle and was about 30 or 40 yards downfield," said Bresciani, "and Marlowe (Pelletier) came over and decked a guy who was coming at me." There was a trick 39-yard pass to Bresciani, who flipped the ball to Pelletier, who ran the rest of the way for the touchdown. There was the fumble Ron Senger recovered for a touchdown. There was an interception by Mark Becker that set up a three-yard touchdown run by Wendell Toth.

"We had two big plays by Bresciani and a defensive touchdown and an interception," said McCrystal. "You're talking 28 points. If you take those away, it's a different ball game. I really don't think the score is indicative of how close the game could have been."

Picton completed 10 of 24 passes for 255 yards. Hammond got into the game in the fourth quarter, to get off some of the rust from his layoff, and completed three of six passes for 91 yards.

Life was good in Ramville. They had two solid quarterbacks. They had an abundance of running backs. There was a sureness and an explosiveness in their pass receiving corps. Their defence was solid. Oh yeah, and nobody could beat them.

The defence carved a notch on the post in the third game of the season, posting a shutout as the Rams kept their undefeated streak alive with a 53-0 crushing of the Edmonton Huskies. Ram's defensive backs Rick Lavoy and Cliff Rusconi each returned interceptions for touchdowns. Lavoy also had a 95-yard punt return that set up a one-yard touchdown plunge by Picton. They held the Huskie offence to less than 170 yards.

Picton started the game and played the first half, completing eight of 18 passes for 154 yards. With a 15-0 lead in his pocket, Hammond came in during the third quarter and the Rams put 38 points on the board, 24 of them in the fourth quarter, 14 of those on interception returns. Hammond completed 8 of 11 passes for 171 yards.

McCrystal made his decision on the starting quarterback issue. "I'd say we have two starting quarterbacks," McCrystal said. It was a subtle reminder that Frank's nickname is Slick.

The Rams played that game without Bresciani, who had injured his shoulder. But their depth again showed itself, with rookie Brian Forrest filling in. Forrest, whose nickname was Animal, caught three passes for 55 yards and scored a touchdown. Dan Johnston, playing in Bresciani's slotback spot, caught five passes for 132 yards and a touchdown. It was all fun that day.

Dan Johnston

Bresciani had been drafted in the fifth round by the Roughriders. He went to their training camp, but was cut and returned to the Rams. In September of 1985, he signed with the Calgary Stampeders as a free agent. He played eight games with the Stampeders as a return specialist.

The Rams finally received a serious test in the fourth game of that season. They finally played the Hilltops, who came to Regina with a 2-1 record. "In my 12 years as a player and coach with the Rams, I've never been at ease going into Hilltop games," McCrystal said.

For the first 30 minutes of the game, McCrystal might have thought he'd seen this movie before. The Hilltops held a 6-5 lead. At halftime McCrystal changed quarterbacks – sending starter Picton in for starter Hammond. The move seemed to ignite the Rams. They scored 14 points in the third quarter, and 21 more in the fourth, to leave the Hilltops in the dust and win 40-16. The onslaught started when Senger recovered a Hilltops' fumble and ran it back 33 yards for the touchdown, something that was becoming old hat with the Ram's defensive end.

Johnston again had a huge game for the Rams, filling in for the still-injured Bresciani, catching six passes for 160 yards and scoring three touchdowns. The Rams' defence did a number on the veteran Gagnon, holding him to just seven completions for a mere 59 yards. Becker and Lavoy each had an interception.

The Rams would go on to an undefeated season, winning all eight games. But, actually, they had won nine games, and the extra win wasn't a playoff game, either. It might even have been regarded as more important than that in some circles.

In a gracious move that upset some of his university cronies, University of Alberta Golden Bears' coach Jim Donlevy called McCrystal and asked him if the Rams would be interested in playing the Bears in an exhibition game. The game was set for September 7th, a Saturday night, in Taylor Field. Donlevy was a forward-thinking coach who could see nothing wrong in a junior team taking on a college team. And he had a tremendous amount of respect and admiration for the Rams and their tradition.

"My bottom line for playing this game was simple," said Donlevy, "I think it's great for football in Canada, because junior football has got to be there. Regina, for example, doesn't have a university football program. And, I mean, if I was a young man coming out of the high-school system here and wanted to play the game and I could play for the Rams and I could go to the University of Regina and still have mom's home cooking, why do I want to go to Saskatoon?"

The game promised to draw one of the biggest crowds ever to Taylor Field – for an event that didn't involve the Roughriders. The closer it got, the more excited people became, especially because the Rams were on such a tear in the PJFC. Both head coaches said that they were not treating the game as an exhibition, that they would be going with their starters, that they would be trying to win.

"We need to be challenged," said McCrystal, "and the Golden Bears will do that. They'll make us a better football team. We're excited."

Said Donlevy, "We're going for the win. It's a very important game for us, no question about that."

One thing would be for certain. It was going to be a fun evening. After the game, McCrystal had arranged for players and coaches from both teams to get together in the Green and White Lounge at Taylor Field for something to eat. "It's important that the players from both teams get to know each other, talk to each other. We want this to be a fun thing, something both teams will have good memories from, no matter who wins."

On a chilly night, a crowd estimated to be upward of 5,000 fans turned out to Taylor Field. The game pitted the best team in junior football against the top-ranked team in university football. It was a battle of sorts. The Rams trailed only once, 1-0 after the first quarter, and then gradually took over the flow of the game.

By halftime, Picton had put the Rams ahead 8-4 on a touchdown by Belisle and a convert and single by Mike Lazecki. The Rams blew the game open in a 14-point third quarter that saw Picton go to the air. Lightning was striking as Picton fired a 53-yard touchdown bolt to Sutcliffe and then hooked up with Forrest on a 109-yard pass and run touchdown. The Rams led 22-4 going into the final quarter, withstood a late Alberta rally, and won the game 22-17. Lavoy had a tremendous game on defence, intercepting three Alberta passes.

Was it worth it?

"Excellent football game, I knew it would be," said Donlevy. "The Rams are a quality football team. They are well-coached, well-disciplined and they execute exceptionally well. What else can you want from a football team?"

McCrystal said, "Maybe now people in this country, and in the Canadian Football League, will realize that junior football is a quality game."

The Rams won that game with their best receiver not playing, Pelletier had suffered a mild concussion the previous week. The Rams' offence never missed a beat, though, with Picton playing the whole game and running a show that produced 445 yards. Picton himself threw for 270 yards and ran for another 77. How sweet it was. And how big a feather in the Rams' helmet it was.

Doug Dorsch

The Rams continued on their way, disposing of one team after another, with new stars emerging on almost a weekly basis. For instance, in a 40-15 win over the Wildcats, and with Picton hurling the ball for 325 yards on just 11 completions, it was wide receiver Doug Dorsch who stepped into the spotlight. Or, make that sped into the spotlight. Dorsch, the son of former Roughrider player and general manager Hank, caught three passes for 128 yards and two touchdowns. Brian Forrest continued as an explosive receiver, catching only one pass, but taking it 60 yards for a touchdown.

The Rams closed off their perfect season with a 38-32 win over the Hilltops in Saskatoon, something that was never hard for them to take. Ron Senger was at it again in this game. For the third time in the season, he had a fumble recovery and his 81-yard return set up a Ram's touchdown. Lavoy had a mixed game on defence. He intercepted two Tony Gagnon passes. But he was also beaten for a touchdown by Gagnon. "That's the first time all season I've been beat for a touchdown," Lavoy said. "I screwed up the coverage."

The Rams had no trouble in the PJFC semifinal, beating the Calgary Colts 39-13, gaining 567 yards in total offence. Picton's hot hand continued. He dealt out 232 yards passing on 13 completions.

The win sent the Rams to the league final, against the Hilltops, in Regina.

The rivalry was resumed. It was nothing new to McCrystal or his Hilltops' counterpart, Kevin Scott. They had played against each other and now they were coaching against each other. An interesting statistic came out the week of the game, involving all the games the Rams and Hilltops had played against each other since McCrystal had joined the Rams in 1972. The Rams had won 32 games, lost 12 and tied two. The Rams and Hilltops had met seven times in league championships since 1972, and the Rams had won every time.

Here we go again. Another of those upsets-in-the-making disasters was just around the corner of Hope Street and Hopeless Avenue. No matter how well the Rams played over the course of the season, they could not get out of the playoffs. The Hilltops came rolling into Taylor Field and belly-laughed their way home with a stunning 31-24 victory over the Rams. Simply put, the Rams were impaled on their own sword. The Rams lost two fumbles, Picton threw three interceptions, and the Rams turned the ball over on downs three times.

For the second straight year, the Rams had hung an 8-0 season on the door, only to have it slammed in their faces when they tried to get in.

"The bottom line is, it's really tough to win a Canadian championship," said McCrystal. "There's a certain degree of frustration, certainly."

The Hilltops went on to win the Canadian championship, and Tony Gagnon's six-year career ended on the highest note.

As if the Rams'-Hilltops' rivalry wasn't enough, another one was born. The Rams grew more than a little upset when the University of Saskatchewan Huskies attempted to recruit some Rams' players to come to Saskatoon. This went over not at all well with McCrystal, who got on the phone to the Saskatoon campus with a please-get-the-hell-out-of-our-backyard kind of conversation. The Huskies, of course, ignored McCrystal. One of those doing the recruiting in Saskatoon was apparently Brian Towriss. He and McCrystal would eventually have their day in the sun, down the road, in Rams' history.

FRANKIE'S FIRST CHAMPIONSHIP

1986

Okay, so maybe this winning every game in the regular season wasn't such a good idea, after all. If it was, then why, after going 8-0 his first year as head coach, and 8-0 his second year as head coach, would Frank McCrystal finish each year with such a bad taste in his mouth?

"We play every year to win the national championship," said McCrystal. "That's it."

And, so, every year, along come the playoffs and out go the Rams. And McCrystal spent the off-season wondering why.

"I'd be lying if I said it didn't bother me," McCrystal said on the eve of the 1986 season. "But as soon as the thought entered my mind, we sat down as a coaching staff and a team and said, 'Look we're doing the right things.' You don't get to be 16-0 doing the wrong things. I think, though, we have to improve. I believe a major problem we had was youth. When you get down in a playoff game, the intensity and the pressure at the time can frustrate the younger fellows more easily than it will a four- or five-year veteran. And the nucleus of our team has been made up of those 18- and 19-year-olds the past two years. I really believe the inexperience in pressure situations has gotten to us in the big games."

McCrystal also felt that more attention had to be paid by the coaches to the offence. When Tim McGeough resigned as an assistant coach because his job as a bus driver conflicted with his ability to spend time with the Rams, McCrystal saw an opportunity. And he took it. He brought in a successful high-school coach named Ray Pitre as an assistant coach. Then, he did some shuffling. McGeough had coached the linebackers. McCrystal said he would take over coaching the linebackers and that Pitre would coach the running backs and assist offensive co-ordinator Bernie Schmidt.

Ray Pitre

"We're going to be better organized in charting plays and recognizing what's available," explained McCrystal. "We want to keep track of what we're doing well and what we're not doing well. We're not going to force those things we're not doing well. Maybe we did that in past years. From my perspective as a head coach, we're going to play a game at a time – we're not going to look past any teams. I have to slow things down and put things in perspective so that we are taking it a game at a time."

On the first weekend of June in 1986, the temperature was mid-summer hot and the Mount Pleasant practice field was overtaken by mosquitos. There wasn't a cloud in the sky. This was the weekend McCrystal had chosen to stage a three-day rookie camp for graduating high schoolers and others who wanted to become Rams. Despite the intense heat and the swarming mosquitos, 119 kids turned out. McCrystal, his five assistant coaches and 15 guest coaches handled the three days of camp, ending with a Sunday afternoon scrimmage in which every player got at least 10 plays.

"We're looking for kids who are going to play for us down the road," said McCrystal. "It generally takes three years before a kid becomes a starter for us and becomes an impact player."

When the Rams went to training camp, weeks later, they knew that come the start of the season they would have a veteran-laden team, more capable of winning a national championship, perhaps, than the teams from the previous two years. The anchor, of course, would be quarterback Dean Picton, who had firmly established himself as not only the Rams' starting quarterback, but also as perhaps the best quarterback in the country. With Picton the quarterback, the guy he had shared the spot with the two previous seasons, Tim Hammond, was moved to tight end. Hammond had no problem making the switch. "I just want to play," he said. "This is my last year and I don't want to be tagging along while all my friends are playing. I'll do whatever the coaches want me to do. And if they need me to play quarterback, I'll do it. I want that Canadian championship, I want to be a part of it." The Rams were not sure if they would have receiver Rob Bresciani back. He was on the roster of the Saskatchewan Roughriders, but there was still talk he might get cut. If so, he would likely come back to the Rams. Three games into the 1986 season, Bresciani did return to the Rams' lineup.

Wendell Toth would be back at fullback, Phil Hulet at slotback and the offensive line would be anchored by all-star centre Kevin Ostapowich and tackle Kelly Handy. The Rams figured to have Jason Belisle and Rich Sutcliffe handling most of the running game. Both had suffered injuries in training camp. Sutcliffe injured his hamstring and would return once it healed. Belisle's, though, was more serious. He had a damaged ankle and there was a good chance he might miss the season. The Rams compensated by moving Cliff Rusconi and Sam Khuber to the offensive backfield from the defensive backfield. But perhaps the most startling development was that the Rams intended to not be the running team they had nearly always been. No, now they wanted to throw the ball. Put it up in the air, on first down, second down, any down. Even kicker Mike Lazecki was going to have to learn to become a passer. It's not that the Rams would totally abandon the run, but it was going to have to share some playing time with the passing game. At least, that was the plan.

When the Rams opened the 1986 season, they did it without having played an exhibition game, and McCrystal knew they would not be as smooth as they would become later in the season. They opened against the Edmonton Wildcats before over 2,700 fans in Taylor Field and won 21-10 in a game in which the Rams' new passing attack was unveiled. Picton was as sharp as a new razor blade. He completed 18 of 31 passes for 355 yards. Hammond was his favourite receiver, catching five passes for 147 yards. The Rams ran the ball only 22 times, with little success, outside of a brilliant 95-yard touchdown run by Dan Johnston. Take Johnston's run off the total, and the Rams rushed for only 77 yards on 21 ground plays.

If anything started alarm bells in McCrystal's head about the first game, it was the number of penalties the Rams took, especially the objectionable conduct calls. The Rams took 17 penalties in the game. Ostapowich was thrown out of the game in the fourth quarter for objectionable conduct. "A problem the last two years was immaturity and that came front and centre again," said McCrystal. "We allowed ourselves to be frustrated and lost control of our emotions. That's a real factor if we intend to be champions – we have to maintain control of ourselves."

Before the Rams would hit their stride in 1986, they had an old score they wanted to settle. The loss to the Hilltops in the 1985 PJFC final had eaten at them all winter long. Now, in their second game of the season, they would get the chance, in Saskatoon. "I've been looking forward to this game since last October," said McCrystal. "It's got to be more than just a regular season game. Almost 40 guys on this team went through the experience of losing to them last October. This will be something of a test of their character in how they respond in the first opportunity to answer the defeat."

The Rams got the message from their head coach. They, in turn, delivered one to the Hilltops. The message came in the form of a 46-10 Rams' victory. It was pretty clear. The Rams were never behind in the game and blew it open in the third quarter with a 22-point outburst. A balanced attack and a pressure defence were the keys for the Rams. They rushed for 199 yards. Picton completed 12 of 24 passes for 180 yards, didn't give up an interception and had two TD throws. Rusconi was the top Rams' rusher with 61 yards, while Johnston and Doug Dorsch were the leading receivers.

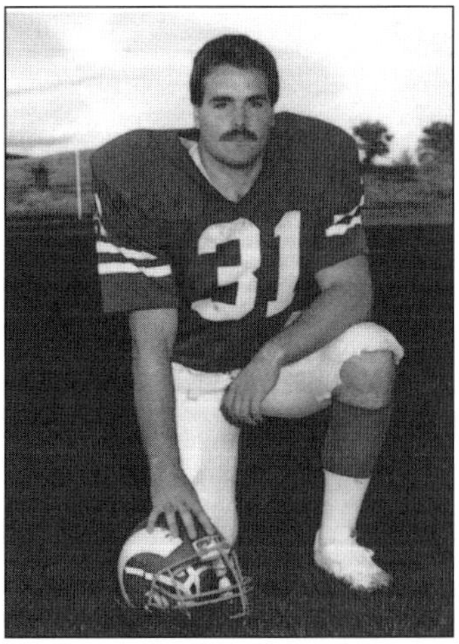
Dave Gebert

The Regina defence, with linebacker Dave Gebert leading the way, had an outstanding game. Gebert pressured rookie Hilltops' quarterback Mark Andrews from start to finish, sacking him three times and forcing him to unload the football sooner than he wanted to on numerous other occasions. One pass was intercepted by Rams' defensive back Jamie Anderson, who returned it 17 yards for a touchdown. Andrews and Anderson had been high-school teammates at Peacock in Moose Jaw. The Rams' defensive backfield of Rick Lavoy, Mark Becker, Gord Lupanko, Darcy Koch and Dave McEachern stuck to the Hilltops' receivers like cotton candy to the fingers of a five year old. They were all over them. The Rams were undefeated after two games, with number three next up.

By now, people were beginning to wonder if the Rams were on their way to yet another undefeated season – such an accomplishment was beginning to look like a curse. The Rams continued to win, beating the Calgary Colts 38-14, despite taking 240 yards in penalties. The Rams, if you can believe it, took 24 penalties. Bresciani played his first game, catching two passes for 57 yards and returning a punt 79 yards. But those penalties – they had become an all too familiar statistic for the Rams. "If we're going to win a national championship, we're going to have to change that," said veteran offensive lineman Tim Relke.

The Rams also got some bad news from the game. Dave Gebert, a veteran and one of the best linebackers around, left the game with a knee injury suffered with 14 seconds to go in the fourth quarter. It was expected he would miss the rest of the regular schedule.

McCrystal was furious with the way the injury had happened. He accused the Colts of deliberately going after Gebert. "One guy posted Dave and another one blew out his knee. It was blatant."

The Rams also were accused of dirty play by both the Hilltops and the Colts. The Rams' 24 penalties against Calgary and 19 against Saskatoon the week before were entered as evidence of the Rams' play.

"We play hard and tough football," said McCrystal. "There is no question we have no desire to win the Lady Byng in this league."

What triggered a reaction in Regina was a newspaper story out of Saskatoon headlined "Coaches of Hilltops, Colts question Ram tactics."

Even Rams' president Paul Barnby got into the act, saying that the team did not like the kind of "bad press" it was seeing out of Saskatoon.

"In the Calgary game, we took 100 yards of talking penalties out of 240," he said. "That upsets us as much as anything. There's no need to do that even if you get bad calls. You've got to live with it, that's all you can do. I'd be the first to admit that we lost our cool . . . we're the Regina Rams and we try to act with as much class as we possibly can. But the kids are human, the coaches are human, the directors are human. We stand for something higher than other teams aspire to and it's unfortunate when we can't maintain that level."

Rob Bresciani put it all into perspective. "No matter what our coaches say, we've got to stop ourselves. We've got to get it into our heads that we're not going to win the big game or a national championship if we keep getting too many penalties."

The Rams ran their winning streak to five games, which meant they had won 21 straight league games,. Then the Hilltops came to Regina. The streak stopped there, the Hilltops won, 45-24. The Rams took 18 penalties for 170 yards, but that wasn't the killer. The Hilltops' offence, especially running back Floyd Collins, were just too much for the Rams to handle on that day. Collins rushed for 220 yards and scored three touchdowns as the Hilltops overcame a 17-7 Regina lead.

"In the last two years, losses ended our season," said McCrystal. "We didn't have an opportunity to regroup after and see what we're made of in terms of team character. This year we can regroup and turn a loss within the season into a positive thing."

The Rams finished off the season with two straight wins, starting with a 78-15 massacre of the Colts in Calgary, with Picton throwing five touchdown passes. The final score was the most lopsided in Prairie Junior Conference history. The Rams' total offence was 688 yards. They closed out the schedule with a 59-14 win over the Edmonton Huskies, clinched first place with a 7-1 record and started to get ready for the playoffs.

Picton established a PJFC single-season yardage record with 2,216 yards. He completed 125 of 226 passes for 16 touchdowns and only gave up three interceptions. Lazecki won the scoring championship on the strength of his leg. Leading receivers were Tim Hammond (33 catches for 602 yards), Rob Bresciani (21 for 467 yards) and Doug

Rob Bresciani

Dorsch (17 for 350 yards). The Rams would play the Huskies in the league semifinal. They'd beaten Edmonton twice by a combined score of 100-22. The playoff game turned into a mugging. The Rams won, 75-0. Finally, a playoff win.

"Our guys have to reach their peak in the playoffs, get better every week," said McCrystal. "This was one step."

The next step was a bigger one. They would go up against the Hilltops for the Prairie Junior Football Conference championship.

The season, and even the first round of the playoffs, was strange in some ways. The Rams were winning, which is what was expected of them. And they were winning a lot of games by big scores. Even the passing attack they had worked on back in the dog days of training camp had clicked. Picton had gotten even better. And Hammond had made a remarkable transition to tight end, which was no big surprise, given the kind of athlete he was. He also played hockey in the winter with the University of Regina Cougars.

Everybody felt that the Rams' season would boil down to the final three playoff games – the PJFC championship, the western final and the national final. The town was starting to feel a buzz, the excitement of the playoffs was in the air.

First, to the PJFC final in Taylor Field against the Hilltops. Neither of the Rams' starting running backs played in this game – Sutcliffe had a sprained ankle and Toth a bruised kidney – so it would fall on the Rams' defence to come up big. "I've always believed, going back to my playing days, that it's defences that win championships," said McCrystal. The Rams' number one target would be the Hilltops' great running back, Floyd Collins.

The Rams built a 15-0 lead, but the Hilltops came back to narrow it to 15-14 at halftime. The Rams owned the second half and went on to a 29-14 victory. The key was the defence. They never gave up a point. The Hilltops' touchdowns came on a 100-yard kick return by Paul Leier and a Darren Hockman interception return for a touchdown off a pass from Lazecki on a botched third-down punting play. They contained Collins, stopping him once on a critical third-quarter, third-down gamble in which the Hilltops needed less than a yard.

Rams' cornerback Rick Lavoy had a stunning game. When McCrystal had said that the veterans had to step their games up a notch in the playoffs – BAM! – Lavoy did just that. The holder on place kicks, he corralled a bad snap and got the ball down perfectly for Lazecki to kick a big field goal in the third quarter. Lavoy also ran two Saskatoon kicks out of the end zone rather than concede a single point. He took one back 41 yards to set up another Lazecki field goal and he took one out 30 yards, which started a Rams' touchdown drive. More? With the Rams leading 21-14, and the Hilltops at the Regina 24, Lavoy forced a fumble that the Rams recovered. The game ended with the Hilltops' Mark Andrews throwing an interception. Guess who made the interception? That Lavoy kid did. He was everywhere. And a week later, he and the Rams would be in Vancouver to take on the Richmond Raiders in the Western final.

Rick Lavoy

Oh, yes, and the Rams only took five penalties.

The game turned into a back and forth contest, with both offences strutting their stuff. Picton guided the Rams' offence to 603 total yards, 331 of it off his 14 completions. Richmond's offence totaled 494 yards, 380 of it in the air. The Raiders opened by taking a 17-1 lead, but the Rams

Dean Picton

came clawing back, knotting the score at 17-17 on a Lazecki field goal. After three quarters the Rams were ahead 24-17, but with eight minutes to go in the game the Raiders had a 25-24 lead. They upped it to 28-24 with about six minutes left.

Then, the Rams struck. Picton found Johnston on a deep pass for a 51-yard touchdown. Wendel Toth ran in for a touchdown from 10 yards out and Picton fired a 19-yard touchdown pass to Dorsch. Lazecki converted the three touchdowns. All this with less than five minutes to go in the fourth quarter.

"We knew when we came in here, there'd be distractions playing in their park," said McCrystal. "We knew there'd be jitters before the game and we thought we'd be down 14 points right away."

The victory sent the Rams to the Canadian final, on November 15, in Regina's Taylor Field. They would be playing the Ottawa Sooners.

The Sooners were a big team with experience. They had 14 players back from the 1985 team that had lost in the Canadian final to the Saskatoon Hilltops. Their quarterback, Rick Boudreau, had been named the east's nominee for the Schenley award for the most valuable player of the year. He didn't win it. He was up against Dean Picton, and Picton was named the winner at a classy banquet the night before the game.

The Rams were never in danger of losing this game. They had pointed to it all season, never forgetting the anger and frustration and empty feeling they had after the playoff losses in 1984 and 1985. They had improved with every playoff game. They had peaked at just the right time. The last game was one of the most complete team efforts a Rams' team had ever produced at this level of the game. Offence. Defence. Specialty teams. The Rams were on their game in every phase.

The Rams led 7-3 after the first quarter, 19-3 at the half, and 33-3 after three quarters. They ended up winning 53-12. Frank McCrystal had his first Canadian championship.

The game was played in -10°C temperatures in front of 8,454 fans. Sitting in the crowd, wearing a winter coat, a toque and thick winter gloves, was Roger Aldag, smiling and holding his hand in the air, the Number One sign. Not far away sat Gord Currie, his face ruddy and healthy looking, smiling and enjoying the game. Mel Fiissel was there. Doug Killoh was there. The stands were filled with people who had played or coached or been executives with the Regina Rams over the years. Once a Ram, always a Ram. And this is what it was all about on that Saturday afternoon in Taylor Field in 1986.

Kevin Ostapowich and Brian Eltom

Two In A Row

1987

Now what?

The price of success can be heavy. But it comes with the territory. Once you win a championship, you're expected to keep right on winning. The Montreal Canadiens knew the feeling. Muhammad Ali knew the feeling. The Pittsburgh Steelers knew the feeling. Wayne Gretkzy knew the feeling. The Edmonton Eskimos know the feeling. The New York Yankees know the feeling. And the Regina Rams also know the feeling.

That sort of tradition caused a chain of events in every one of those organizations. It starts at the top, where some of brightest minds in the business world want to attach themselves to the team, want to contribute to it. It is good for the community, and some of the business people enjoy the attention that comes with being president or a member of the executive. It can get to be an ego thing, but mostly it's not. Mostly, they are individuals who want to improve the community they're in and find their niche. There is more. Successful teams with rich traditions have no difficulty in attracting the best coaches around. And since the Rams were reborn in 1965, that's exactly what they've had – the best coaches around. And, of course, if you are a winner, then players want to play for you, and so the best of the crop of graduating high schoolers flock to the Rams every year. It becomes an endless circle of success. They come as winners, to winners, and they want to leave as winners.

CFL all-star and Hall of Famer Roger Aldag remembers well that Rams' tradition. "The Rams were always money in the bank when I played with the Riders," said Aldag, now a Regina Beach resident, and a golfer. "We would always bet the Saskatoon guys on the team, whenever the Rams would play the Hilltops. Easy money. What I remember most about the Rams is the tradition of winning. In the four years that I did play, we won two Little Grey Cups and were in the final three of my four years. The tradition of winning was really exciting. It just seemed like a guy was expected to win all the time. We had a great winning tradition that we took with us to the Roughriders." Obviously, for much of Roger's career with the Riders, there weren't enough Rams on the roster.

So, when the Rams went to training camp in 1987, it was obvious what the challenge ahead was. To get to the Canadian championship. And win it. Nothing else would suffice.

Frank McCrystal was confident right from the start that the Rams could win a second straight title. They had finished 1986 with a blistering 53-12 victory over the Ottawa Sooners in the Canadian championship. While they did lose some players to graduation, they had such a stock of returning veterans that the shelf life for this team looked good.

Of course, leading the veterans was quarterback Dean Picton, entering his fourth year, and easily the best quarterback in Canadian junior football. This incredibly nice young man, who usually let his play do his talking, had already filled his trophy case with awards his first three years. He was on a Canadian championship team, was the Canadian junior football player of the year, the Prairie Junior Football Conference MVP, and the league's all-star quarterback, all in 1986. He was named the Rams' MVP in 1985 and 1986. This guy could play, as they say. He was the Tiger Woods of his era.

The Rams had 35 players returning, including running backs Rich Sutcliffe, offensive lineman Tim Relke, kicker Mike Lazecki and defensive lineman extraordinaire Dave Gebert, who was coming off torn knee ligaments that had

Dave Gebert

Mike Lazecki

resulted in his missing most of 1986. Relke, Sutcliffe and Lazecki also attended the Roughriders' training camp before heading back to the Rams. The popular Lazecki, a guy who never seemed to stop being a kid, and who always wore a toothpaste commercial grin, had the strength of leg that would give him a chance at a pro career. In the 1986 Canadian final, he had boomed one punt 81 yards and kicked a 52-yard field goal with a frozen football. I am not sure many CFL kickers ever had an 81-yard punt.

The Rams had lost two of their top receivers from the previous year – Tim Hammond and Phil Hulet, both of whom had graduated. But the Rams never skipped a beat, they still had veterans like Dan Johnston and Doug Dorsch and a slew of others.

There has been much made of the passing of the torch from player to player, from coach to coach, from season to season. But in the background, keeping the organization strong and also growing, was the ever-changing guard that was the Rams' executive. I called it guard because that was precisely what every Rams' executive member was doing – guarding the tradition and the expectations of the organization.

The 1988 addition to the Rams' clubhouse saw the new era of Rams' executives move into place. The Rams came to build their $150,000 addition to the clubhouse in typical Rams' fashion – get it done for nothing, if possible, but as cheaply as possible if that wasn't, ah, possible.

They got Regina architect Bob Ellard to design it. They went out and brought in donations from business and community. But the key might well have been a voice from their past. Mel Fiissel, a former Rams' player, assistant coach, head coach and member of the executive, owned a company called Alsort Construction. He counted former Rams among those he employed, such as his brother Ken and Gary Wilson, a tough-as-steel defensive back. Alsort oversaw the construction of the clubhouse in a spirit of volunteering its time and labour. One more time, former Regina Rams had stepped to the plate because they believed in this organization and knew, first hand, what it could do for young players. The Rams were simply building on Scotty Livingstone's dream.

The Rams continued to progress in giant steps in this new era. A year after the clubhouse addition went up, they moved toward starting up an educational scholarship program. They wanted their players to attain an education at the post-secondary level, and they were more than willing to provide the road map and the money. The Rams were never just about football. They were always about contributing to the development of young people who would, in their lives, contribute to the place in which they lived. It was the Rams' way.

Okay, so now what? Well, in order to establish such an educational program, a fund first had to be built up. The Rams' executive hit the street running. And begging. Said former Rams' president Paul Barnby, "Since its inception in 1989, the scholarship program has distributed more than $400,000 to eligible players. The scholarship program also laid the foundation for the Rams to eventually join the university of Regina."

But, there was still some football to be played as all of this was going on.

The Rams opened the season with three straight victories over some of the lesser powers in the league. In their second game, against the Calgary Colts, they had a 35-22 win, McCrystal clearly was on edge. He felt his players were not playing tough enough football. If there wasn't blood on the green carpet, McCrystal was not likely to be happy. "I think we're hesitating, not going completely full out on our hits," he growled. "This is a violent game and my football team will play with violence. That's the way it is. That's the way I was coached, that's the way I played, that's the way I coach and that's the way this football team is going to play. We are not quite doing that yet."

The Rams' first real test game came in the fourth game of the season, when they played their rivals from the north, the equally undefeated Hilltops, for the first time. That game turned into a thriller. And just as they had done the year before, the Hilltops hung the Rams' only loss of the season on them. It was a 35-32 hair-lifter for the Hilltops, on the strength of a last-play 42-yard field goal by Rick Barrack.

Both coaches thrived on the caliber of play when these two teams played each other.

"We really do make each other the best in the nation," said Hilltops' coach Kevin Scott. "If we played in two separate leagues, I don't think we'd be as good as we are."

McCrystal agreed. "I'd like to play a team like them eight times during the season. We beat the Huskies 75-0 last year and it wasn't a lot of fun for them or for us."

McCrystal was asked what effect the loss might have on his team. He shrugged. "Winning or losing was no big deal. We'll see who's playing in the snow."

The Rams continued winning, finishing with a 6-2 record and in second place in the standings. The Hilltops beat them one more time, in the last meeting of the schedule, again by a close score. The Rams had taken a 38-36 lead after Picton engineered a brilliant downfield drive that produced the go-ahead touchdown with 1:08 to go in the fourth quarter. But as had been the case all night, the defence couldn't hold and once again Rick Barrack kicked the game-winning field goal, this time from 25 yards out. The final score was 39-38. Picton had an outstanding game. He completed 17 of 30 passes for 431 yards – just six yards short of his Canadian Junior Football League record for most yards passing in a game.

Still, despite the two losses to the Hilltops, the Rams didn't necessarily regard their performance in the regular schedule as a disaster. They were confident they could turn it around for the playoffs, and the season had produced a lot of successes.

One of the reasons they had so many successes was the play of their defensive backfield. The Rams had lost all but one of their defensive backs, Lance Lascue, to graduation. Led by second-year player Blaine Pearce, who was a back-up quarterback in 1986, but was moved to the defence in 1987, the Rams' backfield of rookies Dean Mihalicz, Blaine Coupal and Cliff Rusconi had more than held their own. Another rarity was that a rookie had started at linebacker. That was Roger Reinson, who was so good right off the bat that the Rams had to play him. "It usually takes a player two or three years before he's ready to start," said McCrystal. "But Roger is ready and he's playing now."

"I don't think of myself as a rookie," said Reinson. "If you think of yourself as a rookie, you'll play like a rookie. I think I fit in. I'm a Ram." The linebackers always received special attention from McCrystal, who, of course, had played as a linebacker. "When we're practicing," said Reinson, "and you see him walking over here, you say, 'Here we go again we're going to do some heavy practicing.' I like his attitude. He's a no-nonsense guy and he wants to kick teams. Defensively, he wants us to punish teams and I love that. That's the way the game's supposed to be played."

The way the game is supposed to be played.

The Rams went into the playoffs as huge favourites over the Edmonton Wildcats in the semifinal. But you would never have known it at the beginning of the game in Regina. The Wildcats scored 14 points in the first four and one-half minutes of the first quarter. It served as a wakeup call for the Rams. Before the first half was done, the Rams had taken a 22-15 lead and were on their way to a 41-15 victory.

The Rams' offence, while not overwhelming, was steady and proficient. Running back Sam Khuber carried the ball 23 times and gained 92 yards. He also scored a pair of touchdowns. Picton, who completed nine passes for 185 yards and threw touchdown passes to Al Hendren and Doug Dorsch, also ran the ball himself – nine times for 53 yards.

But the difference in this game was the Rams' defence, just as it had been the week before in the loss to Saskatoon. They shut down the Wildcats completely in the second half, with Tim Burnie, Ryan Hall and Glen Sawa each intercepting a pass in the third quarter.

"McCrystal put in a rugged, crazy style of defence that the Rams played two or three years ago," said Bernie. "We just played a wild and crazy defence, blitzed them and they couldn't stop us."

The Rams geared up for the PJFC championship game against the Hilltops in Saskatoon. It would be the fourth straight year, and the seventh time since the formation of the PJFC in 1976, that the Rams and Hilltops had met in the final.

"Death to the Hilltops. I hate them with a passion," is how Rams' defensive back Cliff Rusconi summed up his feelings about playing the Hilltops.

The Hilltops went into the game as favourites, mostly because of their two, one-point wins over the Rams during the season. It didn't bother the Rams. "All that meant was they got first place," said Picton.

During the week leading up to the game, McCrystal went to veteran running back Rich Sutcliffe. This was Sutcliffe's last year, he would graduate after five seasons with the Rams. Talented, Sutcliffe's career had been dogged by injuries. He had been scratched from the semifinal because the Rams weren't sure he had recovered from a shoulder injury. Sutcliffe wondered if he would ever get to play again. This was his last year. He did not want it to end on the bench. Just a few days before the game in Saskatoon, McCrystal went to see him.

Rich Sutcliffe, Ken Neiszner, Dwayne Lamontagne.

"Rich," McCrystal said, "We're going to start you. You're one of the guys who has to do things for this team to win."

Sutcliffe had one of those rare games. Going against a Hilltops' defence that was as tough against the run as anybody in the league, even tougher, Sutcliffe was given the ball 21 times and gained 187 yards in just three quarters of play. That performance, combined with a solid effort from the Rams' defence, took Regina to a 34-18 victory before 3,000 fans at Gordie Howe Bowl.

The Hilltops had made a defensive move for the game, one which would come back to haunt them. They had moved all-Canadian linebacker Dale Solie to safety. Coach Kevin Scott wanted to stop the Rams' passing attack, which it did, Picton passing for just 80 yards. But it opened the Regina running game, and in case anybody out there thought the Rams could no longer run the ball, they found out differently. The Rams rushed for 317 yards, won the game, controlled the ball, and it was just another day at the office.

The Rams trailed only after the first quarter in that game, 3-0 at the end of the first. They scored 14 unanswered points in the second quarter and another 13 in the third to take a 34-3 lead with them into the fourth.

Dan Johnston

Dan Johnston had a big day, carrying the ball nine times for 44 yards and scoring three touchdowns.

McCrystal was about as happy as he could be over the play of his defence, a part of his team that he still felt was not playing to its potential. "They're playing 100 times better than they played during the course of the season," he said, patting them on the back. Then, he spanked them. The Slick One giveth and the Slick One taketh. "They still, in some sense, lack the killer instinct. We've got to not allow teams to drive the ball on us. There were times in the third quarter when they allowed Saskatoon to put together a few first downs. We can't let that happen. We're going all the way to our Super Bowl and we can't let that happen."

First, though, the Rams had to get past the Okanagan Sun, who had beaten the Richmond Raiders 18-17 in the B.C. final. The western final would be played in Regina. The Sun, who played out of Kelowna, were relatively new to junior football. But they knew all about the Rams, if only because when they had started up they had sought the Rams' advice on how to go about putting together a successful junior organization. The Rams would find out how fast they had learned.

Not fast enough. In a game in which the Rams physically beat the Sun into submission, putting seven players out with injuries, on what were clean hits, Regina won the western final in a breeze, 45-23.

It was a total victory. The Rams rushed for 201 yards and passed for 263. Sutcliffe again had a big game, running for 102 yards. Picton was deadly, completing 14 passes for 263 yards and three touchdowns. Johnston caught seven passes for 104 yards and a touchdown; Dorsch had three catches for 108 yards and two touchdowns.

Dean Picton

The Rams also got something out of a pair of rookies who found themselves playing in what was the biggest game of the season. Rod Flahr, a wide receiver, was used on punt returns. He brought 10 of them back 126 yards and also caught a pair of passes from Picton. Brent Barkman, a rookie running back, briefly got into the game as the Rams stuck with their program of giving rookies as much playing time as they could, because the payoff would come down the road. Barkman only ran the ball once, but he dazzled everybody with a 45-yard jaunt.

When the game was over, McCrystal sat in a chair in the Rams' clubhouse with a beer in one hand and a cigarillo in the other and a look on his face that suggested somebody had just stolen his car.

"We didn't play as well as we should have," he said. "This organization is so geared to winning and winning national championships. It is so intense about it that often anything less is viewed as a failure. We've come away from a Western Canadian championship, winning 45-23, and I'm not celebrating. Name another organization that would be like that."

The national final would be played in Regina. The Rams' opponents would be the St. Vital Mustangs from Winnipeg. It would be their first trip to the Big Show of junior football.

As he tended to do, McCrystal grew more and more philosophical about the Rams as the game drew closer. He talked about what drove the organization and each year's team.

"In 1975, we had lost two games to the Saskatoon Hilltops," he said. "And Gord Currie, in one of the few times I heard him being upset, said 'Losing is not acceptable to the Regina Rams.' And it still isn't. There are a lot of ghosts out here and, as a result, the tradition is such that when you come out here you have to make the commitment to win. You almost feel like there's someone looking over your shoulder. You walk down the hallway and have the line of pictures of all the previous teams. Last year, we lost to the Hilltops and I took all the pictures of all the Canadian championship teams and threw them down on the field and asked the players, 'What have you guys done? These guys are champions. What are you?' We never looked back after that. The essence of our being out here is to win."

The St. Vital Mustangs were a huge team, by any standards. There were linemen on both sides of the ball who were in the 300-pound range. They were coached by Rod Outhwaite, who had played on the Rams' offensive line in 1974 and 1975.

On the eve of the game, McCrystal started to get a little worried. He knew all about the Mustangs' size and who their best players were. He knew what to expect from them offensively and defensively. But the night before the game, at a league banquet with both teams in attendance, Frank saw something and felt something that made him instantly respect what the Rams would be up against.

"They (St. Vital) were very well-behaved and respectful at the banquet. They didn't hot dog it. They didn't try to stare us down or intimidate us. They were just very well behaved, and I respected that. It told me they were a good organization with standards and that they had character. That worried me because teams that have that are the toughest teams to beat," said McCrystal.

The Rams felt that it would be important to get the jump on the Mustangs. They thought that St. Vital would have a big case of nerves because this was their first Canadian championship and it was being played in Regina's backyard. The Mustangs had also never played on artificial turf.

The Rams got off to a jump start. They were ahead 15-1 after the first quarter and 26-8 at the half. But as McCrystal had suspected, the Mustangs had heart, and they clawed their way back in the second half. Two minutes into the fourth the Rams' lead was only five points, 28-23. That was as close as the Mustangs came. The Rams had been forced to go to the well and come out with their best effort of the season. That's what they did. That's why they are the Regina Rams. They ended up winning 31-23 before 7,492 fans in Taylor Field. It was the Rams' 10th Canadian championship. A new chapter had been added to the Rams' tradition. It also marked the first time since the Rams had done it last, which was in 1980 and 1981, that a team had won back-to-back Canadian championships.

Sutcliffe was named the game's outstanding player, rushing for 201 yards on 25 carries. Picton completed 14 passes for 184 yards.

For nine members of the Rams, this was the saddest and happiest of days. It was their last game and they were graduating. But they went out as champions. Included in the list of Rams' graduates in 1987 were Mike Lazecki, Rich Sutcliffe, Jamie Anderson, Tim Burnie, Dave Gebert, Tim Relke, Cliff Rusconi, Rob Sillinger and Al Hendren. What memories they took with them of their time with the Regina Rams.

Rich Sutcliffe

Their pictures would be up on the walls to remind those who were coming after them of what was expected.

THOSE DAGNABIT HILLTOPS

1988

By 1988, Frank McCrystal was entering his fifth year as head coach of the Regina Rams. In his first four years as head coach, the Rams had three Prairie Junior Football Conference championships, two Canadian championships and a winning percentage of .891, with a 41-5 won-lost record. The Rams had just won their second straight Canadian championship. Frank and his wife, Wendy, had a young family, a son, Charlie, and a newborn daughter, Hailey. Life was good.

When McCrystal came to training camp in 1988, graduation had stung the Rams. But they still had some key ingredients left that would allow them to take a serious run at a third straight national championship. "We'd be kidding people if we didn't say we're looking for three championships in a row," said McCrystal on the eve of training camp, where over 100 players would show up dreaming of playing for the Regina Rams. "We feel it's a valid and attainable goal."

The team would again sink or swim on two things. One, of course, was quarterback Dean Picton, whose career with the Rams was one of the most noteworthy of any Ram in any era. Picton had set passing records all over the place. He was twice the PJFC player of the year. Once, he was named the outstanding player in the country. Quiet and unassuming, much of the load would again fall on his sloped shoulders.

The Rams were in good shape offensively. Wendall Toth was back, healthier than ever. Sam Khuber would now get the chance to step out of Rich Sutcliffe's shadow. Receivers Doug Dorsch and Dan Johnston were also back. The offensive line was grounded by veterans Sinisa Stefanovic, Darrell Harle, Ken Neiszner, Steve Tunison, Jim Wenzel and Steve Bryce.

Defensively, the Rams were solid. Greg Karpa and Bill Keith would anchor the three-man front. Glen Sawa, Dave Rezansoff and Roger Reinson would be tough as linebackers, and the backfield of Lance Lascue, Dean Mihalicz, Jeff Kallichuk, Rob Nistor and Ryan Hall was more than capable.

With the season set to start, McCrystal was oozing confidence. "I don't know about the other teams out there," he said, "but I know we're going to be good." As usual, the Rams' stiffest competition was expected to come from the Hilltops. But nobody knew for sure what to expect out of them. In a bizarre move, the Hilltops had fired head coach Kevin Scott, who had taken the team to a first-place finish, only to lose in the final to the Rams the year before.

The Rams opened the season in Edmonton against the Huskies. It was their first game. The Rams rarely played any exhibition games and, as a result, were usually a little rusty come the opener.

They were rusty, sort of. Picton picked up where he left off, completing 18 of 30 passes for 164 yards. The Rams beat the Huskies 30-14. Picton threw two touchdowns to wide receiver Brent Barkman and one to tight end Dwayne Lamontagne. Khuber rushed for 119 yards on 18 carries. McCrystal even used the game to get backup quarterback Randy Zbytnuik some playing time. Zbytnuik was the son of the former Rams' coach – he played most of the fourth quarter.

As the Rams prepared for their second game of the season, against the Edmonton Wildcats in Taylor Field, McCrystal declared that he thought this team could be the best one ever. "There is not one area of this team that I can point to as being a weakness," he said. "This team should win a Canadian championship."

The Rams looked the part against the Wildcats. They scored touchdowns on their first four possessions, and that was the end to the story. They won 41-10. Picton completed 10 passes for 185 yards, didn't give up an interception, and fired four touchdown tosses – twice to Dan Johnston, once to Lamontagne and once to Dorsch. Khuber was again the Rams' leading rusher with 97 yards on 16 carries.

The Rams' defence was nothing short of superlative. Even McCrystal couldn't say enough about them. "That's as tough as we've played defensively in my five years as head coach here."

Edmonton coach Bob Dolman, who had played high-school football for Gord Currie at Balfour, said he didn't even want to watch the video tape of the game. "The pressure of the Rams' tradition is so great, it's like a steam-roller – it gives them a big edge to begin with."

The Rams looked forward to their next game, against the undefeated Calgary Colts. McCrystal welcomed the challenge the Colts would give his Rams in this battle of the undefeated. "There are times when you play games you know you will win and it is boring and not good football for anybody," he said. "I'm glad the Colts are undefeated. I know they are good. I want them to be great. I want our guys to be challenged."

The Rams discovered something about themselves. They found a new weapon in their already formidable offence – the deep pass. Picton threw touchdown passes of 36, 43 and 50 yards as the Rams stopped the Colts 38-20. Dorsch caught two of them and Johnston caught one.

"That's the first time all season we've completed long passes," Picton said. "Usually, they're 20 to 25 yards and it's harder to win like that. Those three long passes are important because it makes the defence change and it makes those short passes a lot easier. It instills fear in the defensive backs and they always think they don't want to get beat deep."

The Rams went into the game with Khuber, who was a late scratch with a hamstring injury. To make matters worse, his backup, Kollin Erichsen was out with a shoulder injury. The Rams went with two rookies, Mark Pachiorka and Chris Curran. But, in the end, the Rams didn't need the running game, the passing game worked on all cylinders.

"We've taken the first step to becoming a championship team," said McCrystal, alluding to the fact that the Colts were undefeated. "We needed adversity to make us stronger."

Dean Picton

Adversity of another kind was on its way. With a 3-0 record in their back pocket, the Rams boarded the iron lung and chugged on up to Saskatoon to take on the Hilltops, who were 2-1 under new coach Dave Hardy.

Hardy, a rookie coach, was trying to convince people that there was nothing special about games with the Rams, that he was treating it as just another game, no more or less important than any other. Hardy said he wasn't going to get caught up in the rivalry.

"He can't help it," offered McCrystal. "I've been tempted at times to negate the fact there is a rivalry and found we got caught not preparing our people. There's no way you can be a member of the Regina Rams or Saskatoon Hilltops and ignore the fact there is a rivalry."

Picton let everybody in Saskatoon know that this was one game that got his juices going. He laid a one-man licking on the Hilltops' defence, completing 23 of 34 passes for 466 yards and five touchdowns. Dorsch caught 10 passes for 221 yards, including a 75-yarder for a touchdown. Johnston caught six passes for 124 yards, and three of them went for touchdowns.

"I just want to prove myself each and every game so no one thinks I am a fluke," said Picton after it was over and the Rams had won 53-34. "I don't want to be a flash in the pan."

Some flash. The Rams did not lose a game throughout the regular schedule in 1988. Picton won his second Canadian player of the year award, made the all-star team and led in passing.

Included in the undefeated season was the 62-17 demolition of the Edmonton Huskies, which did not leave McCrystal happy.

"If we wanted to, we could have scored 100 points on these guys," he said. "We can't get better by playing one quarter or taking people out. We can't allow ourselves to step down to their level. If they want to play with us, it's their responsibility to realize our level of football doesn't work the other way. If you do not come prepared mentally, physically and technically, we make no excuses for the outcome."

The Rams hit the playoffs with first-place secured and an 8-0 record in the bank.

Picton had had another incredible season throwing the ball. He had completed 141 of 243 passes for 2,445 yards and 30 touchdowns. Johnston caught 46 passes for 835 yards and 14 touchdowns, and Dorsch had caught 44 passes, scoring 10 touchdowns off them. Not bad. They opened the playoffs at home against the Edmonton Wildcats. The Wildcats did give the Rams a game before falling 23-15. The Rams were never particularly safe in this game and, in fact, were outscored 10-7 in the fourth quarter, which is usually when they were just licking up the crumbs. But Picton did get his passing game going so that the Wildcats could not complete their comeback. His 12 completions went for 310 yards. Khuber was the Rams' main ground gainer with 109 yards on 20 carries.

Once again, the Rams met the Hilltops in the league final. The game was played in Taylor Field.

In an absolute shocker, the Rams' goal of winning three straight Canadian championships ground to a halt. It was as if they had sped around a corner and run smack into a wall. Splat! The season had ended.

The Hilltops marched into Taylor Field and laid a 36-34 loss on the Rams. Their season was over.

That was another one of those statistics are for losers scenarios. The Rams had well over 600 yards in total offence. Picton passed for 334 yards on 24 completions in 35 tries. Johnston caught 12 passes from his old Central Collegiate high-school chum. Dorsch hauled in seven passes. The Rams rushed for 301 yards, with Erichsen getting 215. Enough to win with? Of course. But the Rams' defence could not control the Hilltops' offence, which totaled 462 yards, 339 of it coming along the ground.

Kollin Erichsen

"Football is a special sport," said McCrystal, as his dreams of three straight lay in ruins all around him. "In anything else, it's a best-of-seven or a best-of-three, or a two-game, total-points. Here, it's sudden death. You go through an entire season at any level from peewee to the NFL and you'll find that teams that should win don't always win."

There was little doubt that McCrystal would be back as head coach in 1989.

Brian Eltom

"I'm not going to go out like that," he said. "It might have been easier to leave if we had won three in a row. Our coaching staff talked about next year. We said that we blew it; we weren't hungry; we didn't want it; we played poorly on defence."

Whatever, the Rams were no longer the kingpins of Canadian junior football. And to make things even a little more pressing, their list of graduating players would gut the offence. Playing their last games as juniors were Picton, Johnston and Dorsch, running backs Wendell Toth and Sam Khuber, and linemen Brian Eltom, Darrell Harle and Ken Neiszner. The only defensive player to graduate was back Lance Lascue.

Those were the holes that would have to be filled if the Rams were to get themselves back in championship mode. McCrystal and his coaching staff, Bernie Schmidt, Doug Zimmerman, Jerry Orban, Ray Pitre, Rick Seaman and Campbell Hackney were not dealing with a full deck, just yet. They had a lot of work to do in the off-season, and the rest of the Prairie Junior Football Conference could hardly wait. You could hear the smacking of lips before winter had even taken hold.

Were the mighty Rams dead?

CORRALLED BY THE COLTS

1989

There are expectations and there are expectations. The realistic ones you can deal with. The unrealistic ones can drive you to despair. "If we don't win the national championship, our season is a failure," stated Frank McCrystal, the Rams' head coach and chief philosopher. "It's a pretty high target that every player here is given, but there is no other way I would rather have it."

As the Rams headed into the 1989 season, they were dogged by that tradition and its demands. It was something McCrystal relished. He said, "That is what it is all about." But the optimism that had accompanied the 1988 season wasn't quite as bright in 1989. The biggest task on McCrystal's table was to replace Dean Picton at quarterback. The guy who got the job was Blaine Pearce, a two-year defensive back starter with the Rams. Pearce, entering his fourth year with the Rams in 1989, was backed up by second-year player Randy Zbytnuik.

"Anybody who is the next quarterback after a guy like Dean Picton will feel some pressure," said Pearce. "But there's more immediate pressures that I have to deal with, like preparing for the season and performing well."

What had happened to the Rams in 1988 had left a bad taste in McCrystal's mouth. "The best word we can use to describe last season is bitter," he said. "We were the best team in Canada. Some people might not like to hear it, but I think in their hearts they know it is true."

With Pearce installed as the starting quarterback for the start of the season, the Rams went about replacing receivers and running backs who had graduated, taking with them one of the deadliest offences in junior football.

It wouldn't be easy. But the Rams always seemed ready to handle challenges like that, and they usually succeeded.

They figured they had two dependable wide receivers ready to step into starting roles in third-year Ram Rod Flahr, who had caught 20 passes in 1988, and lanky rookie Brad Bork, whom the Rams felt would develop into a star.

Blaine Pearce

The running backs were Greg Fiddler and Kollin Erichsen, and the offensive line was anchored by centre Sinisa Stefanovic and guard Steve Tunison.

The big change on defence was linebacker Roger Reinson shifting to Pearce's rover position. Reinson's biggest challenge would be to learn how to defend against the pass. "He's still got to work on his pass defence," said McCrystal. "But if there's a choice between going after the ball or the receiver, he'll go after the receiver. That's my kind of player." Reinson's attitude was best expressed by Reinson. "If we ever come up against a team that wanted to pass across the middle all day, I'd be drooling," he said. "They'd have to haul me off in a straight jacket."

The Rams had linebacker Kelly Trithart back after some time with the Roughriders, and had high hopes at linebacker for rookie Aaron Runge. Cornerbacks Ryan Hall and Steve Klein solidified the defensive backfield.

"Other teams might think we'll be a little weaker this year after losing guys like Picton, Johnston and Dorsch," offensive backfield coach Ray Pitre said. "That would be poor coaching on their part. They know the Rams have a strong team every year."

The Regina Rams hadn't lost the opening game of the season since 1980. And they weren't about to let it happen in 1989. They didn't.

With Erichsen rushing for 212 yards on 29 carries, behind some superb blocking from the offensive line, the Rams rolled over the Edmonton Huskies 37-14 to get the season off to a winning start. Pearce's first game as a starter was sufficient to allow the Rams to be comfortable. While most of the yardage came on the ground, Pearce did complete seven passes, for 102 yards. He also gave up a pair of interceptions.

"Physically, we dominated them," said McCrystal. "The offensive line was simply outstanding. Outside of 12 minutes or so, we controlled the game."

While most were expecting the 1989 season to turn into a playoff showdown between the Rams and the Hilltops, there were rumbles coming out of Alberta that the Calgary Colts were major contenders, and could seriously challenge both Saskatchewan teams.

The Rams got a taste of what the Colts had to offer in their second game of the season. Whatever it was, it wasn't enough to counter what Rams' running back Kollin Erichsen threw at them.

Kollin Erichsen

"It was one of the really great performances in Ram history," is how McCrystal described it. "I don't know if I've ever seen anyone play any better. And I've been here a long time."

Erichsen, in his first full season as a starter, was practically the whole story in the Rams' 25-10 win over the Colts. He rushed for 269 yards in 29 carries, caught two passes for 86 yards, and scored all three Regina touchdowns.

The Rams ended up with 569 yards in offence. But their happiness was short-lived.

For the first time since McCrystal had become head coach of the Rams in 1984, an Alberta team beat Regina. The Edmonton Wildcats, who had taken some serious beatings at the hands of the Rams over the years, beat the Rams 14-8, in Edmonton, in the third game of the season.

"Within this team, we have to work out some attitude situations," said McCrystal. "We had guys missing the bus and others who just weren't prepared to play." Erichsen, the hero of the Rams' second game of the season, gained only 51 yards on 21 carries against the Wildcats. The Wildcats stopped the Rams' ground game by lining up as many as eight defensive players on the line of scrimmage. The Rams' passing attack was unable to take advantage of the obvious shortage of players in pass coverage. Pearce completed 11 of 26 passes for 178 yards. The Rams' offensive totals were terrible. They managed only nine first downs, 70 yards rushing and 184 passing. Not only that, but the Rams lost safety Roger Reinson for six weeks with torn knee ligaments. He would be replaced by rookie Sheldon Thomas.

One guy who wasn't happy that the Rams had lost was the Saskatoon coach, Dave Hardy. His Hilltops would be playing the Rams next. "I would rather have seen them win 55-0," Hardy laughed. "They won't be in a good mood. They won't be fat this weekend, that's for sure."

McCrystal agreed. McCrystal always had a certain degree of cockiness, wherever he coached or played. It was more a matter of speaking what he believed than thinking he was perfect. It rubbed some people the wrong way over the years. But his record speaks for itself.

For instance, leading up to the Hilltops' game, this was what Frank had to say. "The only way to describe the

Regina Rams after the game in Edmonton is we're embarrassed. We're ashamed of our performance. I wouldn't want to be in the Hilltops' shoes this weekend."

If there was any place where the Hilltops had a definite edge over the Rams, it was at quarterback. Now that Dean Picton had left the game, Hilltops' quarterback Shane Reider was regarded as the best quarterback in the PJFC. "He's an amazing kid," Hardy said. "You don't think of him as a great passer. He looks brittle and fragile and not very athletic. He just gets the job done." McCrystal also had respect for Reider. "He's a winner, and those guys are always dangerous." On the eve of the game, the Hilltops announced Reider would not be dressing for the game, having injured a knee the week before.

The Rams won the game, 31-29, but it was remembered more for the moment a Rams' third-down gamble almost backfired and gave the Hilltops an opening to tie. With less than three minutes to go, the Rams were leading 31-23, and facing a third down and two yards to go decision. McCrystal decided to gamble. The play was stuffed, the Hilltops took over and scored to make it 31-29. The victory was saved when Regina defensive back Jeff Kallichuk batted away a pass on an attempted two-point convert.

Blaine Pearce

"I'm really upset with myself," McCrystal said. "We shouldn't have used that play. But as far as gambling, when I came here as head coach, I said we'd play aggressive ball, that we'd try to drive it down the opposition's throat. I guess it's the old adage of more courage than brains."

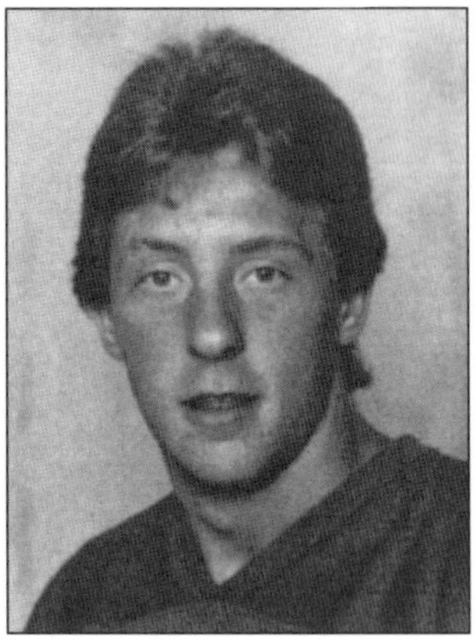

Brent Ripplinger

That game was one where the Rams' rookies came through. Punt returner Brent Ripplinger watched a punt sail over his head, scrambled to pick it up, then scooted 45 yards to the Saskatoon 32. From there, rookie receiver Bork caught a touchdown pass. Bork ended up catching five passes for 89 yards. Ripplinger, who McCrystal called, "one of the best rookies to ever play for the Rams," supplied 134 yards of total offence.

Pearce had his best game passing the ball. He completed 14 passes for 171 yards and didn't give up an interception. He also ran for two touchdowns on gains of one yard and 17 yards. Rams' kicker Darcy Smycniuk had two field goals.

The Rams came out flat a week later. They looked sloppy from start to finish, but they still managed to beat the Edmonton Huskies 21-10.

Pearce spent the game getting knocked down by the Huskies' defence. "He took a big-time beating," said McCrystal. At one point, Pearce threw nine straight pass incompletions. The Huskies tried to hit him every time he threw the ball and they pretty well succeeded.

If there was a bright lining in this dark cloud, it was that the Rams had won a game they probably should have lost.

The Rams got a week off from the Prairie Junior Football Conference. But they didn't get a week off from playing a football game.

The Rams have always looked for ways to enhance not only their own image, but also that of Canadian amateur football. Witness their exhibition game with the University of Alberta Golden Bears, which the Rams won.

Now, they had arranged to play a football team from Europe, in Taylor Field, in what was billed as the Euro-Can

Bowl. The Cologne Red Barons, the defending champions of the West German American Football League, arrived in Regina the week before the game to get themselves used to Taylor Field's artificial turf, and to playing the game under Canadian rules. In Germany, they had played American rules. The team was made up in large part of American soldiers based in Germany. The Red Barons had only two coaches, one of whom was quarterback Mel Crandall, who was also the head coach.

The Rams had hoped for a big crowd, about 10,000 fans. That would have given them sufficient profit from the game to enable them to return to Europe for a rematch a year later. But only about 3,000 fans turned out. The Rams won 54-7; the Red Barons were having a lot of trouble trying to adjust to the different rules.

Still, just the fact that a game like that had been played was looked upon as boosting the game in both Canada and in Europe.

The Rams ran their PJFC record to 5-1 a week later by going into Calgary and sticking a 55-28 beating on the Colts. The Rams' offence hit full stride for the first time that season. With Pearce mixing things up well, the Rams totaled 621 yards in offence – 399 rushing and 222 passing. Erichsen gained 178 yards on 26 carries, which took him to 1,000 yards on the season. Pearce completed 14 passes for 180 yards and two touchdowns – to Bork and Ripplinger.

"We were hopeful that, by game six, our offence would start to connect," McCrystal said. "Our offence took a step forward. We accomplished all that we wanted to do at this time of the season."

Rolling right along, the Rams' offence continued to fire real bullets as they went after the Edmonton Wildcats, remembering well that it was the Wildcats who had beaten them a few weeks earlier. The Rams clinched first place in the PJFC with a 48-36 victory, in a game that left McCrystal less than overjoyed with the play of his defence. "We can't win championships playing defence like this," McCrystal said.

The Rams closed out the season with a loss to the Hilltops. The game meant nothing to the Rams. They already had first place nailed down. But something significant came from it. Kollin Erichsen, the running back who had come into the season needing to prove he could be a starter, rushed for 186 yards on 26 carries to get his name into the Canadian junior football record book. The 186 yards boosted his rushing total to 1,393 yards in 217 runs, which set a new Canadian junior single-season rushing record. Erichsen also broke the PJFC record of 1,239 yards held by former Ram Terry Cochrane.

With the Rams finishing first and the Hilltops second, everybody was sure that once the semifinals were out of the way, these two familiar rivals would see each other again in the PJFC final.

But, first, the Rams had to beat the Calgary Colts in the semifinal.

Even though the Rams had beaten the Colts twice over the regular schedule, the Colts were still a team that had some weapons. The biggest was running back Steve Thompson, who had finished second to Erichsen in the league rushing race. McCrystal felt that if the Rams could hold Thompson to around 100 yards in total, the Rams had a good chance of winning the game. The Rams did a good job on him in the first half, holding him to just 48 yards on nine carries. The Rams were ahead 23-16 at the half, but the game was a tossup. Regina had opened with 15 unanswered points in the first quarter, but were outscored 16-8 in the second. Thompson took over in the second half. He carried the ball 15 times and gained 194 yards as the Colts upset the Rams 38-33 in Taylor Field, one of the most stunning playoff losses in Rams' history. This marked the Rams' earliest exit from the playoffs since 1978.

"Thompson did it all by himself," Rams' defensive lineman Bill Keith said. "He's a one-man show."

The Rams had had defensive problems for much of the season. In the end, it killed them. For the second straight year they would be home and in bed long before the playoffs even got going.

The Colts went on to win the Canadian championship. The Rams went through another soul-searching off-season – they had again failed to win a Canadian championship.

Although the Rams' season had ended much earlier than they would have liked, they had a tremendous impact on the success of the 1989 Grey Cup Champion Saskatchewan Roughriders – no fewer than nine former Regina Rams were with the Riders in one capacity or another.

Former Rams who contributed to the Riders' 1989 Grey Cup Victory.
Back Row: Dr. Jack Alexander, Tom Shepherd, Roger Aldag, Norm Fong,
Rob Bresciani, Larry Mueller and Don McDougall
Front Row: Bob Poley, Bryan Illerbrun

Corralled Again

1990

If you want to know what pressure is, consider this. As the Regina Rams moved into a new decade, one question was being asked incessantly. It wouldn't go away. It was like a fly that buzzes your eardrums in the dark of night and you can't swat it. "What's wrong with the Rams?" That's what they kept getting. It was as if the Rams were locked in their worst losing streak ever. After all, they had not won a Canadian championship in two years. Go figure.

The pressure occurred because the Rams, like any other sports team, were not perfect. They were guaranteed nothing. When teams grow to be as successful as the Regina Rams, then the expectations to maintain that level of achievement are huge. And people tend to forget just how much planning, work, sacrifice, foresight, dedication and passion have to go into the mix to produce winner after winner after winner. One thing, though, is always certain. The Rams can virtually be assured they will be in the playoffs every year, and will usually finish in the top two. Anything less would be a genuine disaster. The Edmonton Wildcats would be deliriously happy with making the playoffs every year. The Edmonton Huskies would be overjoyed. But the Rams had different standards to live by. The Rams had different rivers to swim, different mountains to climb. The Regina Rams always sought the widest river and the highest mountain. They had to live what to others may well have been the impossible dream. They didn't always achieve it. But they never quit trying because they knew, the organization was sure enough of itself, there were championships out there that they could reach. "They never quit," that is what every Regina Rams' coach wanted to say when every season ended.

As the Rams entered the 1990 season, they were in a championship drought. And it would be prolonged for a few more years. It's not that they lost many games, it's just that they lost the wrong ones. Regardless of how good the teams were that they fielded, they would not be bringing home the Armadale Cup, the trophy that symbolized the Canadian championship, until 1993. But even through this drought, they never once lost focus of who they were and what was expected of them. When you are a Regina Ram, you cannot escape it. And who would want to? Who would want to play for a team that expected anything less than your best? It is a feeling that brings home the hurt that always envelops those who lose. Pride makes it more meaningful. There is never any shrugging off a premature season ending in the Rams' clubhouse. The walls, which display the team pictures of all those Rams' teams that won Canadian championships, won't let them forget. The walls beckon them to go the extra mile, and join the other championship teams in their immortality.

The Rams also paid a tribute to their past in 1990. They named their practice field the Scotty Livingstone Field, after the man many felt was the architect of all that the Rams had become and still are.

The Rams plunged into the 1990 season full of pith and vinegar. McCrystal was buying none of this "the 1989 season was a complete writeoff" stuff because the Rams didn't go the distance. "We were 6-2 in 1989," he said. "We had a great season. Yes, we would like to be Canadian champions, but if we fail in becoming Canadian champions, it doesn't mean we failed as a team." Frank was cleverly doing some damage control. He was not dismissing the 1989 season as a failure because there was no championship at the end of the rainbow. He was handing his players a pat on the back, letting them know that they had succeeded, and that now they were getting closer to taking the next step. In many ways, McCrystal was like Currie in that he knew how to motivate his players. It is a wonderful attribute for any coach to have. Slick was also quite adept at deflecting any criticism from the team and the players to himself.

The Rams had a veteran-laden team. On offence, running back Kollin Erichsen (1,393 yards, 13 touchdowns) was returning. Quarterback Blaine Pearce was looking forward to an even better season now that he had a year as starting quarterback under his belt. Pearce, who threw for 1,386 yards in 1989, was happy to have his two starting wide receivers returning – Rod Flahr and Brad Bork. The offensive line was anchored by veteran Sinisa Stefanovic, guard Tim Huber and tackle Tom MacCallum.

Sinisa Stefanovic

Safety Roger Reinson and linebacker Aaron Runge – aggressive, hard-hitting, smart players – brought everything McCrystal wanted to the defence. Rookie Dwayne Ell impressed the coaches enough that they planned on giving him some playing time on the defensive line to see if he was for real.

The Rams went on the road for their first game of the season, busing the nine hours up to Edmonton, and then busing it back after they had whipped the Huskies 34-6. There is a telling force at work here in that a Rams' victory is no big news. It is like a dog bites man headline in the newspaper. Nothing unusual about that. And after all, the Rams had won their season opener for 10 straight years.

McCrystal sluffed off the streak of opening victories. "I don't really put much stock in streaks and records," he

Aaron Runge

Roger Reinson

said. "When you start putting faith in that sort of stuff, you're just setting yourself up to get caught."

McCrystal figured the Rams would win the game for more compelling reasons. "We started preparing for this game and this season nine months ago. When we lost the semi-final in 1989, we started the next day making preparations for this season."

There were the usual mixups in the game, caused simply because this was the Rams' first game. "We're pretty happy with what we were able to do offensively," McCrystal said. "The overall defence was pretty good. They made some mistakes and our young defensive line needs to keep working. But I'd say we're better at this point than in 1989. There are a lot of good things we can build on."

The Rams didn't put any big numbers up on the statistics board, just numbers that suggested they were efficient and methodical when they had to be. Pearce completed nine passes for 153 yards; backup Randy Zbytnuik completed one; five different receivers each had two catches. Erichsen rushed for 78 yards on 18 carries. And the Rams only turned the ball over once.

The Rams came back to Regina happy with how they had played in Edmonton, and determined to make sure that this year their mindset was to improve every game out and to play with intensity, which is what McCrystal was demanding of them. They fired a 49-8 victory over the Edmonton Wildcats in the Rams' home opener at Taylor Field. The Rams put up 642 yards in offence – 290 on the ground and 352 in the air. Erichsen bolted for 114 yards on 15 carries in the two and one-half quarters he played. Pearce completed 11 passes for 290 yards and three touchdowns. Rams' offensive coordinator, Bernie Schmidt, was looking for a more balanced attack, and the Rams achieved it. They ran the ball 37 times and passed it 31 times.

The Rams' defence flattened Edmonton's offence with an unrelenting blitz that saw the Wildcats' quarterbacks get sacked 11 times. "Going after them is our game," said Rams' linebacker Jeff Kallichuk, who had four sacks himself. "We want to go out there and hit and defeat the offence. We want to hurt people. That's the philosophy of our defence."

The Rams received their toughest test when they went to Calgary to take on the defending Canadian champion Colts, the team that had eliminated Regina in the playoffs the year before. It looked as if the Colts had the Rams' number as

Jeff Kallichuk

they rolled to a 22-0 lead in the second quarter. But the Rams struggled back. Having received their wakeup call from the scoreboard, they went on to a 36-29 victory. The comeback was actually lightning fast. Down 22-0, with 12 minutes to go in the second quarter, the Rams had tied the game at 22-22 by halftime.

McCrystal and his brilliant offensive coordinator, Bernie Schmidt, immediately began preparing for their next game, against the Hilltops in Taylor Field. They figured that while they might well want to be more of a passing team, they could run the ball on the Hilltops. They knew they could. And they knew what the dividends would be. For one thing, the Hilltops would not expect the Rams to come at them on the ground. For another thing, if the Rams succeeded in running the ball, the passing game would open right up and all hell would break loose.

Sure enough, the Rams came out running. The Rams' first possession started at their own 29. Pearce called nine straight running plays and the ball moved steadily to the Hilltops' 27. By then, the Hilltops' defensive backs were snuggling closer and closer to the line. That's when the Rams struck, like a viper's tongue. Pearce faked a handoff, stepped back, and fired a pass to Brent Ripplinger, who was wide open and on his way to the end zone. The dye was cast. The game's map was laid out.

The Rams, controlling the football from start to finish, rocked and rolled to a 24-16 victory over the Hilltops to run their winning streak to four straight.

"We wanted to get them – Boom! Boom! – right off the bat," said Ripplinger, who had scored two touchdowns off passes. "We wanted to put them out of the game."

The Rams ran 73 offensive plays, the Hilltops 51. In the first quarter alone, the Rams had 26 plays to Saskatoon's seven. The ground game produced 284 yards by itself, which was 18 yards more than Saskatoon's total offence. Pearce completed eight passes for 103 yards and two touchdowns. He scored another touchdown himself. The amazing Kollin Erichsen had 123 yards on 21 carries, and played only half the game. He was thrown out for trying to kick a Hilltops' player who had grabbed his knee and was twisting it. Nice, that. But it gave Chris Curran a chance to play, and play he did. He gained 73 yards on 14 carries.

The Rams' defence was there, too, sacking Hilltops' quarterback Brent Schneider three times and keeping him under steady pressure from start to finish. "The defence was getting off the ball quickly and we were well prepared," said rush end Sonny Faugno, who had two sacks.

Hilltops' head coach Dave Hardy pretty well summed up what happened when he said, "We wanted to run the ball in the first half. But it's pretty tough when you don't have the ball very much."

The Rams just kept winning after that. Their biggest victory saw them run their undefeated streak to 7-0 when they clobbered the Calgary Colts 33-8. Erichsen was again there, rushing for 217 yards on 29 carries. He had to take on tough Calgary linebacker Cooper Harris, the son of CFL Hall of Famer linebacker Wayne Harris, who had established himself as perhaps the best middle linebacker in CFL history during his storied career with the Calgary Stampeders.

The Rams ended the schedule by losing 27-22 to the Hilltops in Saskatoon in a game that didn't affect where the Rams would finish. The talented Ian Hamilton of the *Leader-Post* wrote: "Even in defeat, Frank McCrystal spoke of victory."

In his usual fashion, McCrystal was getting worked up for the playoffs. "One thing I learned from a 27-22 loss in Saskatoon is we're the best football team in the conference. We're going to win this conference and we're going to win the Canadian championship."

The Rams were off and . . . whoops!

The Calgary Colts came into Regina, still the Canadian champions, and in a shocker they blasted the Rams to smithereens – beating the hometown boys 45-14 in the conference semifinal. Nobody could explain what had happened, except that the year before the Colts had learned how to win the big games, and it was something they obviously hadn't forgotten.

For the Rams, it was going to be another one of those high-pressure off-seasons.

THE RAMS LOSE A GREAT FRIEND

It sits out on the north edge of town, an enduring monument to a town that cared. When the Regina Rams were formed in 1954, it was an historic moment, because it was the beginning. When they were reorganized in 1965, it was a time of dramatic change. When they built the clubhouse, on the sweaty backs of volunteers, members of the executive, coaches, players and families, that was when the Rams really took root in this community. It was a miracle. Soon after, they would spread their wings and the whole country would be awakened by this football giant from the flatlands of Saskatchewan.

Above all, it is the clubhouse that is the standing monument to the vision of people like Scotty Livingstone, Joe Kanuka, Rafe Chadwick, Erwin Strass, Peter McCaffrey. In the beginning, they were the local businessmen who rallied around the Rams' flag and answered the call for help coming from the Rams' ancient digs on south Albert Street.

The clubhouse went up in 1966, the year the Rams won their first Canadian championship. It was built in the shadow of what had once been the city's garbage dump; where sea gulls circled above before gliding into the day's fresh garbage. When the city's residential area began expanding north, the garbage dump was covered with dirt, grass was planted, and it was given the name Mount Pleasant so people would forget its beginnings. The Hill looks down on the Ram's clubhouse and the practice field, which was named Scotty Livingstone Field.

During the day the clubhouse sits mostly empty, except perhaps for equipment people doing the wash and getting things ready for practice. In the late afternoon it comes alive. Dust fills the air as cars carrying players and coaches and executive members show up, coming off Winnipeg Street. There is always noise in the place. Happy noise.

Scotty Livingstone

You could go out there in the dusk of the day and watch the players going through their paces under the lights that went up and down the sides of the field. You could go inside the clubhouse and, if you were lucky, the old boys' club would be gathered around a table telling stories. The place would be filled with laughter and shouts and good-natured ribbing.

Always, at the centre of it all, was Scotty Livingstone. His sidekick, the gravely-voiced Reg Forsyth, would be close at hand. Scotty was a long-time Reginan. He was from the north end of town, and had been in the navy in World War II. He walked with the help of a cane; had a neck that never let him turn his head fully, and spoke in a voice that, the more excited he got, the higher the pitch became. Scotty had held a number of jobs during his working life. If the right party was in government, that's where he would be. If it got turfed out by the voters, Scotty would be turfed out right behind it. He had worked for the Regina Real Estate Board; had been general manager of the Wascana Country Club. He never had trouble making a living. And he never had trouble enjoying life.

If there was a single person responsible for what the Rams became, it was Scotty Livingstone. He was there in 1965, bringing his vision to the Rams' executive. He dreamed big. But it happened. He got Gordon Currie as head coach. He got the clubhouse built. And he watched in absolute glee as the Rams became the most dominant team in junior football. Scotty was their biggest cheerleader. He went on the road with them, he and Kanuka and Forsyth and other members of the executive. The nights would be long and the drinks would be poured and the talk would never end. If the game they were attending was for a championship, then the side bets would flow and Scotty would be taking on all comers who doubted the Rams would win. Year after year this went on. They were fun times.

The 1966 Canadian junior championship in Saskatoon saw Scotty and his partner Reg in heaven. Just one year after the Rams had signed Currie, they were in the national final. By the start of the game, Scotty and Reg were well-primed for the afternoon. They were standing on the sidelines as the teams were being introduced. The Montreal Notre-Dame-de-Grace Maple Leafs wore uniforms similar to the Rams', green and white and red. As they were coming onto the field, Scotty started cheering for them in a voice that carried all over the place.

"Scotch! Scotch!" Reg yelled at his buddy. "That's the wrong team!"

"What the hell are you talking about?" Livingstone snapped back. And kept on cheering.

A few moments later, the Rams began to stream onto the field. Scotty looked, then he saw the Ram horns on the sides of the helmets, and his jaw dropped.

"Oh my God!" Scotty went beet red, redder than normal. He charged onto the field, toward the Montreal players, and he began yelling at them, "(Bleep) you guys! I didn't mean a thing I said to you. I didn't mean none of it, anyway!"

The Rams went on to win, and Scotty recovered from his momentary lapse.

There was something more that linked Scotty to the Rams. It was Currie. Scotty worshipped Currie. They were great friends who understood each other. They spent hours and hours in each other's company, never tiring of it, simply enjoying the rapport. It was Scotty who had talked Currie into coaching the Rams. It was Scotty who had talked Currie into running for politics.

A few days before Scotty died in 1991, he was in the General Hospital. His son, Dick, was sitting with him. Every noon hour, Dick would go the hospital to visit his father. He always stopped at A & W on the way there, to get his dad a hamburger, which Scotty would devour.

"The old man would make me eat his hospital lunch," Dick said. "Then, the nurse would come into the room and say, 'Oh, Mr. Livingstone, you ate all your lunch. Good for you.' "

In the final days of his life, Scotty took to planning his own funeral. One day, he said to Dick, "I want Gord to do the eulogy. Call him up and tell him."

"Is that right?" said Dick.

"Yes, that's right. You phone Gord up."

The next morning, at eight o'clock, Dick phoned Currie.

"Gord, will you do Dad's eulogy?"

There was silence. For 15 to 20 seconds, Currie didn't say a word. Then, he spoke. "God, Dick, I'm so sorry to hear that your dad has died."

"He's not dead, Gord. He just wants to get everything done. You know how he is, he has to be in charge."

"I'd love to do it. No, no, not love to do it. I'd be honoured to do it."

Scotty died late at night on March 31, 1991, in the General Hospital. A few days later, the family and Currie and the minister got together. They talked about the funeral service and about Scotty.

Currie laughed. "This man is making me do things I don't want to do, even in death, just like he did when he was alive."

The funeral was held in Knox-Metropolitan United Church in downtown Regina. One of Regina's largest and most beautiful churches, just across the street from Victoria Park, its bells chimed the day of the funeral. The weather was sunny and it was comfortable. The church was filled with people who knew Scotty. They filled the pews of the main floor, and they filled the upstairs' balconies. Currie gave the eulogy, as only he could.

Bill Clarke, Scotty Livingstone, Rafe Chadwick and Ron Atchison

SASKATOON GETS IN THE WAY AGAIN

1991

For as long as anybody could remember, the Regina Rams could always count on one thing. They went into every season reasonably settled at quarterback. Usually, they were more than settled. They knew pretty well exactly who they would have at the position. Players such as Grant Becker, Richard Seitz, Len Knoll, Marshall Hamilton and Dean Picton all established themselves early in their careers as more than capable quarterbacks. Some were even acknowledged as the best in the country. It was something the Rams were very good at, finding quarterbacks and developing them.

That's why the 1991 season was so unusual. The situation that would unfold come training camp was set up by the graduation of quarterback Blaine Pearce, and the decision by third-string quarterback Shaun Anderson not to return to the Rams.

That left the Rams with Randy Zbytnuik as their starting quarterback. Zbytnuik had been with the Rams for three years, playing behind Picton and Pearce. But he had hardly had any playing time at all. In three seasons, Zbytnuik had only thrown 53 passes, completing 20 of them for 263 yards and five touchdowns. Behind him were three rookies – Kevin Dureau, Corey Goff and Jason Meier. And the Rams had moved tight end Jim Lawson to quarterback. Lawson had played the position with the Balfour Tech Redmen – he would end up as the backup quarterback.

"I feel pretty comfortable," said Zbytnuik. "I feel comfortable reading defences and I know the pass patterns well. I've worked with the receivers for so long that I'm pretty familiar with their speed and moves." He had veteran receiver Brad Bork back. And receiver Don Blair, a rookie, joined the Rams and made an impression right away. Blair, of course, went on to a good career in the CFL.

Elsewhere, the Rams were solid going into the season. Kollin Erichsen had graduated, ending a brilliant career, a career in which he had established himself as one of the best running backs in Rams' history. But in Chris Curran, a four-year veteran, they had a replacement ready, able and willing. "I want to have the years Kollin had. I don't want to be anything less than he was. He was such an unselfish player," said Curran.

Chris Curran

The Rams' offensive line was a solid bunch of muscle – manned by Jim Bryce, Jim Wenzel, Tim McFadden, Tim Huber and Tom McCallum.

The Rams also received a boost when the PJFC's best linebacker the previous two seasons, Jerry Holik, showed up looking to play. Holik, a former Edmonton Huskie, was in Regina attending the Saskatchewan Roughriders' training camp. The Riders wanted to keep him around, on the practice roster. Holik wanted to play. So, he turned out with the Rams, all six feet, three inches and 230 pounds of him. "I'm on the Riders' roster so I get to practice with them and I also get to play amateur football in my final year of eligibility. Things have

Tom McCallum

really worked out well." Holik joined veteran Rams' linebacker Aaron Runge, giving the Rams the top linebacking duo in perhaps the whole country.

On the eve of the season opener, head coach Frank McCrystal knew exactly what would be the key for the Rams in 1991. "The real key for us is how well the quarterbacks perform. We have great receivers and good running backs. If our quarterback handles the ball well and throws the ball well, we'll be in business. But we're still going to look to our defence for leadership and to turn the ball over."

The Rams added to their linebacking prowess by moving rover Roger Reinson to linebacker, a position he had started out at when he joined the Rams. And they still had all-Canadian cornerback Steve Klein.

The Rams took their new act into Calgary to open the season against the Colts. The Colts had eliminated the Rams from the PJFC playoffs the two previous seasons, but McCrystal was more interested in how his team would play than he was in going after a frivolous revenge. After all, nothing was going to change the Rams' recent playoff ousters.

For the 11th straight year, the Rams started the schedule off with a victory, but it wasn't the usual one-sided affair people had come to expect. It took a Herculean effort from the defence for the Rams to escape Calgary with a 14-10 victory. The Colts, who had won the last two Canadian championships, were held to just eight first downs and 200 yards in total offence.

"The defence did what was expected of them," McCrystal said. "One game does not a season make. We met our goals and expectations we had set for the first week of the season. The gravy was we came away with a victory in our first game – and it was in Calgary."

The Rams' offence struggled somewhat, but not enough to get it in any serious trouble. Blair had one touchdown pass from Zbytnuik called back because of a penalty. Tailback Chris Curran, replacing Erichsen, had a solid game running the ball, getting 85 yards on 21 carries and scoring the Rams' only touchdown. Rookie kicker Matt Kellett, from Campbell Collegiate, gave a glimpse of what the Rams could expect from him with field goals of 40 and 38 yards, a convert and a single.

Kellett showed even more promise in the Rams' second game of the season. In fact, he performed so well that, for

Matt Kellett

the first time since Mike Lazecki had played with them, the Rams knew they had a kicker with professional football potential.

The Rams' home opener saw them dismantle the Edmonton Wildcats 66-11 in a game in which Regina took no prisoners. They scored nine touchdowns against the hapless Wildcats – it was a walk in the park.

But it was Kellett everybody was talking about. Kellett kicked off 10 times, converted all nine Rams' touchdowns, and kicked a 50-yard field goal.

Kellett was clearly the surprise of training camp. "Going into training camp, I just wanted to show them what I could do," he said. "I wanted to show them the kicking game is something that should be paid attention to. In high school, it isn't. In junior, it should be."

McCrystal was definitely paying attention. "He's made a really big difference. When we drive the ball 60 yards to the 20, now we'll come away with points. When you drive all that way and don't score, it's really discouraging."

The following weekend, the Rams went to Edmonton to take on the Huskies. This game was a no-brainer. At least, it always had been. In the 26 regular-season games, and the six playoff games the teams had played against each other in PJFC play, the Rams had never lost to the Huskies. But all good things have to come to an end, or something like that. And this streak ended with the Huskies posting a 31-22 victory.

"You're not going to beat one team all the time," commented McCrystal, not at all phased by this bit of misfortune. "It's a fact of life. You're going to lose at some time. This can be a good thing. The pressure of being undefeated is off our backs."

Randy Zbytnuik

The Rams actually played a strong game offensively, totaling 484 yards. Zbytnuik completed 11 of 38 passes for 217 yards and a touchdown, and didn't give up an interception. Blair caught four passes for 82 yards. And the ground game produced 267 yards, with Brad Flavel getting 79 yards on six carries and Curran 66 yards on 12 carries.

Curran, the Rams' leading rusher, had a huge game a week later against the Saskatoon Hilltops in Taylor Field. In fact, it was the best game of his four-year career with the Rams. He rushed 29 times for 164 yards, and scored a pair of touchdowns, as the Rams beat the Hilltops 25-21 in an exciting game that saw the Hilltops score 19 unanswered points in the fourth quarter to almost pull off the comeback of the season.

Curran went into the game against the Hilltops in a confident frame of mind. "I didn't think I had been contributing to the team," he said. "Frank came up to me and said, 'You're as strong as you can be and as fast as you can be, so don't worry about anything. Relax, and when you wake up the next day, be proud of what you did.' So, I did. I relaxed, read my blocks and just ran, and it came a lot easier." The Hilltops' defence also got to Curran a little bit. "The first couple of times I carried the ball, I didn't really go that far, and they said, 'You're not going anywhere tonight, Curran. We've got you.' "

The Rams' offence had 281 yards along the ground. Zbytnuik completed only eight passes for 104 yards, and for the fourth game in a row didn't give up an interception.

The Rams' defence hounded Hilltops' quarterback Brent Schneider all game long, intercepting three passes, and chasing him out of the pocket or forcing him to throw early by alternating blitz packages involving linebackers Doug Huber or Jerry Holik. Sheldon Thomas returned one of the interceptions for a touchdown.

"Even if we had won this game," said Schneider, "we wouldn't have deserved to. They outplayed us."

There was a feeling, now, at this stage of the 1991 season, that Zbytnuik was improving. His three years of being with the Rams had, mostly through practicing, at least taught him enough to give him the confidence not to panic. He

Chris Curran

Brent Ripplinger

knew the pass patterns being run; he knew enough not to take off and run at the first sign of danger, or to throw the ball into coverage.

Still, the Rams' passing game was not at the level they wanted. "We're still a ways off, but I think we're getting better," said McCrystal. "It's definitely a part of our game we'd like to improve on." The lack of zip in the passing game was evident in the statistics of the four games. The Rams had wanted to get the ball into the hands of receivers Brent Ripplinger and Don Blair. Ripplinger, who had caught 25 passes for 465 yards the year before, had made only five catches for 77 yards. He had also run the ball 15 times for 103 yards from his slotback position. And Blair had only nine catches for 149 yards. Not much of a four-game accumulation.

"When we went into the season," said McCrystal, "we wanted to put the ball into Brent's hands 15 times a game because he's such an awesome player. And with Blair, you throw the ball anywhere near him and he's going to catch it."

The Rams won their next two games – 42-22 over the Colts and 58-8 over the Wildcats – but in neither game did either Ripplinger or Blair catch more than two passes each. However, Blair did catch one big one – a 96-yard pass and run for a touchdown from Zbytnuik. That Blair was a threat every time he got the ball was no surprise. In the game he scored his 96-yard touchdown, he also got a touchdown by returning a punt for 60-plus yards.

The Rams killed the Edmonton Huskies 57-9 before 5,000 fans in Taylor Field in their last regular-season game at home. It was the running game that told the offensive story. Curran rushed for an astounding 248 yards and scored three touchdowns as the Rams gained 421 yards on the ground, 648 yards in total. Wide receiver Michael Ball caught two touchdown passes – one a 61-yarder from Zbytnuik, the other a 59-yarder from backup Jim Lawson.

It set up perfectly – a first-place showdown with the Hilltops in Saskatoon's Gordie Howe Bowl. The Rams talked it up the week before the game.

"This can definitely be classed as a playoff game," said Rams' centre Tim McFadden, who had yet to win a game at Gordie Howe Bowl in three PJFC seasons. "First place is on the line and so is homefield advantage throughout the playoffs."

McCrystal got into the mood of the playoff season, too. "That's what makes this game so exciting – it's meaningful for a lot of reasons. Number one, it's for first place – that's the obvious thing. Number two, it's a challenge. They're a good football team. That is what this is all about. We play good athletes and good football teams so we get a chance to measure ourselves."

A bus was arranged to take the Rams' faithful north to Saskatoon. Both cities were caught up in the electric atmosphere of yet another showdown between these two teams. It had been going on since 1954, and nobody was ever sure of what to expect. Some of the greatest games ever played in junior football had been between these two rivals. Some of the biggest upsets had taken place when the Rams and Hilltops met.

The game wasn't even close.

Not even close.

In the end, that is.

The Rams looked as if they might run away with the game, and maybe that's what they thought after they had stormed into a 22-8 lead in the first half. The Rams had scored 22 straight points, after the Hilltops had opened with an 8-0 lead. First, Rams' defensive player Ian Kydd recovered a Hilltops' fumble in the end zone, then Steve Klyne made a 70-yard interception return, then Brent Ripplinger caught a 10-yard pass from Zbytnuik. Matt Kellett added two converts, and Ripplinger scored a two-point convert. The Rams were in control.

They were for a while. The Hilltops, instead of folding, grew stronger. They gave up on the passing attack and started to run the ball. They ran and they ran and they ran some more, and before the Rams knew what had hit them, the Hilltops had scored 36 straight points to take a 44-22 lead on their way to a 54-29 victory.

The Rams slumped to second place, and got ready to take on the Calgary Colts in the semifinal. What they wanted most was another crack at the Hilltops in the PJFC final. "I've been here before," Rams' linebacker Roger Reinson said. "In 1987 we lost to them in this game and then came back up and beat them."

The Colts had knocked off the Rams the two previous playoff years, so McCrystal had little need to do anything to get his players motivated. The Rams, who had once, not so many years ago, danced over the playoff graves of the Hilltops and Colts, were now dancing to a different tune. And it wasn't one of their favourites.

Roger Reinson

The Rams got past the Colts, ending their two-year reign as PJFC and Canadian champions, with a 22-14 win in Taylor Field. It was again the running game and the defence that won the game. Curran, playing as well as everybody knew he could, and finding his place in that long line of great running backs who had played for the Rams, rumbled for 225 yards on 38 carries. The defence held the Colts to 199 yards in total offence.

On to Saskatoon. Again. The Rams had gotten their wish, just like in 1987. They would get one more crack at them.

And the Rams were looking forward to it. Offensive lineman Tim Huber was practically frothing at the mouth waiting for this game. "People downplay the rivalry, but the players know it's there. On the field, it's really obvious."

Reinson, in his last year as a Ram, was ready too. "I hate the Hilltops. Nobody specific, I just hate the Hilltops. I see you up there wearing your Hilltop jacket and I want to drive my car over you – but don't take it personally."

The Hilltops didn't. They showed up for the game, let quarterback Brent Schneider loose, and the Rams were wondering, "Who let the dogs out?"

The Hilltops' bite was worse than the Rams' bark on that Sunday afternoon

With Schneider zinging early touchdown passes, the Hilltops took a 17-3 first-quarter lead, upped it to 29-3 at the half, and then the rains came. The skies opened up and it poured. The combination of the rain and cleats ripping through what was left of the grass turned Gordie Howe Bowl into a mudpie that swallowed up both offences for the rest of the game. The Hilltops went on to win 32-9.

The Rams' season was over, once again a little too early for their liking.

Paul Barnby

"Our season was not unsuccessful," said McCrystal in what was becoming a familiar refrain. "Our season was a success."

There was one totally bright spot for the Rams. President Paul Barnby, a dedicated member of the Rams' executive since 1977, and still is, was named the Canadian Junior Football League's executive of the year.

WIN THE LEAGUE . . . STALL IN SURREY

1992

Enough was enough.

The last time the Regina Rams had won a Canadian championship the year was 1987. For the Rams to go this long without winning a Canadian championship almost warranted a Royal Commission. Like, this was serious stuff. After all, these were the Regina Rams. There were certain very well-defined expectations.

There was a difference, though, when the Rams went to training camp in 1992. The headline in the *Leader-Post* told the early story. "Rams deep at pivot" it read. Where, a year earlier, they had been short on experienced quarterbacks, they now had two veterans returning – Randy Zbytnuik and Jim Lawson. There was also the possibility that one of those two players could be shifted to another position, and one of the younger quarterbacks on hand moved to a backup position. The problem with going with Zbytnuik and Lawson at quarterback was that both were fifth-year players, and in their last seasons of junior eligibility. This was not a good situation.

The Rams always wanted to have a younger quarterback developing behind the older quarterback, for a smooth transition. Offensive coordinator Bernie Schmidt knew what problems could develop down the road if he went with two last-year quarterbacks. "We're going to keep three people," he said. "The bottom line is, we would not want to put ourselves in a hole for next year by keeping two fifth-year guys and one second-year guy this year."

The Rams had five quarterbacks at camp. Along with Zbytnuik and Lawson, there was returnee Jason Meier and rookies Todd Grychowski and . . . oh, what's his name . . . oh, yes, that's it . . . some kid from Bob Poley country by the name of . . . ah . . . oh, yes, here it is . . . Leason . . . yes, Darryl Leason.

The year before, the Rams' passing game had never really taken hold. Any big successes were because of the running game or the defence. Zbytnuik, in really his first full season as a playing quarterback, completed 65 of 154 passes for 1,256 yards and nine touchdowns, and he gave up five interceptions. He started all eight games. Lawson saw some action, but not very much.

The Rams had some rebuilding to do along their offensive line. They had lost three starters to graduation, leaving veteran centre Tim McFadden and tackle Tom McCallum as the lone returnees. The new faces to starting positions were Gary Bresch, Doug Clark and Scott Waters. All had been with the Rams as backups, so they knew what was going on and what would be expected of them.

The Rams' so-called security at quarterback received a serious jolt when Zbytnuik decided to quit the team and move to British Columbia to work. That left Lawson as the starting quarterback. And this kid Darryl Leason, from Hudson Bay, Saskatchewan, who had only played nine-man football, got the job as backup.

The Rams had lost three of their four starting linebackers from 1991 to graduation, and they moved the fourth, Doug Huber, to the defensive line. But McCrystal was confident that his new crew of linebackers, led by Randy Srochenski and Michael Milo, would do the job.

As the Rams headed toward their first game, the talk carried a familiar ring. Nobody ever asked a Rams' coach if he thought the team had a chance at making the playoffs. It was always, "Do you have a team that can win the Canadian championship?" The Rams had become the Montreal Canadiens of hockey dynasties, the Ohio State Buckeyes of American college football, the UCLA Bruins of basketball fame.

Randy Srochenski

"I think we always have a chance," said McCrystal. "That chance is provided by this program. Anybody involved with this program has a chance to be a Canadian champion. Any time we field a football team, given the work done by this program, that football team has the potential to be a Canadian champion."

The Rams opened the season against the Edmonton Wildcats. This would be a season like many they had experienced before. But it was the kind of season that would plant the seeds that would produce a bountiful crop down the road.

The Rams broke with a tradition of sorts when they lost their opening game, 19-18, on a last-second, two-point convert in a game against the Edmonton Wildcats. It was the first time the Rams had lost a season opener since August 26, 1989.

The ever optimistic McCrystal, who was steady in his absolute refusal to find anything seriously negative about any team he had ever coached, found something worth talking about in this loss. "We have to keep it in perspective with our goals for the season. We're aware we have young players and we're inexperienced. We had to get them playing. As far back as the spring, we set certain goals for individuals and the team. We accomplished them. We wanted to improve our passing game – we did that. We wanted to maintain our running game – we did that, too. It was better for us to lose it (the first game) by one point than win it by them missing the two-point convert. At that stage, we would rather win it than have them lose it. The point of that game will be driven home harder by the loss."

Lawson played the whole game at quarterback, his first as a starter with the Rams since joining the team five years earlier. He completed 11 of 19 passes for 248 yards and two touchdowns. Not bad. Matt Kellett kicked a 39-yard field goal, two converts and a 70-yard single.

There was a time in that season when McCrystal became reflective, philosophical. He had been the head coach of the Rams since 1984, so it had become almost ritualistic that, at the end of each season, Frank was asked if he was thinking of retirement. His accomplishments were glowing. He had coached teams to a 56-9-0 regular season record, three PJFC championships, and two Canadian championships. At 38 years old, he and his wife, Wendy, had two children, their son, Charlie, who was seven in 1992, and their daughter, Hailey, who was four.

When asked about his future for the umpteenth time, Frank replied, "I may be here into the next century, until I get it right." He may have said that in some jest, but it turned out to be true. He would still be around in the next century. Coaching is measured only by the number of challenges that come at you. And how you deal with them. Coaching the Regina Rams was a revolving door of challenges, year to year to year, because of the turnover of players and the lofty expectations the organization was always expected to satisfy.

"The opportunity to work with the people here has made me a more patient person, a better father, a better husband," he said. "I really believe I'll be here for a while yet." McCrystal had actually joined the Rams in 1972, as a player under Gord Currie. He had been a linebacker. It says a lot about his heart and his tenacity, Frank was only five feet, seven inches and 170 pounds. That is hardly big enough to be a water boy, let alone a linebacker. But Frank was not only a starting linebacker with the Rams, he was an all-star.

Said Gord Currie:

> He was a fierce competitor. To him, that was a top priority all the time. Sometimes, in the expression of his individuality, he would take the odd uncalled-for penalty. But one thing I would say after saying that is how impressed I was, that he came to control that individuality and blend it in so that he thought of everybody instead of just Frank McCrystal. It became an attribute instead of a liability. He

came to understand that in order to truly be a winner, you have to be under control. When he accomplished that, along with his competitive skills and the leadership skills he always had, he became a winner.

Frank McCrystal 1976

McCrystal learned the basic assumption, that the team always had to come first, during his high-school years under the Jesuits at Campion College. And he learned much from Currie. "I try to follow his leadership and his instruction as well as I can," Frank said. "He and the Jesuits and that education of succeeding through competition are a big part of what we try to do out here and our philosophy. It has to be more than winning. As Gord always said, 'If all you're just out here doing is pushing the pigskin up and down the field, what an incredible waste of time and energy it is.' There has to be more to it. There has to be growth as a person and growth as an athlete. We try to make the players feel important. We tell them, 'To be important, you have to contribute to your world – family, work, school, all of those things.' "

What does the kind of success McCrystal had had up to 1992, in his 20 years as a Ram, in his years as a player, an assistant coach and a head coach, do to you? It drives you, that's what, to do more, to accomplish more.

"I feel pressure because of the tradition," said Frank, who was coaching a team that in 1992 had won 10 national championships. "But a lot of that pressure comes from the commitment of the people involved. I've won seven national championships with the Rams and have been a participant and coach in nine national championships. I've had that experience and I want that experience for the people who work hard to make this go – parents, players, coaches, directors, trainers.

"The problem is, when we lose everybody asks me what went wrong."

The 1992 season saw McCrystal asked the question again. The Rams again finished in second place, behind the Hilltops, who had hung another 7-1 record on the board. The Rams were 5-3, their worst record since 1968, when they were also 5-3.

In the third game of the season, something significant happened, other than the fact that the Rams beat the Calgary Colts 18-6 on a cold and rainy August day. Darryl Leason's career with the Rams was officially launched. He only had a few plays, but he displayed the talents that, down the road, would make him an outstanding member of the Rams. He ran four times for 81 yards and only tried three passes, all of which were incomplete. This is what McCrystal had to say about Leason, "Potentially, Darryl could be one of the greatest quarterbacks to play on a Rams' football team – and we've had some good ones. He has all the tools."

By the seventh game of the season, a 39-16 win over the Edmonton Wildcats, Leason was the starter.

The Rams went on to cross a major hurdle in 1992. They went into Saskatoon and beat the Hilltops 22-17 to end a four-year jinx in trying to win the PJFC championship.

To get to the national championship, the Rams had to travel to Vancouver to play the Surrey Rams. Leason was intercepted four times, turning two of them into touchdowns, and the Rams, the Surrey Rams that is, went on to win the Western final by a 21-10 score.

For the Regina Rams, it was another disappointing ending to the season. But they slept well that winter. They knew that, in Darryl Leason, they had something special and it would just take time for it to develop.

The best, truly, was yet to come.

BACK ON TOP AS NATIONAL CHAMPS

1993

Hudson Bay, Saskatchewan sits in the northeast part of the province. It is a small place, set in tall timbers that seem to wrap themselves around you, isolating you. Known as a lumber town, it is a place that draws hunters from everywhere.

I have been to Hudson Bay twice, flying into it each time from Regina. I went there the first time with Jack Gotta, the head coach of the Saskatchewan Roughriders, and Bob Poley to speak at a sports dinner. The next year, I returned to the same dinner with Poley and Bill Quinter, who was the general manager of the Roughriders.

The first dinner was the most bizarre. Gotta, Poley and I flew into town, were met at the airport and driven to a hall. That place was filled with people – their voices were loud and you knew they were there to have a good time. "These people know how to have a good time," Poley said. Poley was a product of Hudson Bay., where he had played nine-man football. He had also played for the Regina Rams, and he had had a great career in the Canadian Football League with the Roughriders and the Calgary Stampeders.

Poley is big, well over six feet tall, and he has a moustache you could hide a football in. His eyes are always alive, and always he seems to be laughing. His voice would carry through a cement wall. He always seems in a good mood. That night in Hudson Bay, the room reverberated with excitement. He seemed to know everyone. I remember thinking that it was going to be a long night. I thought this as the Happy Hour headed into its second hour. There was only one break. That came when they ran out of beer and liquor in the hall. They had to break into the curling club to get more, because the manager had the key and he was in Saskatoon. I remember sitting down with Bob Poley's father. He poured me a drink. I told him, "There's no room for mix." He said, "You don't need any." I wasn't going to argue. His hands were as big as I was.

Every small place in this province that I have been to, and I have been to hundreds of them, has its own special character. Hudson Bay was obviously a place of hard-working people who knew how to enjoy themselves. It was a place of beauty. It was a place to be in the great outdoors. It was a place for families to be together, to be insulated from some of the temptations of the bigger cities. It was a place that cared about its children. It was a lively and active sports town. Hockey, curling, football, baseball. Whatever. Hudson Bay had a team, or even a league.

Hudson Bay is not a place you would expect to produce talented players for the Regina Rams. But it did. It had a team that played a nine-man league. The first player from

Mike and Darryl Leason

that league that had come to the Rams was, of course, Poley, and his story is well known. Just as the Gull Lake and Shaunavon areas of Saskatchewan had funneled good players to the Rams, all it took to get it going in Hudson Bay, and give the kids hope that they could play at that level, too, was the first one. In Gull Lake, it was Barry Aldag who went from the Rams to the Riders. His brother Roger followed him. The Nicolson brothers followed from Shaunavon, a town just down the highway from Gull Lake.

Once Poley had carved his niche, the door was open in Hudson Bay. Bill Lozinski, a talented wide receiver who would return to Gull Lake to teach school and coach football, played with the Rams. Brian Soyko, Glenn Nowosad and Dwayne Siki all came from Hudson Bay and played with the Rams. In the early 1990s, Hudson Bay's name again appeared on the football map. The Leason brothers began to arrive.

The first was Darryl. He had started playing football in 1987, with the Hudson Bay Riders, as a Grade 8 kid. His athletic ability and leadership skills, his streak of competitiveness, all made him a natural to play quarterback. Darryl showed up at the Rams' camp in 1992.

The second was Michael. He was a tight end in Hudson Bay, and when he came to the Rams, in 1993, they turned him into a slotback. He had the speed and he had a way of catching the ball that made him a natural for the position.

Darryl's first year with the Rams was a matter of being in the right spot at the right time with the right stuff. The Rams had an idea they were getting something special when this kid from Hudson Bay showed up in 1992. He was well over six feet in height and he carried more than 200 pounds. He was obviously an athlete. The Rams had Jim Lawson, a fifth-year player, as their starting quarterback. Leason started the 1992 season as the backup. By the third game of the season, he was getting a fair amount of playing time. By the seventh game, he was the starter. The rest, as they say, is history. Leason went on to one of the most storied careers any Rams' quarterback has ever had.

His talents had not gone unnoticed by other teams. He had caught the eye of a number of American colleges that were waving football scholarships under his nose. Of course, the Rams wanted him too. Rams' coach Frank McCrystal knew that Darryl Leason could be the missing piece in the puzzle that would get them back on track in the Canadian championship derby they had missed out on since 1987. He told the Rams' board of directors, "He is a special player who will win us a national championship."

McCrystal drove to Hudson Bay to see Leason, to talk to him, to get to know him, to convince him that his place in football was with the Rams. "I knew there was something there when I drove up in the winter," McCrystal said. "There was something in the way he walked and the way he talked. He was an athlete." McCrystal would eventually call Leason, "the most competitive athlete I have seen in the last 20 years."

Leason had quarterbacked the Hudson Bay Riders from 1987 to 1991. They had won three provincial nine-man championships, and while he was there their win-loss record was 46-3. He was used to winning. He was one of those rare athletes who, on the basis of his own skills and performance, can make a profound difference in the outcome of every game. He was that good.

The first year that Leason put his mark on the Rams, and solidly entrenched himself as the backbone of this team, was 1993. That was the year he came to training camp as the starter, and the year the Rams finally returned to their championship ways. They would go on an incredible streak of winning Canadian championships, a run that would see them win the Big Show of junior football in 1993, 1994, 1995, 1997 and 1998.

It started in the summer of '93, before the Rams even went to training camp. McCrystal was thorough in taking every avenue available to him in preparing his team from year to year. He had introduced a rigorous off-season physical conditioning program made possible by the expansion of the Rams' clubhouse in 1988 to include a superb physical fitness centre. He had also made use of the Regina Sportsplex running track. The off-season program began in mid-January. And Leason was sent to the Roughriders' training camp in 1993. Nobody expected him to make the Riders, but the training he would get there would make him a better quarterback. He spent a considerable amount of time with Rider quarterback Kent Austin.

When the Rams opened their camp, the difference in Leason from the previous year was immediately obvious. "He is really looking good," slotback Brent Ripplinger said. "If everything goes together with Darryl like it should, the season should be incredible."

"My second year will be a lot better," said Leason. "There were times last year when I stepped in and didn't know what was going on. My biggest improvement from last year

Darryl Leason and Bernie Schmidt

is in reading the defence. As soon as I get to the line, I can tell within a couple of seconds what the defence is. I know where our good matchups are and where our strong points are."

McCrystal was about as excited about the 1993 season as he could be. He oozed confidence that everything was in place, that this would be the Year of the Ram. "After the 1991 season," he said, "we made a commitment to improve our passing game. We worked really hard on passing the ball better. The biggest part of the solution was Leason. He can run and he can pass."

The Rams got even more good news. Ken Stasyshyn, a 1992 all-star nose guard with the Edmonton Wildcats, had decided to move to Regina so he could play with the Rams.

"I wanted to come to Regina just to play for another team," the six-foot, six-inch, 280-pounder said. "I felt I needed a change from Edmonton. I plan on pursuing football after junior and I felt Regina was a good avenue as far as that was concerned. I always kind of admired the Rams. They played honestly. They weren't dirty or anything, they played good solid physical football. It's tough to begrudge a team when they beat you honestly with better skills than you have."

McCrystal felt the addition of Stasyshyn would solidify his defence. The line had only one starter returning from the year before, rush end Doug Huber.

"At that height and that size, and with his wingspan, he's going to be hard to run on and pass over," said McCrystal. "He's going to be very difficult to play against."

The Rams opened the 1993 season on a winning note, of course. They went into Edmonton, scored 23 unanswered points in the fourth quarter and cruised to a 44-25 victory over the Wildcats. "What I'm really happy about," said McCrystal, "is that the players now realize the rewards of our off-season training, our winter program. It came front and centre in the fourth quarter."

The Rams' ground game got off to a good start with seven different ball carriers totaling 277 yards and, despite some dropped balls, Leason produced 259 yards passing on just ten completions, including one 75-yard touchdown throw to receiver Michael Ball. Mark Bernard, Jamie Baillie, Darryl Leason and Mike Rutten each had rushing touchdowns for the Rams. Kicker Matt Kellett produced five converts, two field goals and three singles.

Derek Fink

Defensively, the Rams found a gem in first-year starting cornerback Derek Fink, who intercepted three passes off all-star quarterback Sean Zaychkowsky. Fink had taken over the position from the graduated Sheldon Thomas. Todd Fuchs held down the other cornerback spot.

The Rams kept rolling. With Leason running an offence that produced 518 yards, and with the defence following assistant coaches Alex Smith's and Rick Seaman's thorough game plan, the Rams dropped the Edmonton Huskies 28-14 in Taylor Field. Game three, a 36-22 victory over the Calgary Colts, was cornerback Todd Fuch's turn to shine. Fuchs had five solo tackles, two assisted tackles and two interceptions as the Rams went to 3-0. Running back Mark Bernard found himself busy, carrying the ball 14 times for 70 yards and catching a 54-yard pass from Leason, who threw for 215 yards and ran the ball himself seven times for 57 yards.

Doug Huber

The Rams next went into Saskatoon and recorded their first regular season victory there since August 27, 1988, beating the Hilltops 26-13 in a game that was dominated by the Rams' defence.

The Rams' defence felt that coach Smith had again given them a superb game plan. "Alex is probably one of the most intelligent coaches I've ever had," said rush end Doug Huber. "He scouts teams unbelievably well. We know what teams are going to do, what they're going to run in different situations. He's the leader of the defence."

Sitting comfortably in first place in the Prairie Junior Football Conference, with a 4-0 record, everything was going the Rams' way. Four of their defensive backs, for instance, were in the top seven in the league in interceptions. Cornerback Derek Fink was tied for the league lead with five, halfback Jeff Hagerty and cornerback Todd Fuchs had four each, and halfback Marco Ricci had three.

Mark Bernard

Lloyd MacDonald

The Rams won their next four games to finish the regular season undefeated in eight games, and were assured of home field for the playoffs. The Rams closed out the schedule by whipping the Hilltops 33-17. It was the running game that did in Saskatoon. The Rams rushed for a whopping 412 yards. Darryl Leason ran for 136 yards on six carries; tailback Mark Bernard had 135 on 18 carries; slotback Brent Ripplinger had 104 yards on eight carries.

It was the Rams' first undefeated season since 1988, but that year they hadn't even made it past the PJFC playoffs.

"We have to forget about our undefeated record," said Rams' linebacker Lloyd MacDonald. "If we don't, we'll get cocky and lose."

The Rams were not about to suffer the deadly cramps that can follow an outbreak of over-confidence. If anything, they were dedicating themselves to playing even better in the playoffs. They knew, from past experiences, there were no guarantees, no matter how good your team was, no matter how splendid your record was. The Rams were learning to win all over again.

The Rams opened the playoffs against the Calgary Colts. They opened the first quarter by taking an 18-0 lead, and going on to win the semifinal 50-19. Calgary coach Wayne Harris Jr. knew his team was in over its head right from the start. "The big difference was, 12 or 13 minutes into the game we're losing 18-0 – and we're not playing that badly."

The win sent the Rams to the PJFC final against the Hilltops in Taylor Field. The Rams, who had been having remarkable success running the football, ran it again against the Hilltops, and that was all it took. With Bernard rushing for 148 yards, and Darryl Leason running for another 101 yards, the Rams ran the Hilltops out of Taylor Field with a 30-15 victory.

The Rams had made it to the Western final. The national championship was so close – just two wins away – that the Rams could taste it. They took on the Surrey Rams from Vancouver in the Western final in Taylor Field. The winner would be going on to the Canadian final, which would be played in the home of the Western champ.

This one was never really in doubt. The Rams had regained their killer instinct. They just let it carry them to a 43-12 victory over Surrey. Strange, but that game is still remembered for the ferocious hit that Rams' defensive halfback Jeff Hagerty laid on Surrey receiver Chris Solonynko early in the third quarter. Hagerty leveled Solonynko as he came across the middle of the Rams' defence, just not paying attention.

There are lots of big hits over the course of a game, and over the course of a season. But very few of them are ever remembered the way this one was. It was the kind of hit that could be felt throughout Taylor Field; the kind of hit that would lead the roll call on any Plays of the Year video.

"Mentally, it gets you so into the game, so pumped up," said cornerback Derek Fink, who said he heard the hit from 50 yards downfield.

"Psychologically, it gives you a feeling of control," said Rams' veteran centre Tim McFadden. "It tells you no one's going to change your destiny." McFadden, in a few days, found himself at the top of a hit parade of his own. He was the unanimous choice as the PJFC's outstanding offensive lineman of the year. At the same time, Leason was named the conference's most valuable player. McCrystal was the only Ram to win a national award. He was named the Canadian Junior Football League's coach of the year. He won the Gord Currie Award.

With the championship within reach, the Rams began their preparations for the game in Taylor Field. Five years of failing to win a championship was gnawing away at them, the need to restore the organization to its winning ways was motivating them. They would be playing the Hamilton Hurricanes.

On the eve of the game, Darryl Leason received what he needed to ensure that, in this Canadian final, he would be at the top of his game. He lost the CJFL's outstanding offensive player of the year award to Hamilton quarterback Jason Hayes.

"This will add something to the game," said Leason. "I'm going to go out there and prove to him that I'm as good as he is, or maybe even better. The only way I'm going to do that is to put the W in the win column."

With a crowd of 7,000 fans in a chilly Taylor Field on Saturday, November 13, 1993, the Rams embarked on their championship cruise, riding the wave that was Darryl Leason's finest hour in his Rams' career so far. The Rams won the Canadian championship, beating the Hurricanes 23-11 and sending shivers of worry across the rest of Canadian junior football. The Rams were back, and they were only just beginning. It was the 11th national title for the Rams, the 10th for McCrystal in his career as a player, assistant coach and head coach. The victory was the 12th of the season for the Rams. It was the third time in club history the Rams had gone unbeaten and untied on the road to a Canadian championship. The 1971 and 1981 Rams' teams had also turned the trick.

The story of the game was Darryl Leason. He was named the game's outstanding offensive player. And how could he not have been? Where the Rams had, throughout the season, had some outstanding rushing games, on this day Leason went to the air to get the win. The second-year Ram, the kid from Hudson Bay, Saskatchewan, completed 25 of 36 passes for 439 yards and a touchdown. He also ran with the ball seven times for 35 yards. And the Rams' defence stuffed the ball back down the throat of Hamilton quarterback Jason Hayes, who was harassed from start to finish by an unrelenting Rams' defence. Hayes, who said he had an "off game," completed only 12 passes for 179 yards and gave up three interceptions.

Darryl Leason

"We've really been known as a running team," said back Mark Bernard, who carried the ball for 38 of the 116 yards the Rams' ground game totaled. "I'm sure that's what they were geared up to stop. They really overcommitted on the run, so we passed."

The Rams had put the season to bed. And another dynasty was born.

THE 12TH NATIONAL CHAMPIONSHIP

1994

Whenever the Regina Rams have enjoyed great success, such as they had in 1993, they might just as well have painted big bulleyes on the fronts of their sweaters. Like gophers in Saskatchewan fields, everybody, it seemed, would be taking shots at them.

The 1994 Rams were no different from any of the other Rams' teams that had won Canadian championships. Everybody wanted a piece of them, even, it seemed, the University of Saskatchewan Huskies. But more on that later. For starters, the Rams went into 1994 as targets for every other team. It was not something that coach Frank McCrystal minded. He felt that knowing every team the Rams faced would likely up the level of their game, would force his team to respond to the challenge, and make them better. Challenges were what McCrystal coached for.

"I'd rather be champions than not," he said. "If you take a good hard look at it, the alternative is that you lost. I'd rather win it and deal with the consequences than lose it."

The Rams lost seven starters from the 1993 championship team – fullback Bob Aldridge, wide receiver Brad Bork, rush end Doug Huber, centre Tim McFadden, slotback Brent Ripplinger and defensive tackle Ken Stasyshyn – to graduation. And wide receiver Michael Ball decided he had had enough of junior football.

The Rams knew that the players lost would be difficult to replace, but their program of continually grooming younger players to be ready to start, in the second or third year of their junior careers, ensured that they would have players ready to step in. Jamie Baillie, who was the team's fifth leading rusher in 1993, started at fullback in 1994. Returnees Josh Shaw, Garth Schill and Geoff Deck had the inside track on the wide receiver positions. Michael Leason, who had some playing time in his rookie year, seemed ready to start at slotback. Leason to Leason was about to become a familiar refrain. Darryl Leason was back at quarterback, and if he just repeated what he had done the year before, it would be enough. Of course,

Jamie Baillie

Darryl Leason

Leason was only going to get better and better.

Trent Langford replaced the talented all-Canadian Tim McFadden at centre. Having this kind of talent waiting to bloom was what had kept the Rams near the top of the pack or at the top of the pack for years and years. And, it was happening again.

"I think we're going to be pretty good," said McCrystal. "We have a quarterback and we have linebackers and those are the focal points on both sides of the ball."

The Rams began the defence of their title at home to the Edmonton Huskies and rang up a shutout, 41-0. Boooooring, seemed to be the cry that went up. The game staggered; the pace was interrupted by 45 penalties, 30 of which were called against the Rams.

Mark Bernard

"It's going to happen when you have those lopsided scores early in the season because we virtually play everybody," said McCrystal. "I'm disappointed that we had some calls against veterans. We have to address that and we have to address the procedure penalties and objectionable conduct penalties."

As for the game, Darryl Leason threw two touchdown passes of 19 and 35 yards to Josh Shaw, and a 48-yarder to Shawn Harvey. Mark Bernard scored on a seven-yard run and Chad Ehman on a five-yard run. Matt Kellett kicked a 50-yard field goal, had five converts and three singles. Ho-hum.

The Rams just kept on winning, stopping the Wildcats 30-10 to go to 2-0; beating the Calgary Colts 21-7 and 39-9 in back-to-back games to go to 4-0; running their undefeated streak to 16-0 at the halfway mark of the schedule.

There was little doubt the Rams were confident about where they were heading. "I certainly think we have to challenge ourselves in the second half (of the schedule)," McCrystal said. "I think the other teams have resigned themselves to the fact that we'll finish first . . . we have to make sure we don't become complacement, dull and lazy in the next half of the season."

For the Rams, their next game represented a test. It was against the Hilltops, in Taylor Field, the first meeting of the rivals of the '93 season. The Rams were without linebacker Randy Srochenski, who had gone to the Saskatchewan Roughriders, playing on the special teams in his first game. He played because of a hamstring injury to Peter Miller. He returned to the Rams before the end of the season.

The Rams took the night off against Saskatoon. While their defence had a strong game, holding the Hilltops to just 253 yards in offence, and not giving up a touchdown, the Rams' offence had its miseries. They fumbled the football five times and gave it up one more time on a Leason interception. The Hilltops turned their good fortune into a 16-12 victory. So much for a second undefeated season.

Derek Fink

"It was simply a wakeup call," Rams' defensive back Derek Fink said. "You can't win every game. We just have to start from scratch again."

McCrystal promised a tough week of practice. But he seemed more unhappy with what he perceived to be the Hilltops' reaction to winning the game. "If you let it, what bothers you the most when you lose a game is the attitude of the other team," he said. "When we get beat, the team that beats us is not very gracious. Sometimes that has a tendency to grind on you. When we beat them, I hope we don't act like that. I guess teams aren't used to beating us – and they shouldn't get used to it either."

The game carried a double whammy for Rams' tailback Mark Bernard. He had not only fumbled the ball three times, he had also suffered a serious knee injury. The torn ligaments ended his season, and the Rams' running game appeared to have suffered a serious blow.

The Rams got back on the winning track, beating the Wildcats 41-21, and they picked up where they had left off before the Hilltops' loss. They won the remainder of their scheduled games, including a 24-9 win over the Hilltops, to finish at 7-1 and clinch first place in the PJFC. Leason turned it on in the Hilltops' game, rushing for 161 yards on 18 carries, scoring one touchdown, and completing six passes for 43 yards and a touchdown.

The Rams shot into the playoffs with their play improving, their health not all that bad, and their optimism unlimited. It showed.

They opened against the Wildcats in the semifinal, winning 28-3, with Leason hitting on 16 of 36 passes for 273 yards and a pair of touchdowns.

That set the scene for the Rams and Hilltops to once again meet in the PJFC championship game, in Regina's Taylor Field.

It took the Regina Rams just 44 seconds to serve notice on the Hilltops that they had run into a blind switch. Jason Bula ran the opening kickoff 67 yards to the Hilltops' 33. A roughing penalty moved the ball to the 18 and two plays later the Rams' Darryl Leason scored from a yard out – the Rams were ahead 7-0. By the end of the first quarter the Rams were ahead 17-0 and on their way to a 34-7 victory and a third straight PJFC championship.

Jason Bula

"Right from the opening kickoff, they jumped all over us. They caught us reeling," was how Hilltops' head coach Dave Hardy described it.

"Everyone brings it up a notch for the Hilltops," said Rams' running back Jamie Baillie. "We wanted a quick start, got one, and that set the tempo for the whole game."

The Rams put Hilltops' quarterback Sheldon Ball out of the game with a mild concussion midway through the second quarter. Saskatoon fullback Brad Churchill said there came a time in the game when the Hilltops knew they weren't going to win, but they wanted to play their best.

"If there's a team you don't want to lose to as a Saskatoon Hilltop, it's the Regina Rams," said Churchill, a fourth-year player. "It's good to have these rivalries but I wish we could come out on the winning end once in a while."

Next up for the Rams was the Western Canada semifinal. The opposition this time came in the form of the Winnipeg Hawkeyes. The Hawkeyes were an invitation to gorge themselves as far as the Rams were concerned. The final score told it all, Rams 73, Hawkeyes 7. Only 200 fans took in the game in Taylor Field.

Leason threw for three touchdowns, and ran for one himself, as the Regina offence totalled 515 yards.

In the understatement of the year, McCrystal said, "We have a lot of momentum. We're in the middle of a peak situation and we're going to ride it out."

Ride it out, they did.

The Rams went after the Surrey Rams in the Western final, firing on all cylinders, gaining 516 yards in total offence, and winning 64-3. Running back Jamie Baillie only carried the ball nine times for 90 yards, but he scored four touchdowns.

The victory put the Rams in the Canadian final. This time, they met the Quebec champions, the St. Leonard Cougars, on November 12 in Montreal.

The Rams knew virtually nothing about St. Leonard. "All I know is they're in the way," said linebacker Wavell Starr.

The Rams toured Montreal when they got there. And one of the stops was at the fabled Montreal Forum, the home of the Canadiens. McCrystal said the Forum was a natural stop. Laughing, he said, "Because the Montreal Canadiens are the Regina Rams of the NHL." McCrystal wanted to underline just what was at stake for his players. He had all of the trophies the Rams had won in previous years put into the middle of the dressing room. "It's so the players see it all the time," McCrystal said. "It's a reminder of where we're going. We can have that trophy, or we can give it to somebody else and have it sitting in their dressing room."

Perhaps, it's a good thing the Rams didn't know too much about the Cougars. If they had, it might have been worse.

The Rams beat St. Leonard 52-6 to win the 12th national championship in the club's history, the second in a row. Darryl Leason was named the outstanding player of the game for the second year in a row. He completed 19 of 28 passes for 353 yards and threw touchdowns to Baillie and Chad Ehman. Leason also ran the ball eight times, for 111 yards, and scored a pair of touchdowns.

St. Leonard coach Tony Iadeluca sounded like somebody who knew a runaway train was coming and just stayed put until it had run over him. "They're a great team, we knew it all the way," he said. "We scouted them. We knew they were powerful, had depth at every position and could overpower us. But, hey, we're not the only ones to get that treatment. I'm sure Winnipeg and Surrey were strong teams and they got it. Heck, we were happy to score a touchdown."

The question begged to be answered: "Had the Regina Rams become too good for junior football?"

A couple of interesting and controversial items surfaced in the wake of the Rams' playoff run. One came about when Darryl Leason openly challenged the University of Saskatchewan Huskies to an exhibition game. This brought nothing but anger from the Huskies' Saskatoon campus. They accused the Rams of envying them. Huskie coach Brian Towriss said the Rams were jealous because the Huskies would be playing their national championship in front of 30,000 fans at the Skydome and that they regularly appeared on national television.

To which McCrystal replied, "So does Mr. Dressup."

But the issue that really caused some heads to turn, and some minds to start working, was the suggestion that the Rams did need something more competitive, that they had outgrown junior football.

That brought about the suggestion that the Rams should join the University of Regina and represent the school in Canadian university football. After all, the Rams had 27 players attending the U of R already.

But nothing came of the idea at the time. The University of Regina's dean of the faculty of Physical Activity Studies, Dr. Ralph Nilson, said the university simply didn't have the money to start up another team.

A familiar scene.

It was one idea that was indeed ahead of its time. But not by much.

LEASON'S LAST HURRAH . . . KIND OF

1995

Every sports team in the world, especially those that are able to endure the pitfalls of sport, has something in common. There is always a beginning and there is always an ending. As simplistic as that may sound, it is significant in the big picture because it is how those milestones are handled that tells the story. You have to be able to build a bridge from one year's team to the next, from one era to the next. Trip, and you'll soon find yourself back with the pack. The Rams have always been able to do that. They have managed to stay ahead of the pack. It is why they are the Regina Rams.

The Regina Rams came into the 1995 season with a clear goal in mind. They wanted to win a third straight Canadian junior football championship. It was not out of reach, not with the talent they had. They were also aware that 1995 would mark the end of an era of sorts for the Rams. It was quarterback Darryl Leason's last year. He would be graduating out of junior football when the season ended, whenever that would be.

The Rams had lost the usual load of players from their 1994 team to graduation but, as usual, they had players waiting in the wings to step into starting roles. There were always apprentices on the Rams' roster. Their rookie camp produced players who got invited to the main camp and, in the most part, found themselves practicing during the week and watching games from the sidelines until the time came when they were needed and were ready to play. One player who showed up at the rookie camp was Campbell Collegiate Tartans' slotback Kris Aldag. He was the third Aldag in the history of the Rams. The first was Kris' uncle Barry; the second was Kris' father Roger.

The Rams were delighted when linebacker Randy Srochenski came back to them after trying out with the Saskatchewan Roughriders. The return of Srochenski became even more important when standout linebacker Lloyd MacDonald accepted a scholarship from Minot State University in North Dakota. The Rams also went into the season without running back Mark Bernard, who was still recovering from a serious knee injury suffered during the fifth game of the 1994 season. He was replaced by Mike Maurer, who had split playing time a year earlier with fullback Jamie Baillie, who had graduated.

Mike Maurer

The Rams came out of the starting gate cracking the whip. They opened the season with a 57-10 thrashing of the Calgary Colts. Both the running and passing games were clicking. With Maurer starting, and gaining 168 yards on 16 carries, the Rams once again let the PJFC know who the boss was going to be. Leason had a hot hand passing the ball, completing 16 of 28 passes for 338 yards and three touchdowns. In all, the Rams had 604 yards in offence – 258 yards rushing, 346 passing.

It was not uncommon for the Rams to win their season opener and then go on a rampage of sorts. And that is what happened in 1995. They followed their opening win with two more to run their undefeated mark to 3-0. But once again, as they had done the previous year, the Saskatoon Hilltops put the brakes to the Rams' unbeaten record. They beat Regina 33-20 in Saskatoon. The Rams completely collapsed in the second half, getting just 18 yards rushing and 123 passing in the third and fourth quarters.

"We played with no intensity at all; no intensity and no passion," said McCrystal. "They knocked us around, which is very embarrassing. We're very shaken. We're not poor sports, but we don't take it very well. We're very bitter."

The Rams took it out on the Wildcats the next weekend, shutting them out 52-0. They didn't lose another game the rest of the schedule. They finished in a tie for first place with the Hilltops, each with a 7-1 record, but the Rams were rewarded first place in the PJFC.

Once they had disposed of the Calgary Colts, 49-16, in the semifinal, the Rams looked up and saw the Saskatoon Hilltops staring back at them in the PJFC final. This was nothing new for either team. McCrystal was looking forward to the game, especially because it would be played in Taylor Field. "I don't like them, I don't like their fans and I don't like their referees," he said on the eve of the game.

It turned into a low-scoring defensive struggle. The Rams were lucky they had Matt Kellett as their kicker. Kellett banged four field goals through the goalposts and the Rams won 19-8 to advance to the Western Canadian junior football final against the Okanagan Sun. The Hilltop game, though, ended on a controversial note. On the last play of the game, with the Rams leading 19-8, and no time showing on the clock, Leason took the snap from centre, started to go down on one knee, then quickly stood up and threw a touchdown pass to an obviously wide open Josh Shaw. The play was called back because of a penalty, but the Hilltops were angry and the Rams were embarrassed.

As the days went on, the feelings were still strong. "We've seen a much greater awareness of the consequences that go along with his actions," McCrystal said. "Without a doubt, we've seen a very definite maturing." And linebacker Wavell Starr said, "He's a very competitive person who let his emotions get the best of him."

Wavell Starr

While the Hilltops sat home and fumed, the Rams showed up at Taylor Field to play the Western junior final. They had forgotten about the Hilltops and about Leason's last-second play. None of that mattered now. They were one win away from getting to the Canadian championship game.

The Western final turned into another defensive battle, with the Rams winning 11-8. New concerns began to surface. Through three playoff games, Leason had thrown only three touchdown passes, none in the game against the Sun.

The Canadian Bowl would be played in Regina's Taylor Field, and standing between the Rams and a third straight Canadian title would be the Ottawa Sooners.

The Sooners arrived in Regina, showing no signs of being afraid of the big, bad Rams.

"They've got a good football team," said Ottawa head coach Mike Morris, "but as superior as they are, they're not the Dallas Cowboys."

Said Sooners' nose guard Chuck Sincennes: "They might come out cocky, feeling the west is best. But will they be able to handle the hard-hitting Sooners. They're the champs. We have to come into their house and take it away from them. But we do have the players and we do have the intensity. Whether it's cold, hot, clear, snowy or rainy, we'll be here. We're just a bunch of guys who love to play ball. If they beat us 56-0, I guarantee you they're going to have to work very, very hard for those 56 points. If we win 56-0, they're going to cry."

The night before the game, the Canadian Junior Football League held its annual awards show and, after being shut out in two previous years, the Rams' Darryl Leason was finally acclaimed as the outstanding offensive player in the country.

The Hudson Bay native, now just hours away from his final game as a junior, took it all in stride. "Honestly, I think it's about time," he said. "I think my play over the last couple of years has been good enough to win this award. I'd like to thank my teammates, my offensive line and my receivers. They're the ones who make me look good." Leason's stats for the regular season were impressive. He had completed 158 of 260 passes for 2,749 yards (third highest in Canadian junior history) and had 31 touchdown throws. He had also run the ball 64 times for 615 yards and scored eight touchdowns.

The day of the game, Taylor Field was caught in the grip of winter weather. Overhead, snow fell from dirty-looking grey clouds and the winds picked up. It was cold. Only 1,300 fans showed up to watch the game.

The Rams didn't let those brave souls down. They took a 20-0 lead on the Sooners and went on to a 26-10 victory to accomplish something no other Regina Rams' team had ever accomplished – a third straight Canadian junior football championship.

Leason ran with the ball 10 times and gained 118 yards in another remarkable showing. He completed 13 of 27 passes for 118 yards and three touchdowns. He was, obviously, for the third straight year, named the game's outstanding offensive player.

The Rams' defence came up huge. They came into the game determined to stop Ottawa running back William Green, an American from Dallas, who had rushed for at least 150 yards in each of his previous four games. Against the Rams he gained just 39 yards on 13 carries before Ottawa coach Mike Morris put him on the bench. And left him there for the rest of the game.

"I got nuthin' to say about nuthin'," Green said after the game. "All I'm going to say is, How can you win if you don't play your running back?"

Morris also had nuthin' to say about Green.

The field conditions were, to say the least, treacherous. The snow, the wind, the -18°C temperature all combined to turn Taylor Field into a skating rink, in parts, and that killed Ottawa's fast-hitting running game. They couldn't get enough traction.

Leason, meanwhile, adjusted well. He threw touchdown passes to his brother Mike, Chad Ehman and Mike Maurer.

When the game had ended, and the season was over, the subject of McCrystal's future with the Rams again surfaced. Even his mother (Millie) asked him, "If you win three in a row, are you going to quit?"

"I have to admit, I have thought about it," McCrystal said. He was only 41 years old, and he had just wrapped up his 12th season as the Rams' head coach. "One of the things that creates some conflict within one's self is I probably started too early," he said. "I've been a coach here for 17 years. It would be so weird in the fall not to coach football. But I am starting to think about taking my own lessons to heart: Is there anything else I can do for the community? I just have to reflect on whether I am the best person right now to lead this program and whether it's right for me."

McCrystal reflected on everything. And even though he had long had nothing to prove to anybody, he still found an excitement in the yearly challenges that awaited the Rams' coaches. It was too deeply embedded in him, this thrill of the chase after excellence. He enjoyed it too much. He was too good at it. It was a big part of his life. In some ways, it was his life.

Frank McCrystal would be back in 1996. Darryl Leason wouldn't.

ANOTHER HILLTOPS' SPEED BUMP

1996

There was definitely a vacuum at the Regina Rams' training camp in the year 1996. Anybody who had wandered out to Scotty Livingstone Field on those warm summer nights, when the sun was slowly drifting lower and lower in the sky and the mosquitos were coming out, would have seen some familiar sights. The field would be covered with players, perhaps 100 of them, going through various drills. There would be the sounds of plastic on plastic, voices rising and falling, whistles blowing. But something was missing. For the first time since 1992 Darryl Leason was not the starting quarterback. His unequalled career, which had started out with a nine-man football team in Hudson Bay, had come to an end with the winning of a third straight Canadian championship – something no other Rams' quarterback had ever done.

There had been great Rams' quarterbacks in the past. Richie Seitz was a tremendous ball handler. Len Knoll could throw the ball. Dean Picton could throw it, and he possessed an inspiring quiet leadership, and understood the game so well. But no Rams' quarterback ever possessed the overall package that Darryl Leason had. He was a great runner, he could throw the ball, and he was such a competitor that the word defeat was just not a part of his vocabulary. Now, he was gone. He had graduated, run out of eligibility.

And from that came a sense of excitement. Without Darryl Leason, how far could the Rams go in their quest for a fourth straight championship? It was the kind of situation that brought real drama to the Rams, the kind of situation the Rams had been through before. They knew all about replacing great players. They had been doing it since 1965, when Gord Currie became their head coach.

The new quarterback in the huddle was Chad Ehman, who had operated in Leason's shadow, a backup who really had not received a whole lot of playing time, but the Rams were confident he could do the job. While the 1996 season may not have been as successful as the three previous years, it was hardly a failure.

Chad Ehman

In some ways, in most ways, this was a transition period for the Rams. They had lost not only Darryl Leason, but kicker extrordinaire Matt Kellett, who also had graduated. Kellett might well have been the most reliable punter and placekicker the Rams had ever had. His leg was as powerful as Mike Lazecki's, and he also possessed an accuracy that would take him to the CFL.

1996 marked the arrival of some new players who would be heard from down the road. Running back Cory Olynick and linebacker Jeff Zimmer were two new players who would be heard from in 1996, and for years to come. It also was the year slotback Jason Clermont showed up on the Rams' roster.

Jeff Zimmer

Most times, when a team loses players the caliber of Darryl Leason and Matt Kellett, the next year can be catastrophic. Not with the Rams.

The Rams went through their first two games with a win and a tie. In their third game, against the Edmonton

Huskies, in Edmonton, they played their best game so far.

It was there that McCrystal saw some positive signs emerge. The Rams won the game 28-20, mostly on the strength of a first half that saw them build a 22-7 halftime lead. They hung on in the second half, in the face of an Edmonton comeback, to preserve the victory.

"We were really disciplined in the first half," McCrystal said. "We did some positive things throwing the ball, running the ball. Our defence was great. We had a great first half and we didn't blow it in the second half. In the second half we didn't perform as well. We're okay. We've got something to build on. What the heck, we're in first place. We feel good about that."

Through the first two quarters of the game, the Rams had put together 276 yards in offence while holding the Huskies to just 58 yards.

Mike Maurer (on a three-yard run), Michael Leason (on a 52-yard run) and Olynick (on a three-yard pass from Ehman) had scored Regina touchdowns, all of which were converted by kicker Todd Pinkney.

Dan Paskiw

The Rams put the game away in the fourth quarter when linebacker Danny Paskiw returned an interception 37 yards for a touchdown. The Huskies scored on the last game play to make the score closer than the game actually was.

Ehman had a promising game throwing the football, completing 12 of 17 passes for 125 yards. He also showed he could run the ball, taking off with it 12 times for 70 yards.

The Rams' running attack was clicking through the first three games, for a couple of reasons. One was the play of the offensive line. The other was the running of tailback Mike Maurer, who led the PJFC in rushing with 456 yards on 70 carries. But the big reason was the blocking of fullback Todd Orthner, in his fifth season with the Rams. Orthner's leadership ability and experience were factors in his being named the Rams' team captain.

"Our fullback, along with the offensive line, is the key to our running attack," said offensive co-ordinator Bernie Schmidt. "Most teams key off where Todd is going because they know that where Todd is going, the ball is going. He

Mike Maurer

does a tremendous job. He is totally unselfish. He may only carry the ball once or twice and catch a couple of passes, but he never complains. He's the key to our offence."

The Rams seemed to hit their stride against the Edmonton Wildcats, thrashing the visitors 61-14 in Taylor Field.

The Rams had about as balanced an offence as you could have. They rushed for 295 yards and passed for 282 yards. Nine different Rams ran the ball, with none of them going over the 100-yard mark. Maurer was the top rusher with 80 yards. Ehman completed 11 of 17 passes for 180 yards and threw three touchdowns. Clermont completed three of five passes for 61 yards.

The Rams received a bit of a scare in their next game, against the Colts in Calgary, when all they had, with less than six minutes to go in the game, was a 10-8 lead. Then, they exploded. Ehman found Leason on a 35-yard touchdown pass, he threw a three-yard touchdown dart to Olynick and Jason Melnechenko returned an interception 97 yards for a touchdown. The Rams won, 32-8.

Cory Olynick

The Rams had turnover problems early in the game. "It would have been very easy for us to self-destruct with the number of things that weren't going right earlier in the game," said McCrystal. "We didn't let that happen. We maintained our discipline and remained consistent with what we wanted to happen. Our defence was very impressive. They did a great job."

In a bizarre game in front of 2,500 fans in Taylor Field, the Rams beat the Edmonton Huskies 28-25 and acted as if they had actually lost the game.

The statistics told the story. The Huskies had a total offence of 654 yards, with tailback Dean Jones getting 327 yards on 32 carries.

The Rams were no slouches themselves offensively, putting together an attack that totalled 459 yards.

But the yardage they gave up is what people were talking about. McCrystal couldn't remember anyone getting that much yardage against the Rams in his five years as a player and 18 seasons as a coach.

But he wasn't about to join those who looked upon the game as some sort of loss for the Rams. "It doesn't do us any good to dwell on the things we didn't do," he said. "We have to look at what we were successful at. First and foremost, we won the game. In our worst-case scenario, we'll get second place and be at home in the semis. We accomplished something with the win – we secured second place. Sometimes, we're really hard on ourselves."

The Rams had played the previous couple of games without their top running back, Mike Maurer. He had been undergoing tests for possible heart trouble but, after undergoing examinations and tests, he was cleared to return to the team and play. Maurer had a rapid and irregular heartbeat, which was corrected by a surgical procedure.

The regular season for the Rams came down to the final game, as it always seemed to. First place was on the line when the Rams travelled to Saskatoon to take on the Hilltops, both teams owning 7-1-1 records. In 1996, two more games were added to the schedule, because the Winnipeg Hawkeyes had joined the PJFC.

With 2,500 fans on hand in Gordie Howe Bowl, the Hilltops rocked the Rams with a 45-0 shutout in a game that saw the Rams' offence held to just 206 yards.

"They physically defeated us – offensively, defensively and on special teams," McCrystal said. McCrystal could not recall the Rams being shut out in the 23 years he had been with them.

The Hilltops seemed as shocked as the Rams. "It's kind of a shock," said Hilltops' cornerback Mike Lang, whose father Gordon had played with the Rams in the Canadian championship years of 1975 and 1976.

"Obviously, the outcome is surprising," said Hilltops' head coach Dave Hardy.

The shutout sent the Rams reeling back to Regina to play the Edmonton Huskies in the semifinal. The Rams easily disposed of the Huskies, 30-2, and prepared for a rematch with the Hilltops, who had beaten the Edmonton Wildcats 35-25 in the other semifinal.

The PJFC final was played in Saskatoon and, for the first time in a long time, the Rams did not go into the game as favourites.

"This is what we wanted," said cornerback Craig Briere.

Not exactly. The Rams went into Saskatoon determined to avenge the 45-0 shutout, and through the first half it appeared as if they would do exactly that. The Rams held a 23-3 halftime lead and seemed well on their way to their fifth straight PJFC championship. To make matters worse for the Hilltops, starting quarterback Sheldon Ball had been put out of the game on what the Toppers felt was a late hit. It meant that backup Brad Williamson had to go into the game, and he had not played a whole lot.

With the whole season on the line, the Hilltops rallied behind Williamson. They mounted a stirring comeback that produced a hair-raising 27-23 Saskatoon victory and the PJFC championship. Williamson was the hero of the night. He completed 16 of 23 passes for 207 yards and one touchdown in just 30 minutes of playing time. The Rams could do nothing about it.

McCrystal was not happy with the officiating, especially in the second half. But he said the Rams should be proud of what they did in coming back from a 45-0 shutout and playing as well as they did.

For seven Rams, the game was the last of their junior careers. Graduating were Trent Langford, Todd Orthner, Josh Shaw, Shawn Harvey, Devin Gusa, Derek Fink and Danny Paskiw.

Fink summed it all up quite nicely. "It would have been nice to come up here and beat them," he said. "I'm happy with the five years I had. I won three championships and made lots of friends."

It wasn't the end of the world, after all.

Derek Fink and Tom McCord

FATE & ANOTHER CHAMPIONSHIP

1997

As time went by, just what the Regina Rams had accomplished in winning three straight Canadian junior football championships began to register. And people began to realize, perhaps even understand, the kind of commitment it takes to win, not just one championship, but three in a row. There is so much that has to go into producing the kind of team that is capable of being competitive enough to even attempt to go the distance. And then there are the intangibles – things like breaks, a good bounce from the ball, weather, officiating. Each of those things can either combine to make dreams come true or destroy them. All that a team can really control are the technical and emotional aspects of the game.

The Rams went at the game for most of the year. When they weren't practicing and playing during training camp and the season, they were involved in their winter fitness program. They included everything they could into their program, everything that would give them an edge down the road, in the fourth quarter, in overtime, when it really mattered. The measure of this organization was its record. You can look it up.

There are times, not many, when teams appear that have something special about them. They seem almost too good to be true. And most of the time, their feelings that success awaits them are little more than illusions. But on those rare occasions, those special occasions, they become destiny's child. Simply put, they are destined to win. It is their fate.

That kind of aura seemed to insulate the Rams as they prepared for the 1997 season in the Prairie Junior Football Conference. They did not go into it as the defending champions, and that was unusual. They did not go into it as the favourites, and that was unusual. But they did go into it with a veteran-laden team that oozed experience and included a huge reservoir of talent. And, their playoff elimination a year earlier at the hands of the Hilltops served only to refresh them. It was the cold shower the Rams needed.

Frank McCrystal was back for his 14th season as head coach. It does not take much to get McCrystal fired up. He was fired up as the Rams went into training camp with one thought in mind – they would be back in 1997.

"Our players will be hungry again," McCrystal said. "I don't want to say we're complacent, but it's difficult to maintain that intensity game in and game out, week in and week out. We made that run (of three national titles) with many of the same players. Even so, last year we came within a couple of inches of winning that game (against the Hilltops). As far as the win-loss, championship, non-championship thing, we didn't meet the expectations of other people last season. But we don't feel poorly about the season. It gave us a breather, we'll regroup and go for it again."

The Rams had, perhaps, more experienced players going into the 1997 season than they had had in years. Quarterback Chad Ehman was in his fifth and last year with the team, his second as the starting quarterback. Slotback Michael Leason was back. A new face, receiver Chris Warnecke showed up. Warnecke was a superb athlete with a tremendous work ethic. He had been an outstanding receiver and quarterback in high school in Regina, with the Riffel Royals, but hadn't played football since leaving high school in 1995. Instead, he was a starting guard with the University of Regina Cougars basketball team. He continued to play for the Cougars as well as the Rams.

The defence was backboned by a number of veterans, veterans who could play this game. There was defensive tackle Chad Zipchian, linebackers Jeff Zimmer and Derek Wolbaum, and defensive backs Craig Briere, Jason Melnechenko and Chris Frankowski. Rush end Brent Dancey was headed for an outstanding season.

Over the winter, McCrystal had thought about what had happened to the Rams in 1996, and he came to the realization that he had let it happen. "All of us took things for granted," he said in one of his reflective moments. "I believe we have to renew our work ethic and our commitment to excellence and to our seeking out our potential. We let things happen to us instead of working toward making them happen."

The flavour for 1997 had been chosen. There would be no letting up on this team of destiny.

There was a considerable amount of pressure on Ehman, and he seemed to welcome it. The 22-year-old did not have a bad season in 1996, but it had been his first year as the starting quarterback and there were growing pains to go through. He had passed the test; the future had arrived; he just needed to reach out and grab it.

"I'm a lot more comfortable, at least at the beginning of the year," he said. "I'm not saying I doubted myself last year but I didn't have the experience of being a starter. As the year went on, I started to build up my confidence and hopefully that will carry over to this year."

Chad Ehman

The shadow of Darryl Leason also hung over Ehman. "I tried to shield it out, but it was tough," Ehman said. "This year, I won't have to deal with it."

In his first season as a starter, Ehman had led the Rams to an 8-1-1 record. He completed 123 of 188 passes for 1,839 yards and stacked 16 touchdowns against just six interceptions. He led the PJFC in yardage and completion percentage (65.4) and he was tied for second in touchdowns.

"At the beginning of the year, I had a lot of expectations," he said. "As the year went on, they faded. But the expectations of the team weren't met. The Rams don't like finishing second to anyone. There's nothing more valuable than experience. You can take all the practice snaps you want, but there's nothing like taking snaps in a meaningful game. I don't like to live on last year. This is a new start."

The Rams got off to their expected strong start. They opened the season with a 28-14 victory over the Edmonton Huskies in Taylor Field in front of 2,500 fans. Ehman had a so-so game, but it was enough to win. He was sacked and pressured throughout the game, but still managed to complete 16 passes for 254 yards, and he fired off a couple of touchdown tosses.

Ehman threw touchdown passes to Michael Thomas and Lonnie Hayes. Olynick ran for another. The Rams had the Huskies in deep trouble, trailing 21-6 after the first quarter, but the Huskies rallied.

"Two years ago, when we won the Canadian championship, we'd go into halftime leading a team 28-7 and then come out in the second half and outscore them 21-0 – really put them away," Ehman said. "Last year and this year, we've been letting teams back in games. We've got to get that killer instinct."

If there was one player who did not have to be taught what the killer instinct was all about, it was linebacker Jeff Zimmer. In his third year with the Rams, Zimmer also was emerging as an outstanding linebacker. He had actually been slated to play linebacker in high school at LeBoldus for the Golden Suns, but in his Grade 11 year, an injury to the LeBoldus quarterback saw coach Paul Dawson move Zimmer to the position. "Jeff was the only guy we had who knew enough about football and who wouldn't make a lot of mental mistakes," said Dawson, who was an assistant coach with the Rams in 1997.

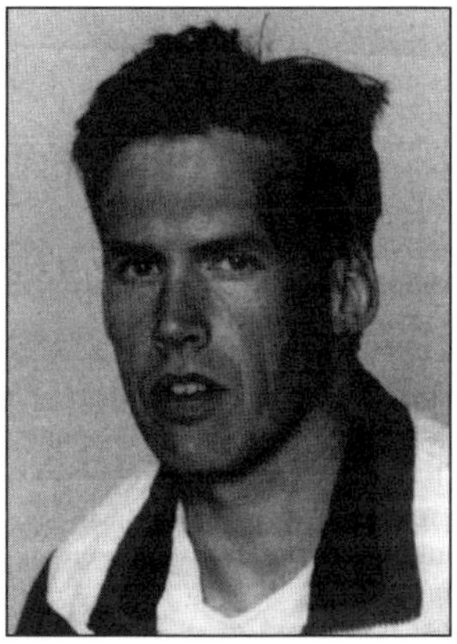

Paul Dawson

"He would have been a killer linebacker in high school. But he had to make a sacrifice for the squad. He had to give up being a potential all-star in order for the team to have a few good games." In 1994, Zimmer was again going to play linebacker for the Golden Suns, but a knee injury finished his season and he had to wait until he joined the Rams in 1995 before he could return to the position. He started out as a middle linebacker with the Rams, but was moved to the outside because it was felt he didn't have the size to handle the middle.

Zimmer was the kind of player the Rams have always looked for. He was talented, had good size and always put the team first.

The Rams' first real test of the 1997 season came at the halfway mark of the schedule when they went up against the Hilltops. They went into the game feeling pretty good about themselves. They were undefeated in three games, as were the Hilltops, and they were coming off a 77-3 win over the Calgary Colts. "This sends out a message that we're ready," said running back Tim Lynchuk after the Colts' game. Lynchuk, who had gained 113 yards on 13 carries against the Colts, added, "Saskatoon had better be ready to play some football."

The rivalry between the Rams and the Hilltops continued to intensify. Jason Clermont, relatively new to all of this, had seen it first-hand. "I have a buddy, Ryan David, who tried out up there last year," said Clermont. "As soon as he cracked the Hilltops' roster, it was a totally different friendship. I'd go up there and he wouldn't take me out to dinner to the normal place because the Hilltops hung out there and he was sure there would be a fight. It's not like that here. I'll take him to the bars where we hang out and there won't be a problem."

The Hilltops went out and whipped the Rams 35-17, to remain as the only undefeated team in the PJFC.

For the Rams, the season's first disappointment had been dealt. But it had happened during the season. The Rams were gearing themselves for the playoffs. It was there that they didn't want to lose.

From game to game to game, it surfaced that the Rams were becoming a multi-faceted team. They could hurt you in so many ways.

Chris Ashman, who had missed the 1996 season because of a broken heel, had turned into an extraordinary punt return man. In a 49-3 win over the Edmonton Wildcats, Ashman ran back two punts for touchdowns The five-foot, six-inch, 170-pound Ashman, who had moves and timing more than blinding speed, ran one back 90 yards and the other 56 yards.

Chris Ashman

Then, there was Cory Olynick. The five-foot, eleven-inch, 198-pound Olynick was almost a team in himself. He played slotback, tailback and fullback, was on the field goal, punt return and kickoff teams. "I'd be happy if I was on defence too," he said.

The Rams were also using all of their quarterbacks as much as they could. They didn't want to go into the playoffs with the backups to Ehman not having received any playing time. So, when the game's outcome had been decided, Clermont found himself leaving his slotback position to play quarterback. And third-stringer Mike Wong also found himself under the centre, taking snaps.

The Rams and Hilltops closed out the 1997 regular season in Taylor Field. The Rams had to beat the Hilltops by 19 points if they wanted to finish in first place, otherwise it would be second place again. The Rams didn't come close, losing 42-24. It was on to the playoffs.

The Rams beat the Edmonton Huskies 25-16 in one semifinal, and the Hilltops stopped the Edmonton Wildcats 55-3 in the other semifinal to set up yet another PJFC showdown between them.

The Hilltops had swept the Rams in the season series. They had also won their semifinal with ease, while the Rams had to work to put the Huskies away. It figured that Saskatoon would be favoured, even more so because the final would be played in Gordie Howe Bowl.

The Rams had moulded their whole season to fit the playoffs. It was there, in the playoffs, that the lessons of the season would produce results. On this Saturday night in 1997, it all did come together for the Rams.

They used something they hadn't used a lot over the course of the schedule. They unleashed their deep passing game, using their two wide receivers, Chris Warnecke and Michael Thomas. And they let Chris Ehman's arm do the rest, as the Rams ousted the Hilltops 46-27.

Warnecke, a first-year Ram, had three catches, all for touchdowns – from 84 yards, 67 yards and 24 yards. Thomas had six catches for 141 yards and one touchdown.

Ehman had perhaps the most daringly efficient game of his career with the Rams. He completed 16 of 26 passes for 451 yards and five touchdowns. "We decided to put the ball up and let our athletes make plays," said McCrystal. "That was Chad believing in the system. It's hard to stand back there and say 'If I throw the ball waaay out there, we'll have success, but he did just that."

The Rams only gained 72 yards rushing, but they didn't need the ground game. On this night, it was bombs away. Hilltops' head coach Dave Hardy resigned a few days after the game.

The win moved the Rams into the Canadian Junior Football League's semifinal. They had to travel to Windsor to play the AKO Fratmen. The winner would go to the Canadian Bowl in Kelowna.

The Rams ran into a buzzsaw in Windsor. The Fratmen appeared well on their way to a victory, taking a 31-10 lead, before the Rams got their engine going, scored four unanswered touchdowns and won 38-31. The game was costly to the Rams. They lost Olynick for the rest of the season with a knee injury.

It was off to Kelowna. And the Rams had company. About 80 Rams' fans made the trip from Regina. Among them was their number-one fan and good luck charm, Jarrod Livingstone. Jarrod was the grandson of Scotty Livingstone, who had been the driving force behind the rebirth of the Rams in 1965, and the son of long-time Rams' supporter Dick Livingstone.

Jarrod has spina bifida, and despite being in a wheelchair you'll find him at Rams' practices and games with his dad, Dick, or his mother, Valerie. He's the focal point for a lot of fun with the players, coaches, trainers and equipment people. "One time they taped me to the floor of the dressing room," Jarrod said.

During the 1997 season, Jarrod had to be admitted to hospital in Regina. The doctors were not sure he would survive. "When I was in hospital and real sick, the entire team came to see me," he said. "I thought if they were that dedicated, I would come to Kelowna." The Rams dedicated their next game to Jarrod while he was in hospital and they won. When Jarrod watched the game film he quickly recovered. His dad promised him that if he got better, and the Rams made it to Kelowna, they would make the 12-hour trip.

And, so, there was Jarrod Livingstone, the grandson of one of the architects of the Rams' organization, in his wheelchair on the Rams' bench, wearing his Rams' hat, and watching what would turn out to be one of the greatest Canadian junior football championships ever played.

Dick & Jarrod Livingstone

The Rams were up against it in this one. They were playing the Okanagan Sun, the hometown team, and the biggest crowd – more than 4,500 fans – to ever watch a game in the Apple Bowl was on hand and making the noise of thousands more.

That game went to a second overtime period before the

Jason Clermont

winner was decided, before the Rams were miraculously able to score the winning touchdown, with but 11 seconds to go, for a 23-20 triumph.

The first quarter was scoreless, but Chad Ehman got the Rams going in the second quarter. When they went to the dressing room at halftime, they were ahead 17-3 on touchdown runs of four yards by Clermont and five yards by tailback Ikenna Ngoka, who was replacing Olynick. Todd Pinkney converted both touchdowns and kicked a field goal. The third quarter was also scoreless, in what had turned into a ferocious battle between two good teams. But in the fourth quarter, with their backs against the wall and the crowd lifting them, the Sun rallied. They outscored the Rams 14-0 on a pair of touchdowns, the last one with two minutes and ten seconds to go, to tie the national championship at 17-all and send the game into overtime.

Neither team scored in the first overtime, so the game moved into the second overtime period. The Sun put together a drive that carried them to the Rams' 10-yard line. There were only two minutes left in overtime, but the Rams' defence held, and the Sun were forced to kick a field goal. It gave them a 20-17 lead. Time was now a huge factor.

There was only one minute and 16 seconds left when Ehman and the offence took to the field, the ball sitting on the grass at the Rams' 35-yard line. Ehman, who had established himself as another in a line of great Rams' quarterbacks, put together a drive that took seven plays to conclude.

Two plays stand out. Both of them centred around Clermont. Two plays from the end of the drive, the Rams faced a third-down and 10-yard situation from the Okanagan 45. Ehman called for a pass. He threw the ball, Clermont was seven yards down the field, he caught it, broke two tackles and roared down the sidelines, past the Sun's bench, and was finally pushed out of bounds on the three-yard line.

With 11 seconds left in overtime, Ehman handed the ball off to Clermont, who powered his way into the end zone for the winning touchdown. The Rams had won their Canadian championship. The air went out of the 4,500 fans who, for hours, had roared their approval at one of the greatest junior playoff games ever.

Ehman had had himself a game for the ages, the last of his junior career. He completed 17 of 32 passes for 231 yards and ran the ball himself 16 times for 66 yards. On what was the biggest drive of his life, he had ice running through his veins. Ngoka replaced Olynick in style, rushing for 115 yards in 19 carries. Clermont, Warnecke, Leason, Briltz, Ngoka and Thomas all made big catches over the course of this heart-stopper.

Chris Briltz

The defence, led by Zimmer, who had been named the outstanding defensive player in the country, had been there when it was needed.

The game left everybody speechless.

"I never used to believe in fate," McCrystal said. "But after watching that one, I'm not so sure."

Destiny's darlings had done it again.

THE RAMS PASS THEIR SAT'S

The date was May 6, 1998. The place was Vancouver. Dick White, the University of Regina's director of recreation and athletics, was at a meeting of the Canada West Universities Athletic Association. On the table was an application by the University of Regina to play football in the CWUAA in 1999. Reject it. Or accept it. It was that simple. The vote was taken. The application was unanimously accepted. Once again the Regina Rams had made a profound change to the face of football in Regina.

The Regina Rams were leaving junior football. The 1998 season would be their last. In 1999, they would be the University of Regina Rams. They would keep their team name, not change it to the Cougars, and their uniforms would be basically the same, with a splash of gold added to go along with the university's colours of green and gold.

It was not unexpected that the Rams were moving to university football. The subject had come up a few years earlier. But by 1998 the Rams had reached a point in their history where there was nothing left for them do in junior football. They had dominated the game so much that, if it wasn't becoming boring, it certainly was totally predictable. They would always be in the top two teams in the PJFC.

The Rams needed a new challenge, that's all there was to it. There were endless meetings with the University of Regina's Dick White and Dr. Ralph Nilson. The Rams' point man was former player Larry LeBlanc, a Regina lawyer and a man still devoted to the Rams. LeBlanc was focused in his belief that the Rams had to make the move for their own survival, for their own growth. There were naturally some on the Rams' executive who were not sure about the move. But LeBlanc was able to sway everybody his way, and he deserves a tremendous amount of credit for how it all unfolded. He and Rams' president Tom McCord, also a former Rams' player, worked tirelessly on making the arrangements fit both the Rams and the university. Former president Paul Barnby, a long-time Rams' executive member, was another who was heavily involved.

Larry LeBlanc

The arrangement would not really change a lot for the Rams. They would foot the bill, but they had such a vast network of fundraising that not a whole lot of tinkering would be needed there.

"That's important," said White, "but what's more important is that they're bringing their whole commitment and organization to us. That's important because we don't know how to run a first-class football operation. They do."

The Rams would continue to practice out of their clubhouse at Mount Pleasant Park until new facilities were built for them on the university campus, a campus which has seen spectacular growth in the last several years.

And, of course, the Rams would bring their history and their tradition to the University of Regina. The image of the University of Regina would be enhanced.

McCrystal welcomed the move. He knew the Rams could compete, he didn't know how long it would take to put together a team that would measure up to the level of competition the Rams would be facing.

The announcement of the move was made at a press conference held at the University of Regina's Physical Activity Centre.

"We're confident we've done our part in working toward the betterment of junior football," McCrystal said. "Now that rests with others." For McCrystal, the move to the University of Regina would see him leave his teaching career in the Regina high-school system and become a fulltime employee of the Rams.

There was some concern expressed that, by leaving junior football, the opportunities for young people wanting to play at that level would decrease. "Our leaving junior football may limit the access for some people," he said. "But we're confident, by giving a year's notice, that we've given those players an opportunity to make other plans." As it turned out, the Prairie Thunder team was formed in Regina and they joined the Prairie Football Conference.

The Rams were joining a league that included the University of Manitoba Bisons, the University of Calgary Dinosaurs, the University of Alberta Golden Bears, the University of British Columbia Thunderbirds and, of course, the University of Saskatchewan Huskies.

McCrystal knew that moving into college football would likely bring him some good-natured ribbing. Over the years, he and some of his players had challenged university teams to exhibition games. He had taken shots at universities for using players in their late 20s.

He got that impish grin on his face when he was reminded of that. "I'm sure I've left myself open to a great deal of criticism. Not only am I expecting that, but maybe I am looking forward to it."

But, first, McCrystal had one more challenge awaiting him. The 1998 Prairie Junior Football Conference season. It would be the last year of junior football for the Regina Rams, who were first formed in 1954. They knew how they wanted to finish it.

RAMS GRADUATE WITH HONOURS

1998

Sometimes, things moved quickly for the Regina Rams. When they headed into the 1998 season, needing a replacement for the graduated Chad Ehman, they figured it would be a no-brainer. They would simply take the versatile Jason Clermont from his slotback spot and put him in as the starting quarterback. It was something Clermont had wanted to do since he had joined the Rams a couple of seasons earlier. He had been a quarterback in high school and that was his position.

Sometimes, the best laid plans of men and Rams go down the tube. Clermont was out at quarterback before he even got in.

It was an old wound that did him in. He aggravated an injury to his throwing shoulder, something he had hurt in the 1996 Senior Bowl high-school all-star game. He initially had tendinitis in his rotator cuff, but the joint got worse after he had separated it during his rookie year with the Rams. So, just a few weeks before the 1998 season was over, Clermont returned to his slotback position. "You want to put the ball in the hands of your best player as much as you can," said McCrystal. "Is that at slotback, quarterback, tailback? We might be better off with Jason at slotback anyway."

That left Mike Wong as the Rams' starting quarterback. In his rookie year in 1997, Wong had been the third-string quarterback behind Ehman and Clermont, and as a result saw very little playing action. "There's a little bit of pressure, but with the receivers, and the offensive line and the running backs we have, I can't do a bad job."

Defensively, the Rams were anchored by linebacker Jeff Zimmer, who had had an outstanding season the year before, an all-star and award-winning kind of year. Zimmer had developed into perhaps the best linebacker in junior football. In the Canadian Bowl victory over the Okanagan Sun, Zimmer played the game of his life, making 14 solo tackles and recovering a fumble.

"He can take his game to another level," said Rams' defensive co-ordinator Erwin Klempner. "He's learned a lot. He's a lot smarter. Last year, he was just reacting to the ball. This year, he'll recognize things before they happen. He'll have the confidence to go make those plays."

The Rams were ready for what surely would turn into a nostalgic season. "At some point this season," said McCrystal, "it'll be our last time at Gordie Howe Bowl and our last time at Clarke Stadium. It won't necessarily be sadness, but there will be some feelings and emotions when we leave."

If McCrystal had any worries, it was that the Rams were looking toward next year. He wanted them to stay focused on the 1998 season, and approach it as they had every season. Certainly he wasn't worried about the talent he had on hand. Wong had at his disposal the best set of receivers in the country – Clermont and Chris Warnecke as slotbacks, Michael Thomas and Ryan Smith as outside receivers. He had two experienced running backs in Cory Olynick and Chris Briltz.

Defensively, there were Zimmer and Royal Harden at linebacker positions, and a secondary manned by five veterans, including halfbacks Jason Melnechenko and Corrie McKee.

There was also a handful of impressive rookies among the new faces recruited – tailback Neal Hughes and defensive end Lee Cherkas were two of the best.

The Rams opened the 1998 season on the road and Wong got off to a blistering start in his first game as a starter. He passed for 490 yards and three touchdowns as the Rams beat the Wildcats in Edmonton 34-24.

"I thought I'd do all right, but I couldn't have imagined myself doing this well," Wong said. "I had a lot of help from my teammates. J.C. (Clermont) was telling me things in the huddle and so were the linemen."

Mike Wong

Wong led the Rams to 642 yards in total offence and completed 14 of 26 passes. His first pass filled him with confidence – an 82-yard touchdown to Clermont, who later caught a 15-yard touchdown toss. Wong also hit rookie wide receiver Ryan Smith on a 70-yard touchdown play. Smith had come to the Rams after two seasons with the University of Saskatchewan Huskies. Warnecke caught four passes for 85 yards and Thomas hauled in a pair for 70 yards, as Wong used all his receivers.

Rookie tailback Neal Hughes rushed for 113 yards, replacing Olynick, who sat the game out with a hamstring injury.

Shane Ostapowich

Meanwhile, the Rams realized that they had found another truly versatile player, Shane Ostapowich, who came to junior football from the LeBoldus Golden Suns. Ostapowich was being used as a backup tailback, backup wide receiver, third-string quarterback, first-string punt returner and first-team kickoff returner in his rookie year. "He's a natural athlete," Rams' offensive coordinator Bernie Schmidt said. "Some people are naturals." Schmidt just shrugged. "You can't explain it."

Wong found out early in the season that there were going to be some bad moments in his rookie year as starting quarterback. He found out in the Rams' third game of the year.

The Hilltops came to town. Wong threw five interceptions and Saskatoon left with a 21-16 victory.

"There's no excuse for what I did," Wong said. "I can't throw interceptions. When it all comes down to it, that's what cost us the game."

McCrystal wasn't worried. "We've been involved with this too long to push the panic button. We'll play them again and Mike will have four more games under his belt. Things will be different."

The Rams suffered a serious loss when wide receiver Michael Thomas injured a knee so badly that doctors figured it would take him eight weeks to recover. The Rams did have sufficient backups – Chris Ashman, returning from a knee injury suffered while playing soccer, Shane Ostapowich and Troy Gordon.

If there was anything the Rams displayed in 1998, it was that they were not always going to be predictable. In a game against the Huskies in Taylor Field, rain and wind were the order of the day. It should have set up the Rams' running game perfectly. Not so. Wong went to the air and, despite the wet conditions, he put on a show as the Rams won 40-11.

Wong, who called only 15 running plays, completed 18 of 38 passes (he had a number dropped) for 295 yards and three touchdowns. Clermont caught seven of them for 120 yards. The Rams also got a big game out of their specialty teams. Ostapowich had a 59-yard kickoff return and returned five punts for 91 yards. Hughes had 88 yards of punt returns and another 45 on kickoff returns, giving the Rams good field position virtually every time.

As usual, where the Rams finished depended on how they did against the Hilltops in the last game of the schedule. It was also the Rams' last trip to Gordie Howe Bowl. That, they would never miss.

The Rams needed to beat the Hilltops by five points to finish in first place. They did. They beat them 32-13. McCrystal had promised after the first game between these two, when Wong served up five interceptions, that the Hilltops would see a different Mike Wong the next time. They did. Wong completed 24 of 39 passes for 266 yards and two touchdowns. And he only gave up one interception.

Chris Warnecke

It was a game for a while. At one point, early in the third quarter, the Hilltops had cut the Rams' lead to 15-13. But come the fourth quarter, the Rams took control. Their defence wrapped the Hilltops' offence in a suffocating hold, not giving them anything. And the Rams' offence exploded for 17 points – Warnecke caught a 23-yard touchdown pass from Wong and Clermont scored on a three-yard run. Both touchdowns were converted by Todd Pinkney, who also kicked a 33-yard field goal.

Clermont had a big game, catching 11 passes for 128 yards. Smith had five catches and Warnecke had four as the Rams spread their passing game around.

For Wong, his first season as starting quarterback was something to write about. He was the regular season's leading passer with 142 completions in 252 attempts for 2,570 yards, 12 interceptions and 25 touchdowns. Clermont led the league in scoring and pass receiving with 13 touchdowns and 39 catches; Hughes was fourth in rushing as the Rams ended up with a first-place finish and home field in the playoffs. And McCrystal was named the PJFC's coach of the year.

The Rams hosted the Edmonton Wildcats in the PJFC semi-final, handing them a 54-25 loss.

It took a while for the Rams to get untracked against Edmonton. At one point in the first half, the Wildcats had taken a 17-11 lead, but the Rams weren't rattled. "No one gets down on this team," said Wong. "We knew that as long as we played our game and kept plugging away that things would work out."

The Rams scored 43 unanswered points. Wong completed 16 of 32 passes for 288 yards. The running game churned to 222 yards. Hughes led the ground game with 149 yards in 16 carries; Olynick had seven carries for 84 yards and two touchdowns; Wong ran one touchdown into the end zone. Wong also threw touchdown passes to Smith and Troy Gordon.

The Rams were set to play their final game ever against the Hilltops – in the PJFC final in Regina's Taylor Field on Saturday, October 24, 1998.

The Rams had managed to avoid reliving memories throughout the season, staying riveted on getting by their next game. They carried that same attitude into the game against the Hilltops. Those who yearned for a barnburner were disappointed. But nobody else in Regina was.

The Rams uprooted the Hilltops 48-10 and put Saskatoon's season on the shelf.

Mike Wong

Wong only threw 20 passes, completing 14 of them for 177 yards. He never gave up an interception. The Rams ran the ball 46 times, gaining 197 yards, Olynick was the leader at 66 yards in 14 carries. It was the Rams' defence that got much of the credit for this victory. They forced seven turnovers and held Saskatoon to just 275 yards in offence, and only 76 of that came via the pass.

For the Rams, the game meant only that they got to play one more time – in the Canadian Bowl for the national championship. Fittingly, the game was played in Regina. And, once again, it was the Rams against the Okanagan Sun.

On Saturday, November 14, 1998, the Regina Rams played their last game of junior football. They had been at it since 1954. They had begun to meet with success in 1965. And now, near the end of the century, their journey was over. They wanted to leave behind one more good memory, because they had no idea what to expect once this game was over.

The game, the last one, was actually over fairly early. The Rams were as fired up for this game as they had been for any. They were ahead 15-0 after the first quarter and 22-3 after the second. They won their 15th Canadian junior football championship by a score of 36-13.

"We never really talked about it, but we felt pressure to not let anybody down who ever had been a Ram and all the people who made the decision to go to the CIAU," said Clermont. "We wanted to go out with a bang. There's no better way to go out – by taking the trophy with us."

Jason Clermont

Clermont had a superb game, catching eight passes for 124 yards and scoring two touchdowns, one of them a one-handed circus kind of catch off of a tipped pass that went for 24 yards. Olynick scored two touchdowns on short runs. Zimmer got one when he recovered a fumble. Wong completed 19 of 26 passes for 269 yards and didn't throw an interception. Warnecke had five catches for 61 yards.

Chris Warnecke

The Rams' defence was one step ahead of the Sun's offence all day. Okanagan quarterback Chris Orban, the son of former Ram Jerry Orban, couldn't get his passing game going and completed only eight passes. When he was a boy growing up, his dad had taken him to Rams' practices every night. By the end of that day, he had seen enough of the Regina Rams, thank you. He was intercepted three times.

The Rams' domination of junior football was complete. They had won five of the last six Canadian championships.

"We're closing this chapter," said McCrystal, "but we're opening a new chapter next year."

Back in the Rams' clubhouse, the celebration was long and loud. The place would never be the same. The Canadian Bowl trophy sat on the carpet. McCrystal stood near the hallway leading into the dressing room. He was just standing there, with a somewhat weary look, his hair tossed and his eyes staring down at the trophy that, for a moment, stood alone.

"I wonder," McCrystal said to nobody in particular, "I wonder what the Vanier Cup looks like." He smiled, turned and walked down the hall.

The Rams Go To College

1999

Before you run, you have to learn to walk. And before you walk, you have to learn to crawl. Or, as my good friend Joe Kazeil often says, "Every journey starts with a small step."

In the winter of 1999, the last year of the decade, the century and the millennium, the University of Regina Rams ordered new uniforms. They were adopting a darker green, there would be gold trim, the horns on the helmets would be gold, the pants would be gold. The Rams were now ready. And so was the city.

If anything had ever disappointed the Regina Rams in their junior football life, it was that they rarely received the kind of support at the gate they should have received, given how successful they were. Crowds of around 2,000 were the norm. Even when they played the Canadian championship games at Taylor Field, they did not always command big crowds.

Dick White and Dr David Barnard ceremonial kickoff

But in 1999, as they prepared for their first season of Canadian college football, the Rams had suddenly become a hot item in town. Where they had sold around 500 season tickets in junior football, they sold 2,500 for the university schedule.

Denis Losie
long-time player and coach

Nobody knew what to expect from the Rams in this first year. In some ways, it was a bit of a contradiction. The Rams were so well-known across the country. But, in this new situation, they were also unknown. In a perfect world, the Rams would go undefeated in their first season in university ball, sweep through the playoffs, and win the Vanier Cup on a triple overtime field goal by a backup kicker.

The real world, though, had something different in mind.

The Rams had prepared for this game for a long time, the first game of their new life. It was against the University of Manitoba Bisons in Taylor Field on Saturday, September 4, 1999.

The day before, McCrystal was clearly happy the big moment had arrived. "Thank God we're almost at the game," he said. "We've been talking about this for 19 months. I'm at the point now where I'm thinking, 'Let's just play.' We're really excited about it. There's a rejuvenation and there's new excitement. There's a new challenge and a new conference. It's just different. As such, people are excited about the newness. That's something we have to maintain."

On a pleasant Saturday evening, a crowd of 7,012 people streamed into Taylor Field for the University of Regina Rams' coming-out party. And a party it was. Two hours before the game, there was a barbecue, prize draws and music by the band GoKart Mozart.

The Rams were a young team, certainly younger than most of the teams in the league. Many of them had come from the 1998 championship team. Others were new to the Rams. All of them attended the University of Regina. They also were not a big team.

Manitoba head coach Brian Dobie didn't know what to expect from the Rams. He had watched them in the Canadian Bowl, seen film on them, talked to people about them.

"The first thing you've got to do is respect them," he said. "And that's not just a token coaching line. They're the Regina Rams, they're emblematic of junior football in Canada. We know what they're about. One thing they have going for them before the ball is even snapped is tremendous pride, tremendous tradition and tremendous confidence because they know how to win. They go into games expecting to win – and that's the Regina Rams."

McCrystal said, "It's more excitement that we're going into a new challenge. It's not scary and it's not frightening. It's exciting and something to look forward to. One of our trophies in the clubhouse which quotes Tennyson's Ulysses says, 'To strive, to seek, to find and not yield,' so that's what we're doing."

When Manitoba coach Brian Dobie walked out onto the turf at Taylor Field on the Saturday night, he couldn't believe his eyes, a big smile spread across his face. "Hey," he said after the game had been played, "this is the best football province in the country and look at that crowd. There's no question – our players talked about it on the bench – that when Regina started to roll in the third quarter and the crowd really got into it, you could see they were playing on a ton of emotion."

As many had suspected, the Rams lost their opening game of college football, 37-28, to the Bisons, who were just too big and perhaps a little more experienced at this level than were the Rams.

But, at least, the Rams didn't get blown out of the game. They held their own, sending sparks of electricity through the 7,000-plus fans when Chris Ashman returned a kickoff 95 yards for a touchdown. In the third quarter the Rams came to life and mounted a comeback that had the Bisons reeling.

Chris Ashman

Trailing 21-9 after two quarters, the Rams came out to prove something in the third quarter. And prove it, they did. The Rams erupted for 13 unanswered points on touchdowns by Jason Clermont, on a nine-yard pass from Mike Wong, and by Clermont on a one-yard run. It put the Rams ahead 22-21, but the Bisons answered with points of their own before coming home with the win.

Mike Wong served up four interceptions in the game, finishing with 20 completions in 41 attempts for 280 yards. Clermont caught 11 passes for 149 yards, introducing the Bisons to a player who was unstoppable. The Rams ran the ball for only 51 yards. Jeff Zimmer had a big game at linebacker, making 10 tackles and getting one sack.

The Bisons were able to run the ball at the Rams, with tailback Craig Carr doing most of the damage. He carried the ball 28 times and gained 259 yards. Carr figured the Rams had some maturing to do now that they were in university football. "I noticed a few times we'd get a big play and they'd be 'Man, what happened?' They'd break down right after that. In this league, you've got to regroup right away. This game is so mental, you've got to learn to just turn the page. They're used to dominating their league. They're not used to teams coming in here and getting up on them or basically battering them around. God, they've got talent everywhere. They've got to just turn the page."

The Rams, if anything, came out of the game encouraged. "This was a benchmark," said Clermont. "Now we know where we're at. We competed with that team. Not to spite them – they've got a good team – but we faced as good if not better teams in junior football and beat them. We can play here."

In some ways, the Rams' first season in university football paralleled the Rams' first season in existence. The Rams did not win a game in the college league in 1999. They went 0-8 and missed the playoffs. In 1954, their first year ever, the Rams lost all seven games and missed the playoffs.

Everybody was waiting for the first game between the Rams and the University of Saskatchewan Huskies. It came one week after they had lost to Manitoba. There was a huge crowd in Griffiths Stadium, over 6,000 fans, on a cold, wet Saturday afternoon, and they were on the Rams as soon as they came out for their pre-game warmup.

The Rams came out firing, and immediately caught a few breaks. The Huskies turned over the ball twice and the Rams turned the two gifts into an 11-0 lead. But the Huskies caught fire when running back Doug Rozon tore off on a 70-yard touchdown run. "That gave us life and then we pinned them deep in their own end in the second quarter and we took over physically," Huskie head coach Brian Towriss said.

The Huskies scored 42 straight points after the Rams had taken the 11-0 lead and went on to win the first meeting between the two teams, 56-12. "It's nice to lay a licking on them," said Huskie wide receiver Kelly McNairn, who had taken a few beatings from the Rams when he was with the Hilltops. "But they're going to be ready the next time."

Clermont sounded off after the game. "If we've got a game at 1:30, we'd better be ready to play at 1:30, to whatever time the game ends. We didn't play football today."

The media was all over McCrystal, asking him if he was embarrassed or humbled. "Those are words for creative writers," Slick replied. "What we're going to do is keep working. We'll build on the things we did well and we'll be at Taylor Field next Saturday afternoon. We don't have quitters on this team in any capacity – not directors, not coaches and not players. We don't quit."

The Rams lost the following weekend, 32-19, to the University of British Columbia Thunderbirds, and then took a hammering in Edmonton the week after that, getting throttled 57-14 by the University of Alberta Golden Bears. That was not how it was supposed to be. Didn't these people recognize THE Regina Rams?

The Alberta loss was unsettling to McCrystal. "We're very disappointed," McCrystal said, "and 'very' is a pathetic modifier. It was certainly a team effort. We didn't cover, we didn't move the ball and we didn't make plays. We had dropped balls, missed tackles, missed reads and missed blocks. We believe we'll bounce back. If not, if we thought the four quarters were long and if we thought the bus ride back from Edmonton was long, the rest of the season could be a lifetime."

The Rams' next loss, 44-24, their fifth straight, was handed to them by the University of Calgary Dinosaurs.

Some good things did emerge for the Rams. They had their best offensive game of the season. They got 29 first downs and 533 yards in total offence, 364 yards of which came from the passing of Wong. Shane Ostapowich caught five passes for 89 yards and the Rams got touchdowns from Warnecke, Clermont and Craig Schweitzer (on his first carry as a Ram).

Calgary coach Tony Fasano was impressed with the Rams. "They're not a bad football team. The thing here is it's their first time in the league and the first time seeing these teams. They'll get better. It's just going to take some time. Rome wasn't built in a day."

The Rams were officially eliminated from the playoffs a week later when they went to Winnipeg and lost to the Bisons, 24-10, in a game that saw the Rams' defence excel and the offence out-yardage the Bisons. But the Rams

Frank McCrystal

made some costly errors and it cost them their first win. Clermont scored the Rams only touchdown, on a pass from backup quarterback Mark Anderson, with less than 30 seconds to go in the game.

The playoff elimination was felt in the Rams' dressing room. The reality of their failure in their first season hit home. "That bothers us," said McCrystal. "One of our goals was to make the playoffs and we felt that that was something that was possible for us. Now we'll try to play like we always have, for the pride and the dignity and the tradition of our organization. We've come a long way from the Edmonton fiasco."

The Rams dropped to 0-7 when the Huskies came to town and beat them 24-7. But what was significant about the game was that the Rams pulled starter Mike Wong and put backup Mark Anderson into the game. Wong started the game throwing well. He completed seven of his first eight passes, but he was pulled when he threw an interception in the second quarter. The Rams' offence really did little, though, getting just 242 yards in total, and Clermont caught only one pass.

The Rams closed out the season with a 35-7 loss to the University of British Columbia Thunderbirds in Vancouver. It was an 0-8 baptism.

"This isn't the end of the world. We had an exhibition season," said McCrystal. "We have to be able to run the ball. Obviously, that means we need some offensive linemen who are strong enough and have the size to get it done. That's going to be our focus from this moment on."

Year Two - Vanier Cup Finalists

2000

If you had to pick two words to describe the difference between the University of Regina Rams from 1999 to 2000, they would be Darryl Leason. He was back. The one-time brilliant Rams' quarterback had taken the Rams to three Canadian championships. He then went to the University of Calgary Dinosaurs in 1996. In 1997, he was named the CIAU's first team All-Canadian, but a year later he was the backup quarterback. When he returned in 1999, Leason was again listed as the backup. It was too much for him. He quit the Dinosaurs, sat out the season, and would not be eligible to return until the 2000 season.

Darryl Leason

Leason, his wife and their two children moved back to Regina. He came to the Rams' 2000 training camp looking as if he hadn't lost a step or developed any rust from the layoff, having played some senior football in Calgary during his year away from university.

Just like that, the Rams went from a team with the stigma of an 0-8 record to one that would surely be a bonafide contender. Leason had that kind of aura. The move also obviously solidified the Rams' quarterbacking position. The year before, neither Mike Wong nor backup Mark Anderson had had a great year. With Leason on board, Wong became the backup. In order to play more, Anderson decided to leave the Rams and join the Prairie Thunder, who were in their first year as the new junior football team in Regina. "I came back to win the Vanier Cup," Leason said.

The Rams had spent the off-season recruiting for size and strength, and they had found some talent in, of all places, Quebec – linebacker Jon Cormier and offensive lineman Eric Beauchemin. More than a few players would come to the Rams from La Belle Province in the future. Despite the travails of the previous year, the Rams' reputation remained strong.

The Rams and Bisons played an exhibition game in Taylor Field to tune up for the season openers. It was two games in one, with the Bisons winning 28-22. Manitoba dominated the first half of the game, running up a 24-7 halftime lead. The Rams took over in the second half, out-scoring the Bisons 15-1, and almost winning it when they drove the ball to the Bison eight, only to fail to get it into the end zone.

Leason and Wong shared playing time, but neither was sharp throwing the ball. Leason completed only six of 17 passes for 144 yards, and Wong had eight completions out of 20 throws for 121 yards.

The game served its purpose. It gave both coaching staffs a look at their charges under the fire of a game as opposed to practices and scrimmages.

What the Rams needed most of all in the 2000 season, if they were to have any chance of rebounding from 1999, was a win. The longer it took them, the harder it would be to get it.

It didn't take long at all. The Rams opened at home against the University of Calgary Dinosaurs, who came bearing gifts. They turned the ball over eight times. The Rams pounced quickly, building a 24-1 halftime lead. The University of Regina Rams won their first game ever by a 31-25 score, but there were times in the second half when it looked as if they were going to give it back to the Dinosaurs. Twice, in the fourth quarter, Leason threw interceptions on back-to-back possessions when everybody agreed the Rams should have been running out the clock. "The guys on the sidelines were probably having heart attacks," Leason said. McCrystal was not amused. "In years gone by, when we've gone up 24-1, we've buried teams. Some of the things we did in the fourth quarter were out of character. But some of the things we did last season were out of character too."

Neal Hughes

Leason picked up good yardage throwing the ball, completing just 11 passes but gaining 264 yards. But it was the run that the Rams' offence depended on in this game. They rushed for 286 yards, with Leason getting 90 of them on 10 carries, and Neal Hughes getting 176 yards on 20 carries. Cory Olynick caught 30- and 20-yard touchdown passes from Leason. Clermont and Ron Arnold ran majors into the end zone. Rookie kicker Jon Ryan, an outstanding player from Sheldon-Williams Collegiate in Regina, had four converts, and Mark Wernikowski kicked a field goal.

The impact of the Rams' victory was felt immediately.

"This removes the distraction of winning the first game," said McCrystal. "Now we're almost part of the university fraternity."

Running back Neal Hughes said, "This will make the other teams aware that we're not a Mickey Mouse team anymore. We're in this."

The Rams went out to Vancouver for their second game. They lost 33-30, in a game which also saw them lose Hughes with a broken forearm that would keep him out of the lineup for at least three weeks.

Marco Ricci

The Rams had put an emphasis on finding defensive backs that could cover the passing attacks that came at them in college football. It was part of the transition. "Before, we used to have bigger backs as run stoppers," said Rams' defensive coach Marco Ricci. "Now, these guys have to cover receivers all over the field. You just didn't see that much throwing in junior." The Rams' defensive backfield of Sheldon Gray, Corrie McKee, Matt Dean, Ian Bonnell and Nick Billings was making the adjustment and the Rams were becoming a tougher team to throw against.

The 2000 season was indeed a strange one for the Rams. But if it did anything, it underlined their philosophy that they would never quit, and that they would always play to make the playoffs.

But as the season wore on and the Rams lost more than they won, they reached a critical point that called on all of their determination. With two games to go, and with the chance to still grab a playoff spot, the Rams were 2-4. They had to win both games, there was no alternative.

The Rams were on a three-game losing streak when the University of British Columbia Thunderbirds came to town. Twenty-four seconds into the second quarter, the

Thunderbirds held a 17-0 lead. But the Rams, with a strong wind at their back and hope in their sails, took off on a 30-point surge. Leason shone in the quarter, throwing four touchdown passes – 55 and 30 yards to Shane Ostapowich, 21 yards to Jason Clermont and 25 yards to Neal Hughes.

"That quarter was our guys playing like we know they can play," said McCrystal. "Darryl was the old Darryl. He ran. He threw. He did all the things he used to do before. And Hughes was outstanding. We were dominant in that quarter."

The second half started with the Rams still on fire. Hughes took the opening kickoff and ran it back 84 yards for a touchdown. Still, the Thunderbirds wouldn't buckle. The Thunderbirds were still in it in the fourth quarter when they went on a 17-point scoring run.

But the game was decided with 5:46 left. The Rams assumed possession of the ball at their own 22, leading 47-37. With the wind in their faces, the Rams went on a 10-play, 64-yard march before Ryan tried and missed a field goal attempt. By the time the Thunderbirds got the ball, there was only a little over a minute left, not enough time. The Rams won 47-37 to keep their playoff hopes alive.

Chris Warnecke

"I just sat back and watched the O-line take on the D-line," said Rams' Shane Ostapowich. "I watched Hughes gain yards, and saw Warnecke and Clermont make big catches on second down."

Said Leason, "They had us backed up but we came out fighting and delivered. It was like that the whole game. When push comes to shove, we showed everybody what we're capable of doing."

Leason had a big night, obviously. He had completed 22 of 30 passes for 345 yards and rushed 16 times for 62 yards.

But it was Hughes who tallied the huge figures for the Rams. He had 263 combined yards – 107 on kickoff returns, 85 on 15 carries, 55 on six catches and 16 on a punt return.

Neal Hughes

The Rams were back. And they were for real. They nailed down a playoff spot in the last game of the season, beating the Golden Bears in Edmonton 28-20. The Rams finished the season at 4-4 and in third place.

"We really didn't think of making the playoffs our second or third year," said McCrystal. "How long it was going to take we really weren't sure. We weren't far off last year. I still don't think our record was indicative of how we played. This year we had experience and some age maturity."

There had been times in their history when it seemed that absolutely nothing could stop the Regina Rams. And that is what happened in the playoffs.

The Rams travelled to Calgary to take on the Dinosaurs in the Canada West semifinal.

In a wild game, the Rams took control in the fourth quarter. Trailing 25-10, two minutes into the quarter, the Rams scored on each of their next four possessions to win the game 33-32 and advance to the Canada West final.

Leason put on a show, that's what did it. He completed

14 of 15 passes in the final quarter for 238 yards and three touchdowns, two to Clermont and one to Ostapowich. It left the teams tied at 32-32.

With just under three minutes to go, the Rams had the ball at their 15. Leason worked his magic. It took Leason 11 plays to move the Rams 79 yards to the Dinosaurs' 16. There were two seconds showing on the clock. Ryan was sent in to punt the ball. If he made it the Rams would win by a point. If he didn't, there would be overtime. Quite a spot for a rookie to be in. But Ryan caught all of the ball and sailed the punt through the end zone, giving the Rams their heart-stopping, last-second victory.

Leason finished the night with 30 completions in 43 attempts for 440 yards.

The Rams would have to travel to Winnipeg to take on the Bisons in the final.

It was the same old script. Heading toward the end of the fourth quarter, with just over two minutes left, the Bisons scored to take a 22-18 lead. It wasn't enough. In a stirring march that drained everybody in the stadium, Leason took the Rams 87 yards in 12 plays. On third down from the Manitoba 10, Leason fired a pass to Hughes, who caught it in the end zone to give the Rams their second straight comeback win – 25-22.

The Rams had won their first Hardy Cup championship in their second season.

"I've never experienced that," Manitoba coach Brian Dobie said of the final drive. "It's all on Darryl Leason. It was a fantastic game by Darryl Leason."

Leason was 25 for 44 for 416 yards, and he ran the ball 18 times for 121 yards and two touchdowns.

Hughes had also had a sensational game. He finished with 345 yards – 206 on 10 catches, 102 on four kickoff returns, 28 on six rushes and nine on two punt returns. Just another day at the office. Clermont caught seven passes for 104 yards.

The Rams were now just one win away from the Vanier Cup. But to get to Toronto they first had to go through Halifax. The Rams had to play the hometown St. Mary's Huskies in the Atlantic Bowl.

It was mandatory, when the Rams went somewhere new, that the team take a tour of all the places of interest. When they hit Halifax, McCrystal put them on a bus and off they went, tourists. Peggy's Cove was on the agenda, and offensive lineman Junior Gohn got too close to the water. He fell into the Atlantic Ocean and was still wringing water from his clothes when he got back to the hotel.

Todd Krenbrink

The Rams enjoyed these little side trips. "Everybody has to do the same thing instead of being off on their own," said offensive tackle Todd Krenbrink. "It also gives everybody the opportunity to experience something they may miss if they're off on their own."

The Rams-Huskies game was televised on national television, and anybody who didn't watch it until the end missed it all. It was simply a case of different town, same script for the Rams, who were definitely on a roll.

With seven minutes to go in the game, the Huskies held a 36-24 lead. Then the Rams took charge. Hughes ran back a kickoff 84 yards for a touchdown and the Rams scored a safety. Finally, with just over a minute and a half to play, Leason threw a 12-yard touchdown pass to Chris Warnecke. That was all she wrote, the Rams won 40-36.

McCrystal had once wondered what the Vanier Cup looked like. He was about to find out. The University of Regina Rams were in the Vanier Cup.

"At the start of the season, never in my wildest dreams did I think we'd get here," said Rams' defensive end Lee

Cory Olynick

Cherkas. "I thought we'd get here some day but not this soon."

Olynick had had the game of his life. He caught 10 passes for 147 yards, and they were key catches. "They just weren't covering me," he said. Olynick had played through a series of injuries. There had been so much pain in his foot the day before the game, he shouldn't have been able to play. "Neal Hughes made the outstanding plays, but the unsung hero of the game was Cory Olynick," said McCrystal.

Next stop for the Rams was the Vanier Cup in Toronto, where only the University of Ottawa Gee Gees stood between them and the Cup.

How much longer could this Cinderella story go on?

The Rams had lived by the comeback in the playoffs, and they died by it.

It was a familiar story to start. The Rams' defence didn't receive its wake-up call and, as a result, the Gee Gees, quarterbacked by the game's MVP, Phil Cote, ran up a 35-10 halftime lead. The Rams came alive in the second half, especially in the fourth quarter, out-scoring Ottawa 29-7,

Jeff Zimmer

but it was a case of too little too late. They lost the Vanier Cup, 42-39, before 18,209 fans.

The Rams' offence had certainly played well enough to win. They had gained 563 yards, 207 along the ground and 356 in the air. But Ottawa's offence was also cooking, going through the Rams' defence for 539 yards. The defense had lost linebacker Jeff Zimmer with an ankle injury three Ottawa possessions into the game. Cote completed 16 passes for 275 yards.

Jason Clermont

Leason was Leason, that's all. He completed 28 of 44 passes for 356 yards, and was the game's leading rusher with 116 yards on 12 carries. Jason Clermont played the second half with a separated shoulder. He caught three passes for a game total of six catches for 106 yards. It was a courageous performance.

But none of that was enough.

"Maybe winning this one wouldn't have helped us," McCrystal said. "Maybe winning this one would have made it seem too easy."

McCrystal now knew what the Vanier Cup looked like. But he had yet to hold it.

NOT QUITE VANIER BOUND

2001

The cute little guy with the shiny face and glasses showed up in the late spring and everybody stared at him. Even the hair looked neat, well, sort of. Maybe the new look was what the University of Regina Rams needed to win a Vanier Cup. The cute little guy with the new look was none other than Rams' head coach Frank McCrystal.

Off had come the moustache that had wriggled above his top lip like a caterpillar. And on had gone the glasses. McCrystal had shaved off the moustache on Easter Monday. It wasn't his idea. It was his wife Wendy's. "She says, 'Take the moustache off.' I say 'Why?' She says 'Just to try something different.' " It was quite the change. "After I did it, everybody looked at me very strangely. The guys look at me and say 'Why?' I say, 'I wasn't getting enough attention.' I didn't realize how people would react. I'd better bring it back."

The 2001 Frank McCrystal edition had changed. Some thought it was for the better. Some didn't. The 2001 edition of the University of Regina Rams had changed, too, and for the better. Or, so it seemed.

Making the playoffs, and then going on that miraculous playoff run where every victory was a comeback, and in the final moments, and then coming within seconds of winning the Vanier Cup – it was all the Rams needed to get their confidence level back to where it had been in junior football. After all, in just one year the Rams had been transformed from a team that had lost all eight of its games to one that had almost won the Vanier Cup. And they had also learned that, in college football, you have to play 60 minutes every game. The caliber and the competition were that good.

The Rams weren't bad themselves, mind you. Linebacker Jeff Zimmer had been drafted in the fifth round of the Canadian college draft by the Calgary Stampeders. He attended their training camp, but an ankle injury resulted in his being sent back to Regina. And quarterback Darryl Leason tried out with the Winnipeg Blue Bombers. Both came back to the Rams.

The biggest loss for the Rams was the graduation of wide receiver Chris Warnecke, one of the greatest athletes to ever play for the team. But Jason Clermont was back; Neal Hughes was back; Cory Olynick was back; Michael Leason was back; Shane Ostapowich was back; Jon Ryan was back; Michael Thomas was back. As well, quarterback Mark Anderson had returned after a year of playing with the junior Prairie Thunder in Regina. Clermont had come back bigger and stronger than he had been the year before. He had added nine pounds to his six-foot, three-inch frame, bringing his weight up to 234 pounds. The offensive line was strong, with all-star centre Tony Plett and six-foot, seven-inch, 300-pound tackle Todd Krenbrink anchoring it.

The biggest chore facing the Rams was on defence. The Rams had rebuilt the offence in 2000. Now, it was the defence's turn. Linemen Kyler Jukes and Tony Presidente, and defensive backs Jason Ulley and Mike Kissinger figured to strengthen the defence. Linebacker Jeff Zimmer was moved to the middle from the outside, and his brother Craig, a rookie, would see action at outside linebacker. The Rams were, obviously, gearing up to stop the run.

The Rams started off the season with three straight victories, and included in that package was their first win over the University of Saskatchewan Huskies. The Rams toppled the Huskies 31-21 in Taylor Field with a crowd of 7,238 fans on hand. They moved to 4-0 when Leason, Clermont

Kyler Jukes

and Hughes proved too much to handle for the University of British Columbia Thunderbirds in a 59-21 shellacking before 5,121 fans in Taylor Field.

Leason passed for 364 yards, Clermont caught seven passes for 151 yards and Hughes ran nine times for 109 yards.

With the 364 yards passing, Leason established a new Canada West career passing yardage record of 8,657 yards. The old record had belonged to University of Calgary quarterback Greg Vavra.

The Rams suffered their first loss in Game 5 against the Calgary Dinosaurs, losing the game 35-33. They were worried that they had lost Leason for the season with knee ligament damage. Defensive end Lee Cherkas was definitely finished for the season, having broken his ankle and torn the ligaments during the game.

Mark Anderson took over at quarterback, and now the Rams had their work cut out for them. They had their worst offensive game of the season against the University of Manitoba Bisons, gaining only 175 yards total offence, 99 yards of that coming on one play, as they lost their second straight game, 47-11.

But they rallied in their game against the University of Alberta, traveling to Edmonton and laying a 40-14 licking on the Golden Bears. The win officially clinched a playoff spot for the Rams, who were 5-2 with one game to play.

The Rams' defence was as sturdy as the Great Wall of China. They stamped a "Return to Sender" label on every play the Bears threw at them, mercilessly harassing Alberta quarterback Blair Zahara, sacking him five times.

Anderson played his second full game at quarterback, and threw three touchdown passes, completing 16 of 30 passes for 213 yards.

The Rams dazzled the Bears with a couple of trick plays, both involving kicker Jon Ryan. On a punt, he threw a 39-

Jon Ryan

yard pass to Neal Hughes. On a field goal, he took the direct snap and ran 17 yards for the first down. Both plays led to Rams' touchdowns.

The Rams closed out the schedule in Saskatoon against the Huskies – on the line was second place. To get second place, though, the Huskies had to do more than beat the Rams, they had to win by 11 points.

The Rams lost the battle, but they won the war. The Huskies beat them 34-28, not a big enough margin, so the Rams got second place. The two teams returned to Regina the following week and met in the semifinal.

The Huskies victory might well have made some of the Rams happy that they had at least finished second. But Jason Clermont was furious with his teammates after the game. "The players looked like cowards," he said. He was upset that the Rams just ran out the clock in the final moments of the game, instead of trying to go for the win.

McCrystal was asked about it. "Why'd we do it? Because we're smarter than the players are," laughed McCrystal. "That's why we're coaches and they're players."

The Rams and Huskies in the semifinal – it was a matchup made in heaven; that rivalry had sown its roots in 2001.

"Oh, it'll be exciting and it'll be bitter," said McCrystal. "We always used to say the Rams and Hilltops made each other better for the playoffs. That's going to happen here. You're not going to find anything more intense in Canada in the next week."

The big news the week of the semifinal was that Darryl Leason would play, his knee wrapped in a special brace. Leason went into the game wanting a piece of the Huskies, who had said he wouldn't be the same quarterback he was before he was injured. Oh? The Rams won the game, 58-31, and now the rivalry had some sting to it.

Leason shredded the Huskies defence. It took him three plays to give them something to think about. He hit Clermont, the league's leading receiver, with a 51-yard touchdown pass. Before he was done, Leason had completed 20 passes for 418 yards and five touchdowns. He threw touchdown passes to Ostapowich and Jon Ryan, and twice hit Neal Hughes for touchdowns. Clermont got another touchdown on a run and cornerback Chris Ashman returned an interception 54 yards for a major. Ryan had two field goals and seven converts.

For the second straight year, the Rams were in the Canada West final, and for the second straight year they traveled to Winnipeg to play the University of Manitoba Bisons.

This was Leason's last year in university football. He wanted to go out holding the Vanier Cup. But the Bisons had other ideas.

Leason had been banged around by the Huskies in the semifinal, and had taken a few shots on his wounded knee. But he was still able to start against the Bisons. He even had some mobility this time.

In the end, it didn't matter. The Bisons, remembering their loss in the final the previous year to the Rams, hung on for a 23-17 victory. The University of Regina's season was over. Just like that.

"I don't think we're discouraged," said McCrystal. "We feel poorly about the loss but it's important to keep it in perspective and keep our heads about us."

Leason was the only player who definitely would not be back in 2002. His eligibility had run out. But there was speculation that Jason Clermont also had played his last game as a Ram. Clermont figured to be drafted in the first round of the college draft, and he was ready to play at the pro level.

For the Rams, 2002 seemed another year they could genuinely look forward to with high expectations.

Jason Clermont and Imperial Potentate Ken Smith at East-West Shrine Bowl
A United States college all-star game played at Paolo Alto, California

THE BATTLE CONTINUES

2002

In 2002, quarterback Darryl Leason and slotback Jason Clermont, likely the two best players to ever play those positions with the Rams, were no longer with the team.

Leason had used up his eligibility and moved back to Calgary, where he was playing senior football with the Calgary Wolfpack. Although Clermont still had a year's eligibility left, the six-foot, three-inch, 240-pounder was drafted in the first round by the B.C. Lions, made their team, and went on to have a season that saw him win the Canadian Football League's rookie of the year award.

You would think that any team which had lost its one-two punch offensively might be plunging to the depths of despair. Or, at least, experiencing a little panic. Not the University of Regina Rams.

The Rams, though, were ready with a new starting quarterback. He was Mark Anderson, who had been the starting quarterback before the Rams had gone to the university level. Anderson had played four years earlier, when

Mark Anderson and Bernie Schmidt

Leason was playing college football at the University of Calgary. Anderson also had spent a full season as a starter with the Prairie Thunder, Regina's new junior team. So, there was no waiting around for him to develop into a starter. He already was. All he had to do was play the game.

The 2002 season was, in part, still a rebuilding season for the Rams, who after their 0-8 first year at the college level, had established themselves as one of the league's most consistent contenders. It was a reputation they had brought from junior football. "We've got a really interesting mix of young, really good athletes and older, experienced athletes," coach Frank McCrystal said. "We have to find a way for both of those groups to contribute."

It didn't hurt that the Rams still had some key veterans back – players such as Cory Olynick, Shane Ostapowich, Neal Hughes, Jeff Zimmer and Matt Dean. They would be expected to show the way, along with, of course, Anderson.

Zimmer also was a key. The 2001 defensive player of the year in Canada had had a tryout with the Winnipeg Blue Bombers, but he was released. He had not been planning on playing, and had approached the Rams about the possibility of becoming a coach. But Zimmer's family talked him into playing one more year. So, he decided to return to the Rams. Right off the bat, Zimmer had an impact. The Rams opened the season with a 15-10 victory over the UBC Thunderbirds at Taylor Field, and Zimmer virtually shut down the UBC offence all by himself. He had nine tackles, three assists, two big hits on quarterbacks and a sack for a safety. "He's unbelievable," said defensive coach Paul Dawson. That said it all.

Offensively, the Rams kept tripping over themselves. Anderson completed only 11 of 33 passes, but eight of his throws were dropped.

Michael Thomas

The Rams rolled to a second straight victory with a decisive 31-7 thrashing of the University of Saskatchewan Huskies. Anderson completed 20 of 33 passes for 33 yards and three touchdowns. He didn't throw an interception. Anderson hooked up with receiver Michael Thomas on a 75-yard touchdown throw early in the fourth quarter. And the Rams scored two more before the quarter was out to get the win.

The season had gotten off to a better start than some had expected. The Rams kept it going. They went to 3-0, riding a big game out of running back Neal Hughes to a 14-7 win over the University of Alberta Golden Bears. Hughes carried the ball 28 times for 185 yards. Although the Rams still did not look sharp throwing the ball – Anderson had only 11 completions for 182 yards – they were still undefeated.

The team to beat in Canada West was the University of Manitoba Bisons. And the Rams found out why. They took their 3-0 record into Taylor Field and took on the Bisons. With 4,813 fans on hand in Taylor Field, the Rams took it on the chin, 35-8. The Bisons took the Rams apart in the first half, and McCrystal wasn't happy about it. "In the 30 years I've been associated with this team," he said, "that half of football was the worst I can remember us playing." McCrystal pulled Anderson at halftime and put backup Jon Schneider into the game.

The loss sent the Rams into a bit of a tailspin. They lost 24-12 to UBC, lost 23-4 to the Huskies and wondered if they would ever win again. They did, closing out the schedule with a 41-10 victory over the Simon Fraser University Clansmen. They finished in third place.

The Rams were not the favourites going into the playoffs. They had lost Neal Hughes with an injury. They had to go to Calgary and take on the second-place Dinosaurs in the semifinal. No problem – the Rams had a reputation for turning it on in the playoffs. When the tap was shut off they whipped the Dinosaurs 39-17. But the biggest upset came two provinces over. In one of the most unpredictable playoff results in a long time, the University of Saskatchewan went into Winnipeg and knocked off the unbeaten, top-ranked University of Manitoba Bisons 37-18.

The fourth-place Huskies went to the Hardy Cup final. You couldn't have asked for a better matchup. The game was played in Taylor Field, on a snowy November Saturday afternoon. The Huskies capitalized on numerous Rams' mistakes and beat them 44-28.

It ended the Rams' season. Maybe next year.

MUCH MORE THAN JUST A FOOTBALL TEAM

Nothing ever stops with them. They are like a wheel that just keeps on turning. They go from year to year, from decade to decade, from quarter century to quarter century, and it is always pretty well the same. With the University of Regina Rams, there is always success, there is always a contending team and there is always a championship just around the corner. Oh, there may be the odd hiccup. But it is never that serious and it certainly never lasts.

The Rams, you see, are a work in constant recreation. No matter what they are doing and when they are doing it, they are always building for tomorrow. Because, in junior football and university football, tomorrow comes every year. Every season marks the end to somebody's career. They all eventually graduate. They all have to be replaced. That is why the Rams always keep the best rookies around. They may not play a whole lot, but they play some. They, for sure, practice a lot. And they learn all about the history of the Rams, of what went before them, and what will be expected of them when they become starters. And most of the rookies the Rams keep will start. And they will be ready to. That is part of the Rams' way, and it is among the reasons the Rams are the Rams.

The Rams are much more than a football team.

They try to shape the lives of these young people so that when they head out in the real world, they understand and want to be a part of their community. They find out about volunteering in their community, no matter what community they become part of. They learn about the satisfaction that comes with volunteering and making a contribution. That is part of the Rams' way.

The players are assisted by the Rams' educational fund. But it is not just a handout of a few thousand dollars for some kid's tuition. In order to get the financial help, the players must maintain a certain grade level. Thus, they not only save money, but they also learn that if you work hard, there is a reward. That is part of the Rams' way.

The players learn about the massive amount of fundraising that goes on to ensure the health and future of the team. They learn about all of the directors who prowl the stands of Taylor Field during Roughrider games, selling 50/50 tickets to raise money. They learn about the annual mixed sports dinner which has become a fixture on the calendar since the first one in 1966. It takes serious effort to sell 800 or 900 tickets, but the directors are devoted to this team and so they do it. That is part of the Rams' way.

They learn the importance of getting to know one another and the importance of being team players. They learn it when Frank McCrystal takes them out to the Retreat on a hill in the Qu'Appelle Valley, overlooking the highway and the town of Lumsden. That is a part of the Rams' way.

They learn about all the players and coaches and directors and presidents who have gone before them when McCrystal takes them to the top of the hill at Scotty Livingstone Field and talks to them about everything from the Rams' history to great events in world history. That is a part of the Rams' way.

Playing for the Rams is more than just a football experience. It is why years after they have finished playing for the Rams, many of them stay on. They stay on as coaches, or managers, or members of the executive. They never want to leave the organization. It has that kind of pull on people's emotions and their lives.

When the Rams ended the 2002 season with a playoff loss to the University of Saskatchewan Huskies, they never skipped a beat. They knew they had been faithful to their history of always looking ahead, of always preparing for the future.

In the searing heat of August of 2003, the Rams poured onto Scotty Livingstone Field from their clubhouse. If you watched it from the hill at the north end, the scene looked exactly as it has looked since the Rams moved there in 1966. And you knew, just as they had known virtually every other year since then, that those players down below on that field would be right in the thick of the hunt. And, who knows, maybe this will be the year they win the Vanier Cup. That's what they always prepare for, success and a shot at the championship. It is the Rams' way.

Much More Than Just A Football Team 227

THE BUILDING BLOCKS

The Regina Rams Football Club, as a junior football team and as the University of Regina Rams, has always held in high esteem its building blocks – the thousands of players, coaches, directors, trainers, equipment staff and volunteer doctors who have donated their time, talents and energy to ensure the success of their team. On the following pages are the rosters (as history has best provided us) and the team pictures from the clubs' first 50 years.

1954 REGINA RAMS

Players: Jack Ashenbrenner, Bev Bell, Ed Boychuk, Murray Buranen, Ken Burgess, Jack Chandler, Pat Chapman, Dick Christianson, Al Deck, Larry Dumelie, Ron Dundas, Roger Eccleston, Bill Finnegan, Gordon Flaman, Frank Flegel, Gib Forbes, Pete Heidt, John Hudson, John Johns, Jack Klein, Wayne Klinck, Gary Larter, Johny Mann, Enos Marchtaler, Glen MacDonald, Bill (Duke) McEachern, Doug McVety, Pete Morin, Steve Nazarchuk, Wayne Nichol, Bill Nixon, Dale Parsons, Gerry Probe, Frank Roberts, Brian Roland, Edward Sheffield, Bernie Sebastian, Stan Shoeman, Regent Smith, Al Thompson, Art Uhren, Marvin Vandale, Don Vassos, Bert Vinet, Jerry Wasnik, Gerry Williams, Ralph Wittich, Brian Wittich, Jerry Worden, Don Young.

Coaches: Toar Springstein (Head Coach), Wayne Pyne, Lindsay Holt.

Staff: Joe Sullivan (Equip. Manager), Doc Patrick (Trainer), Carl Sullivan (Mascot), Al Wessell (Team Mangager), Pete Martin (Pubilicity), Dr. A.D. Baker (Dentist), Dr. Campbell Dixon (Dentist), Dr. Irwin Bean (Physician), Dr. E. Jones (Physician).

Directors: John Rowand (President), Martin Grudnitski (Past President of Bomber Dales), Tom Drope (Secretary), Max Amon (Treasurer).Roy Beale, Joe Brehm, Bill Ciz, Paul Dojack, Don Graham, Earl Houston, Beattie Martin, Cliff McLeod, Bill Peacey, Ken Preston, Lionel Ray, Al Relkey, Bob Ritchie, J. Smith, Ross Sneath, Jack Stewart, Earl Wismer.

1955 REGINA RAMS

Players: Bill Aumuller, Murray Balfour, Stan Barber, Len Biden, Pat Chapman, Denny Cochrane, Bill Diamond, Larry Dumelie, Ron Dundas, Ken Edwards, Gordon Flaman, Gib Forbes, Garry Ford, Mickey Garvey, Pete Heidt, Martin Howe, John Johns, Jerry Kleisinger, Patrick Klock, Len Kram, Don Leskun, Glen MacDonald, Erv Marchtaler, Del Mayes, Kev McKinney, Doug McVety, Butch Miller, Harvey Mohr, Bill Moldovan, Paul Nazarchuk, Wilf Oberthier, Dale Parsons, Marvin Pidhorny, Gerry Probe, Brian Roland, Edwin Schmidt, Lawrie Schmidt, Bernard Sebastian, Edward Sheffield, Gerald Tanouye, Clair Treleaven, Art Uhren, Cliff Uhren, Ted Urness, Jack Urness, Bert Vinet, Fred Wagman, Jerry Williams, Ralph Wittich, Jack Wood, Alf Zimmerman.

Coaches: Toar Springstein (Head Coach), Wayne Pyne, Bill Ciz,

Staff: Andy Charuk (Equip. Mgr.), Ted Stawarz (Trainer), Dr. Irwin Bean, Dr. Campbell Dixon,

Directors: John Rowand (President), Martin Grudnitski, Tom Drope, Max Amon, Earl Houston, Paul Dojack, Cliff McLeod, Lionel Ray, Harry Hilsden, John Lord, Al Wessel, Ken Preston, Jack Stewart, Ross Sneath

1956 REGINA RAMS

Players: Bob August, Willie Aumuller, Danny Banda, Stan Barber, Ron Blom, Harvey Campbell, Denny Cochrane, Fred Cochrane, Pete Connellan, Duane DeCorbey, Ed Delaronde, Leo Delsnyder, Jim Dick, Ken Don, Larry Dumelie, Ken Edmonds, Bill Forbes, Gib Forbes, Garry Ford, Mickey Garvey, Pat Klock, Woody Langfield, Hugh Lennon, Don Leskun, Don Lubiens, Glenn MacDonald, Wayne Mang, Rod McGrath, Pete McLean, Gord Millin, Bill Moldovan, Luke Moser, Paul Nazarchuk, C. Page, Bob Pettigrew, Marvin Pidhorny, Gerry Probe, Erwin Schmidt, Laurie Schmidt, Siggy Splett, Gerry Tanouye, Clair Treleaven, Bill Treleaven, Cliff Uhren, Jack Urness, Ted Urness, Fred Wagman, Gilbert Wagner, Ralph Wittich, Alf Zimmerman.

Coaches: Bill Ciz (Head Coach), Wayne Pyne,

Staff: Tom McRadu (Equip. Mgr.), Ted Stawarz (Trainer), John Robertson (Manager), Dr. Campbell Dixon (Dentist), Dr. E. A. Jones (Physician), Dr. Irwin (Physician).

Directors: Tom Drope (President), John Rowand (Past President), Jack Finlayson (Secretary), Max Amon (Treasurer), Martin Grudnitski, Harry Hilsden, John Lord, John Malone, Jack Stewart, Al Wessel, Roy Wright.

1957 REGINA RAMS

Players: Doug Aikens, George Anderson, Lyell Armitage, Danny Banda, Wayne Barber, Ron Blom, Harvey Campbell, Gil Collins, Al Collins, Ray Crebo, Ken Culham, Jim Dick, Barry Dixon, Ken Don, Larry Dumelie, Bob Erickson, Tom Fahlman, Bill Forbes, Garry Ford, Mickey Garvey, Max Geisthardt, Pat Hengen, Dave Howie, Dennis Junior, Jack Kennedy, John Klein, Woody Langfield, Clarence Long, Norman Lorenz, Donald Lubiens, Doug Lyons, Pete McLean, Dennis MacPherson, Bill Metcalfe, Gordon Millin, Bill Mondovan, Luke Moser, Bryan Noonan, Ernie Pawliw, Marv Pidhorny, Ken Plante, Gerry Roy, Lionel Ruhr, Bill Sides, Dennis Silzer, Siggy Splett, Gerry Tanouye, Ken Townsend, Bill Treleaven, Claire Treleaven, Jack Urness, Fred Wagman, Bill Wright, Alf Zimmerman.

Coaches: Bill Ciz (Head Coach), Wayne Pyne,

Staff: Tom McRadu (Equip. Mgr.), Ted Stawarz (Trainer), John Robertson (Team Manager), Dr. Campbell Dixon (Dentist), Dr. E.A. Jones (Physician), Dr. Irwin Bean (Physician).

Directors: Harry Hilsden (President), Tom Drope (Past President), John Gareau (Secretary), John Malone (Treasurer), Max Amon, Allan Day, Jack Finlayson, Martin Grudnitski, Cass Lambrecht, Doug Ramsay, John Rowand, Al Wessel.

1958 REGINA RAMS

Players: Trayton Adair, Doug Aikens, Lyle Andrews, Wayne Barber, Brian Bowerman, Jack Brandt, David Butts, Harvey Campbell, John Chobaniuk, Al Collins, Vince Collins, Ken Culham, Jim Dick, Barry Dixon, Mickey Donnelly, Henry Dorsch, Tom Fahlman, Bob Fedor, Gary Fitz, Morley Fleischhaker, Gil Graboski, Terry Harper, Trevor Holfeld, Dave Howie, George Jaeger, Ed Jerome, Bob Jerome, Dennis Junior, Jack Kennedy, John Klein, Woody Langfield, Bill Lecaine, Bob Leskun, Larry Leslie, Clem Long, Doug Lyon, Dennis MacPherson, Tom McCallum, Bill Metcalfe, Cyril Moore, Brian Noonan, Bernard Osiowy, Ernie Pawliw, Ken Plante, Tom Pollock, Henry Riplinger, John Rusu, Bill Sides, Dennis Silzer, Louis Sylvestre, Clair Treleaven, Bill Ursaki, Dymetry Warnyca, Bill Wright, Paul Yaciw

Coaches: Bill Ciz (Head Coach), Wayne Pyne, Nick Blum,

Staff: Tom McRadu (Equip. Mgr.), Ted Stawarz (Trainer), Dr. Campbell Dixon (Dentist), Dr. E.A. Jones (Physician), Dr. E.L. Weekes (Physician).

Directors: Al Wessel (President), Harry Hilsden (Past President), Jack Stewart (Team Manager), John Malone (Vice President), Max Amon, Tom Drope, Jack Finlayson, John Gareau, Martin Grudnitski, Cass Lambrecht, Doug Ramsay, John Rowand.

1959 REGINA RAMS

Players: Bob Bateman, Chris Batley, Ray Blender, Jack Brandt, Harvey Campbell, John Chobaniuk, Vince Collins, Al Collins, John Connellan, Sam Decorby, Jerry Dombowski, Henry Dorsch, Al Edwards, Bill Elsom, Tom Fahlman, Bob Fedor, Gary Fitz, Morley Fleischhaker, Graham Ford, Gilbert Graboski, Trevor Holfeld, Dave Howie, George Jaeger, Dale Johanson, Jack Kennedy, John Klein, Al Lang, Don Lavoie, Bob Leskun, Randy Lorenz, Gary Mather, Bob McMillan, Bill Metcalfe, Cyril Moore, Phil Moynihan, Vern Pachal, Don Paterson, Ernie Pawliw, Rick Purcel, Jerry Roy, Dennis Silzer, Tony Spooner, John Starzynski, Louis Sylvestre, Ray Trembley, Bill Ursaki, Dymetry Warnyca, Paul Yaciw

Coaches: Bert Iannone(Head Coach), Wayne Pyne, Nick Blum

Staff: Tom McRadu (Equip. Mgr.), Ted Stawarz (Trainer)

Directors: Gordon Mitton(President), Bill Ciz, Judge E.M. Culliton, Daryl Heald, Bill Spicer, Jack Stewart, Al Wessel

1960 REGINA RAMS

Players: Stan Agopsowicz, Dareau Ashenbrenner, Bob Bateman, Chris Batley, Stan Biden, Brian Bowerman, Tom Ceare, Wayne Chappelle, Dick Dirk, Henry Dorsch, Gerry Dumboski, Bill Elsom, Owen Enich, Bob Fedor, Gary Fitz, Orville Fitzgerald, Reg Folk, Maurice Fortif, Dan Gallagher, John Guerin, Vernon Herley, Jack Kennedy, Brian Kittleson, James Kuster, Gerry Lafontaine, Dale Laird, Al Lang, Don Leader, Bob Leskun, Nick Lipon, Murray Lowey, Gary Mather, Dan Maxim, Dennis Messier, Bill Metcalfe, Bob Mirwald, Ately Morrow, Phil Moynihan, Ron Pachal, Robert Peacock, Mal Perkins, Art Sorrenson, Ken Tyson, Bill Ursaki, Dick Wiest, Paul Yaciw.

Coaches: Bert Iannone (Head Coach), Wayne Pyne, Harvey Cambell, Tom Fahlman.

Staff: Ted Stawarz (Trainer), Tom McRadu (Equip. Mgr.)

Directors: Gordon Mitton (President), Scotty Livingstone (Vice President), Tom Drope (Past President), Ron McGuigan (Secretary), Al Wessel (Treasurer), Jack Stewart (Registrar).

1961 REGINA RAMS

Players: Dareau Ashenbrenner, Gordon Bowerman, Bob Bulmer, Wayne Chapelle, Garnet Christianson, Al Collins, Dan Daniels, Dick Dirk, Gary Elgear, Gary Fitz, Barry Forester, Lorne Gale, Dan Gallagher, Andrew George, John Guerin, Mike Hockenhull, Ken Johns, Ron Johnstone, Len Kleisinger, John Konoff, Benny Kuzmic, Murray Kyle, Dale Laird, Al Lang, Joe Larson, Don Leader, Leo Ledohowski, Bob Lochbaum, Murray Lowey, Gary Mather, Dan Maxim, Dan McGowan, Dennis Messier, Ately Morrow, Phil Moynihan, Vic Osiowy, Norm Parisien, Mal Perkins, Art Pluntz, Warren Potts, Don Savage, Gerald Schmidt, Terry Shercliffe, Vern Simonson, Alex Smith, Ed Snyder, Jim Street, Randy Swedburg, Ken Tyson, Barry Urness, Larry Van Moorlehem

Coaches: Bert Iannone (Head Coach), Wayne Pyne, Tom Fahlman, Martin Ruby .

Staff: Ted Stawarz (Trainer), Tom McRadu (Equip. Mgr.)

Directors: Gordon Mitton (President), Scotty Livingstone (Vice President), Tom Drope (Past President), Rafe Chadwick, Jim Dickens, Ron McGuigan, Jack Stewart, Al Wessel .

1962 REGINA RAMS

Players: John Arnot, Gordon Bateman, Grant Becker, Gordon Bowerman, Rennie Bradley, Ron Cobbledick, Marty Collins, Pat Dailey, Ed Deutscher, Jim Dickson, Lorne Dunsmore, Gary Elgear, Reg Folk, Barry Forrester, Terry Gordon, Mike Hochenhull, Ted Hogan, Paul Houston, Ken Johns, Kevin Kearns, Jim Kuster, Joe Larson, Don Leader, Rudy Lipp, Dan Maxim, Bob McAfee, Art McAvoy, Don McGowan, Ken McNabb, Bill Millar, Ately Morrow, Jim Oliver, Norm Parisien, Bill Paterson, Mal Perkins, Warren Potts, Art Plunz, Gerald Reinson, James Reinson, Neil Robinson, Robert Rusu, Don Savage, Gerald Schmidt, Andy Schuck, Terry Shercliffe, Vern Simonson, Alex Smith, Lyle Sinkewicz, Barry Urness, Larry Van Moorlehem, Bob Walker, John Woodard, Dave Wirth, Donald Zerbin.

Coaches: Bert Ianonne (Head Coach), Paul Anderson (Head Coach), Russ Haines, Nellie Green, Jack Urness, Ron Adam.

Staff: Paul Yaciw (Equip.Mgr.), Ted Stawarz (Trainer), Jim Dickens (Team Manager),

Directors: Scotty Livingstone (President), Rafe Chadwick (Vice President), Gordon Mitton (Past President), Ron McGuigan,
Jack Stewart, Al Wessel.

1963 REGINA RAMS

Players: John Arnot, Don Bahnuik, Bill Baker, Art Belanger, Rennie Bradley, Henry Bzdel, Keith Chow, Ron Cobbledick, Marty Collins, Lyle Culham, George Daurie, David Davies, Bob Decker, Ed Deutscher; Lorne Dillabaugh, Jim Doan, Ken Dobra, Fred Dorsch, Ernest Grundy, Ted Hogan, Ken Huber, Ken Johns, Gerald Kambeitz, Jim Kambeitz, Gary Karpiuk, Tom Kellough, Hartley Kerr, Gary Korvan, Ben Kusmic, Jim Kuster, Joe Larson, Glenn Lawson, Rudy Lipp, Bob Lochbaum, Byron Lopes, Al Lott, Bob Lowe, Bob McAfee, Art McAvoy, Ken McNabb, Bob Orban, Norm Parisien, Bill Paterson, Mal Perkins, Mel Puscas, Gerald Reinson, James Reinson, Neil Robinson, Robert Rusu, Grant Rusconi, Vern Simonson, Alex Smith, Larry Van Moorlehem, Bob Walker, Dan Zerbin,

Coaches: Paul Anderson (Head Coach), Russ Haines, Jack Urness, Nellie Greene, Galen Wahlmeier,

Staff: Gary Mather (Equip. Mgr.), Jackie Lewis (Trainer), Ted Stawarz (Trainer)

Directors: Scotty Livingstone(President), Rafe Chadwick(Vice), Gordon Mitton(Past), Bill Ciz, Jim Dickens, George Johns, Joe Kanuka, Peter McCaffrey, Roland McGuigan, Mac McLean, Gary Miles, Jack Stewart, Allan Wessel, Ken Wheeler.

1964 REGINA RAMS

Back Row: Mel Puscas, Ed Deutscher, Barry Aldag, Ken Huber, Gord Clark, Rod Smith, Dick Leech, Fred Dorsch, Ron Cobbledick, Pat McAvoy, Frank Abdou, Rob Shorten.
Third Row: Jim Reinson, Bill Cheers, Ken Hranchuk, Cam Clark, Gary Rumpel, Larry Van Moorlehem, Dave Orban, Art McAvoy, Don Chadney.
Second Row: Gerry Reinson, Bob Lochbaum, Bob McAfee, Neil Robinson, Ken McNabb, Garth West, Russ Marchuk, Don Bahnuik, Grant Becker, Murray Redhead, Al Lott, Doug Wass.
Front Row: Vic Brodoway (Equipment Mgr.), Nick Blum (Assistant Coach), Paul Anderson (Assistant Coach), Dr. Rafe Chadwick (President), Bill Ciz (Head Coach), Ted Stawarz (Trainer), Kevin Kearns (Team Manager).
Missing: Players: Bill Stevenson, Rick Sawa, George Daurie, Bill Luzecky, Ron Thompson, Ken Walters, Dr. Paul Schwann. Directors: George Johns, Joe Kanuka, Scotty Livingstone, Ron McGuigan, Max Bahnsen, F.C. Bell, Jim Dickens, Bob Hutton, Cliff Lamb, A.J. MacDonald, Ray Shooter, Jack Stewart, Dr. A.P. Strudwick, Ken Wheeler, Peter McCaffrey, Reg Forsyth.

1965 REGINA RAMS

Back Row: Gord Ciuca, Neil Robinson, Cam Clark, Mel Puscus, Garth West, Dick Leech, Ken McNabb, Dick Hearn, Bill Luzecky.
Fourth Row: Lloyd Dobie (Trainer), Ron Cobbledick, Murray Redhead, Raymond Legault, Gary Rumpel, Rod Smith, Barry Aldag.
Third Row: James Reinson, Les Miller, Garry Andrews, Bill Stevenson, Al Chase, Bob Shorten, Ken Walters, Bernie Brandt, Alex Kerr (Equip. Mgr.).
Second Row: Larry Van Moorlehem, Pat McAvoy, Gerald Dobra, Paul Cocks, Frank Abdou, Dave Orban, Joe McGrath, Don Bahnuik, Ken Huber, Barry Radcliffe, Doug Wass, Grant Becker.
Front Row: Jack Stewart (Dir.), Ken Wheeler (Dir.), Ron McGuigan (Mgr. Sec), Dr. Rafe Chadwick (Pres.), Al Relkey (Assistant Coach), Gord Currie (Head Coach), Gib Wagner (Assistant Coach), Scotty Livingstone (Past Pres.). Directors: Kevin Kearns, Ken Culham, Vic Moore.
Missing: Players: Daun Daum, J. Dumalski (Water Boy), Don Chadney, Al Lott, Fred Dorsch, Victor Zipchian. Directors: Joe Kanuka, Reg Forsyth, Peter McCaffrey.

1966 REGINA RAMS – NATIONAL CHAMPIONS

Back Row: Doug Griffith, Barry Radcliffe, Ken Newman, Fred Ward, Carl Blashill, George McLeod, Paul Cocks, Brian Duckett, Pat McDonnell, Doug Chekay, Rich Seitz, Larry Van Moorlehem.
Third Row: Lloyd Dobie (Trainer), Ken Huber, Frank Abdou, Al Johnston, Rod Brown, Mel Fiissel, Bill Locke, Gerald Dobra, Stan Crawford, Bill Deal, Bob Millar, Rod Smith, Alex Kerr (Equip. Mgr.), J Dumalski (Assistant Equip.).
Second Row: Bernie Brandt, Garry Andrews, Doug Morice, David Orban, Stan Mustatia, Ron Stengler, Dick Hearn, Daun Daum, Barry Aldag, Cam Clark, Vince Germann, Bill Waters.
Front Row: Gord Currie (Head Coach), Ken Walters, Gord Ciuca. Directors: Vic Moore, Scotty Livingstone, Joe Kanuka (President), Rafe Chadwick, Ken Wheeler, Ken Culham, Ron McGuigan (Manager), Al Relkey, (Assistant Coach), Gib Wagner (Assistant Coach), Erwin Strass (Dir.).
Missing: Players: Garry Chappelle, David Hazan, Bob Hornsberger, Doug Morrison, Bill Salloum. Directors: Reg Forsyth, Peter McCaffrey, Jack Stewart.

1967 REGINA RAMS

Back Row: J. Dumalski (Equip. Boy), Gordon Ciuca, Rod Smith, Rich Seitz, Bob McKenzie, Bob Foley, Wayne Commodore, Eric Harbottle, Jim Charter, Alex Kerr (Equip Mgr.), Doug Killoh (Assistant Coach).
Fourth Row: Ken Pielak, Dave Hall, Richard Kearns, Tom Ireton, George McLeod, D. Brandick, R. Rohrick, Bob Hornsberger, Vince Germann, Ron Nicolson, Bob McFadyen.
Third Row: Lloyd Dobie (Trainer), D. Snowfield, Gordon Brown, Alistair Johnston, Bill Pastuch, Rod Brown, Mel Fiissel, Bill Locke, Dick Hearn, Doug Morice, Frank Ens, Tom McCallum, David Hazen.
Second Row: Al Relkey (Assistant Coach), Gord Currie (Head Coach), Don Tingle, Stan Crawford, Ken Newman, Stan Mustatia, Barry Radcliffe, Bob Millar, Bill Waters, Pat McDonnell, Bill Deal, Frank Abdou, Bill Salloum.
Front Row: Directors: Erwin Strass, Vic Moore (Vice Pres.), Jerry Joynt, John Holash, Gerry Probe, Rafe Chadwick, Reg Forsyth, Scotty Livingstone, Ken Wheeler (Vice Pres.), Ron McGuigan (Manager), Jack Stewart, Dr. Paul Schwann, Brian Closs, Doug Griffith, Don Schmidt.
Missing: Players: Wayne Borys, Brian Duckett, Joe Kanuka (Pres.)

1968 REGINA RAMS

Back Row: Bob Hornsberger, Wayne Commodore, Gord Brown, Don Tingle, Brian Closs, Jim Charter, Tom Ireton.
Fourth Row: Ron Scrimbitt, Don Schmidt, Murray Ruhr, Doug Zimmerman, Rich Seitz, Henry Schubach, Ron Nicolson, Rich Ackerman.
Third Row: Stan Crawford, Bob McFadyen, Bob Millar, Dieter Pelzer, Eric Harbottle, Pat McDonnell, Bill Pastuch, Gerry Walker, Bill Salloum.
Second Row: Dave Seeley, Wayne Borys, Stan Mustatia, Rick August, Ken Newman, Alistair Johnston, Bob Johnstone, Ray Manz, Mike Hill, Frank Abdou.
Front Row: Reg Forsyth (Vice-Pres.), Al Relkey (Assistant Coach), Gord Currie (Head Coach), Stew Harrison (Dir.), Ron McGuigan (Sec. Mgr), Ken Wheeler (Pres.), Rafe Chadwick (Dir.), Jerry Joynt (Dir.), Vic Moore (Dir.), Lloyd Dobie (Trainer)
Missing: Players: Bob Helman, Monte Ziola, Bob Brennan, Randy Cobbledick, Doug Morice. Directors: Joe Kanuka, Scotty Livingstone, Jack Stewart, John Holash, Erwin Strass, Alex Kerr, Larry Ast.

1969 REGINA RAMS

Back Row: Doug Killoh (Assistant Coach), Jim Charter, Wayne Borys, Jim Hopson, Dieter Pelzer, Don Tingle, Brian Closs, Alex Nicolson, Ron Nicolson, Murray Patzwald (Equipment Assistant)
Fifth Row: Wayne Staudt, Murray Ruhr, Bob Kerr, A. Northcott, Randy Cobbledick, Bill Brennan, Rae Pratt, Rick Kellet, Arnie Tiefenbach, R. MacDonald, Alex Kerr (Equipment Mgr.)
Fourth Row: Lloyd Dobie (Trainer), Eric Harbottle, Rae Haverstock, Rich Ackerman, Dan Eaglestone, Larry Schwentke, Gerry Walker, Rick August, Wolfgang Pelzer.
Third Row: Gord Currie (Head Coach), Don Schmidt, Rob Pyne, A. Braun, Monte Ziola, Barry Polowick, Peter Schaefer, Bill Pastuch, Kim Ziola, Dave Seeley, Al Relkey (Assistant Coach).
Second Row: Ray Manz, Mike Hill, Bob McKenzie, Peter Springstein, Tony Husli, Henry Schubach, Bob MacFadyen, Bill Deal, Ron Scrimbitt, Garry Wilson.
Front Row: Directors: Vic Moore, Jack Stewart, John Holash, Jim Anderson, Gary Mather, Jerry Joynt (Vice Pres.), Ken Wheeler (President), Reg Forsyth (Vice Pres.), Scotty Livingstone, Ron McGuigan (Secretary-Manager), Reg Salter.
Missing: Directors: Erwin Strass, Rafe Chadwick, Joe Kanuka, Stew Harrison. Players: G. Barber, Doug Zimmerman.

1970 REGINA RAMS – NATIONAL CHAMPIONS

Back Row: Reiner Brittner, Alex Nicolson, Rae Pratt, Bob Kerr, Rocky Treleavan, John Broderick, Bob McFadyen.
Sixth Row: Doug Killoh (Assistant Coach), Alex Kerr (Equipment Manager), Roy Shiplack, Dieter Pelzer, Brian Closs, Don Tingle, Jim Charter, Jim Hopson, Irwin Ottenberg, Mel Fiissel (Assistant Coach).
Fifth Row: Murray Patzwald (Equipment Assistant), Al Relkey (Assistant Coach), Blake Walker, Tony Husli, Gord Glass, Peter Schaefer, Gord Selinger, Henry Schubach.
Fourth Row: Jim Francis (Trainer), Garry Wilson, Don Schmidt, Rich Akerman, Eric Harbottle, Doug Zimmerman, Monte Ziola, Ken Dobra, Bryan Dimen, Gerry Walker, Peter Springstein, Gord Currie (Head Coach).
Third Row: Rob Pyne, Mike Hill, Ray Manz, Dave Seeley, Jerry Orban, Barry Polowick, Terry Renwick, Ken Fiissel, Larry Kratt, Ron Scrimbitt.
Second Row: Dr. Frank Samuels, Dr. Jack Alexander. Directors: Eli Fluter, Gary Mather, George Hambley, Scotty Livingstone, Joe Kanuka, Ron McGuigan, D. Gibson, Dr. Rafe Chadwick (Manager), Jim Anderson.
Front Row: Directors: Stew Harrison, Jack Stewart, Ken Wheeler, Wilf Gee, Jerry Joynt, Reg Forsyth (President), Reg Salter, Tom Shepherd, Vic Moore, John Holash.
Missing: Director: Erwin Strass. Players: Rick Kellett, Dave Sawa.

1971 REGINA RAMS – NATIONAL CHAMPIONS

Back Row: Doug Killoh (Assistant Coach), R. Winter, Peter Schaefer, Roy Shiplack, Jerry Orban, Dieter Pelzer, Jim Hopson, Blake Walker, Terry Renwick, Mel Fiissel (Assistant Coach).
Fourth Row: Jeff Donison, Ron Cherkas, Marvin Messner, Rich McCullough, Kim Ziola, Rich Storey, Larry Kratt, Larry LeBlanc, Brian Saip.
Third Row: Norm Fong (Equipment Manager), Ken Dobra, Garry Wilson, Dave Sawa, Rocky Treleaven, Ray Manz, Mike Hill, Rob Pyne, Tony Husli, Steve Mazurak, Don Schmidt (Assistant Coach).
Second Row: Al Relkey (Assistant Coach), M. Riley, John Broderick, Ken Fiissel, Bob Lane, Doug Zimmerman, Dave Wormsbecker, Gord Selinger, Malcolm Adams, Gord Currie (Head Coach)
Front Row: Jim Francis (Trainer), Ron McGuigan (Manager). Directors: Stew Harrison, George Hambley, Jerry Joynt, Reg Forsyth (President), Reg Salter, Rafe Chadwick, Barry Mang, John Holash.
Ball Boy: Vic Klein.
Missing: Players: Gordon Glass, Bryan Dimen, Alex Nicolson, Terry Hincks, Greg Treleaven, Reiner Brittner, Don Monk, Dave Seeley. Directors: Eli Fluter, Wilf Gee, Joe Kanuka, Scotty Livingstone, Gary Mather, Vic Moore, Tom Shepherd, Jack Stewart, Erwin Strass, Ken Wheeler, Dr. Frank Samuels, Dr. Jack Alexander.

1972 REGINA RAMS

Back Row: Norm Fong (Equipment Manager), Ron Brooks, Darryl Herauf, Dave Zerr, Rod Laporte, Mike Gebert, Frank McCrystal, Jim Francis (Trainer).
Fifth Row: Reg Forsyth (Past President), Darryl Puscus, Augie Bernstein, Mickey Adams, Erwin Klempner, Joe Herauf, Brian Saip, Darryl Cherkas, Bob Milton (Director), Rafe Chadwick (Director).
Fourth Row: Doug Alexander (Director), John Holash (Director), Ken Dobra, Bernie Schmidt, Bob Lane, Rocky Treleaven, Dale Weisbrot, Scott Meikle, Rich Delnea, Ron Winkler.
Third Row: Gary Mather (Director), Gord Glass, Steve Mazurak, Bryan Dimen, Greg Johnson, Stu Scalf, Larry Kratt, Dave Wormsbecker, Don Young, Lloyd Holtzman, Tom McCord, Jack Stewart (Director).
Second Row: Doug Killoh (Ass't Coach), Don Schmidt (Ass't Coach), Jeff Donison, Pete Schaefer, Roy Shiplack, Terry Hincks, Larry LeBlanc, Jim Hopson, Blake Walker, Randy Labatte, Gord Currie (Head Coach), Mel Fiissel (Ass't Coach).
Front Row: Roger Aldag, Lorne Hubick, Lenny Knoll, Rick Storey, Pete Byars (Manager), Reg Salter (Vice-President), Jerry Joynt (President), Tom Shepherd (Treasurer), John Broderick, Dave Sawa, Don Wilde, Jack Lichtenwald.
Ball Boys: Vic Lein, Jack Roenspeiss
Missing: Players: Mark Kellendonk, Barry Polowick, Dr. Frank Samuels, Dr. Jack Alexander, Al Relkey (Ass't Coach). Directors: George Hambley, Eli Fluter, Stew Harrison, Joe Kanuka, Scotty Livingstone, Barry Mang, Ron McGuigan, Ken Wheeler.

1973 REGINA RAMS – NATIONAL CHAMPIONS

Back Row: Doug Alexander (Director), Bob Poley, Dennis Brooks, Roy Shiplack, Terry Hincks, Larry LeBlanc, Scott Meikle, Brian Saip, Bob Lane, Brian Illerbrun, Al Jensen (Director)
Fourth Row: Jim Francis (Trainer), Phil Paskaruk, Dale Weisbrot, Mark Constable, Dwayne Thurmeier, Erwin Klempner, Frank McCrystal, Larry Kratt, Don Young, Rod Simaluk, Harvey Johnson (Director), Eli Fluter (Director).
Third Row: Dr. Jack Alexander; Norm Fong (Equipment Manager), Terry Evans, Bernie Schmidt, Dave Sawa, Darryl Herauf, Preston Young, Len Knoll, John Kreikle, Greg Johnson, Ted Dolinski, Don Wilde, Peter Byars (Team Manager).
Second Row: Tom McCord, Roger Aldag, Randy Labatte, Bryan Dimen, Rick Storey, Jack Lichtenward, Ken Dobra, Mike Gebert, Don Mosher, Terry Reed, Les Ludwig.
Front Row: Directors; Reg Forsyth, Norbert Thurmeier, Bob Milton, George Hambley (Vice-President), Reg Salter (Vice-President), Jerry Joynt (President), Gord Currie (Head Coach), Mel Fiissel (Ass't Coach), Al Relkey (Ass't Coach), Gerry Orban (Ass't Coach). Directors: Gary Mather, Reg Houston, Stan Ward, Jack Stewart.
Ball Boys: Vic Klein, Jack Roenspiess.
Missing: Don Schmidt (Assistant Coach). Directors: Rafe Chadwick, Ken Wheeler, Tom Shepherd, Scotty Livingstone, Stu Harrison, Dr. Frank Samuels, Erwin Strass, Don McDougall. Players: Rich Delnea, Larry Kozakevich, Stu Scalf, Darryl Puscus, Jim Limmerick.

1974 REGINA RAMS

Back Row: Vic Klein (Ball Boy), Jerry Orban (Ass't Coach), John Kriekle, Michael Sim, Jim Morgan, Vern Ell, Kelly Reardon, Erwin Klempner, Craig Kenyon, Jim Limmerick, Tom Parker, Shane Armstrong, Gordon Currie (Head Coach), Jack Roenspiess (Ball Boy).
Fourth Row: Doug Killoh (Ass't Coach), Mike Mushansky, Greg Johnson, Jack Lichtenwald, Frank McCrystal, Brian Illerbrun, Eugene Larocque, Don Mosher, Mike Gebert, Bob Poley, Don Young, Preston Young, Mark Constable.
Third Row: Jim Kenyon, Dennis Brooks, Bernie Schmidt, Randy Labatte, Tom McCord, Scott Meikle, Roger Aldag, Rod Outhwaite, Bob Lane, Darrel Puscus, Ted Dolinski, Mel Fiissel (Ass't Coach).
Second Row: Doug Wilson (Director), Terry Evans (Equip. Mgr.), Rod Simaluk, Darryl Herauf, Larry Kozakevich, Len Knoll, Les Ludwig, Don Wilde, Rick Storey, Charles Obrigewitsch, Mike Hanson, Tim Almas, Terry Read.
Front Row: Dr. Frank Samuels (Team Doctor), Eli Fluter (Director), Stan Ward (Director), Bob Milton (Vice - President), George Hambley (President), Don McDougall (Sec.), Reg Houston (Director), Norbert Thurmeier (Team Manager), Doug Alexander (Director), Peter Byars (Director).
Missing: Directors: Gary Mather (Vice-Pres.), Reg Forsyth, Scotty Livingstone, Tom Shepherd, Ken Wheeler, Jack Stewart, Rafe Chadwick, Al Jensen, Harvey Johnson, Jerry Joynt, Dr. Jack Alexander, Jim Francis (Trainer). Players: Dale Weisbrot, Dave Wormsbecker.

1975 REGINA RAMS – NATIONAL CHAMPIONS

Back Row: Doug Killoh (Coach), Tim Ziegler, Kevin Harle, Doug MacKenzie, Craig Kenyon, Jeff Reimer, Gord Lang, Bernie Schmidt, Dave Hall, Frank McCrystal.
Fourth Row: Doug Zerr, Rene Glenn, Dale Von Hagen, Jim Kenyon, Tim Almas, Eugene LaRocque, Don Mosher, Tom McCord, Bob Poley, Jim Limmerick, Les Ludwig, Don Wilde.
Third Row: Vern Ell, Mike Mushanski, Shane Armstrong, Brent McConnell, Mark Constable, Don Young, Kerry Berryman, Darryl Herauf, Richard Reitmeier, Thom Parker, Kelvin Derkson.
Second Row: Stan Ward (Director), Bruce Lipinski, Randy Labatte, Chuck MacDonald, Scott Meikle, Roger Aldag, Mike Sim, Bob Lane, Gerry Fellner, Len Knoll, Ted Dolinski, Harvey Kozakevich, Jim Francis (Trainer).
Front Row: Don McDougall (Sec.); Norbert Thurmeier (Manager); George Hambley (President); Jack Roenspiess (Equipment); Joanne Lemieux (Assistant Trainer). Coaches: Mel Fiissel, Gord Currie (Head Coach), Jerry Orban. Directors: Reg Houston, Al Jenson, Peter Byars, Dr. Jack Alexander, Dr. Frank Samuels, Barry Roenspiess (Ball Boy).
Missing: Player: Brian Illerbrun, Rodney Kobsar (Ball Boy). Directors: Don Black, Eli Fluter, Harvey Johnson, Alex Kerr, Gary Mather, Bob Milton, Jack Stewart, Doug Wilson, Ken Wheeler, Rafe Chadwick, Reg Forsyth, Scotty Livingstone, Tom Shepherd, Jerry Joynt.

1976 REGINA RAMS – NATIONAL CHAMPIONS

Back Row: Eugene LaRocque, Bob Moore, Craig Kenyon, Vern Ell, Tim Almas, Steve Sebastian, Greg Nesbitt, Boyd Richards, Alex Camponi.
Sixth Row: Alex Kerr (Director), Brian Illerbrun, Rich Reitmeier, Charlie Obrigewitsch, Dave Hall, Frank McCrystal, Terry Read, Jim Limmerick, Doug Killoh (Assistant Coach).
Fifth Row: Maurice Butler, Doug MacKenzie, Greg Fieger, Len Knoll, Kelvin Derkson, Les Ludwig, Jim Kenyon, Bob Poley.
Fourth Row: Norm Fong (Equipment Mgr.), Rich Crawford, Dale Von Hagen, Tom Parker, Darryl Herauf, Bruce Lipinski, Bill Lozinski, Brent McConnell, Jack Roenspiess (Equipment Assistant).
Third Row: Grant Becker (Director) Clarence Sacawayacappo, Chuck McDonald, Scott Meikle, Kerry Berryman, Kevin Harle, Mike Sim, Bob Lane, Randy Labatte.
Second Row: Jo-Anne Lemieux (Assistant Trainer), Dieter Pelzer (Director), Eli Fluter (Director), Al Jensen (Director), Dr. Frank Samuels, Dr. Jack Alexander, Jim Francis (Trainer).
Front Row: Don McDougall (Sec.), Bob Milton (Vice-Pres.), Mel Fiissel (Assistant Coach), Gord Currie (Head Coach), Gary Mather (Pres.), Reg. Houston (Director), Norbert Thurmeier (Director), George Hambley, (Past Pres.).
Ball Boys: Murray Falkenstein, Barry Roenspiess, Allen Wielgoz.
Missing Players: Cory Elson, Gerry Fellner.
Missing Directors: Don Black, Jeff Bugera, Pete Byars, Harvey Johnson, Tom Shepherd, Jack Stewart, Doug Wilson, Lorne Warnes; Jerry Orban (Assistant Coach), Bernie Sebastian, Erwin Strass.

1977 REGINA RAMS

Back Row: Craig Kenyon, Rich Reitmeier, Dave Hall, Brian Illerbrun, Rene Glenn, Terry Read, Jim Kenyon, Dr. Jack Alexander.
Fifth Row: Paul Barnby (Dir.), Bryan Dimen (Assistant Coach), Dave Badowich, Don Finn, Steve Sebastian, Bob Euteneier, Bob Moore, Boyd Richards, Jerry Orban (Assistant Coach), Val Vlanich (Dir.).
Fourth Row: Jack Roenspiess (Equipment Mgr), Larry Mueller, Darrell Baiton, Mark McCulloch, Glen Farrow, Vern Ell, Glen Elford, Julien Hulet, Greg Nesbitt, Jerry Zbytnuik (Assistant Coach).
Third Row: Eric Harbottle (Dir.), Doug MacKenzie, Kelly Hamilton, Greg Fieger, Thom Parker, Tim Almas, Len Antonini, Bruce Lipinski, Paul Richardson, Bill Lozinski, Jeff Bugera (Dir.).
Second Row: Chuck McDonald, Brent McConnell, Kevin Harle, Mike Sim, Clarence Sacawayacappo, Jeff Reimer, Dr. Frank Samuels.
Front Row: Jim Francis (Trainer), Don McDougall (Dir.), Dr. Don Benz, Pete Byars (Dir.), Mel Fiissel (Head Coach), Gary Mather (President), Lorne Warnes (Dir.), Reg Houston (Manager), Norbert Thurmeier (Dir.), Al Wielgoz (Ball Boy).
Missing Players: Maurice Butler, Tim Probe, Corey Elson, Dale Von Hagen, Mike Mushanski, Kerry Berryman, Jim Limmerick, Bob Poley.
Missing Directors: Bob Milton, George Hambley, Don Black.

1978 REGINA RAMS

Back Row: Cam Clark (Assistant Coach), Bryan Dimen (Assistant Coach) Kelly Hamilton, Tim Wiens, Greg Jones, Rich Reitmeier, Dave Hall, Chuck McDonald, Marty Hamilton, Len Antonini, Calvin Sikorski, Wes Clifford.
Fourth Row: Randy Pollock (Eqp't Mgr.), Vern Ell, Les Krentz, Les Mironuck, Darrel Baiton, Greg Fieger, Thom Parker, Tim Almas, Bill Lozinski, Bruce Lipinski, Doug MacKenzie.
Third Row: Gerry Harris (Assistant Coach), Drew Ward, Larrry Mueller, Bill Parker, Tim Probe, Tim Garvin, Blair Bucsis, Greg Nesbitt, John Hartung, Julien Hulet, Randy Smith.
Second Row: Don Seaman (Dir.), Grant Becker (Dir.), Wayne Mulligan, Martin Altwasser, Kevin Harle, Brent McConnell, Kerry Berryman, Clarence Sacawayacappo, Paul Richardson, Glen Farrow, Dave Badowich.
Front Row: Eric Harbottle (Dir.), Carla McGillivray (Assistant Trainer), Dr. Frank Samuels, Don McDougall (Dir.), Reg Houston (Manager), Pete Byars (Dir.), Norbert Thurmeier (Dir.), Bob Milton (President), Lorne Warnes (Dir.), Val Vlanich (Dir.), Jerry Zbytnuik (Head Coach), Jim Francis (Trainer).
Ball Boys: Gary Falkenstein, Terry Wielgoz.
Missing Player: Gary Klotz.
Missing Directors: Gary Mather, Don Black, Eli Fluter, George Hambley, Dr. Jack Alexander.

1979 REGINA RAMS

Back Row: Directors: George Hambley, Peter Byars, Dave Whitteker, Val Vlanich, Lorne Warnes, Gary Mather, Paul Barnby, Norbert Thurmeier, Don McDougall.
Fifth Row: Al Pylatuk, Brad Cocks, Perry McCormick, Wayne Obrigewitsch, Larry Mueller, Julien Hulet, Cal Sikorski, Randy Smith, Tim McGeough, Jim Sinnaeve, Marty Hamilton, Dave Badowich, Jim Stirr.
Fourth Row: Bill Parker, Mel Ell, Gerry Straeker, Tim Wiens, Kelly Hamilton, Drew Ward, Doug MacKenzie, Tim Probe, Tim Garvin, Greg Fieger, Len Antonini, Wes Clifford.
Third Row: Rod Sisco, Hal Webber, Doug Currie, Darrell Baiton, Les Krentz, Marshall Hamilton, Blair Bucsis, Greg Nesbitt, Kerry Berryman, Lyle Mosiondz, Craig Hammond, Hal Wilkie.
Second Row: Perry Smales, Tim Spelliscy, Gary Frank, Terry Solonynko, Terry Zerf, Wayne Mulligan, Brent McConnell, Don Finn, Paul Richardson, Blair Thompson, Clarence Sacawayacappo, Glenn Farrow, Greg Wilchuck.
Front Row: Dr. Frank Samuels, Randy Pollock (Equip. Mgr.), Frank McCrystal (Assistant Coach), Gerry Harris (Assistant Coach), Cam Clark (Assistant Coach), Jerry Zbytnuik (Head Coach), Bob Milton (President), Marj Leach (Assistant Trainer), Jim Francis (Trainer), Carla McGillivray (Assistant Trainer) Eric Harbottle (Team Manager), Terry Wielgoz (Ball Boy).
Missing Players: Craig Edwards, Dennis Ziegler.
Missing Directors: Grant Becker, Don Black, Gary Fitz, Eli Fluter, Ken Hagerman, Bill Nelson, Don Seaman, Doug Wilson, Dr Jack Alexander.

1980 REGINA RAMS – NATIONAL CHAMPIONS

Back Row: Directors: Paul Barnby, Bob Milton, Eric Harbottle, Reg Houston, Bob Millar, Val Vlanich, Eli Fluter, Norbert Thurmeier (Vice President), Keith King, Wayne Hunter, Gary Mather.
Fifth Row: Bernie Knoll, Greg Brock, Randy Lewis, Bill Parker, Terry Eisler, George Heuck, Hal Wilkie, Len Antonini, Marty Hamilton.
Fourth Row: Galan Walhmeier, Gary Klotz, Rodger Hutchinson, Chris Hamilton, Murray Ell, Brent Taylor, Dave Munroe, Larry Mueller, Tim McGeough, Calvin Sikorski, Randy Smith, Al Pylatuk, Jim Sinnaeve, Julien Hulet, Larry Geni, Chuck Toth.
Third Row: Randy Bradley, Rob Palmarin, Doug Currie, Tim Probe, Pat Hamilton, Keith Hiller, Les Krentz, Rod Sisco, Tim Wiens, Frank Macera, Lyle Mosiondz, Tim Spelliscy, Mel Ell, Craig Edwards, Kelly Hamilton.
Second Row: Dave Arsenault, Ken Vallevand, Terry Solonynko, Kevin Peyson, Dave Badowich, Blair Thompson, Greg Wilchuck, Wayne Mulligan, Greg Nesbitt, Craig Hammond, Dennis Ziegler, Clarence Sacawayacappo, Glen Farrow, Paul Dawson.
Front Row: Carla McGillivray (Assistant Trainer), Colin Byas (Assistant Equip. Mgr.), Les Rody (Equip. Mgr.), Dr. Frank Samuels, Don McDougall (President), Gerry Harris (Coach), Cam Clark (Coach), Jerry Zbytnuik (Head Coach), Frank McCrystal (Coach), Jim Francis (Trainer), Marshall Hamilton (Coach).
Missing Directors: Bill Nelson (Vice President), Dave Whitteker, Dr. Jack Alexander.

1981 REGINA RAMS – NATIONAL CHAMPIONS

Back Row: Paul Barnby (Team Manager). Directors: Wayne Hunter, Ken Hagerman, Andy McDougall, Bob Millar, Norbert Thurmeier (Vice-President), Val Vlanich (Secretary), Tom McCord, Bill Nelson (Vice-President), Fred Chriest, Jack Kennedy.
Fifth Row: Dave Whitteker (Director), Keith Hiller, Jim Sinnaeve, Keith McLean, Randy Smith, Calvin Sikorski, Larry Mueller, Tim McGeough, Don Gorski.
Fourth Row: George Heuck, Rob Palmarin, Tim Probe, Tim Spelliscy, Hal Wilkie, Mark Kent, Tim Wiens, Les Krentz, Terry Zerff, Doug Currie, Kelly Hamilton.
Third Row: Chris Hamilton, Bill Parker, Rod Sisco, Dave Arsenault, Terry Eisler, Lyle Mosiondz, Bernie Knoll, Julian Hulet, Paul Dawson, Frank Macera, Marty Hamilton.
Second Row: Len Antonini, Charlie Yurkowski, Randy Bradley, Dave Badowich, Craig Hammond, Blair Thompson, Wayne Mulligan, Terry Solonynko, Brent Taylor, Reiny Dundas.
Front Row: Cory Byas (Ball Boy), Rob Jamont (Ball Boy), Carla McGillivray (Assistant Trainer), Jim Francis, (Trainer), Les Rody (Equipment Manager), Dr. Frank Samuels (Team Doctor), Don McDougall (President), Jerry Zbytnuik (Head Coach), Gerry Harris (Coach), Cam Clark (Coach).
Missing: Frank McCrystal (Coach), Don MacRae (Player).
Missing Directors: Dr. Jack Alexander, Gary Mather, Bob Milton.

1982 REGINA RAMS

Back Row: Tom McCord (Dir.), Bob Millar (Dir.), Loring Lascue, Darcy Koch, Rob Predenchuk, Rob Palmarin, Andy McDougall (Dir.), Hal Wilkie, Wayne Hunter (Dir.), Tim Wiens, Marty Hamilton, Gary Uhren (Dir.), Frank Macera, Ed Bankowski (Dir.).
Fifth Row: Don McDougall (Dir.), Rodger Hutchinson, Rod Sisco, Terry Cochrane, Terry Zerff, Chris Hamilton, Murray Hanson, Ron Lancaster Jr., Rick Kachur.
Fourth Row: Ken Hagerman (Dir.), Marlowe Pelletier, Glen Weir, Charlie Yurkoski, Lyle Mosiondz, Kevin Peyson, Paul Dawson, Kevin Ostapowich, Gord Marceca, Jim Francis (Trainer).
Third Row: Mark Kent, Dave Kot, Randy Bradley, Don MacRae, Brent Taylor, Terry Solonynko, Steve Sombach, Brent Molnar, Ben Schoots, Glenn Stevenson.
Second Row: Randy Klein, Al Fink, Don Gorski, Del Palaga, Tim McGeough, Al Pylatuk, Terry Eisler, Mike Grzyb, Mark Becker.
Front Row: Les Rody (Eqp't Mgr.), Cam Clark (Assistant Coach), Bill Nelson (Dir.), Frank McCrystal (Assistant Coach), Norbert Thurmeier (Pres.), Jerry Zbytnuik (Head Coach), Gerry Harris (Assistant Coach), Val Vlanich (Dir.), Jack Kennedy (Dir.), Bob Milton (Dir.).
Ball Boys: Brad Herschmiller, Randy Zbytnuik.
Missing Ball Boys: Jerry Hardy.
Missing Coach: Bernie Schmidt.
Missing Players: Dave Arsenault, Lary Geni.
Missing Directors: Dave Whitteker, Paul Barnby, Don Black, Reg Houston, Bob Pelton, Gary Mather, Fred Chriest, Doug McKillop, Dr. Frank Samuels, Dr. Jack Alexander.

1983 REGINA RAMS

Back Row: Directors: Gary Uhren, Paul Richardson, Ed Bankowski, Andy McDougall, Bob Lane, Wayne Hunter, Fred Chriest, Bob Millar, Bob Pelton, Gary Mather, Tom McCord, Jack Kennedy, Don McDougall.
Sixth Row: Sam Zurawski, Dean Pasiuk, Steve Hammernick, Dave Kot, Tim Hammond, Darcy Koch, Mark Becker, Rick Lavoy, Rob Antonini, Al Fink.
Fifth Row: Mike Pestill, Chris Hamilton, Ken Schofield, Jim Braun, John Papandreos, Rick Kachur, Curtis Standing, Mark Toderan, Doug Goy, Scott Thackery, Doug Brown, Paul Barnby (Dir.), Paul Yaciw (Dir.).
Fourth Row: Mark Kent, Wade Probe, Marlowe Pelletier, Kevin Peyson, Don MacRae, Steve Sombach, Kelvin Ostapowich, Lawrence Gargol, Russ Turgeon, Todd Lewis, Reiny Dundas, Brent Taylor, Phil Hulet.
Third Row: Dave Gebert, Mike Lazecki, Ken Katchur, Gord Marceca, Dave Arsenault, Terry Cochrane, Terry Zerff, Hal Wilkie, Rod Sisco, Lary Geni, Al Hendren, Rich Sutcliffe, Ken Nickel.
Second Row: Brad Herschmiller (Equip. Mgr.), Del Palaga, Randy Klein, Loring Lascue, Terry Eisler, Rob Sillinger, Don Gorski, Rob Palmarin, Tim Relke, Barry Wilkie, Ben Schoots, Randy Zbytnuik (Ball Boy), Gerry Hardy (Ball Boy).
Front Row: Cam Clark (Assistant Coach), Stan Szumlak (Assistant Trainer), Roland Scheuer, Tim McGeough, Bernie Schmidt (Assistant Coach), Gerry Harris (Assistant Coach), Frank McCrystal (Assistant Coach), Norbert Thurmeier (Pres.), Jerry Zbytnuik (Head Coach), Dave Whitteker (Dir.), Bill Nelson (Dir.), Jim Francis (Trainer).
Missing Directors: Don Black, Eli Fluter, Ken Hagerman, Reg Houston, Doug McKillop, Bob Milton, Val Vlanick.
Missing Doctors: Dr. Jack Alexander, Dr. Donovan Brown, Dr. Bill Elliott, Dr. Frank Samuels.

1984 REGINA RAMS

Back Row: Directors: Dave Howie, George Crawford, Doug McKillop, Len Antonini, Ken Hagerman, Val Vlanich, Andy McDougall, Don McDougall, Jack Kennedy, Jon Hammond, Paul Yaciw, Bob Rieger.
Seventh Row: Paul Barnby (Director), Dan Johnston, Jim McDowell, Warren Miller, Kelly Handy, Ron Bresch, Mark Brown, Al Hendren, Randy Klein, Del Palaga, Ron Wasylyshyn, Reg Houston (Director).
Sixth Row: Mel Fiissel (Director), Kevin Chekay, Loring Lascue, Al Wielgoz, Wendell Toth, Charlie Dumba, Randy Shulz, Paul Yanko, Darrell Schmidt, Don Gorski, Rick Lavoy, Gary Mather (Director).
Fifth Row: Norbert Thurmeier (Past President), Darren Benning, Phil Hulet, Darcy Koch, Jason Belisle, Lawrence Larkin, Ken Nickel, Marlowe Pelletier, Terry Eisler, Gord Lupanko, Bob Pelton (Director).
Fourth Row: Larry Mueller (Director), Dean Picton, Stuart Sparvier, Sid Lovegrove, Brent Pollock, Mark Kent, Emil Delnea, Tim Burnie, Lawrence Gargol, Rich Sutcliffe, Doug Dorsch.
Third Row: Gary Uhren (Director), Ken Schofield, Mark Becker, Rob Palmarin, Kevin Peyson, Mike Lazecki, Tim Hammond, Rob Sillinger, Gord Marceca, Ron Senger, Gerry Hardy.
Second Row: Greg Singer, Russ Turgeon, Steve Sombach, Kelvin Ostapowich, Tim Relke, Brian Eltom, Brian Forrest, Dave Gebert, Randy Morrish (Director).
Front Row: Bob Millar (Vice-President), Jim Francis (Trainer), Tim McGeough (Assistant Coach), Doug Zimmerman (Assistant Coach), Frank McCrystal (Head Coach), Jerry Orban (Assistant Coach), Bernie Schmidt (Assistant Coach), Rick Seaman (Assistant Coach), Ed Bankowski (Manager), Brad Herschmiller (Equipment Manager), Dave Whitteker (Vice-President), Bill Nelson (President).
Ball Boys: Jason Sroka, Cory Culling.
Missing Directors: Fred Chriest, Paul Richardson, Rocky Treleavan.
Missing Players: Steve Butler, Rod Chabot, Henry Funke.
Missing Doctors: Dr. Jack Alexander, Dr. Frank Samuels, Dr. Bill Elliott.

1985 REGINA RAMS

Back Row: Directors: Ken Black, Gary Uhren, Norbert Thurmeier, Bob Forrest, Fred Chriest, Bob Mitchell, Don McDougall, Doug McKillop, Bob Rieger, Dave McMahon, Mel Fiissel.
Sixth Row: Wendell Toth, Al Wiegloz, John Simic, Scott Thackray, Kevin Chekay, Jamie Anderson, Troy Grado, Brad Arsenault, Ken Neiszner, Doug Dorsch, George Crawford (Dir.)
Fifth Row: Mark Sombach, Mike Douglas, Ron Froh, Greg Earis, Kent Paterson, Paul Yanko, Bill Keith, Gary Cash, Marlowe Pelletier, Phil Hulet, Sean Wouters.
Fourth Row: Gary Mather, (Dir.), Emil Delnea, Gord Lupanko, Tim Burnie, Lawrence Gargol, Darcy Symcniuk, Glen Sawa, Jim Warnecke, Sam Khuber, Ken Schofield, Dean Picton, Dave Stouse (Dir.)
Third Row: Bob Millar (Vice-President), Jon Rae, Jason Belisle, Lance Lascue, Tim Hammond, Darcy Koch, Al Hendren, Rich Sutcliffe, Dan Johnston, Randy Morrish (Dir.)
Second Row: Jack Kennedy (Vice-President), Dave Gebert, Rob Sillinger, Ron Senger, Kelly Handy, Ed McQuarters Jr., Brian Forrest, Kelvin Ostapowich, Brian Eltom, Paul Barnby (President).
Front Row: Jason Sroka (Ball Boy), Cory Culling (Ball Boy), Jerry Harty (Assistant Equip. Mgr.), Brad Herschmiller (Equip. Mgr.), Terry Cherepuschak (Trainer), Patti Cherepuschak (Assistant Trainer), Rick Seaman (Assistant Coach), Tim McGeough (Assistant Coach), Frank McCrystal (Head Coach), Assistant Coaches: Doug Zimmerman, Jerry Orban, Bernie Schmidt, Ed Bankowski (Mgr.), Ball Boys: Corey Piche, Kevin Baier.
Missing Players: Mark Becker, Rod Chabot, Charle Dumba, Andy Fourlas, Dwayne La Montagne, Lawrence Larkin, Rick Lavoy, Mike Lazecki, Jim McDowell, Warren Miller, Del Palaga, Tim Relke, Cliff Rusconi, Kevin Schiller, Rod Wasylyshyn, Darren Benning, Ron Bresch, Robert Bresciani, Joe Mahnic, Randy Schultz.
Missing Directors: Len Antonini, Jon Hammond, Dave Howie, Andy McDougall, Larry Mueller, Bob Pelton, Paul Richardson, Val Vlanich, Larry Kratt, Bill Nelson, Rocky Treleaven. **Missing Ball Boy:** Jason Diewold. **Missing Doctors:** Dr. Jack Alexander, Dr. Brian Barootes, Dr. Bill Elliott.

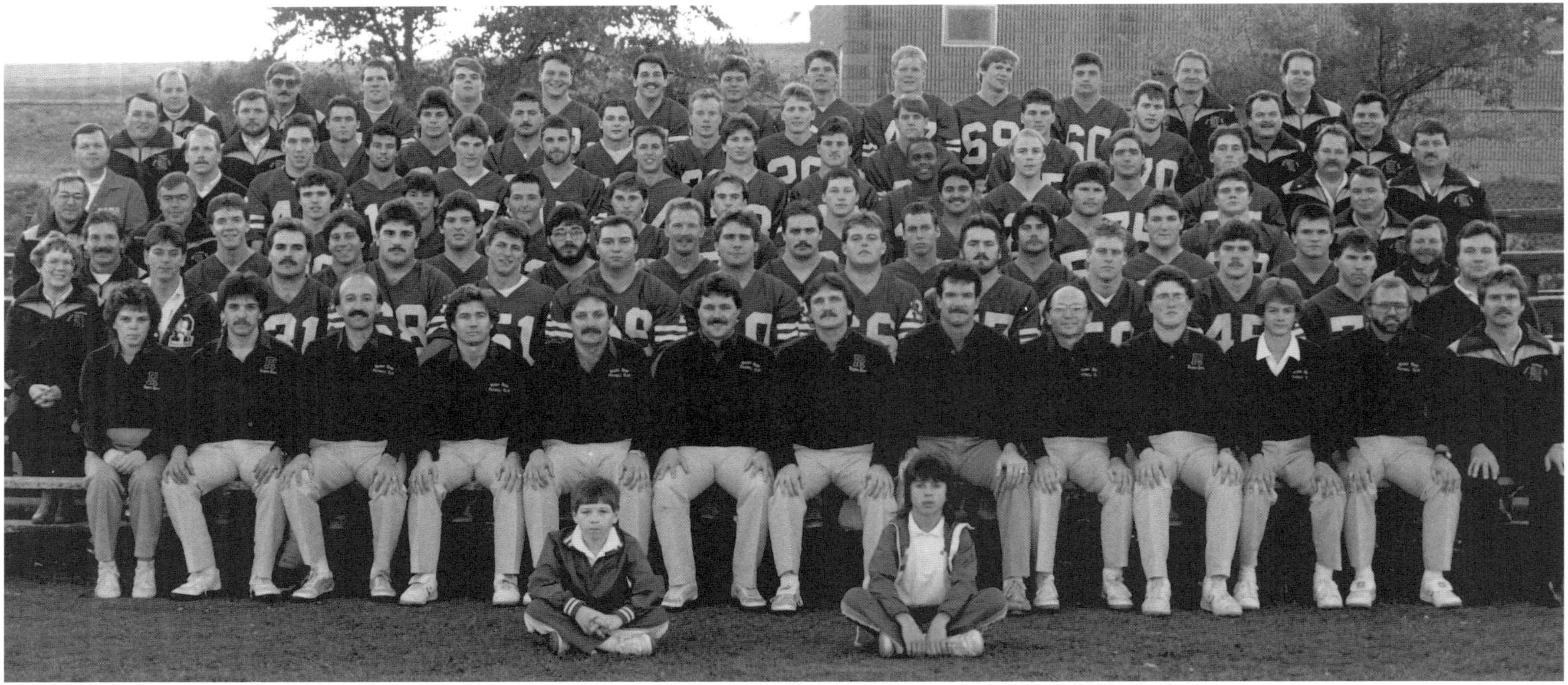

1986 REGINA RAMS – NATIONAL CHAMPIONS

Back Row: Bob Pelton (Dir.), Andy McDougall (Dir.), Rich Sutcliffe, Shane Goodwin, Bill Dinu, Rob Bresciani, Dean Picton, Mike Lazecki, Jon Rae, Bill Keith, Greg Karpa, Norbert Thurmeier (Dir.), Dave Stouse (Dir.).
Sixth Row: Dave Howie (Dir.), Larry Kratt (Dir.), Troy Grado, Wendell Toth, Phil Hulet, Ryan Hall, Ken Schofield, Dan Johnston, Doug Dorsch, Sean Wouters, Gary Cash, Bob Rieger (Dir.), Ken Black (Dir.).
Fifth Row: Don McDougall (Dir.), Len Antonini (Dir.), Kevin Chekay, Lance Lascue, Blaine Pearce, Mark Becker, Darcy Koch, Dave McEachern, Ricky Lavoy, Cliff Rusconi, Gord Lupanko, Brad Arsenault, Jim Warnecke, Randy Morrish (Dir.), Gary Uhren (Dir.).
Fourth Row: Bob Mitchell (Dir.), Jack Kennedy (Dir.), John Ferguson, Jeff Kallichuk, Dwayne Lamontagne, Darcy Smycniuk, Maurice Exner, Kollin Erichsen, Sam Khuber, Greg Cherkas, Scott Harris, Dave McMahon (Dir.).
Third Row: Jon Hammond (Dir.), Steve Tunison, Mark Sombach, Ken Neiszner, Rob Sillinger, Tim Hammond, Ron Senger, Kevin Reimer, Glen Sawa, Laird McLeod, Dave Rezansoff, Gary Mather (Dir.).
Second Row: Cheryl Beitel (Office Sec.), Gerry Hardy (Eq. Assistant), Dave Gebert, Kelly Handy, Lawrence Gargol, Kelvin Ostapowich, Tim Relke, Brian Eltom, Emil Delnea, Al Hendren, Tim Burnie, Jamie Anderson, Larry Mueller (Dir.).
Front Row: Patty Cherepuschak (Tr.), Terry Cherepuschak (Tr.), Jerry Orban (Coach), Ray Pitre (Coach), Bernie Schmidt (Coach), Frank McCrystal (Head Coach), Doug Zimmerman (Coach), Campbell Hackney (Coach), Rick Seaman (Coach), Brad Herschmiller (Eq. Mgr.), Kevin Baier (Eq. Assistant), Ed Bankowski (Mgr.) Paul Barnby (Pres.).
Ball Boys: Robbie Cherepuschak, Jason Sroka.
Missing Players: Rod Brown, Rod Chabot, John Cunningham, Ron Froh, Trevor Grabowski, Scott Hazen, Dean Kuz, Ken Meredith, Dean Mihalicz, Kent Paterson, Brad Pawliw, Kevin Pilkey, John Simic, Paul Yanko.
Missing: Cory Culling (Ball Boy), Corey Piche (Assistant Equip. Mgr.), Dr. Jack Alexander, Dr. Brian Barootes, Dr. Bill Elliott, Bob Millar (Vice Pres.), Bill Nelson (Past Pres.), Doug McKillop (Treasurer), George Crawford (Dir.), Mel Fiissel (Dir.), Bob Forrest (Dir.), Lawrence Gerritsen (Dir.), Paul Richardson (Dir.).

1987 REGINA RAMS – NATIONAL CHAMPIONS

Back Row: Directors: Murray Patzwald, Bob Pelton, Jack Kennedy, Gary Mather, Ken Black, Dave McMahon, Larry Kratt, Basil Chomos (Chaplin), Bob Rieger, Cliff Dacey, Dave Stouse, Paul Barnby, Norbert Thurmeier.
Sixth Row: Rob Tudor (Dir.), Dave Howie (Dir.), Brian Eltom, Rob Sillinger, Sinisa Stefanovic, Bill Keith, Maurice Exner, Dwayne Lamontagne, Greg Fiddler, Kent Paterson, Tim Burn e, Tom McCord (Dir.).
Fifth Row: Jon Hammond (Dir.), Steven Bryce, Zeljko Stefanovic, Darrell Mosiondz, John Ferguson, Jon Rae, Greg Karpa, Terris Chorney, Bill Dinu, Steve Tunison, Laird McLeod, Jim Warnecke, Randy Morrish (Dir.).
Fourth Row: Larry Mueller (Dir.), Rod Flahr, Glen Sawa, Kelly Gorman, Dave Rezansoff, Brad Arsenault, Trevor Blanchard, Cletus Vassos, Roger Reinson, Tim Relke, Jim Wensel, Ken Neiszner, Kelly Sherman, Ed Bankowski (Dir.).
Third Row: Wendell Toth, Dan Johnston, Blaine Pearce, Neal Donovel, Brent Barkman, Dave Gebert, Rob Nistor, Cory Aspelieter, Kollin Erichsen, Sean Wouters, Jamie Anderson, Cliff Rusconi, Wallie Sich, Gary Uhren (Mgr.).
Second Row: Jay Yaciw (Ball Boy), Dean Picton, Ryan Hall, Lance Lascue, Steve Klyne, James Vollhoffer, Jeff Kallichuk, Sam Khuber, Darcy Smycniuk, Rich Sutcliffe, Blaine Coupal, Mike Lazecki, Dean Mihalicz, Bob Millar (Pres.).
Front Row: Rob Cherepuschak (Ball Boy), Patty Cherepuschak (Assistant Trainer), Terry Cherepuschak (Trainer), Jerry Orban (Assistant Coach), Bernie Schmidt (Assistant Coach), Ray Pitre (Assistant Coach), Frank McCrystal (Head Coach), Doug Zimmerman (Assistant Coach) Campbell Hackney (Assistant Coach), Brad Herschmiller (Equip. Mgr.), Kevin Baier (Assistant Equip. Mgr.), Corey Piche (Assistant Equip. Mgr.), Jason Sroka (Ball Boy).
Missing Players: Rod Chabot, Greg Cherkas, Doug Dorsch, Al Hendren, Rick Lavoy, Dwayne Roy, Mark Sombach.
Missing: Rick Seaman (Assistant Coach), Dr. Jack Alexander, Dr. Brian Barootes, Dr. Bill Elliott, Doug McKillop (Vice Pres.), George Crawford (Dir.), Bob Forrest (Dir.), Lawrence Gerritsen (Dir.), Andy McDougall (Dir.), Don McDougall (Dir.), Boyd Richards (Dir.), Ron Stengler (Dir.).

1988 REGINA RAMS

Back Row: Directors: Larry Kratt, Al Picton, Roger Salloum, Lawrence Gerritsen, Gary Mather, Fred Dulmage, Bob Pelton, Cliff Dacey, Dan Maxim, Dennis Junior, Jack Kennedy, Dave Stouse, Tom McCord, Larry Mueller, Doug McKillop.
Sixth Row: Dave Howie (Dir.), Murray Patzwald (Dir.), Bernie Schmidt (Coach), Brenda Stickel (Office Mgr.), Bill Keith, Mark Moellman, Maurice Exner, Dwayne Lamontagne, Sheldon Thomas, Jeremy Pellerin, Steve Bauer, Father Basil Chomos, Ed Bankowski (Dir.), Bob Millar (Dir.), Randy Morrish (Dir.).
Fifth Row: Stephen Bryce, Robin Garchinski, Carlos Buttner, Robin Reid, John Ferguson, Jon Rae, Greg Karpa, Brian Wozniak, Jason Tiefenbach, Steve Tunison, Tom Busch, Jim Warnecke, Brian Eltom, Darrell Harle, Sinisa Stefanovic.
Fourth Row: Rod Flahr, Glen Sawa, Kelly Trithart, Dave Rezansoff, Morley Crawford, Tim Huber, Cletus Vassos, Chuck Carefoot, Sonny Faugno, Scott Felton, James Wenzel, Greg Cherkas, Ken Neiszner, Tom MacCallum.
Third Row: Dean Mihalicz, Wendell Toth, Dan Johnston, Blaine Pearce, Chris Curran, Mark Pachiorka, Brent Barkman, Roger Reinson, Neal Donovel, Greg Fiddler, Kollin Erichsen, Sean Wouters, Brian Ross, James Pillipow, Wallie Sich.
Second Row: Dean Picton, Ryan Hall, Lance Lascue, Steven Klyne, Kelly Hackman, Darcy Dahlem, James Vollhoffer, Jeff Kallichuk, Sam Khuber, Darcy Smycniuk, Randy Zbytnuik, Brad Flavel, Blaine Coupal, Doug Dorsch, Milan Cacic, Gary Uhren (Dir.).
Front Row: Jay Yaciw (Ball Boy), Brad Walters (Ball Boy), Robbie Cherepuschak (Ball Boy), Patty Cherepuschak (Assistant Trainer), Terry Cherepuschak (Trainer). Coaches: Ray Pitre, Jerry Orban, Frank McCrystal (Head Coach), Doug Zimmerman, Campbell Hackney, Rick Seaman, Brad Herschmiller (Equip. Mgr.), Corey Piche (Assistant Equip.), Kevin Baier (Assistant Equip.), Michael Schmidt (Ball Boy), Ryan Zimmerman (Ball Boy).
Missing Players: Steve Gelinas, Robert Nistor, Bob Sheldon.
Missing Directors: Jon Hammond, George Crawford, Norbert Thurmeier, Rob Tudor, Don McDougall, Doug Tunison, Paul Barnby, Andy McDougall, Ken Black, Dave McMahon, Kevin Mason (Ball Boy), Dr. Jack Alexander, Dr. Brian Barootes, Dr. Bill Elliott.

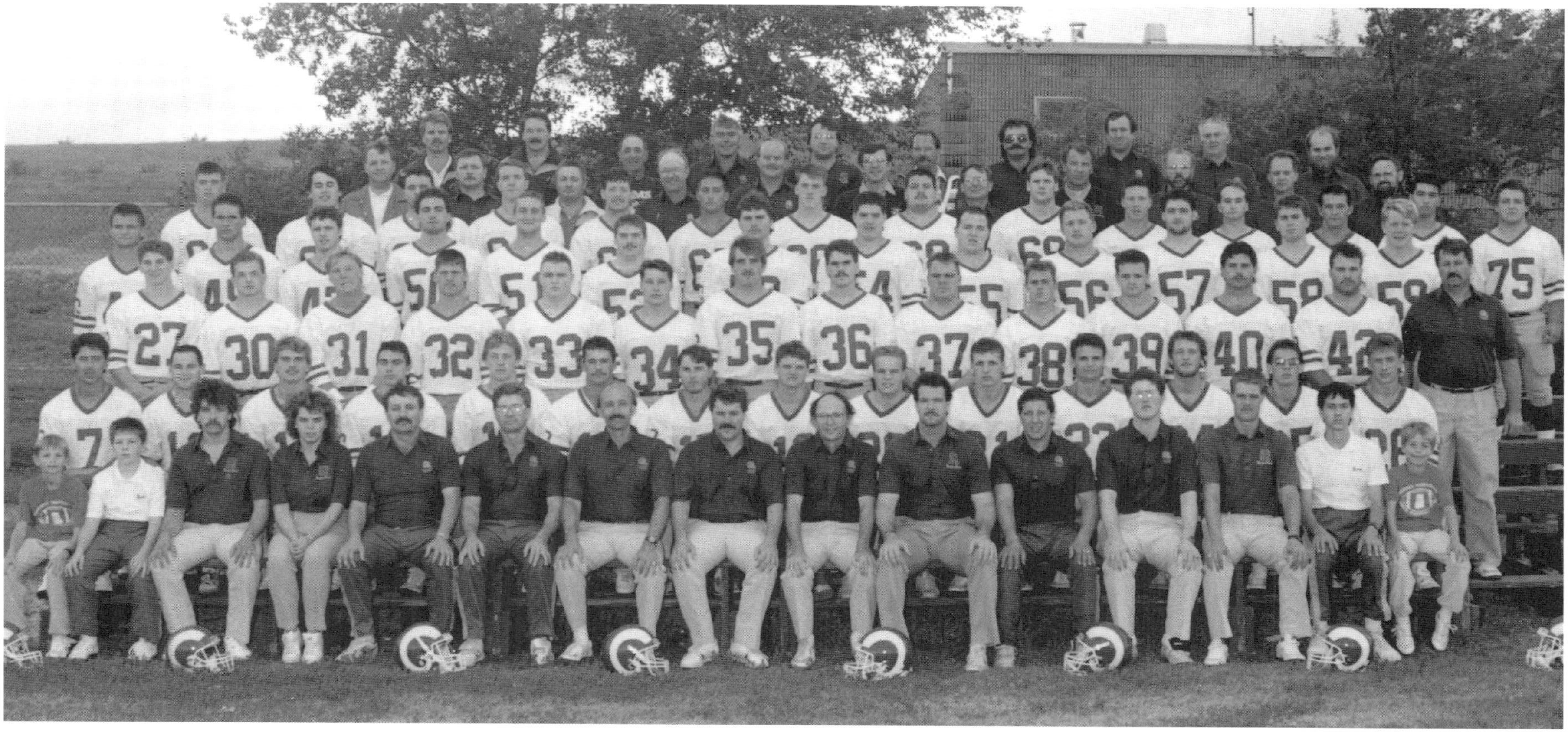

1989 REGINA RAMS

Back Row: Directors: Paul Barnby, Jon Hammond, Earl Kallichuk, Jack Kennedy, Larry Mueller, Randy Morrish, Tom Balkwill, Doug McKillop, Cliff Dacey, Murray Patzwald.
Sixth Row: Directors: Don McDougall, Larry Kratt, Dan Maxim, Doug Tunison, Tom McCord, Bob Millar, Al Picton, Fr. Basil Chomos, Ed Bankowski, Dave Stouse, Fred Dulmage.
Fifth Row: Greg Karpa, Gary Bresch, Jason Tiefenbach, Steve Tunison, Tom Busch, James Warnecke, Tim McFadden, Sinisa Stefanovic, Bill Keith, Kelly Gorman, Maurice Exner, Dwayne Lamontagne, Sheldon Thomas, Steve Bauer.
Fourth Row: Dave Rezansoff, Aaron Runge, John Ferguson, Sonny Faugno, James Wenzel, Tim Huber, Mike Slater, Tom MacCallum, Stephen Bryce, Robin Garchinski, Robin Reid, Corey Renwick, Jon Rae.
Third Row: Blaine Pearce, Brent Barkman, Roger Reinson, Neal Donovel, Greg Fiddler, Kollin Erichsen, Bob Aldridge, Brian Ross, Brad Flavel, Mark Moellman, Rod Flahr, Glen Sawa, Kelly Trithart, Gary Uhren (Mgr.).
Second Row: Shaun Anderson, Ryan Hall, Wade Schekk, Steve Klyne, Brent Ripplinger, Jeff Kallichuk, Darcy Smycniuk, Randy Zbytnuik, Chris Curran, Brad Bork, Milan Cacic, Dean Mihalicz, Mike Rutten, Jeff Banda.
Front Row: Michael Schmidt (Ball Boy), Robbie Cherepuschak (Ball Boy), Terry Cherepuschak (Trainer), Patty Cherepuschak (Assistant Trainer), Bernie Schmidt (Assistant Coach), Ray Pitre (Assistant Coach), Jerry Orban (Assistant Coach), Frank McCrystal (Head Coach), Rick Seaman (Assistant Coach), Campbell Hackney (Assistant Coach), Tim McGeough (Assistant Coach), Brad Herschmiller (Equip. Mgr.), Corey Piche (Assistant Equip. Mgr.), Trevor Herschmiller (Ball Boy), Kent Schmidt (Ball Boy).
Missing Players: Myles Hyland, Mark Pachiorka, Doug Huber, Kelly Busch, Kelly Brennan, Russell Fedak, Wade Shrimpton.
Missing Directors: Ken Black, Grant Engel, Dave Howie, Dennis Junior, Gary Mather, Andy McDougall, Bob Pelton, Roger Salloum, Norbert Thurmeier, Steve Sombach, Kevin Baier, (Equip. Mgr.), Brad Walters (Ball Boy), Dr. Jack Alexander, Dr. Brian Barootes, Dr. Bill Elliott.

1990 REGINA RAMS

Back Row: Directors: Paul Barnby, Fred Dulmage, Doug Tunsion, Jack Kennedy (President), Al Picton, Tom McCord, Earl Kallichuck, Cliff Dacey, Bob Pelton, Dave Stouse, Doug McKillop, Bob Millar.
Sixth Row: Directors Dave Howie, Tom Balkwill, Players: Don Blair, Maurice Exner, Greg Treble, Sheldon Thomas, Marco Ricci, Director Don Mc Dougall.
Fifth Row: Directors Steve Sombach, Dave Gebert, Players: Gary Bresch, Jason Tiefenbach, Dwayne Ell, Carlos Buttner, Tim Seiferling, Tim McFadden, Myles Keyowski, Sinisa Stefanovic, Director Murray Patzwald.
Fourth Row: Leanne LaMontange (Admin. Asst.), Larry Grabeldinger, Steve Bauer, Jason Beals, Sonny Faugno, Jim Wenzel, Tim Huber, Mike Slater, Tom MacCallum, Steve Bryce, Scott Waters, Cory Renwick, Doug Clark.
Third Row: Blaine Pearce, Todd Fuchs, Kelly Gorman, Roger Reinson, Jason Daum, Greg Fiddler, Kollin Erichsen, Bob Aldridge, Brian Ross, Brad Flavel, Hans Larson, Rod Flahr, Jason Kotyk, Dave Rezansoff, Aaron Runge.
Second Row: Shaun Anderson, Michael Ball, Jeff Grund, Steve Klyne, Brent Ripplinger, Jeff Kallichuck, Jim Lawson, Brian Harrison, Randy Zbytnuik, Chris Curran, Brad Bork, Dean Kuz, Cory Doka, Sherlon Husset.
Front Row: Trainer Theresa Seiferling, Assistant. Coaches Ray Pitre, Bernie Schmidt, Jerry Orban, Gary Uhren (Mgr.), Head Coach Frank McCrystal, Assistant Coaches Rick Seaman, Campbell Hackney, Tim McGeough, Equip. Mgr. Brad Herschmiller, Assistant Equip., Trevor Herschmiller, Trainer Cory Piche.
Missing: Player Cory Borsa, Directors Ed Bankowski, Jon Hammond, Dennis Junior, Gary Mather, Andy McDougall, Randy Morrish, Larry Mueller, Tim Relke, Roger Salloum, Wayne Saxby, Norbert Thurmeier, Larry Kratt, Ken Black, Dan Maxim, Team Chaplain Basil Chomos. Ball Boys Kent Schmidt, Michael Schmidt, Dr. Jack Alexander, Dr. Brian Barootes, Dr. Bill Elliott.

1991 REGINA RAMS

Back Row: Directors: Paul Barnby, Norbert Thurmeier, Ed Bankowski, Fr. Basil Chomos, Dave Stouse, Tim Relke, Bob Millar, Wayne Saxby, Doug Tunison, Roger Brandvold, Tom Balkwill, Fred Dulmage, Gary Mather, Dennis Junior, Earl Kallichuk.
Fifth Row: Steve Sombach (Dir.), Doug Clark, Steve Uren, Gary Bresch, Dwayne Ell, Hans Larsen, Tim McFadden, Myles Keyowski, Mark Thomas, Doug Nkeyasen, Greg Treble, Sheldon Thomas, Marco Ricci, Cory Borsa, Grant Engel (Dir.).
Fourth Row: Jason Kotyk, Denis Losie, Lloyd MacDonald, Doug Huber, Randy Srochenski, Joedy King, John Carmichael, Michael Milo, Sonny Faugno, Jim Wenzel, Steve Beach, Tom MacCallum, Steve Bryce, Scott Waters, Corey Renwick.
Third Row: Jack Kennedy (Dir.), Jeremy Kroeker, Jeff Hagerty, Todd Fuchs, Jerry Holik, Roger Reinson, Kyle Ouart, Greg Fiddler, John MacKenzie, Bob Aldridge, Brian Ross, Brad Flavel, Aaron Runge.
Second Row: Leanne LaMontagne (Admin. Assistant), Bo Sanders, Michael Ball, Jason Maier, Steve Klyne, Brent Ripplinger, Scott Sinclair, Wavell Starr, Randy Zbytnuik, Chris Curran, Brad Bork, Matt Kellett, Cory Doka, Ian Kidd, Theresa Seiferling (Trainer), Cathy Sinclair (Assistant Trainer).
Front Row: Larry Kratt (Dir.), Bob Pelton (Dir.), Brad Herschmiller (Equip. Mgr.). Coaches: Ray Pitre, Tim McGeough, Rick Seaman, Doug McKillop (President), Frank McCrystal (Head Coach), Bernie Schmidt, Campbell Hackney, Gary Uhren (Mgr.), Trevor Herschmiller (Assistant Equip.), Cliff Dacey (Dir.), Ken Black (Dir.), Jon Hammond (Dir.).
Ball Boys: Michael Schmidt, Brandon Hackney, Kent Schmidt.
Missing: Players: Don Blair, Tim Huber, Jim Lawson. Directors: Dave Gebert, Dave Howie, Thomas McCord, Andy McDougall, Don McDougall, Randy Morrish, Larry Mueller, Murray Patzwald, Dan Maxim, Al Picton, Roger Salloum, Jerry Orban (Coach), Louise Ashcroft (Team Physio.), Shannon Doig (Team Physio.), Dr. Jack Alexander, Dr. Brian Barootes, Dr. Bill Elliott.

1992 REGINA RAMS

Back Row: Directors Paul Barnby, Dave Howie, Cliff Dacey, Dennis Junior, Ken Black, Bob Millar, Jon Hammond, Tom McCord, Fred Dulmage, Doug Tunison, Murray Patzwald, Wayne Saxby, Wally McCready, Bob Pelton.
Fifth Row: Doug Clark, Steve Uren, Gary Bresch, Mike McGrath, Cory Drechsler, Paul Clark, Trent Langford, Tim McFadden, Myles Keyowski, Josh Shaw, Marty Yaskowich, Greg Treble, Sheldon Thomas, Marco Ricci, Cory Borsa, Earl Kallichuk (Dir.).
Fourth Row: Gary Mather (Dir.), Joedy King, John Carmichael, Michael Milo, Sonny Faugno, Dave Wahl, Darren Bird, Jeff Pennington, Tom MacCallum, Doug Huber, Tim Coucill, Scott Waters, Corey Renwick, Jack Kennedy (Dir.).
Third Row: Don Fuchs (Dir.), Jeff Grund, Brian Harrison, Shawn Harvey, Mike Rutten, Mark Bernard, Bob Aldridge, Damian Hyrnuik, Tom Gardiner, Jason Kotyk, Denis Losie, Lloyd MacDonald, Marco Gustin, Randy Srochenski, Ed Bankowski (Dir.).
Second Row: Darryl Leason, Michael Ball, Jason Maier, Brent Ripplinger, Scott Sinclair, Jim Lawson, Wavell Starr, Dan Paskiw, Chris Curran, Brad Bork, Matt Kellett, Cory Doka, Ian Kydd, Derek Fink, Jeff Hagerty, Todd Fuchs.
Front Row: Leanne LaMontagne (Admin. Assistant), Louise Ashcroft (Physiotherapist), Jeff Kallichuk (Equip. Mgr.), Gary Uhren (Manager). Coaches: Jerry Orban, Ron Senger, Doug McKillop (President), Fank McCrystal (Head Coach). Coaches: Alex Smith, Bernie Schmidt, Ray Pitre, Rick Seaman, Danielle Droder (Assistant. Trainer), Cathy Sinclair (Trainer), Shannon Doig (Physiotherapist).
Ball Boys: Jason Amon, Jamie Kallichuk.
Missing Players: Gerald Daschuk, Marco Gustin, Brian Ross.
Missing Directors: Roger Salloum, Larry Kratt, Tim Relke, Tom Balkwill, Roger Brandvold, Dave Gebert, Dan Maxim, Norbert Thurmeier, Dave Stouse, Steve Sombach, Andy McDougall, Don McDougall, Randy Morrish, Larry Mueller, Al Picton, Dr. Jack Alexander, Dr. Brian Barootes, Dr. Bill Elliott, Fr. Basil Chomos (Team Chaplain).

1993 REGINA RAMS – NATIONAL CHAMPIONS

Back Row: Paul Barnby (Dir.), Chrystal Pelltier (Assistant Trainer), Cathy Sinclair (Assistant Trainer). Directors: Fred Dulmage, Cliff Dacey, Dennis Junior, Jack Kennedy, Wally McCready, Doug Tunison, Don Fuchs, Dave Howie, Wayne Saxby.
Sixth Row: Jamie Zaluski, Jody Gould, Devin Gusa, Josh Shaw, Mike Leason, Garth Schill, Geoff Deck, Marco Ricci, Len Milo, Doug McKillop (Dir.), Thomas McCord (Dir.).
Fifth Row: Earl Kallichuk (Dir.), Jeff Pennington, Doug Huber, Tim Coucill, Scott Waters, Paul Clark, Doug Clark, Chris Seibel, Garry Aveyard, Ken Stasyshyn, Trent Langford, Tim McFadden, Monique Knippel (Assistant Trainer).
Fourth Row: Dave Rezansoff (Dir.), Tom Gardiner, Simon Shaw, Sheldon Cossar, Lloyd MacDonald, Wavell Starr, Randy Srochenski, Mike Moore, John Carmichael, Michael Milo, Denis Losie, Cory Borsa, Darren Bird, Louise Ashcroft (Physio).
Third Row: Ed Bankowski (Dir.), Derek Fink, Jeff Hagerty, Todd Fuchs, Bryce Downey, Blaine Gerein, Shawn Harvey, Mike Rutten, Mark Bernard, Bob Aldridge, Kyle Ouart, Jaime Baillie, Bob Millar (Dir.), Patrick Sinclair (Ball Boy).
Second Row: Ian Saxby (Ball Boy), Darryl Leason, Michael Ball, Jason Maier, Todd Othner, Brent Ripplinger, Scott Sinclair, Chad Ehman, Aaron Saxby, Dan Paskiw, Craig Briere, Matt Kellett, Seth Neuls, Chris Wilke (Ball Boy).
Front Row: Crystal Ward (Trainer), Gary Uhren (Mgr.), Brad Herchmiller (Equip. Mgr.). Coaches: Ray Pitre, Rick Seaman, Ron Senger, Frank McCrystal (Head Coach), Bob Pelton (Pres.). Coaches: Bernie Schmidt, Jerry Orban, Alex Smith, Bill Bissett (Assistant Equip.), Leanne LaMontagne (Admin. Assistant).
Missing: Players: Brad Bork, Ian Kydd, Steve Uren. Directors: Larry Kratt, Larry LeBlanc, Gary Mather, Don McDougall, Larry Mueller, Kelvin Ostapowich, Al Picton, Roger Salloum, Steve Sombach, Norbert Thurmeier, Father Basil Chomos, Phil Kaiser (Assistant Equip.), Len Meyers, Dr. Jack Alexander, Dr. Brian Barootes, Dr. Bill Elliott.

1994 REGINA RAMS – NATIONAL CHAMPIONS

Back Row: Directors: Bob Millar, Cliff Dacey, Jack Kennedy, Gary Treble, Rick McCullough, Earl Kallichuk, Wally McCready, Wayne Saxby, Don Fuchs.
Fifth Row: Steve Uren, Chris Seibel, Mike Moore, Trent Langford, Brent Nicholas, Jamie Zaluski, Devin Gusa, Josh Shaw, Michael Leason, Garth Schill, Marco Ricci, Monique Knippel (Assistant Trainer).
Fourth Row: Randy Srochenski, Royal Harden, John Carmichael, Derek Wollbaum, Denis Losie, Cory Borsa, Darren Bird, Jason Boyda, Tim Coucill, Scott Waters, Cairan Gilmore, Doug Clark, Thomas McCord (Dir.).
Third Row: Ian Kydd, Derek Fink, Jeff Hagerty, Todd Fuchs, Mike Maurer, Rod Geiss, Shawn Harvey, Chris Briltz, Todd Orthner, Kyle Ouart, Jamie Baillie, Heath Walters, Lee Brentnell, Wavell Starr.
Second Row: Darryl Leason, Jason Bula, Chris Orban, Dan Gudmundson, Bereket Woldu, Chad Ehman, Chris Frankowski, Dan Paskiw, Craig Briere, Kevin Hicks, Matt Kellett, Jason Melnechenko.
Front Row: Brad Herschmiller (Equip. Mgr.), Leanne LaMontagne (Admin. Assistant), Chrystal Pelletier (Assistant Trainer), Trevor Herschmiller (Equip.). Coaches: Alex Smith, Rick Seaman, Ron Senger, Gary Uhren (Mgr.), Frank McCrystal (Head Coach), Bob Pelton (Pres.). Coaches: Jerry Orban, Bernie Schmidt, Ray Pitre, Crystal Ward (Trainer).
Ball Boy: Derrick Statt.
Missing: Players: Kelly Bauman, Mark Bernard, Lloyd MacDonald, Chad Zipchian, Anthony Findlay, Michael Milo. Directors: Ed Bankowski, Paul Barnby, Fred Dulmage, Dave Howie , Dennis Junior, Dean Kleisinger, Larry Klatt, Larry LeBlanc, Gary Mather, Don McDougall, Doug McKillop, Kelvin Ostapowich, Al Picton, Dave Rezansoff, Roger Salloum, Steve Sombach, Norbert Thurmeier, Doug Tunison, Louise Ashcroft (Team Physiotherapist), Scott Carson (Ball Boy), Dr. Jack Alexander, Dr. Brian Barootes, Dr. Bill Elliott, Fr. Basil Chomos, Larry Mueller.

1995 REGINA RAMS – NATIONAL CHAMPIONS

Back Row: Paul Barnby (Dir.), Don Fuchs (Dir.), Doug McKillop (Dir.), Brent Nicholas, Adrian Gilmore, Devin Gusa, Michael Leason, Chad Ball, Paul Wilson, Travis Taylor, Gary Treble (Dir.), Wayne Saxby (Dir.), Fred Dulmage (Dir.).
Fifth Row: Bob Pelton (Dir.), Curtis Morgan, Tim Coucill, Brad Jensen, Ciaran Gilmore, Brad Tarry, Steve Uren, Chris Seibel, Trent Poitras, Mike Moore, Brent Dancey, Trent Langford, Thomas McCord (Dir.), Jack Kennedy (Dir.).
Fourth Row: Roger Salloum (Dir.), Rick McCullough (Dir.), Lee Brentnell, Jeff Zimmer, Randy Srochenski, Royal Harden, John Carmichael, Derek Wollbaum, Barry Rees, Dennis Kotsetas, Todd Krenbrink, Chad Zipchian, Fr. Basil Chomos, Tony Theaker (Dir.).
Third Row: Chrystal Pelletier (Assistant Trainer), Jason Melnechenko, Corrie McKee, Derek Fink, Tim Lynchuk, Mike Maurer, Shawn Harvey, Chris Briltz, Todd Orthner, Ikenna Ngoka, Cory Olynick, Stu Russell, Monique Knippel (Assistant Trainer).
Second Row: Curt Heunison (Assistant Trainer), Darryl Leason, Jason Bula, Chris Harden, Chris Orban, Dan Gudmundson, Berket Woldu, Chris Frankowski, Dan Paskiw, Craig Briere, Kevin Hicks, Louise Ashcroft (Physio).
Front Row: Leanne LaMontagne (Admin. Assistant), Brad Herschmiller (Equip. Mgr.). Coaches: Alex Smith, Rick Seaman, Ron Senger, Frank McCrystal (Head Coach), Ed Bankowski (Pres.). Coaches: Jerry Orban, Bernie Schmidt, Ray Pitre, Trevor Herschmiller (Equip. Assistant), Gary Uhren (Mgr.).
Ball Boys: Justin Brenner, Terry Bourassa.
Missing: Players: Chad Ehman, Matt Kellett, Mark Bernard, Wavell Starr, Denis Losie, Josh Shaw. Directors: Dave Howie, Dennis Junior, Earl Kallichuk, Al Kellett, Dean Kleisinger, Larry Kratt, Larry LeBlanc, Gary Mather, Don McDougall, Bob Millar, Dave Rezansoff, Norbert Thurmeier, Doug Tunison, Larry Mueller, Crystal Ward (Trainer), Dr. Jack Alexander, Dr. Brian Barootes, Dr. Bill Elliott, Greg Treble (Dir.).

1996 REGINA RAMS

Back Row: Paul Barnby (Dir.), Fr. Basil Chomos, Sheldon Stener (Dir.), Josh Shaw, Mike Leason, Derek Ford, Derek Woitas, Travis Taylor, Gary Treble (Dir.), Todd Fuchs (Dir.).
Fifth Row: Doug Tunison (Dir.), Brad Jensen, Ciaran Gilmore, Joe Vitkauskas, Matt Gafencu, Mike Moore, Brent Dancy, Trent Langford, Brent Nicholas, Adrian Gilmore, Devin Gusa, Don Fuchs (Dir.).
Fourth Row: Rick McCullough (Dir.), Jeff Zimmer, Ryan Effa, Royal Harden, Jon Illerbrun, Derek Wollbaum, James Schiller, Barry Rees, Dennis Kotsetas, Todd Krenbrink, Chad Zipchian, Curtis Morgan, Gary Block , Tony Theaker (Dir.).
Third Row: Erin Klempner (Assistant Trainer), Corrie McKee, Derek Fink, Todd Pinkney, Mike Maurer, Tim Schultes, Chris Briltz, Todd Orthner, Ikenna Ngoka, Cory Olynick, Juan Serrano, Gregg Strom, Scott MacAulay, Karen Phipps (Trainer).
Second Row: Leanne LaMontagne (Admin. Assistant), Kevin Dueck, Michael Thomas, Jason Clermont, Chris Orban, Dan Gudmundson, Bereket Woldu, Chad Ehman, Chris Frankowski, Dan Paskiw, Craig Briere, Jared Hoover, Mike Surkan, Jason Melnechenko, Bobbi Markewich (Assistant Trainer).
Front Row: Brad Herschmiller (Equip. Mgr.), Gary Uhren (Mgr.). Coaches: Alex Smith, Rick Seaman, Denis Losie, Ron Senger, Frank McCrystal (Head Coach), Ed Bankowski (Pres.), Coaches: Jerry Orban, Bernie Schmidt, Paul Dawson, Greg Treble (Assistant Mgr.), Trevor Herschmiller (Assistant Equip.).
Missing: Directors: Cliff Dacey, Fred Dulmage, Dave Howie, Dennis Junior, Earl Kallichuk, Al Kellett, Jack Kennedy, Dean Kleisinger, Larry Kratt, Larry LeBlanc, Gary Mather, Thomas McCord, Don McDougall, Doug McKillop, Bob Millar, Kelvin Ostapowich, Bob Pelton, Dean Picton, Jason Pylatiuk (Physio), Marco Ricci, Roger Salloum, Wayne Saxby, Steve Sombach, Norbert Thurmeier, Louise Ashcroft (Physio), Dr. Jack Alexander, Dr. Brian Barootes, Dr. Bill Elliott, Ron Ward. Players: Trent Poitras, Shawn Harvey, Tim Lynchuk, Chris Seibel, Stuart Russell.

1997 REGINA RAMS – NATIONAL CHAMPIONS

Back Row: Sheldon Stener (Dir.), Rick McCullough (Dir.), Doug McKillop (Dir.), Larry Paik, Derek Woitas, James Cheke, Wayne Saxby (Dir.), Doug Tunison (Dir.), Gary Treble (Dir.), Don Fuchs (Dir.), Gary Uhren (Dir.), Jack Kennedy (Dir.).
Fifth Row: Gary Block, Jon Heathcote, Ciaran Gilmore, Jon Klassen, Trent Poitras, Kevin Baron, Dave Patenaude, Doug Hill, Chris Warnecke, Michael Leason, Derek Ford, Bob Pelton (Dir.).
Fourth Row: Jeff Zimmer, Ryan Effa, Brett Wagner, Royal Harden, Jon Illerbrun, Derek Wollbaum, James Schiller, Barry Rees, Dennis Kotsetas, Todd Krenbrink, Chad Zipchian, Curtis Morgan, Ed Bankowski (Dir.).
Third Row: Cyndi Munoz (Equip. Mgr.), Corrie McKee, Chris Ashman, Tim Lynchuk, Todd Pinkney, Lonnie Hayes, Chris Briltz, Corey Thackeray, Ikenna Ngoka, Cory Olynick, Scott MacAulay, Karen Phipps (Trainer), Fr. Basil Chomos.
Second Row: Mike Wong, Jason Clermont, Troy Gordon, Jarred Kleisinger, Chad Ehman, Chris Frankowski, Troy Leach, Craig Briere, Jared Hoover, Mike Surkan, Jason Melnechenko.
Front Row: Bobbi Markewich (Trainer). Coaches: Shawn Kuster, Paul Dawson, Blair Thompson, Bernie Schmidt, Frank McCrystal (Head Coach), Thomas McCord (Pres.), Rick Seaman, Erwin Klempner, Denis Losie, Greg Treble (Mgr.), Erin Klempner (Trainer).
Missing: Players: Clayton Murray, Michael Thomas, Dean Lang, Trevor Schoenroth, Juan Serrano, Brent Dancey, Brent Nicholas, Adrian Gilmore, Craig Briere, Carey Gabrielle, Shaun Machdanz, Kevin Phillips, Joe Vitkauskas. Directors: Fred Dulmage, Todd Fuchs, Dave Howie, Earl Kallichuk, Dean Kliesinger, Larry Kratt, Larry LeBlanc, Gary Mather, Don McDougall, Raelene Miller, Aaron Runge, Randy Ryba, Tony Theaker, Norbert Thurmeier, Cleveland Vann, Dean Picton, Jason Pylatiuk (Physio), Dr. Jack Alexander, Dr. Mike Nicholls, Dr. Bill Elliott, Leanne LaMontagne (Exec. Assistant).

1998 REGINA RAMS – NATIONAL CHAMPIONS

Back Row: Directors: Larry Kratt, Ed Bankowski, Sheldon Stener, Bob Pelton, Doug McKillop, Tony Theaker, Gary Treble, Jack Kennedy, Wayne Saxby, Dave Howie, Fred Dulmage.
Sixth Row: Joe McGrath, Nick Srochenski, Doug Hill, Chris Warnecke, Ryan Smith, Derek Ford, Mike Ervin, Derek Woitas, Jason Oglesby.
Fifth Row: Curtis Morgan, Gary Block, Jon Heathcote, Curtis Lawrence, Jon Klassen, Justin Ermel, Trent Poitras, Kevin Baron, Lee Cherkas, Dallas Kronberg, Tony Plett, Denis Losie Sr. (Dir.).
Fourth Row: Jeff Zimmer, Todd Schick, Brett Wagner, Royal Harden, Mischa Bosovich, Derek Wollbaum, James Schiller, Brian Smuk, Neil Coulthard, Todd Krenbrink, Chad Zipchian, Jason Pyatiuk (Physio).
Third Row: Joe Baker (Equip. Mgr.), Chris Ashman, Sheldon Gray, Todd Pinkney, Matt Dean, Neal Hughes, Chris Briltz, Carey Gabrielle, Cory Olynick, Matthew Firnesz, Scott MacAulay, Heather Klempner (Trainer).
Second Row: Mike Wong, Michael Thomas, Ian Bonnell, Troy Gordon, Jarred Kleisinger, Shane Ostapowich, Troy Leach, Cam Strasser, Mike Surkan, Jason Melnechenko, Corrie McKee, Bobbie Markewich (Trainer).
Front Row: Erin Klempner (Trainer), Candice Larson (Exec. Assistant), Cory Borsa (Mgr.). Coaches: Blair Thompson, Bernie Schmidt, Thomas McCord (Pres.). Coaches: Frank McCrystal (Head Coach), Erwin Klempner, Rick Seaman, Paul Dawson, Denis Losie Jr., Shawn Kuster.
Missing: Players: Jason Clermont, Jared Hoover, Dean Lang, Corey Thackeray, Juan Serrano, Jeff Bollinger. Directors: Larry LeBlanc, Bob Dancey, Don Fuchs, Earl Kallichuk, Dean Kleisinger, Gary Mather, Rick McCullough, Don McDougall, Raelene Miller, Marco Ricci, Randy Ryba, Roger Salloum, Norbert Thurmeier, Greg Treble, Doug Tunison, Steve Tunison, Gary Uhren, Cleveland Vann, Dean Picton, Todd Fuchs, Dr. Jack Alexander, Dr. Mike Nicholls, Dr. Bill Elliott, Fr. Basil Chomos.

1999 UNIVERSITY OF REGINA RAMS

Back Row: Directors: Bob Aldridge, Dave Howie, Rick McCullough, Bob Pelton, Jack Kennedy, Gary Treble, Bob Millar, Larry Kratt, Tony Theaker, Ed Bankowski, Sheldon Stener, Gary Uhren.
Fifth Row: Gary Mather (Dir.), Curtis Lawrence, Terry Seidlitz, Ciaran Gilmore, Kevin Baron, Lee Cherkas, Dallas Kronberg, Tony Plett, Kris Miller, Chris Warnecke, Daniel Yaskowich, Brian Luesink, Jason Oglesby, Leandre Gallais (Physio).
Fourth Row: Joe Baker (Equip. Mgr.), Jeff Zimmer, Todd Schick, Craig Zimmer, Neil Coulthard, Mischa Bosovich, Jesse Sakires, Chad Dorsch, Brian Smuk, Dennis Kotsetas, Todd Krenbrink, Devin Gusa, Curtis Morgan, Jeff Yorga.
Third Row: Erin Klempner (Trainer), Corrie McKee, Chris Ashman, Sheldon Gray, Todd Pinkney, Matt Dean, Dean Lang, Neal Hughes, Chris Briltz, Mike Ervin, Dustin Olson, Jon Schneider, Lee Moffatt, Craig Schweitzer.
Second Row: Mike Wong, Mark Anderson, Jason Clermont, Ian Bonnell, Troy Gordon, Jarred Kleisinger, Curtis Wong, Shane Ostapowich, Cory Olynick, Danny Paskiw, J.R. Klisowsky, Sean Jestadt, Jason Melnechenko, Bobbi Markewich (Trainer).
Front Row: Kelly Walker (Trainer), Candice Larson (Exec. Assistant). Coaches: Shawn Kuster, Denis Losie Jr., Blair Thompson, Rick Seaman, Larry LeBlanc (Pres.). Coaches: Frank McCrystal (Head Coach), Erwin Klempner, Bernie Schmidt, Paul Dawson, Cory Borsa (Mgr.), Heather Klempner (Trainer).
Missing: Directors: Paul Barnby, Fred Dulmage, Don Fuchs, Todd Fuchs, Terry Hincks, Earl Kallichuck, Dennis Junior, Dean Kleisinger, Jack Lichtenwald, Denis Losie Sr., Thomas McCord, Don McDougall, Doug McKillop, Raelene Miller, Kelvin Ostapowich, Dean Picton, Marco Ricci, Aaron Runge, Scott Sinclair, Norbert Thurmeier, Greg Treble, Doug Tunison, Steve Tunison, Cleveland Vann, Bob Dancey, Dr. Jack Alexander, Dr. Mike Nicholls, Dr. Bill Elliott. Players: Gary Block, Jeff Smith, Dave Patenaude, Brian Tweitmeyer.

2000 UNIVERSITY OF REGINA RAMS

Back Row: Directors: Bob Pelton, Jack Kennedy, Sheldon Stener, Doug McKillop. Tony Plett, Aaron Schulz, Nathan Walker, Chris Warnecke, Michael Leason. Directors: Cory Borsa, Gary Treble, Joe Ralko, Gary Mather.
Fifth Row: Ed Bankowski (Dir.), Matthew Anderson, Gary Block, Jeff Yorga, Curtis Lawrence, Eric Beauchemin, Terrance Seidlitz, Colin McCannell, Ryan Fowler, Kevin Baron, Lee Cherkas. Directors: Val Livingstone, Denis Losie Sr.
Fourth Row: Dave Howie (Dir.), Jonathan Cormier, Jeff Zimmer, Mike Storey, Craig Zimmer, Morgan Bunce, Mischa Bosovich, Jesse Sakires, Ed Junior Gohn, Craig Hamilton, Todd Krenbrink, Devin Gusa, Gary Uhren (Dir.).
Third Row: Brian Scott, Nick Billings, Corrie McKee, Sheldon Gray, Matt Dean, Dan Yaskowish, Chris Briltz, Mike Ervin, Neal Hughes, Lee Moffatt, Craig Schweitzer, Eric Benson.
Second Row: Don McDougall (Exec. Dir.), Mike Wong, Darryl Leason, Jason Clermont, Ian Bonnell, Jon Ryan, Mark Wernikowski, Shane Ostapowich, Cory Olynick, Danny Paskiw, Justin Skamanis, Bob Aldridge (Mgr.).
Front Row: Joe Baker (Equip. Mgr.). Trainers: Kelly Walker, Kristine Pasqua, Lindsay Corrins. Coaches: Erwin Klempner, Marco Ricci, Frank McCrystal (Head Coach), Denis Losie Jr., Blair Thompson, Bernie Schmidt, Rick Seaman, Paul Dawson, Leandre Gallais (Physio).
Missing Players: Mike Thomas, Jude Werapitiya, Chris Ashman, Ronald Arnold, Juan Serrano
Missing Doctors: Dr. Bill Elliott, Dr. Mike Nicholls, Dr. Dennis Alfano., Dr. Jack Alexander.
Missing Directors: Paul Barnby, Fred Dulmage, Don Fuchs, Todd Fuchs, Terry Hincks, Earl Kallichuk, Denis Junior, Dean Kleisinger, Larry Kratt, Larry LeBlanc (Pres.), Jack Lichtenwald, Thomas McCord, Rick McCullough, Bob Millar, Kelvin Ostapowich, Dean Picton, Doug Rogers, Aaron Runge, Norbert Thurmeier, Doug Tunison, Steve Tunison, Mary Ann Zipchian, Shawn Kuster (Coach), Matt Vukman (Assistant Equip. Mgr.), Don Clark (Academic Advisor), Bob Dancey, Raelene Miller, Scott Sinclair, Greg Treble, Tony Theaker.

2001 UNIVERSITY OF REGINA RAMS

Back Row: Val Livingstone (Director), Curtis Lawrence, Eric Beauchemin, Terry Seidlitz, Collin McCannell, Ryan Fowler, Kyler Jukes, Lee Cherkas, Tony Plett, Sean Kent, Andrew Turbuck, Mike Leason, Denis Losie Sr. (Director).
Fifth Row: Gary Treble (Director), Mischa Bosovich, Jesse Sakires, Tony Presidente, Edward Gohn, Craig Hamilton, Todd Krenbrink, Devin Gusa, Matt Anderson, Gary Block, Jeff Yorga, Todd Fuchs (Director).
Fourth Row: Gary Surkan (Director), Chris Briltz, Mike Ervin, Neal Hughes, Lee Moffatt, Craig Schweitzer, Eric Benson, Jon Cormier, Jeff Zimmer, Mike Storey, Craig Zimmer, Sheldon Stener (Director).
Third Row: Don McDougall (Exec. Director), Marc-Antoine Lamothe, Matt Cherkas, Brian Scott, Nick Billings, Corrie McKee, Chris Ashman, Sheldon Gray, Jason Ulley, Matt Dean, Dan Yaskowich, Morgan Bunce, Dr. Bill Elliott (Team Doctor).
Second Row: Larry LeBlanc (Director), Rick Tiefenbach, Mike Kissinger, Mike Wong, Darryl Leason, Mike Thomas, Mark Anderson, Jason Clermont, Ian Bonnell, Clayton Drouin, Jon Ryan, Shane Ostapowich, Cory Olynick, Gary Uhren (Director).
Front Row: Shawn Kuster (Coach), Matt Vukman (Equip. Assistant), Leandre Gallais (Physiotherapist), Bob Aldridge (Manager), Rick Seaman (Coach), Erwin Klempner (Coach), Frank McCrystal (Head Coach), Paul Dawson (Coach), Marco Ricci (Coach), Denis Losie Jr. (Coach), Bernie Schmidt (Coach), Lindsay Corrins (Head Trainer), Kristine Pascua (Trainer).
Missing Players: Chris Morrison, Geoffrey Rankin, Mark Wernikowski.
Missing: Coach Blair Thompson; Equipment Mgr. Mike Spelliscy; Doctors Mike Nicholls, Dennis Alfano; Trainer Sarah Brentnell; Academic Advisor Don Clark.
Missing Directors: President Rick McCullough, Brent Anderson, Ed Bankowski, Paul Barnby, Cory Borsa, Brian Chapman, Fred Dulmage, Kollin Erichsen, Terry Hincks, Dave Howie, Earl Kallichuk, Dennis Junior, Jack Kennedy, Dean Kleisinger, Larry Kratt, Jack Lichtenwald, Gary Mather, Thomas McCord, Doug McKillop, Bob Millar, Raelene Miller, Kelvin Ostapowich, Tim Owens, Bob Pelton, Dean Picton, Doug Rogers, Aaron Runge, Dan Thibault, Norbert Thurmeier, Greg Treble, Doug Tunison, Steve Tunison, Al Wielgoz, Mary Ann Zipchian.

2002 UNIVERSITY OF REGINA RAMS

Back Row: Directors: Paul Barnby, Dan Thibault, Bob Pelton, Larry LeBlanc, Dean Picton, Sheldon Stener, Bob Millar, Steve Tunison, Jack Kennedy, Dan Johnston, Gary Treble, Dave Howie, Gary Surkan, Gary Mather, Ed Bankowski, Denis Losie Sr.
Sixth Row: Trent Poitras, Charles Quenneville, Peter Nelke, Chris Bauman, Ryan Smith.
Fifth Row: Jon Labonte, Chay LaCoste, Curtis Lawrence, Eric Beauchemin, Travis Kuntz, Sean Brimacombe, Ryan Fowler, Kyler Jukes, Lee Cherkas, Chris Morrison, Tony Plett, Sean Kent, Val Livingstone - Director.
Fourth Row: Eric Earnshaw, Paul Grondin, Matt Nesbitt, Jeffrey Zimmer, Pero Rashovich, Jon Cormier, Craig Zimmer, Mischa Bosovich, Jesse Sakires, Clark Gates, Anthony Presidente, Craig Hamilton, Todd Krenbrink, Vicki Ing - Marketing Director.
Third Row: Chris Stevens, Brian Scott, Nick Billings, Corrie McKee, Chris Ashman, Sheldon Gray, Steven Stone, Matthew Dean, Matt Nelson, Morgan Bunce, Chris Briltz, Mike Ervin, James Seeley, Neal Hughes, Jason Muller.
Second Row: Don McDougall - Exec. Director, Tate Quest, Mike Kissinger, Mark Anderson, Jon Schneider, Mike Thomas, Tim Feasby, Ian Bonnell, Steven Ryan, Jon Ryan, Mark Wernikowski, Shane Ostapowich, Cory Olynick, Marc-Antoine Lamothe, Mathew Cherkas.
Front Row: Lindsay Corrins - Trainer, Matt Vukman - Assistant Equip. Mgr., Mike Spelliscy- Equip. Mgr., Bob Aldridge - Team Mgr., Bernie Schmidt - Coach, Blair Thompson - Coach, Marco Ricci - Coach, Frank McCrystal - Head Coach, Rick McCullough - President, Rick Seaman - Coach, Erwin Klempner - Coach, Denis Losie Jr. - Coach, Paul Dawson - Coach, Leandre Gallais - Physiotherapist, Kristine Pascua - Assistant Trainer.
Missing Directors: Cory Borsa, Brian Chapman, Doug Dorsch, Fred Dulmage, Kollin Erichsen, Todd Fuchs, Don Gorski, Terry Hincks, Earl Kallichuk, Dean Kleisinger, Larry Kratt, Jack Lichtenwald, Thomas McCord, Doug McKillop Kelvin Ostapowich, Tim Owens, Aaron Runge, Norbert Thurmeier, Greg Treble, Doug Tunison, Gary Uhren, Al Wielgoz, Maryann Zipchian, Sarah Brentnell - Assistant Trainer, Dr. Bill Elliott, Dr. Mike Nicholls, Shawn Kuster (Fitness Coach), Don Clark (Academic Advisor), Brent Anderson, Dennis Junior.

2003 UNIVERSITY OF REGINA RAMS

Back Row: Paul Barnby, Cory Borsa, Ed Bankowski, Bob Pelton, Bob Millar, Doug McKillop, Gary Mather, Doug Dorsch, Dan Johnston, Dean Picton (Vice President), Gary Treble, Jack Kennedy, Al Wielgoz, Dan Thibault, Dave Howie
Sixth Row: Doug Tunison (Director), Lee Cherkas, Ryan Ackerman, Wade Nellis, Sean Kent, Trent Poitras, Paul McDill, Peter Nelke, Matt Nelson, Mat Fiedelleck, Matt Miller, Brett Vancise, Ryan Smith, Nathan Dvernichuk (Director), Gary Uhren (Director)
Fifth Row: Denis Losie Sr (Director), Norbert Thurmeier (Director), Clark Gates, Jon Baker, Craig Hamilton, Todd Krenbrink, Kyle McNeil, Jon Labonte, Chay LaCoste, Brian Gatin, Eric Beauchemin, Travis Kuntz, Sean Brimacombe, Ryan Fowler, Kyler Jukes, Scott MacAulay (Marketing Co-ordinator)
Fourth Row: Rick McCullough (Director), Raymond Robertson, Mike Dennett, Neal Hughes, Greg Girard, Eric Earnshaw, Paul Grondin, Matt Nesbitt, Steven Stefankiw, Brendan Hysuik, Jon Cormier, Craig Zimmer, Mischa Bosovich, Jesse Sakires, Gary Surkan (Vice President)
Third Row: Lindsay Corrins (Head Trainer), Aadon Fieger, Brian Scott, Charlie McCrystal, Corrie McKee, Chris Ashman, Sheldon Gray, Dwayne Benkovic, Kyle Lanigan, Matt Dean, Tyler Pokoyoway, Morgan Bunce, Joel Lipinski, Matt Vukman (Assistant Equip. Mgr.)
Second Row: Jessica Kaczmar (Trainer), Tate Quest, Mike Kissinger, Mark Anderson, Jon Schneider, Mike Thomas, Stefan Endsin, Ian Bonnell, Steve Ryan, Jon Ryan, Shane Ostapowich, Cory Olynick, Marc-Antoine Lamothe, Luke Derkson, Val Livingstone (Director)
Front Row: Kristine Pascua (Trainer), Shawn Kuster (Coach), Paul Dawson (Coach), Blair Thompson (Coach), Denis Losie (Coach), Marco Ricci (Coach), Frank McCrystal (Head Coach), Sheldon Stener (President), Rick Seaman (Coach), Erwin Klempner (Coach), Bernie Schmidt (Coach), Bob Aldridge (Team Mgr.) Mike Spelliscy (Equip. Mgr.) Erica Hopkin (Trainer)
Missing: Players: Andrew Turbuck, Tim Feasby, **Directors:** Brian Chapman, Fred Dulmage, Kollin Erichsen, Todd Fuchs, Terry Hincks, Earl Kallichuk, Dean Kleisinger, Darcy Koch, Larry LeBlanc, Jack Lichtenwald, Don McDougall, Kelvin Ostapowich, Tim Owens, Randy Palmer, Aaron Runge, MaryAnn Zipchian, Medical Staff: Dr. Bill Elliott, Dr. Mike Nicholls, Dr. Arnold Endsin, Dr. Dennis Alfano, Leandre Gallais (Physiotherapist), Dr. Don Clark (Academic Advisor).

REGINA RAMS' PRESIDENTS AND COACHES

	President	Coach
1954	John Rowand	Toar Springstein
1955	John Rowand	Toar Springstein
1956	Tom Drope	Bill Ciz
1957	Harry Hilsden	Bill Ciz
1958	Al Wessel	Bill Ciz
1959	Gordon Mitton	Bert Iannone
1960	Gordon Mitton	Bert Iannone
1961	Gordon Mitton	Bert Iannone
1962	Scotty Livingstone	Bert Iannone
1963	Scotty Livingstone	Paul Anderson
1964	Dr. Rafe Chadwick	Paul Anderson & Bill Ciz
1965	Dr. Rafe Chadwick	Gordon Currie
1966	Joe Kanuka	Gordon Currie
1967	Joe Kanuka	Gordon Currie
1968	Ken Wheeler	Gordon Currie
1969	Ken Wheeler	Gordon Currie
1970	Reg Forsyth	Gordon Currie
1971	Reg Forsyth	Gordon Currie
1972	Jerry Joynt	Gordon Currie
1973	Jerry Joynt	Gordon Currie
1974	George Hambley	Gordon Currie
1975	George Hambley	Gordon Currie
1976	Gary Mather	Gordon Currie
1977	Gary Mather	Mel Fiissel
1978	Bob Milton	Jerry Zbytnuik
1979	Bob Milton	Jerry Zbytnuik
1980	Don McDougall	Jerry Zbytnuik
1981	Don McDougall	Jerry Zbytnuik
1982	Norbert Thurmeier	Jerry Zbytnuik
1983	Norbert Thurmeier	Jerry Zbytnuik
1984	Bill Nelson	Frank McCrystal
1985	Paul Barnby	Frank McCrystal
1986	Paul Barnby	Frank McCrystal
1987	Bob Millar	Frank McCrystal
1988	Bob Millar	Frank McCrystal
1989	Jack Kennedy	Frank McCrystal
1990	Jack Kennedy	Frank McCrystal
1991	Doug McKillop	Frank McCrystal
1992	Doug McKillop	Frank McCrystal
1993	Bob Pelton	Frank McCrystal
1994	Bob Pelton	Frank McCrystal
1995	Ed Bankowski	Frank McCrystal
1996	Ed Bankowski	Frank McCrystal
1997	Thomas McCord	Frank McCrystal
1998	Thomas McCord	Frank McCrystal
1999	Larry LeBlanc	Frank McCrystal
2000	Larry LeBlanc	Frank McCrystal
2001	Rick McCullough	Frank McCrystal
2002	Rick McCullough	Frank McCrystal
2003	Sheldon Stener	Frank McCrystal

REGINA RAMS' LIFETIME MEMBERS

Dr. Rafe Chadwick
Joe Kanuka
Scotty Livingstone
Erwin Strass
Gary Mather
Don McDougall
Norbert Thurmeier
Paul Barnby
Bob Millar
Doug McKillop
Bob Pelton
Ed Bankowski
Jack Stewart
Roland McGuigan

REGINA RAMS' HONOURARY LIFETIME MEMBERS

Tom Shepherd
Ken Wheeler

INDIVIDUALS WHO HAVE PLAYED OR COACHED WITH THE REGINA RAMS AND PLAYED OR COACHED PROFESSIONAL FOOTBALL IN THE CFL

Barry Aldag
Roger Aldag
Paul Anderson (Coach)
Dave Badowich
Don Bahnuik
BIll Baker
Danny Banda
Kerry Berryman
Don Blair
Nick Blum (Coach)
Jack Brandt
Wayne Borys
Rob Bresciani
Maurice Butler
Harvey Campbell (Player & Coach)
Ron Cherkas
Bill Ciz (Coach)
Jason Clermont
Cochrane, Terry
Ken Don
Henry Dorsch
Larry Dumelie
Rick Dundas
Ron Dundas
Gerry Fellner
Greg Fieger
Nellie Greene (Coach)
Campbell Hackney (Coach)
Russ Haines (Coach)
Kelly Hamilton
Marshall Hamilton (Player & Coach)
Darrell Harle
Lindsay Holt (Coach)
Jim Hopson
Bert Iannone (Coach)
Brian Illerbrun
Dan Johnston
Matt Kellett
Doug Killoh (Coach)
John Klein
Ron Lancaster Jr. (Player & Coach)
Eugene Larocque
Mike Lazecki
Bob Leskun
Tom MacCallum
Irv Marchtaler
Mike Maurer
Steve Mazurak
Bob McMillan
Ed McQuarters Jr.
Bill Metcalfe
Dale Parsons
Bob Poley
Brent Pollock
Rob Pyne
Wayne Pyne (Coach)
Roger Reinson
Martin Ruby (Coach)
Dennis Silzer
Vern Simonson
Alex Smith (Player & Coach)
Toar Springstein (Coach)
Randy Srochenski
Kelly Trithart
Jack Urness (Player & Coach)
Ted Urness
Preston Young

TEAM RECORDS 1954 - 2002

Year	W	L	T	Pts	Pos	
1954	0	7	0	0	4th	Missed Playoffs.
1955	7	1	0	10	1st	MSJFL finalists. Lost total point series 36-24 to Winnipeg Rods.
1956	6	2	0	9	1st	MSJFL finalists. Lost total-point series 22-8 to Winnipeg Rods.
1957	4	4	0	5	4th	Missed Playoffs.
1958	3	5	0	6	2nd	MSJFL finalists. Lost total-point series 84-39 to Saskatoon Hilltops.
1959	3	4	0	6	2nd	MSJFL semi-finalists. Lost sudden-death 8-0 to Winnipeg Weston Wildcats.
1960	3	5	0	4	4th	Missed playoffs.
1961	2	6	0	4	3rd	MSJFL semi-finalists. Lost sudden-death 22-13 to Saskatoon Hilltops.
1962	3	5	0	5	3rd	MSJFL semi-finalists. Lost sudden-death 21-8 to Saskatoon Hilltops.
1963	4	4	0	6	2nd	MSJFL finalists. Lost total-point series 95-0 to St. James Rods.
1964	3	5	0	5	2nd	MSJFL champions. Defeated Saskatoon Hilltops 35-24 in total-point series, lost Western final 47-8 to Edmonton Huskies.
1965	6	2	0	10	1st	MSJFL champions. Defeated Winnipeg Weston Wildcats 77-44 in MSJFL total-point series, lost Western final 28-10 to Edmonton Huskies.
1966	5	3	0	8	1st	**National Champions.** Defeated Saskatoon Hilltops 41-17 in MSJFL total-point final series; defeated Edmonton Wildcats 17-14 in Western final; defeated Notre Dame de Grace Maple Leafs 29-14 in National final.
1967	5	3	0	8	2nd	MSJFL finalists. Lost total-point series 50-16 to Saskatoon Hilltops.
1968	5	3	0	8	2nd	MSJFL finalists. Lost total-point series 48-32 to Saskatoon Hilltops.
1969	6	2	0	10	2nd	MSJFL finalists. Lost total-point series 23-21 to Saskatoon Hilltops.
1970	6	2	0	9	2nd	**National Champions.** Defeated Winnipeg Hawkeyes 47-46 in MSJFL total-point final series; defeated Vancouver Meralomas 49-21 in Western semi-final; defeated Edmonton Huskies 29-11 in Western final; defeated Burlington Braves 39-8 in National final.
1971	8	0	0	12	1st	**National Champions.** Defeated Winnipeg Hawkeyes 72-31 in MSJFL total-point final series; defeated Edmonton Huskies 48-7 in Western semi-final; defeated Vancouver Meralomas 34-12 in Western final; defeated Burlington Braves 42-13 in National final.
1972	7	1	0	11	1st	Western champions. Defeated Saskatoon Hilltops 74-30 in MSJFL total-point final series; defeated Vancouver Meralomas 57-14 in Western final; lost National final 33-8 to Hamilton Hurricanes.
1973	7	0	1	11	1st	**National Champions.** Defeated Saskatoon Hilltops 88-42 in MSJFL total-point final series; defeated Vancouver Meralomas 30-28 in Western semi-final; defeated Edmonton Huskies 19-17 in Western Final; defeated Ottawa Sooners 9-0 in National final.
1974	8	0	0	12	1st	MSJFL champions. Defeated Saskatoon Hilltops 77-21 in MSJFL total-point final series; defeated Edmonton Huskies 19-10 in Western semi-final; lost Western final 17-11 to Vancouver Meralomas.
1975	6	3	0	12	2nd	**National Champions.** Defeated Saskatoon Hilltops 86-33 in MSJFL total-point final series; defeated Edmonton Huskies 31-25 in Western final; defeated Hamilton Hurricanes 38-19 in National final.
1976	7	1	0	14	2nd	**National Champions.** Defeated Edmonton Wildcats 62-28 in AJFL final; defeated Vancouver Meralomas 48-0 in Western final; defeated Hamilton Hurricanes 45-23 in National final.
1977	6	2	0	12	2nd	PJFC semi-finalists. Lost 35-24 to Edmonton Wildcats.
1978	6	2	0	12	2nd	PJFC semi-finalists. Lost 40-12 to Edmonton Wildcats.
1979	6	1	1	13	1st	Western champions. Defeated Saskatoon; 42-0 in PJFC final; defeated Fort Garry Lions 54-7 in Western semi-final; defeated Vancouver Meralomas 45-21 in Western final; lost National final 13-9 to Ottawa Sooners.

Year	W	L	T	Pts	Pos	
1980	7	2	1	15	1st	**National Champions.** Defeated Edmonton Huskies 33-10 in PFJC final; defeated Vancouver Meralomas 28-5 in Western final; defeated Hamilton Hurricanes 26-15 in National final.
1981	10	0	0	20	1st	**National Champions.** Defeated Edmonton Huskies 33-10 in PJFC final; defeated Vancouver Meralomas 59-22 in Western semi-final; defeated Winnipeg Hawkeyes 30-20 in Western final; defeated Hamilton Hurricanes 46-24 in National final.
1982	8	2	0	16	2nd	PJFC champions. Defeated Saskatoon Hilltops 21-17 in PJFC final; lost Western final 17-14 to Renfrew Trojans.
1983	6	2	0	12	2nd	PJFC finalists. Lost PJFC final 35-28 to Edmonton Wildcats.
1984	8	0	0	16	1st	PJFC champions. Defeated Saskatoon Hilltops 19-15 in PJFC final; lost western final 45-28 to Richmond Raiders.
1985	8	0	0	16	1st	PJFC finalists. Lost PJFC final 31-24 to Saskatoon Hilltops.
1986	7	1	0	14	1st	**National Champions.** Defeated Saskatoon Hilltops 29-14 in PJFC final; defeated Richmond Raiders 45-28 in Western final; defeated Ottawa Sooners 53-12 in National final.
1987	6	2	0		2nd	**National Champions.** Won PFC 34-18 over the Saskatoon Hilltops; won Western Final 45-23 over the Okanagan Sun; won Canadian final 31-23 over the St. Vital Mustangs.
1988	8	0	0		1st	Lost PFC final 36-34 to Saskatoon Hilltops.
1989	6	2	0		2nd	Lost PFC semi-final 38-33 to Calgary Colts.
1990	7	1	0		1st	Lost PFC final 45-14 to Calgary Colts.
1991	6	2	0		2nd	Lost PFC final 32-9 to Saskatoon Hilltops.
1992	5	3	0		2nd	Won PFC final 22-17 over the Saskatoon Hilltops; lost Western final 21-10 to the Surrey Rams.
1993	8	0	0		1st	**National Champions.** Won PFC final 30-15 over the Saskatoon Hilltops; won Western final 43-12 over the Surrey Rams; won Canadian final 23-11 over the Hamilton Hurricanes.
1994	7	1	0		1st	**National Champions.** Won PFC final 34-7 over the Saskatoon Hilltops; won Western semi-final 73-7 over the Winnipeg Hawkeyes; won Western final 64-3 over the Surrey Rams; won Canadian final 52-6 over the St. Leonard Cougars.
1995	7	1	0		1st	**National Champions.** Won PFC final 19-8 over the Saskatoon Hilltops; won Western final 11-8 over the Okanagan Sun; won Canadian final 26-10 over the Ottawa Sooners.
1996	8	1	1		2nd	Lost PFC final 27-23 to the Saskatoon Hilltops.
1997	6	2	0		2nd	**National Champions.** Won PFC final 46-27 over the Saskatoon Hilltops; won Canadian semi-final 38-31 over the Windsor AKO Fratmen; won Canadian final 23-20 over the Okanagan Sun.
1998	7	1	0		1st	**National Champions.** Won PFC final 48-10 over the Saskatoon Hilltops; won Canadian final 36-13 over the Okanagan Sun.
1999	0	8	0		6th	Missed CIAU playoffs in Canada West.
2000	4	4	0		3rd	Won CIAU Canada West league final 25-22 over the Manitoba Bisons; won CIAU Atlantic Bowl 40-36 over the Saint Mary's Huskies; lost Vanier Cup to Ottawa Gee Gee's 34-29.
2001	5	3	0		2nd	Won Canada West CIS final 58-31 over the Saskatchewan Huskies; lost Hardy Cup to Manitoba Bisons 23-17.
2002	5	3	0		3rd	Won Canada West CIS semi-final 39-17 over the Calgary Dinos; lost the Hardy Cup to the Saskatchewan Huskies 44-28.

Abbreviations:

MSJFL – Manitoba-Saskatchewan Junior Football League
AJFL – Alberta Junior Football League
PJFC – Prairie Junior Football Conference
PFC – Prairie Football Conference
CIAU – Canadian Intercollegiate Football Union
CIS – Canadian Interuniversity Sport

A TRADITION OF WINNERS
LEAGUE AWARDS WON BY RAMS' PLAYERS (1955-2002)

1955 Rookie of the Year – Don (Butch) Leskun
1956 Rookie of the Year – Sig Splett
1957 Most Valuable Player – Jack Urness
1958 Rookie of the Year – Dymetry Warnyca
1959 Rookie of the Year – Gary Mather
1962 Most Valuable Player – Vern Simonson
Rookie of the Year – Tom Hogan
Most Gentlemanly Player – Vern Simonson
1963 Most Gentlemanly Player – Mel Perkins
1964 Rookie of the Year – Dave Orban
1965 Rookie of the Year – Ken Walters
1966 Most Outstanding Lineman – Larry Van Moorelehem
1967 Most Valuable Player – Ken Newman
Most Gentlemanly Player – Don Schmidt
1968 Most Valuable Player – Ken Newman
1969 Most Valuable Player – Don Schmidt
1970 Most Outstanding Lineman – Rae Pratt
1971 Most Valuable Player – Rob Pyne
Rookie of the Year – Ron Cherkas
1972 Most Valuable Player – Bryan Dimen
Rookie of the Year – Lenny Knoll
Most Outstanding Lineman – Jim Hopson
1973 Most Valuable Player – Ted Dolinski
Most Outstanding Lineman – Terry Hincks
Rookie of the Year – Preston Young
1974 Most Valuable Player – Lenny Knoll
Most Gentlemanly Player – Ted Dolinski
Rookie of the Year – Les Ludwig
1975 Most Outstanding Lineman – Roger Aldag
1978 Most Outstanding Offensive Lineman – Brent McConnell
1979 Most Valuable Player – Marshall Hamilton
Rookie of the Year – Marshall Hamilton
Most Outstanding Offensive Lineman – Kerry Berryman
Most Outstanding Offensive Back – Greg Fieger
1980 Most Outstanding Defensive Lineman – Greg Nesbitt
Most Outstanding Offensive Lineman – Clarence Sacawayacappo
Most Outstanding Defensive Back – Bill Parker
1981 Most Outstanding Linebacker – Cal Sikorski
Most Outstanding Offensive Back – Doug Currie
Rookie of the Year – Brent Taylor
1982 Most Outstanding Offensive Back – Terry Cochrane
Rookie of the Year – Terry Cochrane
Most Outstanding Defensive Back – Tim Wiens
Most Outstanding Defensive Lineman – Lyle Mosiondz
1983 Most Outstanding Defensive Back – Hal Wilkie
Most Outstanding Offensive Back – Terry Cochrane
Most Outstanding Offensive Lineman – Brent Taylor
CJFL Outstanding Offensive Player – Terry Cochrane
1984 Most Outstanding Defensive Lineman – Dave Gebert
Rookie of the Year – Jason Belisle
1985 Most Outstanding Defensive Lineman – Dave Gebert
1986 CJFL Outstanding Offensive Player – Dean Picton
Most Valuable Player – Dean Picton
Most Outstanding Receiver – Tim Hammond
Most Outstanding Defensive Lineman – Ron Senger
Most Outstanding Offensive Lineman – Kelvin Ostapowich
1987 Western Nominee CJFL Most Outstanding Offensive Player – Dean Picton
Most Valuable Player – Dean Picton
Most Outstanding Defensive Lineman – Dave Gebert
1988 CJFL Outstanding Offensive Player – Dean Picton
Most Valuable Player – Dean Picton
Most Outstanding Receiver – Dan Johnston
Most Outstanding Offensive Lineman – Brian Eltom
1989 Most Outstanding Offensive Back – Kollin Erichsen
Most Outstanding Defensive Back – Dean Mihalicz
1990 Most Valuable Player – Kollin Erichsen
Most Outstanding Running Back – Kollin Erichsen
Most Outstanding Offensive Lineman – Sinisa Stefanovic
Most Outstanding Receiver – Brent Ripplinger
Most Outstanding Defensive Back – Steve Klyne
Most Outstanding Defensive Lineman – Jason Tiefenbach
Coach of the Year – Frank McCrystal
1991 Most Outstanding Linebacker – Roger Reinson
1992 Most Outstanding Defensive Lineman – Sonny Faugno
Rookie of the Year – Darryl Leason
1993 Most Outstanding Offensive Lineman – Tim McFadden
Most Valuable Player – Darryl Leason
1994 CJFL Western Nominee Most Outstanding Offensive Player – Darryl Leason
Coach of the Year – Frank McCrystal
1994 CJFL Outstanding Offensive Back – Darryl Leason
Most Outstanding Special Teams – Matt Kellett
Most Valuable Player – Darryl Leason
1995 CJFL Outstanding Offensive Player – Darryl Leason
Most Outstanding Offensive Lineman – Trent Langford, Tim Coucill
Most Outstanding Placekicker – Matt Kellett
Most Outstanding Defensive Lineman – Derek Fink
1996 CJFL Outstanding Defensive Player – Danny Paskiw
Most Outstanding Offensive Lineman – Trent Langford
Most Outstanding Linebacker – Danny Paskiw
Most Outstanding Defensive Back – Derek Fink
1997 CJFL Outstanding Defensive Player – Jeff Zimmer
Most Outstanding Defensive Lineman – Brent Dancey
1998 PFC Most Outstanding Receiver – Jason Clermont
Most Outstanding Defensive Back – Jason Melnechenko
CJFL Outstanding Linebacker – Jeff Zimmer
CJFL Outstanding Defensive Lineman – Chad Zipchian
PFC Coach of the Year Nominee – Frank McCrystal
1999 none
2000 none
2001 Canada West Russ Jackson Nominee – Matt Dean (Academic achievement, outstanding athletic skills, & community service)
Canada West Hec Creighton Nominee – Jason Clermont (Most Outstanding Player)
Canada West President's Trophy – Jeff Zimmer (Outstanding Defensive Player)
2002 none